Myths and Legends of All Nations

Myths and Legends of All Nations

HERBERT SPENCER ROBINSON
KNOX WILSON

ROWMAN & LITTLEFIELD
Lanham • Boulder • New York • London

Published by Rowman & Littlefield
An imprint of The Rowman & Littlefield Publishing Group, Inc.
4501 Forbes Boulevard, Suite 200, Lanham, Maryland 20706
www.rowman.com

86-90 Paul Street, London EC2A 4NE, United Kingdom

British Library Cataloguing in Publication Information Available

Library of Congress Cataloging-in-Publication Data

The Library of Congress has cataloged the hardcover edition of this book as follows:

Robinson, Herbert Spencer
Myths and Legends of All Nations
A Littlefield Adams Quality Paperback
1. Mythology 2. Legends 3. Folk-lore
I. Wilson, Knox, 1901 - joint author. II. Title
BL310.R6 1967 291.1'3 75-35613 CIP

ISBN 9781538178270 (cloth : alk. paper) | ISBN 9781538178287 (pbk. : alk. paper) | ISBN 9781538178294 (epub)

∞™ The paper used in this publication meets the minimum requirements of American National Standard for Information Sciences—Permanence of Paper for Printed Library Materials, ANSI/NISO Z39.48-1992.

Preface

THIS BOOK brings together in convenient form, for interesting, informative reading and for instant reference, a great wealth of famous myths and legends, from all periods and from all parts of the world. Here in a carefully planned volume are the great stories and folklore of the Greeks, Romans, Oriental peoples, Celts, Norse and Teutons, other European groups, of the Polynesians of the Pacific, the American Indians, and our own American folklore.

The mythologies which have had the greatest influence on our literature and art and on our thinking have of course been presented most fully, since there are frequent occasions for acquainting or reacquainting one's self with their perennially fascinating characters and episodes, but the reader will also find much that is intriguing in the tales and themes from the less familiar sources.

We have divided the book into twenty-two sections, each dealing with the lore of a particular people or group of related peoples. Within sections, in so far as the material permits, we commence with the myths of the gods and continue with the legends of the heroes. The centered headings give the names of the principal figures around whom groups of stories focus; the General Index gives exact page references for individual stories.

We take up first the Egyptians and then the Babylonians, two peoples whose civilizations go back to the very beginnings of recorded history. Next we give some of the ancient legends of the Hebrews which stand apart from the Old Testament yet have their place in the great tradition which molds the work of writers and artists and thinkers of many countries. Next we turn to the rich and varied myths and legends of the ancient Persians and of the peoples of India. And following these we give early beliefs and stories of the Chinese and then of the Japanese.

The mythology of Greece has through the ages provided inspiration and theme, character and plot, to every people who have come into touch with its myriad enchantments. We inevitably give the largest section of the book to this vast treasure of the Greeks. The lore of the Romans is closely connected with that of the Greeks, and we make clear in our section on the Romans just what this relationship is; also telling something of the Etruscans who preceded the Romans in Italy.

Following the lore of the Ancient World we take up the great flowering of myths and legends in the earliest and later periods of the Middle Ages, in various parts of Europe. We have a very inclusive section on the Celts, giving the famous myths and stories of Ireland and Wales as well as the ever-entrancing legends of King Arthur and his Knights in Britain. Our next section is on the vigorous tales of the gods and heroes of the Norse and Teutons, a world of extraordinary vividness, which is perhaps best known today through the great music dramas of Richard Wagner. Then there is a section on certain outstanding figures in Old English lore, followed by sections on great stories from the Romance peoples, then the Slavs, and then the Finns.

We next introduce under the headings "Fairy Lore of Europe and the Orient" and "Various Legendary Figures and Themes," two sections which contain exceedingly interesting material not readily assignable to any single national group and drawing on the folklore of quite a number of peoples. Toward the end of the book we have shorter sections on the myths and legends of some of the African peoples, and then the Polynesians of the Pacific.

The next to the last section is devoted to the lore of the various peoples of American Indian origin, in North, Central, and South America. And the final section deals with some outstanding figures in our own American folklore.

For those who may wish to turn to the book as a source of topical reference for use in a speech or a paper, we have prepared a Topical Index which immediately precedes the General Index. The General Index at the end of the book shows the pronunciation of names and provides a rapid means of locating the passages devoted to any individual deity, hero, or episode.

In the writing of this book, Knox Wilson prepared principally the sections on the Egyptians, Babylonians, Persians, and peoples of India. The sections on the Greeks and Romans and practically all of the other peoples are by Herbert Spencer Robinson. Both authors are tremendously indebted, however, to Dr. Leo J. Henkin, Assistant Professor of English at Brooklyn College, who contributed three sections, those on "Legends of the Hebrews," "Fairy Lore of Europe and the Orient," and "Various Legendary Figures and Themes," and who also assisted with introductions to a number of other sections.

It is the hope of the authors that *Myths and Legends of All Nations* will prove both interesting and useful to many people, and that it will help to bring the fascinating world of mythology closer to those who want to acquaint themselves with these gems of the past while living the life of the busy present.

H. S. R.

K. W.

Contents

Introduction

WHAT WE MEAN BY MYTHS AND LEGENDS. *Myths* are fabulous stories, reaching back into the dim past, which offer an interpretation of some natural phenomenon or some long-established belief or custom. In the absence of scientific knowledge primitive man created imaginative explanations of the origin of things, of the heavens, of the cycle of the seasons, of life and death. There was no science of astronomy to explain that the sunrise is not a rising of the sun out of the earth, but the result of the earth turning on its axis; or that winter follows summer not as the result of some malignant force, but as the natural effect of natural causes. There was no science of geology to tell of the slow evolution of the earth through millions of years; no science of physics to point out that an echo is not another voice responding to a call, but the same voice thrown back by some obstruction.

In our own era, an age of science, we as individuals may not be able to explain some natural phenomenon but we rest secure in the knowledge that it can be explained or has already been explained by someone with more knowledge than we possess. Consequently, we do not exercise ourselves too much in trying to fashion explanations for the changes in the firmament or the earth which, we realize, wiser men must have already given. But the inquiring mind of more primitive man in the dawn of civilization was constantly disturbed by the challenge of the unknown, and he busied himself constantly contriving answers to the questions which troubled him. Roving freely, unhampered by the laws of science, his fancy evolved for him some of the most beautiful stories the world has ever known.

To the people of very ancient times, all nature was animated; all things were, or could be, persons. Assuredly then, so inspiring an object as the sun, illuminating the world when it appeared in the east and darkening the world when it disappeared in the west, was a personality also, but certainly more than human—and thus there grew up the idea that the sun was a god, one of the most majestic and important of the gods. But surely so lofty a creature as a god would not deign to walk across the great stretch of sky between morning and evening, and so, in some accounts, he was given a chariot driven by two or four or six horses. True, his face and form were not visible as he moved across the heavens, but that was because his chariot, his clothing, and his crown were so dazzling. In time the fancy of primitive folk played about almost every natural object, assigning personality to rain and cloud, wind and storm, tree and flower. Not at once but gradually, over a long stretch of time, did these explanations of marvels come to be. They represent the collective imagination of a people or nation, not the inventions of any one man, and they changed with time and circumstance and the mood of the tellers. And the sum total of these stories which a particular folk created for itself is that people's *mythology.*

Legends, as we use the term, tell us the stories of the heroes of old, whereas myths, as we have seen, deal chiefly with the gods and the forces of nature. Tales of heroes often contain mythical and fanciful elements, but many of them are based upon at least some bit, or even a considerable amount, of factual or of historical truth, though it is often impossible to determine just where fact ends and fantasy begins. The great story of the Trojan War is a legend of epic proportions, as are the stories of the Volsung saga and the Ring of the Nibelungs, of Roland of France, of Cuchulain and of Deirdre of Ireland, and many others. Some legends are the bearers of the early traditions of a people, such as the story of Romulus of Rome and the great cycle of tales centering upon King Arthur of Britain.

The legend-making process still continues, and the future will undoubtedly add its store. As time passes, figures of history tend to acquire an almost legendary character, and we see something of this happening in a measure to our own Washington and Lincoln.

There is sometimes only a shadow line between legendary figures who have come down to us as part of a people's folklore and the imaginative creations of one or a group of individual writers whose characters have acquired an almost legendary quality, as is true of Aladdin and Ali Baba in the *Arabian Nights,* of Cervantes' Don Quixote, Shakespeare's Romeo and Juliet, Washington Irving's Rip Van Winkle, and many more. In this book we have necessarily recognized this important distinction, and we have, for the most part, not included individual figures who come to us as creations in works which are literature rather than folklore.

Related to myths, yet standing somewhat apart, is the lore of fairies, and elves, and other imaginary beings, who appear in the folk tales of many peoples. We devote a separate section toward the end of this book to these fascinating groups of tiny spirits.

COMPARISONS BETWEEN THE VARIOUS MYTHOLOGIES. Everyone who reads at all extensively in this book will note considerable similarity between themes, characters, incidents, and even details, in the mythologies of countries that are widely separated by both time and distance. The points of likeness between the myths of the ancient Greeks and Romans and the Egyptians, the Babylonians, the peoples of India, the Celts, the Norsemen and Teutons, the Polynesians of the Pacific, and the American Indians are so marked and of such frequent occurrence that they cannot be easily dismissed or disregarded. In order to account for these resemblances and repetitions, scholars have advanced several theories—none of them completely satisfactory.

According to one theory, "borrowing" accounts for the resemblances. This

Myths and Legends of the Egyptians

It is often pointed out that certain river valleys have been cradles of civilization, and the valley of the Nile illustrates clearly what this signifies. Egypt, enriched by the Nile and protected north and south by good natural barriers, and east and west by burning desert, produced one of the earliest civilizations. For ages it must have seemed a place apart, in Africa but not of it. Egyptian writing, astronomy, knowledge of metals, large-scale engineering—these were extraordinary, almost unbelievable achievements. Yet it was their fears and their constant concern about the state of the dead which accounted for the magnificence and exquisite detail of their tomb-building and their cleverness in mummifying, and at the same time indicated their lack of a broad knowledge and understanding of the world.

In the monotheism of Ikhnaton, with its beautiful hymns, we find an advanced religion, but this was the actual belief of only a small group of Egyptians at a certain favored period of time. In general, the ancient Egyptian religion throughout its long history was conservative in the extreme, retaining to the end traces of primitive animism, of conflicting local traditions, and of henotheism or the tendency to make a number of the various gods of a pantheon supreme one after another. However, what it lacked in logical clarity Egyptian religion more than made up for in picturesqueness (though that word does not properly suggest the Egyptian austerity and augustness), so that even the most cursory treatment of its mythology leaves in the reader's mind vivid impressions of hawk- or scarab- or jackal-headed gods, of human-headed gods, bearing the sun between wings or horns, of stinging asps, of the sun-god in his boat, and of the celestial cow. The sun predominates; and even in the late and decadent animal worship of Apis, the sacred bull of Memphis, one finds, in the monuments, the winged disk of the sun placed above the head of the god.

Egyptian civilization flourished over the course of more than 3000 years (going back as far as about 4000 B.C.), and it was inevitable perhaps that, despite a strong tendency toward conservatism, details of Egyptian mythology should have been modified from time to time. The names of many of the gods were changed and the attributes and powers ascribed to certain gods were shifted in the course of time to other gods. Furthermore, since Egypt was a country with widely scattered centers of culture, each locality tended to contribute its own elements to Egyptian mythology. These two factors, then—long duration and individual regional cultures—explain the variations and inconsistencies found at some points in the following account of the Egyptian deities.

The Creation

In Nu, the world-ocean, existed Neb-er-tcher ("Lord to the uttermost limit"). This god took upon himself the form of the creative Khepri. After uttering his own name and establishing a place upon which to stand, Khepri, or Ra, the sun-god, had union with his own shadow and so begot Shu, god of the dry atmosphere, and Tefnut, god of the waters above the heavens. Then these two opposites were united and had offspring, Nut (the heavens) and Keb (the earth).

All day long, while the sun, the Eye of Khepri, made its trip from east to west, Nut remained in her place above the earth, but as darkness came she gradually descended until she rested upon the bosom of the earth-god, Keb.

Keb and Nut became the parents of Osiris and Isis, Set and Nephthys. Thus was created the circle of the nine great original deities, the Ennead, which—in some form or other—every Egyptian temple recognized: namely, Khepri, Shu, Tefnut, Keb, Nut, Osiris, Isis, Set, and Nephthys.

According to one version, Osiris and Isis were joined even before their birth, with the result that Isis brought forth her son Horus; and to Nephthys was born Anubis, the fruit of a similar union with Set.

Neph and Pthah

Nu, the name for the world-ocean in the above version of the creation, is also another name for Neph, a god who was worshipped at the island of Elephantine in Upper Egypt, at Thebes, at Antaeopolis, and at many other places. He was described as the spirit of God moving on the face of the waters. He had a ram's head with curved horns. His wife, or consort or *sacti,* was Auka. He was called the god who made the world and everything that is in the world, including men and gods. He was represented as a potter at his wheel. Other names under which he was known (besides Nu) are Num, Nef, Cnouphis, Cenubis, Kneph, and Amen-Kneph.

Still another name for Neph is Pthah (or Ptah), the chief seat of whose worship was Memphis. Pthah has been described as an artisan of the world. As a master workman he made the moon, the sun, and the earth. He was invoked as the father of all beginnings, as the first god of the upper world, as the god who holds the world in place with his hands. He was variously represented as a man, walking or sitting, as a mummy wearing a skull-cap, and as a bandy-legged dwarf or pigmy.

Ra

Ra (or Re) was the god of the sun. While according to one creation myth Ra was self-produced and identical with Khepri and Neb-er-tcher, he was also considered the son of Neith, the goddess of Sais (described below). The kings of Egypt looked on Ra as their patron and protector, identified themselves with him, and used his name as a prefix to their own names and royal titles. Ra was represented as a hawk, an animal sacred to him, or as a man with a hawk's head, on top of which was the red disk of the sun or a snake, the latter being symbolic of supreme power. The scarabaeus or sacred beetle was his emblem. As a mighty sun-god, he conquered the forces of darkness, travelling night and day by boat through the heavenly waters and into Tuat, the Egyptian region of the dead.

One of the myths of Ra centers around his destruction of humanity, a task in which he employed Athor (or Hathor), who was both his mother and his daughter. Athor, who was identified with Isis, was the goddess of the sky, of the rising and setting of the sun, and the goddess of love and beauty. She set about her task with such vicious pleasure that she was soon up to her neck in blood, and Ra himself had to call a halt to her violence by flooding the land with an intoxicating beverage, which made her drunk. Athor was also a goddess of the dead and was called the Lady of the Sycamore. She was represented sometimes as a woman, sometimes with the head of a cow, and wearing the sun's disk, horns, and plumes.

Ra's other children were MAAT (or Mat), the goddess of truth and law and order; MU, the personification of light in a physical sense, as Maat was of moral and ethical light; and SHU, the solar light. Keb (or Seb), offspring of Shu and Tefnut in the creation myth already described, is in some versions a son of Ra.

Ra appears in other forms as MENTU and ATMU. Mentu is Ra as the rising sun and Atmu, Ra as the setting sun. (Atmu is also called Tem, Temu, and Atem.)

Also identified with Ra is AMUN, the chief god of Upper Egypt. His name means "the hidden or the concealed one." Amun was also known as and identified with Ammon, Amen, Amen-Ra, and Amun-Num. By his wife and consort, MAUT, he had a son, KHUNS; the parents and the son formed the Upper Egyptian trinity. Amun represented the power—hidden and mysterious—that creates and sustains the universe. As AMEN-RA, the god of the sun, he gave light and life to man and the earth. As AMUN-NUM, he is the breath or spirit of life. His identification with the sun-god was the work of the priests who thus sought to maintain his position and to magnify his importance.

Maut, the wife of Ra or Amun and the mother of Khuns, was called the mother of the gods and the mistress of the sky. She was represented with the head of a lioness or a vulture, or with the head-dress of a vulture, that bird of prey being regarded as a symbol of maternity.

Keb and Nut

KEB (or Seb), a son of Shu and Tefnut or of Ra, was the Egyptian god of earth and its vegetation. In the hieroglyphics he was described as the father of the gods, a term applied to Neph, Pthah, and many other deities. All things on earth were under Keb's authority, and the earth itself was called the Horse of Keb. For his work in producing the cosmic egg he was given the name of the Great Cackler. He was represented as a man with the head of a goose, which was his symbol, and with a disk and a crown on his head.

He married his sister, NUT (also Nutpe or Nepte), and by her became the father of Osiris, Isis, Set, and Nephthys. Nut, who (like Maut) was called the mother of the gods, presided over childbirth and was the patron of nursing.

Osiris and Isis

OSIRIS, one of the great Egyptian deities, was the son of earth and sky, that is, of Keb and Nut, although Neph was sometimes regarded as his father. Osiris was the brother-husband of Isis and the father of Horus. He was the principle of good; his brother, Set, was the principle of evil. Beginning as a local god of Busiris, and regarded as a great benefactor of Egypt, Osiris later became a sun-god and a moon-god through being identified with Ra and Khuns. Osiris was represented either as a man or as a mummy with a white plume crown. His worship was universally observed throughout Egypt. Like many other gods, Osiris was regarded in capacities that seem to be contradictory; he was both the god of the dead, through his lordship in the underworld, AMENTI, and the god or source of renewed life, through Horus, who represented the sun.

ISIS, the goddess of the earth and of the moon, was the sister-wife of Osiris and the mother of Horus. With her brother-husband, Isis was the divinity most widely worshipped by the Egyptians, and there were no limits to her powers. She ruled in heaven, on the earth, on sea and ocean, and in the world below, where she handed out rewards and punishments, decided the fate of mortals, and decreed life or death.

Osiris' traditional foe was Set, the god of darkness, who finally overcame him, locked him in a coffin which he had persuaded him to enter by trickery, and threw him into the Nile. Set later opened the chest and cut up Osiris' body into fourteen pieces and scattered them throughout various parts of Egypt. Isis devotedly collected all the pieces, except one, and buried them in different parts of the country, which explains the confusion concerning the burial place of the god. According to another myth, the cries and prayers of Isis, and the rites and ceremonies she performed with the aid of Nephthys, Thoth, Anubis, and Horus, made the pieces join together, and the body became whole again. By means of a magic formula Isis then brought her husband back to life and he rose from the dead. In this manner, Osiris became the god of resurrection and life eternal, and the lord of the underworld and the judge of the dead. With the assistance of her son, Horus, Isis later killed Set and recovered the ruling power usurped by him.

As the goddess of birth, and the productive principle in nature, Isis' symbol was the cow, which was sacred to her. Monuments usually show her as a young woman, seated, with Horus on her lap. She has a cow's horns on her head and the orb of the moon is between the horns. She holds a metal rattle in her right hand. She is standing with Horus at her right side. The festivals that honored her were symbolic of her grief and joy. Her attributes were the horn of plenty, ears of corn, the moon, a lotus flower, a serpent, and horns. Her chief temples were at Busiris, at Abydos, and at Philae. She was widely worshipped in Greece, and, in spite of opposition on the part of state authorities, in Rome. The Greeks identified Isis with Io because of the Greek legend of Io's finally reaching Egypt after her wanderings and of being restored to her original shape on the banks of the Nile.

Isis, at one time, became jealous of the power of her mighty ancestor, Ra. She lived upon earth, the kingdom of Keb, in the form of a witch-woman, beautiful, crafty, and active. But Ra had become so old that as he walked along he dribbled at the mouth and his saliva fell upon the ground. This gave Isis the opportunity she had long awaited. She obtained some of the god's spittle, mixed it with dust, and molded a poisonous serpent. This creature she left in Ra's path. When the aged god came slowly by, the serpent bit him, and immediately the venom entered into his body. In horrible pain, the god called to him all the gods who had power in magic; but only Isis gave him reason to hope. If he would utter his secret name, he might live, she declared. He then replied that he was Khepri in the morning, Ra at noon, and Temu in the evening. But Isis was sure there was no power in those names, for they were already known to everyone. At last, constrained by the poison, Ra allowed Isis to take from him his heart, with the secret name it held, and also his two eyes (the Sun and Moon). Then Isis quelled the poison, but Ra had lost his supreme power, which now was held by Isis; in time the great Eye of Day came into the possession of her son, Horus.

Horus

HORUS, the son of Osiris and Isis, was the god of light who overcame darkness. He also had some of the attributes of Ra, god of the sun, to whom he to some extent corresponds, and he was believed to be the life-giving power of the sun. The hawk was sacred to him and he was usually represented as being hawk-headed. The circumstances of Horus' conception were most unusual. After the decline of Ra, Osiris was the greatest of the male divinities. His brother, Set, an evil god, had dared to oppose him but had been defeated. So all seemed well. But a new war sprang up between Set and his friends and Osiris and his forces; and this time Set hurled Osiris to the ground and killed him. Isis, the sister-wife of Osiris, took the form of a bird, as did Nephthys, though she was Set's consort; then these two birds with piercing cries of grief alighted on the ground beside the slain body. With her feathers Isis fanned the air, which moved and entered the nostrils of the god. Restored to her own form, she chafed his hands, clasped him to her breast, and drew from him that which enabled her to become the mother of Horus.

Not only did Set, the evil god of the Ennead, encompass the death of Osiris but he also succeeded, for a time, in holding Isis as a captive. Yet at last she escaped, with the help of Thoth, the god of letters (see below), and hid herself on the edge of the Reed Swamps until after her child had been born.

Upon a time she went to a certain temple to perform a religious observance in honor of her late consort. She thought that she had left her child well enough concealed. In her absence, however, a scorpion, sent out by Set, found the child and stung him to death. The sorrow of Isis was great when she saw the dead Horus. At first she could find no cure; and in this there was much irony, for shortly before making her unlucky journey to the temple, Isis had restored to life a child who had been bitten by a scorpion-goddess.

Nephthys came to grieve, too, as she had done after the death of Osiris. "Pray that the sailors in the Boat of Ra may cease rowing," she urged. Isis did so, and, behold, the Boat and the Disk slowed down and drifted and came to a stand, and down from the Boat of Millions of Years came the helping-god Thoth with spells and magic and the great word of life and the fluid of life, itself, which he had from Ra. Then when this fluid of life reached the body of Horus, the poison began to flow out of him and he came to himself again. Ra had acknowledged Horus as his descendant; nor was this all, for Thoth promised that after Horus came to the throne of Egypt and had reigned over the land, both he and Ra himself would be the advocates of Horus in the Judgment Hall of the Dead (see below).

Then, after assuring Isis that his power, great though it had just been shown to be, was less than hers—for was it not her prayer which had caused the sun to stand still?—the helping-god Thoth rose to his place again, the rowers bent to their oars, and the great Boat of Millions of Years resumed its way across the sky.

Horus was also known under the name of HARPOCRATES. Under this name he was worshipped by both the Greeks and the Romans, as well as the Egyptians. He was pictured as a nude child sitting on his mother's lap or on a lotus flower, or standing by his mother's side. He had curly locks, and his finger was on his lips, for which reason the Greeks and Romans thought that he was the god of silence and worshipped him as such. The name Harpocrates is the Greek equivalent of the Egyptian Harpechruti, that is, Har (or Horus) the Child, and the finger-on-mouth pose is a sign or symbol of childhood, not a warning or signal for silence. A distinction was usually made between the Horus who avenges his father's death when he grows up, and the infant Horus, or Harpocrates, who still needs a mother's care.

Set, Nephthys, and Anubis

SET (or Seth), a god representing the powers of darkness, was the principle of darkness and evil, both physical and moral. He was the brother or father of Osiris, brother of Isis, and the brother and husband of NEPHTHYS. He was represented as a curious zoological combination, with the body of an ass, the ears and snout of a jackal, and the tail of a lion. The okapi, a strange mixture of mule and giraffe, and the jerboa, a small mouse-like creature built on the lines of a midget kangaroo, seem to approach the animal suggested. Worshipped at first as a sun-god, Set later became associated with the opposite idea of darkness.

Nephthys (or Nebt-Het) was a goddess of the dead and a personification of the dusk; she was the sister of Isis, the wife of her brother Set, and the mother of Anubis. She helped Isis to recover the drowned Osiris and mourned with her over his body. She was represented as a woman crowned with hieroglyphic symbols that might have meant a house and a basket, and was also shown with horns and the disk of the sun. She was worshipped at Edfu, Dendera, and at Abydos.

Her son, ANUBIS, of whom Osiris and Ra were also said to be the father, was a god of the dead and of the art of embalming. With Nephthys he took part in the funeral rites of Osiris. A somber god, his was the duty of watching the scales and weighing the heart or soul in Amenti, the Egyptian underworld. If the soul of the person did not meet the required specifications, he was eaten by AMMIT, a horrible monster, half-lion and half-hippopotamus, with crocodile jaws. Ammit had found out by experience that many souls were below standard and he used to stand by in the weighing room, right next to the scales. Anubis was represented with the head of a jackal. According to another myth, Anubis swallowed his father.

Thoth

THOTH, the god of letters already mentioned in connection with Osiris, Isis, and Horus, was the registrar and recorder of the underworld in which he dwelt. He kept the accounts of the weight of each soul and handed them to the great judge of the dead, Osiris. The long-beaked, stork-like bird, the ibis, was sacred to him and he was represented with the head of an ibis, as well as with a pen, a writing tablet, and a palm-branch. Killing an ibis was a crime punished by death. Thoth was also the god of the moon, in which aspect he was portrayed with the crescent and disk. He was a god of learning and wisdom, the inventor of many branches of art and science, and a master of magic.

Apis

APIS, the great beast-god of Egypt, was a sacred bull worshipped at Memphis. (The Egyptian name of this sacred beast was HAP, the more familiar name "Apis" being actually a Greek form.) The worship of the animal was widespread and popular because it was regarded as an avatar or reincarnation of Osiris, the most human of all Egyptian deities. The sacred animal, that is, the bull selected for the honor of deification, was required to have certain distinguishing marks: a black hide, a white spot on the forehead in the shape of a triangle, a spot shaped like a half-moon on its right side, and a knot like a beetle under the tongue. When this bull was found, after long searching, it was treated as a god and all honors were paid to it, but its divinity was severely limited. It was not allowed to live for more than twenty-five years, and when it reached that age it was, with great ceremony, drowned in the waters of the Nile. Its death was regarded as a great calamity and the entire nation went into a period of mourning, which was changed to one of joy and thanksgiving as soon as another bull with the necessary qualifications was found. When the animal with the sacred marks was discovered, it was taken in a special boat to Memphis, where it was housed in a splendid apartment and where every attention was paid to its welfare and comfort. The most beautiful cows that could be found were provided for him, and great care was observed in his diet. When thirsty, he drank pure water from a well or fountain, as the river water was thought to be fattening. The embalmed remains of the bull were buried in a magnificent stone coffin or sarcophagus. Less than a hundred years ago, many mummified bulls were found at Memphis, one of the chief centers of Apis' worship. At Heliopolos, the city of the sun, Apis was called Mnevis or Onuphis.

Other Important Deities

NEITH (or Net) has already been mentioned as the mother of Ra. She was the goddess of the upper heaven, or ether. Neith was called the mother, the mistress of heaven, and the elder goddess. As the mother, she was the feminine counterpart of Khem, the father (discussed below).

Although the mother of Ra and of many other gods, she was a virgin goddess. She herself was not born of parents but was self-produced.

She was represented in a standing position, with the crown of Lower Egypt on her head. She held a sceptre in her left hand and a bow and two arrows; in her right hand she carried the *ankh,* or symbol of life. Another representation showed her with bow and arrows and a distaff or shuttle, from which she was identified as a goddess of war and of weaving. (Another Egyptian goddess of war was ANOUKE, of the island of Elephantine.) As an earth-mother, Neith was portrayed with green hands and a green face. After she became identified with Isis, Neith was pictured as a cow, that animal being sacred to Isis. Her worship was not so widespread as that of other divinities, but she was honored especially at Sais and to some extent at Thebes.

KHEM (or Chem) as the father was a counterpart of Neith, the mother. He was the god of generation and production. As a god of reproduction he was identified with RANNO, the god of gardens—an extension of his attribute of fertility. He was the lord of the harvest, patron of agriculture, ruler of the vegetable kingdom, and the giver of fertility to humans, to animals, to all things that grow in the ground. He was represented as a mummy.

BUBASTIS (also Bast, Bastet, or Ubasti), a daughter of Isis, was the cat-headed goddess of the city of Bubastis in Lower Egypt. She was a goddess of the kindly rays of the sun, as distinguished from her sister, SEKHET, who, with the head of a lioness, typified the fierce heat of the sun that causes discomfort and torture. Bubastis was represented with a rattle in one hand, a shield in the other, and a basket on her arm. The temple of the city of Bubastis was sacred to her and contained a cat cemetery covering many acres.

SERAPIS (or Sarapis), the god of healing, was a Greco-Egyptian divinity, whose worship was introduced into Greece at the time of the Ptolemies, and into Rome at the same time as that of Isis. His most famous temple, the magnificent Serapeum, was erected at Alexandria by Ptolemy Soter (367–283 B.C.), about 300 B.C. and destroyed in 385 A.D. Serapis was really Apis in another form and under another name. As Apis was the living Osiris, that is, Osiris living in the body of the sacred Bull of Memphis, so Serapis was the dead Apis or the Osiris who has passed into Amenti, the underworld. Worshipped for his healing power, Serapis had many temples where sick persons came to sleep, to have their dreams interpreted, and to receive instructions from the priests regarding a cure. The worship of Serapis covered the Greek islands, Greece itself, Asia Minor, and Italy. Serapis was represented with a dog, lion, or wolf-headed animal at his side, and a serpent twisted around his body. He had thick, curly locks, a heavy beard and mustache. The symbol of the underworld, a modius or corn-measure, was on his head.

The SPHINX was a benevolent creature, a personification of the food-and-fruit-producing powers of the earth and also a goddess of wisdom. She was represented as a reclining lion, without wings, and with the head and breasts of a woman; sometimes she had the head of a hawk or a jackal. A reproduction of her figure was placed in front of every Egyptian temple. (The Egyptian Sphinx should not be confused with the Greek Sphinx. They are different both in appearance and personality.)

The Judgment Hall of the Dead

The Book of the Dead is a mere title of convenience for any one of a great number of Egyptian papyri containing unmethodical chapters—to the number of one hundred and sixty and more—on the wanderings of the soul after death, its trial in the great hall before Osiris, and the Osirian doctrine of resurrection. The most famous of these, dating from the XVIII Dynasty, is some 3400 years old, and there are others regarded as older still. The core of each of these Books of the Dead is a chapter concerned with what is called the "negative confession" of the dead and the weighing of his heart before the supreme judge of the lower world.

But let us follow what was to many ancient Egyptians a familiar sequence of events—some of them events known through actual experience and other events known only through conjecture. The latter part of the sequence will be based upon the Book of the Dead.

A king or great official, let us say, has died. His mummified body in its painted coffin has been ferried across the Nile in a barge and dragged on a sledge to its resting place in the Valley of the Tomb of the Kings. The paid mourners, the musicians, and the acrobats are distracting the crowd at a little distance, but at the door of the tomb or within one of its chambers the sober-eyed priests are laying out meats and fruits and flowers, unguents, apparel, and a score of other things, reciting, meanwhile, formulas intended to give the dead man's *Ka,* or "double," the power to enjoy the funeral offerings. Now the priests place talismans in niches on all four walls of the burial chamber to protect the dead from evil coming from any quarter. And now at last the priests withdraw and the funeral ceremonies are over.

Meanwhile—and here we begin to follow the Book of the Dead—the *Ka,* wandering through darkness in search of the Judgment Hall of the Dead, has renamed himself Osiris, hoping to be restored to life, as Osiris was restored by Isis and Thoth, so that he now is lord of the land of the setting sun. At last he enters a terrifyingly vast hall, the distant roof of which is supported by massive pillars. Osiris, ten times as great in size as he himself is, sits enthroned above the level of his eyes at the opposite end of the Hall. He wears the towering white crown of upper Egypt. His arms are folded, but in one hand he holds a scourge and in the other a staff which symbolizes justice. Between the great Osiris and his latest namesake are a shrine and a pair of scales. The jackal-headed Anubis and the hawk-headed Horus are standing by to superintend a novel kind of weighing, and the ibis-headed Thoth is at one side, ready to record the result. But upon the shrine there waits a creature, part hippopotamus, part lion, and part crocodile, called the devourer of the dead. If the man is to escape this monster, he must make forty-two negative confessions of sins which satisfy forty-two judges seated in boxes just below the roof of the double-hall; and in the even more important weighing upon the scales, his heart must right the balance when set in the pan over against Maat, the goddess of truth, or over against the feather which represents her. Should he pass these severe tests, however, he will dwell forever in the favor of Osiris, and his own new name of Osiris will not have been assumed in vain.

Myths and Legends of the Babylonians

MESOPOTAMIA, the prodigiously fertile plain north of the Persian Gulf through which the Tigris and Euphrates rivers flow, was the heartland of several ancient civilizations—Babylonian, Assyrian, Chaldean. It had no natural boundaries like those of Egypt, and no such air of protection hung over it. It was the scene of mighty struggles of mountaineers against nomads, and of king against king. Great monuments of one reign, great advances in learning, were lost and perhaps succeeded by others in the continuing conflicts. The inhabitants at almost any period might have taken as their basic saying either "To the victor belong the spoils—for a season" or "Where the body is, there will the eagles be gathered together."

Perhaps that is why (in spite of the presence of certain very primitive elements from the Sumerian age) the dominant tone of the Babylonian mythology is one of disillusionment, of worldly sophistication. It is full of intentional ambiguities on man's position in the universe and his ultimate fate. Life's pleasures, friendship, and initiative and courage are praised and valued, but their transitory nature is always felt; and even those heroes who have the approval of both men and gods find in the end that the cards of life are stacked against them.

The history of the Babylonians, Assyrians, Chaldeans, and other peoples of Mesopotamia goes back as far as 4000 B.C., just as does that of Egypt; and the civilizations of the Babylonians and related peoples also flourished for more than 3000 years.

The Babylonian Pantheon

There were at least ten great Babylonian deities, and there were also about half as many figures less highly regarded but almost equally well known.

ANU was the god of the heavens, the old, unchanging monarch of the North Star. He was the oldest of the Babylonian gods, the father of all the gods, and the ruler of heaven and destiny.

ENLIL was next, the god of the Great Mountain or Earth and the god of the Golden Age. Enlil was said to have possessed the tablets of destiny, but they were stolen by the storm god, Zu. Despite numerous attempts by the other gods, the tablets were never recovered.

EA was god of the water-depths, of springs and rivers, and hence a friend to man. He was born of the sea, from which he carried to man the elements of culture. The trees of life sprouted and grew under his divine protection and were watered by the Euphrates and the Tigris, the two rivers he created at the beginning of everything. He was thus the god of wisdom and of life. In form he was half man, half fish, and was also worshipped as a potter who shaped both men and gods at his wheel. He was also god of the air. His wife was HINLIL, who was the goddess of grain.

Another benign deity was SIN (or NANNAN), the old moon-god. He was the son of Enlil. He and his consort, NINGAL, the Great Lady or Queen, were often regarded as the parents of Shamash and Ishtar. Sin occupied a high place in the religious hierarchy of the Babylonians, as their calendar was based on the moon. He was represented with the symbol of the crescent moon and a long flowing beard, and was worshipped as the lord or giver of wisdom.

The sun-god, SHAMASH, was bringer of light, champion of justice, and giver of good laws. As god of the sun he hated and punished darkness and evil in all its forms. He was also the supreme god of oracles, and as such was the lord and master of the famous Babylonian soothsayers. From Shamash, Hammurabi, the king of Babylon, was believed to have received the code of laws which bears his name. Shamash also possessed the powers of healing and of giving life.

ISHTAR (whom the Phoenicians worshipped under the name of ASTARTE), the daughter of Anu or of Sin, was the queen of heaven, the mother of all life, and the goddess of love and war. TAMMUZ, the husband or lover of Ishtar, was the god of vegetation who each year came to life and then died again. We give details of the stories of these two leading Babylonian deities below.

MARDUK, son of Ea, was the god of the spring sun, of prudence, and of wisdom. By his wife, Zarpanit, he was the father of NEBO, the god of learning, who was also credited with the invention of letters and writing. According to the Babylonian *Creation Epic,* it was Marduk who brought forth the world. This story is given below.

ADAD (or Hadad), god of the thunder-cloud, was good to have as a friend because he brought the needed summer rains, but terrible as an enemy because of the lightning which he cast. He conquered his foes by famine, flood, and lightning, and his worshippers called on him to destroy their enemies. He was identified with the legends of the Great Flood. The cypress tree was sacred to him. His wife was Shala.

Last among the great gods came ASSHUR, whose fame grew with that of his Assyrians until, at the time of their ascendency, almost all that had been attributed to the major Babylonian gods was attributed to him. By those outside his realm he was known, and feared, as the archer, a mighty god of war.

ALLATU (or ERESH-KIGAL) was the goddess of ARALLU, the Babylonian underworld. She almost lost both her life and throne, saving them at the last moment by offering to share her kingdom with NERGAL, a god of war and hunting, who was on the point of killing her because she demanded his death for not honoring her as she deserved. Nergal, who thus became a ruler of the lower regions, was sometimes a god of fertility, but at other times a bringer of fever and death. He was represented with the head of a man, wings, and the body of a lion. As a god of pestilence and destruction, his symbol was a sword with which he destroyed his enemies.

GIRRU, god of the smith's fire and the priest's fire, was the first-born of heaven and the son of Anu. He personified fire in three aspects: heavenly fire, fire on earth, and fire used in sacrificing to the gods.

NINIB, the son of Enlil, was a god with many powers, loved by his worshippers for his eagerness to heal the sick, a kindly work in which he was aided by his wise wife or consort, GULA. Ninib was also a god of vegetation and fertility and, in his less beneficent aspect, the lord or god of battle and the chase. Gula, the Great Physician and goddess of healing, was, like her husband, a vindictive as well as a beneficent deity. Death and the diseases that caused death were subservient to her; she could restore life when she wished to do so but was also able to end it with any of the fatal illnesses that were her weapons.

Ishtar and Tammuz

ISHTAR, one of the great figures in Babylonian mythology, was capricious in love, willful and imperious in action. As the mother goddess, Ishtar was moved to pity and sorrow at the suffering of her earthly children and at the hardships imposed by pestilence and flood, but she was cruel and callous as the goddess of love, her rites being celebrated with such licentiousness by her followers that the name of Ishtar and the centers of her worship became synonymous with wickedness and immorality. As a goddess of war she was so terrible that even the gods trembled at her while warlike people sang her praises.

Though it was sometimes said that the death of TAMMUZ was caused by Ishtar, according to another legend he was killed while hunting a wild boar. The account of Ishtar's descent to the Babylonian underworld to visit Tammuz is one of the most famous Babylonian tales.

Presumably Ishtar had felt remorse for having caused his death, and had made up her queenly mind to restore him to life, if such a thing could be done. So Ishtar, daughter of the moon-god, went down to the land where the inhabitants sit in darkness, where all things are overspread with motionless dust. To the porter of ALLATU, queen of the underworld, she spoke in haste, threatening to break down his door if he did not open at once. Yet the porter did not comply until he had obtained his mistress's grudging consent.

As he caused Ishtar to enter the first gate, he removed her great crown, explaining that such was the ancient custom of Allatu. As he caused her to enter the second gate, he approached and took off the ornaments of her ears, again saying that such was the custom of Allatu. At the third gate, he approached and took off the chains from about her neck, for such was the custom of Allatu. At the fourth gate he took off the ornaments of her breast, for such was the custom of Allatu. At the fifth gate, he took off her studded girdle, for such was the custom of Allatu. At the sixth he took off her bracelets and her anklets, for such was the custom of Allatu. At the seventh he took off the garment covering her nakedness, for such was the custom of Allatu.

Admitted at last to the presence of the dark queen, Ishtar flew at her in a rage. Meanwhile the other came storming at Ishtar, cursing her in every organ and limb, and intent upon making her a prisoner forever.

But the great god Ea knew that while Ishtar was in the lower world all generation among men and among lesser creatures must cease. Ea therefore created a man who went to Allatu and pleased her as much as Ishtar had previously displeased her. But this messenger had his orders. During the wine-drinking, when Allatu's heart was at ease, the stranger suddenly asked for water from a certain water-skin. Then Allatu smote her thigh, for she recognized a power greater than her own. She called Namtar, her own messenger, and told him to sprinkle Ishtar with the water of life and let her return to her own land. This was done, and, as Ishtar retraced her steps, her robe and her adornments were restored to her at door after door.

Marduk

MARDUK was the tutelary god of the city of Babylon. As the power and fame of Babylon grew, his standing in the pantheon also grew until the title of Bel (Lord) was often used to designate him. Marduk was believed to have brought about the creation of the world. TIAMAT, a terrifying goddess who represented the chaotic, overwhelming ocean, was feared by all the gods. By all, that is, except Marduk. At a convocation of the gods, he promised to fight Tiamat and her hated dragons. After a strenuous battle Marduk slew Tiamat and bound the dragons. Out of Tiamat's corpse, after he had cut it into two parts, he created heaven and earth, and added the constellations and the planets and fixed their movements. Then, on the advice of his father, Ea, he created man. For his great deed, as well as for his magical powers, Marduk was created a great god by the other gods. (According to a second version, the world was formed from the ocean, but peacefully, without a struggle between Tiamat and Marduk.)

Marduk was especially considered the compassionate god of mankind, relieving man's ills with the power and knowledge which his father, Ea, had given him.

Adapa and the South Wind

ADAPA, servant of EA, was given by his master a godlike wisdom, but Ea did not grant him a life-span different from that of any other mortal. He was the steward in the house of Ea and also his huntsman and fisher. One day, busy with his fishing, he had steered his sailing boat into the open sea; the South Wind overturned his boat and gave him a ducking.

"South Wind," cried Adapa, as soon as he could reach the surface and breathe again, "I will break thy wing!"

And instantly—it must have been through the will of Ea—the wing of the South Wind was broken. For seven days the South Wind did not blow. Then from his messenger, ANU, god of the heavens, learned of the broken wing. Rising from his throne, he commanded his messenger to bring Adapa before him.

Ea, knowing what would occur next, clothed Adapa in a mourner's garment. Adapa would soon be standing at the gate of Anu before Tammuz and Gishzida, the two gods who repeatedly die and live again. They would ask him whom he mourned, and he was to answer that he was sad because Tammuz and Gishzida had left his land. They would be pleased and they would therefore put Anu in a humor to forgive Adapa for cursing the South Wind. But that would not be all. They would offer him four things: bread of death, water of death, a garment, and oil. He was, of course, to refuse the food and drink, but was to put on the garment and anoint himself with the oil.

Soon the messenger from Anu came, and all took place as Ea had said it would, except that the dying gods called the bread, "bread of life" and the water, "water of life." When, following his master's instructions, Adapa refused to eat and drink, Anu was amazed at Adapa's apparent unwillingness to live forever. For the bread and water would have made him one of the immortals. But there could be no second chance, and all that Anu could do for Adapa was to have his messenger lead him back to his own land.

And how is the myth to be interpreted? Do the gods love man? Do they hate man? Or do they use him as a pawn in a game which they play against each other?

Etana and the Eagle and the Plant of Birth

The consort of ETANA, king of Kish, had brought forth only stillborn children. When she prayed to Anu, the ancient god decided to make the childlessness of Etana an excuse for a test of the king's courage. Shamash was sent to Etana to instruct him to take the road across the mountain. There he would see an eagle, who might be the agent through whom he could obtain the Plant of Birth. Once in possession of this plant, Etana might rest assured that in due time his wife would give birth to a living child.

Having crossed the mountain, Etana found the eagle sorely in need of a friend. The eagle and the serpent had originally sworn to assist each other, but the eagle had wilfully wronged his ally, whereupon the serpent had outwitted the eagle, and, having got him in his power, had broken one of his wings and cast him into a pit to die from hunger and thirst. But the eagle had prayed to Shamash for help, and now help had come in the person of Etana. The king fed the eagle and watched over him, and after eight months the eagle's power of flight was restored and he rose out of the pit.

Then, knowing that the Plant of Birth was held by Anu, Etana and the eagle at length perceived what they must attempt to do. Etana got upon the mighty creature's back, and, while goatherds and dogs looked upward in amazement, the strange pair began an ascent that was to carry them through the spheres. After two hours of flight, the earth below looked like a mountain and the ocean like a mountain lake. After four hours, sea and land were still more shrunken. After six hours, the great sea looked no bigger than a water-ditch dug by a gardener to irrigate his plants. Some hold that Etana and the eagle entered through the gate of Anu and worshipped him, but most say that at length even the brave eagle and Etana lost heart, began to descend, and then fell and crashed to earth. Etana had lost his life without obtaining the Plant of Birth, but he had made a kingly attempt to follow out the instructions of Shamash. That Anu was satisfied appears from the fact that after Etana's death the queen was delivered of a child who lived to ascend his father's throne.

The Epic of Gilgamesh

There was an actual king of Erech, in Southern Babylonia, who bore the name of GILGAMESH. He must have been an unusual man, for in time his name became associated with a number of old stories. These, put into the form of a short epic about 2000 B.C., have been preserved in twelve imperfect tablets which were recovered from the library of Assurbanipal among the ruins of Nineveh. The eleventh tablet, which contains an account of the great deluge, is of the highest importance, but the entire epic is—if viewed in the right perspective—of very real human interest and of rare poetic quality.

Gilgamesh was two-thirds god and one-third man, and there was no one like him, no one to match him. He was shepherd of his folk, but so intent was he upon making the walls of Erech unshakable that he kept his strong men working by night as well as by day. Then the people complained: "Gilgamesh leaves not the son to his father, the maiden to the warrior, nor the wife to her husband." And they cried to the goddess ARURU, "Thou hast shaped Gilgamesh; shape now a rival to oppose him, so that the men of Erech may have rest."

Aruru, the potter, the shaper, washed her hands, pinched up some clay, and molded the wild man ENKIDU. Shaggy and hairy he was, with hair that had sprouted like grain; and little did he know of men and their cities, for he ate herbs with the gazelles and drank with the wild beasts at the water-holes.

The hunter who first discovered him did not dare to face him, and so the wild animals went free. But, acting on the advice of his crafty old father, the hunter went to Gilgamesh with a request which the king was quick to grant.

"Go, hunter," said Gilgamesh, "and take with thee one of the priestesses of Ishtar. When the wild beasts come down to the well, let her cast off her garment. Then Enkidu will draw near to the woman and away from his wild beasts, and they will draw away from him."

This was done, and for a week Enkidu enjoyed the love of the priestess of Ishtar. Next, the woman persuaded Enkidu to eat bread and drink wine with the shepherds, so that he became their friend and drove the lions away from the flocks. At last the priestess spoke of the greatness of Gilgamesh, hinting that he and he alone was worthy of being Enkidu's rival or Enkidu's friend.

In the city the two heroes met in a struggle that shook the streets like an earthquake. Gilgamesh at last had the advantage, but Enkidu had won the king's respect. Then and there the two formed an undying friendship.

Gilgamesh now wished to war against the monster HUMBABA in the cedar forests. Enkidu warned Gilgamesh of the monster's might, but this warning had no effect, and NINSUN, the great queen, complained to Shamash of his having given Gilgamesh too stormy and restless a heart. Her only hope was in Enkidu. She called him to her and said, "Fight at the side of Gilgamesh; protect him and never leave him till the day of his return home from the cedar forests."

Of the actual fight we have no account, but that it was a serious one may be inferred from statements that Enkidu grew faint when he entered the cedar forests, that the two friends did not defeat Humbaba without securing the aid of Shamash.

After the struggle Ishtar urged Gilgamesh to be her consort. Gilgamesh replied to Ishtar in scorn. She had brought sorrow upon Tammuz, her first love. Many later lovers had she had. And which one of them had escaped sorrow? One had been a herdsman. Had she not turned him into a wolf, so that his own shepherd-boys and dogs gave him chase? And Ishullanu, her father's gardener: had she not turned him into a bat? Gilgamesh had no desire to be so treated.

Ishtar, scorned, caused Anu to create a heaven-bull which killed five hundred of Gilgamesh's warriors before it was slain by the king and Enkidu. Ishtar cursed Gilgamesh, whereupon Enkidu threw a thigh-bone of the bull into her face. Ishtar and her priestesses then could do nothing but wail over the thigh-bone of the bull of heaven, but the heroes poured oil into the horns of the monster, then poured out the oil as an offering to Shamash, and finally returned to the palace, where Gilgamesh was hailed as mightiest among men.

By the rejoicing did not last long. Enkidu, with a vision of approaching death before his eyes, took to his bed.

Then Gilgamesh assembled his nobles and said, "Like a wailing woman I cry for Enkidu, my friend. What now to me are my festal robe, my axe, my lance, my sword?" He returned to the hero's bed and called to Enkidu, speaking to him of their old days together. But his friend made no answer; and when Gilgamesh touched him on the heart he knew that that heart had ceased to beat. Then Gilgamesh drew a cover over the still body of his comrade. In his grief he roared like a lion and tore hair from his head. When he grew calmer, he promised the shade of Enkidu that he would cause all Erech to mourn him.

After six days of mourning, Gilgamesh left ramparted Erech and took his way over the steppes, for he was minded to speak with UTNAPISHTIM, his ancestor. Having wandered long, Gilgamesh reached the mountain at the earth's end. There he saw the terrible scorpion-man and his wife who keep watch over the rising and setting of the sun. When challenged by the scorpion-man, Gilgamesh answered, "I would go to Utnapishtim, to that forefather of mine who shares unending life with the gods, in order to ask him about the mysteries of death and life."

Then Gilgamesh went on, though warned by the scorpion-man that the road of the setting sun had never been traveled by man. Twelve miles wide was the inside of the mountain. After eight miles he cried aloud, for the darkness was thick, nor could he see what lay behind him. After nine miles he felt the north wind; after ten, he plucked up his courage; after eleven, he began to see sunlight; and after twelve miles he was in the open again.

Before him lay a grove of the gods. The branches were of lapis lazuli, and rubies hung upon the trees. Siduri, the cupbearer of the gods, was seated there by the rim of the sea, but when she saw Gilgamesh she feared his shape and his woeful visage and therefore locked her gate and the door of her chamber. Yet she talked with Gilgamesh through window and gave him counsel.

"Eat and drink, and have joy in wife and child. Do this while you can, for the gods have allotted death to man and have kept life for themselves."

Gilgamesh paid no heed. "Where is the way to Utnapishtim? If it can be done, I will pass over the sea."

Siduri, the cupbearer, asked how anyone except Shamash could pass over those waters of death. And yet there might be a way. Ur-Shanabi, the shipman of Utnapishtim, might consent to ferry him over.

Ur-Shanabi was found and was won over to sympathy with Gilgamesh in his bereavement. Together they poled the ship along. When they came to the waters of death, which Gilgamesh might not touch, Gilgamesh stripped off his garment and held it aloft as a sail, and thus they came at last to the far one, to Utnapishtim.

Like Siduri and Ur-Shanabi, Utnapishtim was quick to notice the deep signs of grief and pain upon the countenance of Gilgamesh.

"Why should my cheeks not be so wasted, my heart so sad?" asked Gilgamesh. "My friend, who endured all hardships with me, has been overtaken by the fate of mankind. I have mourned him and I mourn him still. My friend, whom I love, has turned into earth. And shall not I, like him, lie down and rise not up again?" And reminding Utnapishtim that he had risked all and endured great pains in order to reach him, he asked for a share of Utnapishtim's wisdom.

Yet what could Utnapishtim answer? Death is ever the slayer of life. Do we build a house believing it will stand forever? Do we always find the river in flood?

Gilgamesh grew angry. Was there no justice in the universe? He and Utnapishtim looked enough alike to be brothers, yet he himself was born to fight and to die, whereas Utnapishtim, like a god, was even then idly enjoying endless life.

Then, partly to compliment Gilgamesh, and partly to turn his mind away from his sorrows, and partly, perhaps, to hint that he, himself, did not know why he had been singled out by the gods for special favor, Utnapishtim began to speak of the days of the great deluge:

Ages ago, the gods ruling over Shuruppak on the Euphrates resolved to send a flood against the inhabitants because of their sins. But Ea warned Utnapishtim, who thereupon began, with the aid of his family and servants, to build a great ship, two hundred feet long, two hundred feet broad, and two hundred feet high. When asked what he was doing, Utnapishtim replied that Enlil had grown to hate him and all other men, and that he, Utnapishtim, was planning to shift his allegiance to Ea and to dwell in his watery kingdom. He loaded his sturdy, decked-over ark with food and drink and treasure, and brought in cattle and sheep and skilled servants and all the members of his family.

When the storm came it was so terrible that the very gods were frightened and withdrew for safety's sake to the remote heaven of Anu. But after six days and nights the hurricane passed away and the torrents of rain ceased.

On the seventh day Utnapishtim opened a window, and wept as sunlight burst inward upon him. At about this time the ark grounded upon the summit of a mountain. Utnapishtim released a dove and then a swallow, but they returned, for the ark was still their only resting place. A raven, released later, did not return; and those within knew that the waters were at last drying up. They drove out the animals, then came out of the ark and sacrificed to the gods.

Enlil at first was enraged that anyone had escaped his storm, but the other gods had been appeased, and Ea argued that good men should not have been made to perish for the sins of the wicked. At length Enlil relented and blessed Utnapishtim and his wife, declaring that he had transformed them into gods and would see to it that they should dwell forever in a distant paradise at the estuary of the streams.

When Utnapishtim ended his tale and Gilgamesh was preparing to leave, Utnapishtim's wife took pity on the weary Gilgamesh and asked her husband to make the heroic voyager a gift.

"At the bottom of the underworld sea," Utnapishtim whispered, "is a briar-plant. If you pluck it, it will pierce your hand, but do not hesitate, for it is the plant of life."

Gilgamesh tied stones to his feet and sank to the bottom of the sea at the designated spot, grasped the plant, cast off the stones, and rose again. At once the boatman and Gilgamesh began the return voyage, Gilgamesh rejoicing at the thought of that which he was bringing back to Erech and calling it the plant of metamorphosis and rejuvenation. But after they had crossed the sea and completed a good part of the land journey, Gilgamesh bathed in a spring, leaving the plant unguarded upon the ground. A serpent smelled the sweet plant, slid up, and carried it away. (That is why the serpent is able to cast off his old skin and renew his youth, whereas man must grow older and older until he dies.)

Now Gilgamesh despaired of bringing the gift of new life to Enkidu, but his longing to see his old friend was not lessened. In Erech again, he brooded over this thought.

Anointed and clad in a clean garment, contrary to the ancient custom of Allatu, he burst into the lower world and began to bestir himself as if he had been at home. Not for lack of courage was he defeated; but the mysterious forces of the dark land of Arallu began to restrain him and to sap his strength. With difficulty he regained the upper world.

Then, since he could not go to Enkidu, he begged Enlil and then Sin and finally Ea to cause the ghost of Enkidu to rise before him. Ea gave orders to Nergal, who opened a hole in the earth, through which the spirit of Gilgamesh's old companion came rushing up like a wind. The heroes embraced, but what comfort could they offer each other? The serpent had stolen Gilgamesh's plant of life; and what Enkidu knew of the laws of Arallu was so melancholy that he refused to share it with his friend lest he be bowed down with weeping.

Gilgamesh nevertheless had one final question. Did a man's actions and decisions on earth make a difference in the land of Allatu and Nergal?

Yes, here at last was a scrap of comfort. Virtue was not scorned but was still itself. He who had died in battle was tended by father and mother and wife; he who had perished without having earned the friendship of his fellows, the leavings of the pot and the crusts of bread thrown into the street made up his portion.

Legends of the Hebrews

The ancient land of Israel, the home of the Hebrew people, lay between Egypt and Babylonia. The faith of the Hebrews lives as religion; the legends and history told for all time in the Old Testament are a part of the knowledge of everyone; there is no need for retelling here. Yet the reader as he acquaints himself with other sections of this book will undoubtedly turn in his mind to the account which the Bible gives: the creation of the world; the Garden of Eden and the fall of man; the Flood; the lives of the patriarchs, Abraham, Isaac, Jacob; the story of Joseph and the journey to Egypt; the exodus from Egypt and return to the Promised Land, under the leadership of Moses; the days of Joshua, and of the Judges, among whom were Deborah, Gideon, Samson; the idyllic story of Ruth; the reigns of Saul, of David, of Solomon, builder of the Temple; the thunderings of the mighty prophets, Elijah, Isaiah, Jeremiah, Amos, Hosea, Ezekiel; the patience and wisdom of Job; the victories of Esther over Haman, of Daniel over Nebuchadnezzar, and, in the *Apocrypha,* of Judith over Holofernes, and the victories of the Maccabees. To these each reader will add countless other names and episodes which are the imperishable heritage of all of us.

Apart from the Old Testament however there are in the traditions of the Hebrew people, of the Jewish people as they came to be called, myths and legends which are often referred to, and which concern themselves with persons and beings for the most part mentioned only incidentally in the Bible. These legends, which tell of Lilith, said to have been the first wife of Adam, of the world of the angels and archangels and demons, and other later figures, were handed down orally by the Hebrew people until the scholars and scribes, the rabbis and preachers began to make use of them for the purpose of education and instruction. They collected the legends and tales, along with writings of their own, in such works as the *Talmud* and the *Midrash,* which are almost inexhaustible repositories of the legends and myths of the Jewish people.

In the later Middle Ages, a body of esoteric knowledge which had been accumulated in the course of 2000 years by mystically minded Jews, came to exercise considerable influence on Jewish legends. This lore, gathered together in the *Cabala,* pictured a shadowy world haunted by unspeakable demons, specters, ghosts, and *dibbukim* (transmigrating souls), and out of these cabalistic superstitions came such legends as that of the *golem* and the *dibbuk.*

We give in the following entries the Hebraic and Jewish legends which, standing apart from the Old Testament, have widely influenced the world of thought and imagination.

ANCIENT HEBREW LEGENDS

Lilith

As the early pages of Genesis give two accounts of the creation of woman, a legend developed that Adam had not one wife but two, and that LILITH was the first wife. Lilith, like Adam, had been created from the dust (*adamah*) of the earth, had been one of the wives of SAMMAEL (or Satan), but, being of a wild and passionate nature, had left her spouse and joined Adam. Lilith refused to be subservient and submissive to Adam on the ground that since both had issued from the dust, they were both equal. They quarreled and Lilith fled.

At Adam's prayer, the Lord sent three angels in pursuit of her, called SENOI, SANSENOI, and SAMMANGELOF. He ordered them to tell her to return, and if she refused to obey, then a hundred of her offspring would die daily. Lilith resisted all their efforts to have her return, and vowed vengeance against little children, infants, and babes. However, she was powerless to do harm in the presence of an amulet bearing the names of the three angels who halted her on her flight.

Lilith is conceived in rabbinical tradition as having consorted with Adam once more during the period of 130 years when he was separated from Eve, after their expulsion from Eden. From their union issued the demons or SHEDIM who rove about the world plaguing mankind.

In medieval times Lilith was identified as a night demon, sometimes also referred to as LAMIA, who attacked those who sleep alone, and seduced men in their sleep. She was represented as a beautiful temptress with alluring long hair.

The Angels

The angels are described as supernatural powers, obeying the command of the Creator and doing his bidding. Their functions are legion. Some are appointed for celestial service, while others are attached to earth and especially to man. They mediate between God and man, carry prayers to the throne of God, and accompany the dead on their departure from this world. There is a special class of angels whom the Creator calls into existence for a very short span of time. They are called forth by the breath of the Almighty from the rivers of liquid fire under the throne of the Eternal. They sing a hymn to his glory, and then disappear. To execute every behest of God a new angel is created who passes away as soon as he has executed the command.

Angels are also the guardians of the nations, seventy nations being so guarded, over whom rules MICHAEL as Israel's angel-prince. With these God sits in council when holding judgment over the world, each angel pleading the cause of his nation. Besides the guardian angels of the nations, sixty-three angels are mentioned as janitors of the seven heavens, and at each of these heavens stand other angels as seal-bearers. The head and chief of all these is ASRIEL. Three great classes of angels are: the SERAPHIM, the CHERUBIM, and the OPHANIM.

The essence of the angels is fire; their fiery breath consumes men, and no man can endure the sound of their voices. The angels of wrath and anger are wholly of fire; but another group called ISHIM is composed half of fire and half of snow. The angel of death is full of fiery eyes, so that anyone who looks at him falls down in dread. The angel who presides over the ERELIM has seventy thousand heads and seventy thousand mouths on each head, and seventy thousand tongues in each mouth.

According to one tradition, each angel was one-third of a world in size; according to another their length is a journey of five hundred years. Their food is manna, of which Adam and Eve ate before they sinned.

On his breast each angel carries a tablet, in which the name of God and the name of the angel are combined. Of the myriads of angels, the names of some are designated. AKATRIEL carries the words and thoughts of man to the celestial regions. GALLIZUR, who is also called RASIEL, listens to what is being proclaimed behind the Veil before the throne of God, and makes it known to the world. BEN NEZ is the prince of the storm; BARAKIEL of lightning; LAILAHEL of night; JORKAMI of hail; RAASHIEL of earthquake; SHALGIEL of snow; RAHAB of the sea.

The angels on earth have the function of accompanying and watching over men. Every man has a special guardian angel, and there are accompanying angels. Thus two angels—one good and one evil—accompany man. Every pious and virtuous act accomplished by man produces a tutelary angel. The tutelary angels also have the function of pleading the cause of the just and the pious before the throne of the Eternal. Whenever one of the heroes or pious men of Israel meets with a calamity, or is in great distress, they intercede for him before God. Thus when Abraham raised his hand to sacrifice his son Isaac, when Pharaoh intended to kill Moses, hosts of ministering angels prostrated themselves before the Lord and pleaded until the Creator saved them.

Great as is the number and influence of the angels, yet in many respects they are inferior to man. ENOCH, translated to heaven, intercedes on behalf of the angels instead of having them intercede for him, and none of the angels could learn the secrets of God which were told to him.

The Archangels

There are four Archangels who surround the throne of the Creator. They are MICHAEL, RAPHAEL, GABRIEL, and URIEL.

MICHAEL is the harbinger and messenger bringing good tidings. He is also the angel of peace, and as such is often called the high priest, ministering in heaven. His name means "who is like God" and he stands to the right of God's throne. He is the heavenly scribe who records the actions of nations and men, and at the same time he is the medium for the transmission of the Law.

Michael's adversary is SAMMAEL, who is also known as Satan (see Satan, below).

GABRIEL, who is next to Michael, standing to the left of the Throne, is the strength of the Lord, as his name signifies. Gabriel is made of fire. He manifests the Divine justice and punishment for the wicked, and only for the latter is he terrible, being mild before the just. It was Gabriel who marked the fronts of the wicked with a letter in blood, and those of the pious and just with a letter in ink, so that the angels of destruction should not harm them.

RAPHAEL personifies the power of healing. He heals and banishes disease. He accompanied the patriarch TOBIAS on his journey and helped him to conclude it successfully, after which he healed TOBIT of his blindness.

URIEL personifies the radiance emanating from the divine nature. He rules over hell and will bring from there the souls of the dead for judgment on the last day. Uriel was the guide of Enoch through the underworld and related to the patriarch the sufferings of the damned. He is also identified as the archangel who was sent to warn Noah of the impending deluge and as the angel who wrestled with Jacob.

Other Angel Princes

The angel SANDALPHON stands upon the earth, while his head reaches the heavens. He surpasses in height all his heavenly colleagues. Sandalphon weaves crowns of glory for his Creator.

REDIYAO is the angel of rain, the genius of the celestial and earthly waters. His terrible voice resounds continually throughout the world.

METATRON is the prince of the world, the superintendent into whose hands the world is given. He is the angel who received the mission to lead the children of Israel into the Holy Land. Metatron is also the preserver and guardian of the law and of the Holy Writ.

The Fall of the Angels

Although all the angels called into being were pure and holy, some of them allowed themselves to be swayed by pride. SAMMAEL, who is also known as SATAN, was one of the Seraphim, with twelve wings. He at first recognized as his superior only the Creator himself, but soon a mad ambition entered his heart and he wished to usurp the throne of God. Sammael's jealousy knew no bounds, especially when he saw the favored position of the first man. He refused to pay homage to Adam, but, on the contrary, plotted with other angels to bring about the fall of man. Against the express command of the Lord he excited the passions of Adam and of Eve who committed the first sin and were expelled from Eden.

As a punishment of his pride and his jealousy Sammael and those angels who had joined with him in the conspiracy were ordered driven from heaven. The Seraph did not submit without a struggle, and there was a war between the rebel angels headed by Sammael and the angelic host headed by Michael. It was the archangel Michael in particular who struggled with Sammael. In his struggle the latter caught the wings of Michael and tried to drag him down in his fall, but the Eternal saved Michael.

Satan

Sammael, or SATAN as he came to be more familiarly known, after his fall came to be prince of hell and the ruler of the devils or fallen angels. He also was appointed as the executioner of the human race, or the angel of death. But the Lord had even further use for Satan—to try men to determine whether they are truly good or at base wicked. Men have the freedom to choose good or evil. Sammael's function was to try to seduce mankind and to involve them in wicked deeds. When he succeeded in this, he appeared before the heavenly tribunal as prosecutor. He was then tempter, seducer, accuser, and executioner.

The Demons

The demons, male and female, in the legends of the Hebrews, fill the world and surround man in all shapes and forms, spreading disease and suffering among mortals. However, they are not always absolutely evil. Sometimes they are, like the sprites, serviceable and kind, and may be made not only innocuous but obedient to mankind.

The demons are divided into SHEDIM, ROUKHIN, MAZIKIN, and LILIN. In three things they are like man, while in three things they are like angels. Like man they take nourishment, propagate themselves, and die. But like angels they have wings, pass through space unhindered, and know the future. They assume the form of human beings or any other form they choose; they see but cannot be seen. They are also supposed to be able to rotate their heads completely. In accordance with their perverse nature, the demons have their dwelling places in spots shunned by mortals—in deserts and morasses, in ruined and desolate houses, and dirty places. To go alone into such places is dangerous, and especially on the eves of Wednesday or Saturday. Demons have no power over anything that is sealed, counted, measured or tied up. The pronouncing of God's name can always overcome them.

Ashmedai

King of the demons is ASHMEDAI or Asmodeus. Of immense strength and cunning, he is intent upon doing harm to man. King Solomon, however, was able to subdue him to his bidding.

A legend tells that when King Solomon set about building the Temple, he faced the problem of cutting the stone, for no iron was to be used in the construction of the Temple. From the rabbis he learned about an insect, called the SHAMIR, which had existed since the creation and which had the power of cutting the hardest stone; Moses had used it to cut the precious stones of the *Ephod*. However, only Ashmedai, it seemed, knew where the Shamir could be procured. To capture Ashmedai, Solomon sent his servant BENAIAH to the mountain where the arch-demon dwelled. There Benaiah discovered the cistern which Ashmedai kept filled with water to satisfy his great thirst. Finding the cistern covered with a stone which was sealed with the demon's seal, the clever servant dug a hole below the cistern and drained off the water. He then dug another pit above the cistern, made a channel from it to the cistern, and by this means proceeded to fill up the empty cistern with wine. When Ashmedai returned he discovered his seal intact, drank of the wine, and, intoxicated, fell asleep. Thereupon Benaiah fastened around the neck of the sleeping demon a magic chain upon which was engraved the name of God. Powerless, the demon was dragged to Solomon's presence and compelled to reveal the whereabouts of the Shamir. Ashmedai remained in the power of Solomon until the building of the temple was completed.

MEDIEVAL JEWISH LEGENDS

The Golem

From the thirteenth century Hebrew mystics comes the legend of the GOLEM (literally, shapeless or lifeless matter), designating a homunculus created by the magical invocation of a name. Rabbi Elijah of Chelm, tradition had it, created such a golem from clay, inscribing upon its forehead the *Shemhamforash,* or secret name of God. He thus gave it the power of life, but withheld from it the power of speech. When the creature attained giant size and strength, the Rabbi, appalled by its destructive potentialities, tore the life-giving name from its forehead, and it crumbled into dust. In some versions of the legend, not the word of God but the word *emet,* or "truth," was cut into the forehead of the golem. The destruction of the creature was effected by erasing the initial letter of *emet,* leaving *met* ("dead").

The Dybbuk

Belief in spirit-possession, the faculty of demons to render a man the physical "vessel" through which the demon could operate, was one of the terrifying superstitions of East European Jews in the Middle Ages. Demons who took possession of a human body, it was believed, exercised such complete control over it that the personality and the will of the victim were extinguished. They could be expelled only by the most powerful exorcisms. In perpetually seeking to make their homes in a man's body, these demons or *Dibbukim* (singular, *dibbuk* or DYBBUK) had as their greatest desire the invading of the body of a scholar.

The initial appearance of a *dybbuk* is in a story included in the *Ma'aseh Book* published in 1602 but containing material whose origin is considerably earlier than that date. In this story the spirit or dibbuk which took possession of a young man was the spirit of one who in this life had sinned egregiously, and the spirit therefore could find no peace. This form of the belief, possession by the restless spirit of a deceased person, is in essence a version of the doctrine of the transmigration of souls.

These strange stories filled with medieval superstition have a curious fascination which has appealed to writers in later periods.

Myths and Legends of the Persians

The Persian or Iranian civilization made very distinctive contributions to the culture of the ancient world. While it laid great stress on efficiency in governmental organization and was able, through conquest, to establish the most extensive empire of its day, it also rose to philosophical and ethical heights in its religion, known in later times as Zoroastrianism, after its founder, Zoroaster, or Zarathustra, who is said to have lived in the seventh century B. C. The teachings of Zoroaster are contained in the sacred writings known collectively as *Avesta,* and it is on this work that we base our account of early Persian mythology. The key to Persian mythology is dualism, with a constant struggle taking place between the forces of good, or light, and the forces of evil, or darkness. As compared with the gods of the Egyptians and Babylonians, the gods of the Persians tended more to be personifications of abstract qualities than actual personages.

Zoroastrianism flourished in Persia until the seventh century A.D., when the new faith of Mohammedanism overwhelmed the ancient religion. Mohammedanism, a monotheistic religion, in its very nature ruled out any further development of Persian mythology. However, the poet Firdausi, under the patronage of the Mohammedan ruler of Persia, created a host of legendary figures supposedly drawn from Persia's great past. His characters are not gods but heroes of epic proportions. Our account of Persian mythology, then, consists of two parts—descriptions of the gods and goddesses of Zoroaster and tales of the folk heroes of Firdausi.

ANCIENT PERSIAN MYTHS

We give in the three entries which follow the ancient Persian beliefs more or less as they are said to have been set and fixed by Zoroaster in the seventh century B.C. It should be noted that the reference to the prophet Zarathustra are to Zoroaster himself under another name by which he is also known.

The Persian Pantheon

The central figure in the Persian Pantheon was AHURA MAZDA (ORMAZD), the Lord of Wisdom, who created all good things. Lesser gods, members of Ahura Mazda's court, were the AMESHA SPENTAS (Immortal Holy Ones); and another step lower were the YAZATAS (Venerable Ones), such as ATAR, the genius of fire, and ANAHITA, genius of water. Over against Ormazd was set the Spirit of Evil, ANGRA MAINYU or AHRIMAN, often called DRUJ (Deception). He had his army of *daevas* (demons), six of whom were sufficiently powerful to oppose the Amesha Spentas.

Ahura Mazda and the Creation

AHURA MAZDA created the AMESHA SPENTAS, and, as each was formed, ANGRA MAINYU shaped his evil counterpart.

Ahura Mazda created the stars, an army ready to do battle against Angra Mainyu's evil spirits. TISHTRYA, the dog star, presided over the eastern stars, HAPTOK RENG over the northern, SATAVES over the western, and VANAND over the southern. Angra Mainyu created the planets to throw the constellation into disorder. The result was a disfiguration of the cosmos, as from fire and smoke.

Typical of the struggles going on above men's heads was the strife between Tishtrya, the dog-star, and APAOSHA, a demon who had captured the rains and caused the drought of the dog-days. In the shape of a white horse, with golden ears and caparisoned in gold, Tishtrya fought against Apaosha, who had assumed the form of a horrible black horse, bald of head and back and tail. After three days Tishtrya gave ground and complained to Ahura Mazda that his loss of strength resulted from his worshippers' failure to sacrifice to him and name his name. But when the worshippers remedied this fault, Tishtrya met Apaosha again and overcame him and drove him from the sea Vourukasha. Then Tishtrya took of the waters of the sea and caused them to become showers watering the earth.

Angra Mainyu and his demons, after a struggle lasting for a quarter of a year, were put down by the Amesha Spentas and Yazatas.

Ahura Mazda created the goddess ANAHITA (the Spotless), the source of all waters, including those that purify the sea and those that fall as dew and rain upon the cultivated lands and all the earth. But at first it was not as it is now, for the creation of waters antedated the shaping of the lands.

The Amesha Spenta AMERETAT caused ten thousand different kinds of plants to grow, including the Tree of All Seeds, which encouraged other plants to grow, and the Ox-Horn Tree (White Haoma), which was better still, since all who ate it were said to become immortal. Angra Mainyu created a lizard to harm the Ox-Horn Tree, but the Good Spirit created ten fish to swim round the tree in the sea Vourukasha, so that it was never left unprotected.

Next came the creation of fire, or rather of fires, since there were five kinds: Berezisavanh, the sacred fire of the temples; Vohu Fryana, the fire which burns within the bodies of men and beasts; Urvazishta, the potential fire within trees; Vazishta, the lightning; Spenishta, the fire which burns in the presence of Ahura Mazda.

The creation of animals was more complicated. Ahura Mazda had created a mighty ox, but it was a mere raging, senseless monster, which could do no good in the world which it encumbered. But the god MITHRA, with torch in one hand and knife in the other, was born out of a solid rock beneath a certain fig tree on the banks of a river. First he clothed himself with fig leaves, and then in godlike manner he made a treaty with the sun. Next, seeing the primeval ox, he seized it by the horns, mounted upon its back, and broke it to his will. But the raven—an incarnation of VERETHRAGNA (Victory)—came with a message from his master and Mithra's friend, the sun. Mithra was to take his knife and kill the monster. When the youthful god did so, all species of animals sprang up at once from the limbs and the flowing blood of the sacrificed creature.

It is to be observed that the Verethragna-raven existed before this particular creation, and the same seems to have been believed of other mythical birds held in high reverence by the Persians. SAENA, the simurgh, a bird similar to the roc of the *Arabian Nights,* rested on the tree of good remedies in the sea Vourukasha, and shook down from it the seed of all plants. His feathers had magic powers, as shown in the story of Zal and his descendants, soon to be related. When Rustam was brought into the world with the aid of the sword, Zal healed Rudabeh's wound with a stroke of the simurgh's feather, and Rustam himself, when wounded by Isfandyar, was brought back from death's door by the same means. Second among birds was CAMROSH, whose duty it was to collect the seeds shaken down from the tree and to see that Tishtrya rained them down with the waters which reinvigorate our earth. Remarkable also was the bird KARSHIPTAR, who preached the religion of Zarathustra within the *vara* or enclosure of Yima (described below).

Human beings were the last creatures to be formed. The spirit of the first man, GAYA MARETAN, coexisted for three thousand years with the spirit of the primeval ox, but at last, from the sweat of Ahura Mazda, was formed his body, that of a tall and handsome youth of fifteen. Gaya Maretan repelled a thousand evil daevas sent against him by Angra Mainyu, but after thirty years he succumbed to hunger and disease, and a poison poured over his body by the Spirit of Evil. Various parts of his body became various metals. Gold was his seed. After his body had been preserved for forty years by Spenta ARMAITI, the genius of the earth, it brought forth the first human pair, MASHYA and MASHYOI. At first one could not have foreseen their future, as they were joined together and made their first appearance as a *rivas*-plant, with one stem and fifteen leaves, the last detail signifying that like Gaya Maretan they were born at the age of fifteen years.

Men were made for the good kingdom of Ahura Mazda, but they often fall away and join with Angra Mainyu in the apparently unending struggle of Good against Evil. But the struggle will end. The last man, the final Saoshyant, or savior, will appear in kingly glory and will completely put down forever the Druj and all the evil creation.

The Vara of Yima

On a certain day the prophet Zarathustra asked Ahura Mazda: "Who was the first man with whom thou didst converse?"

The answer was that that man was YIMA, the great shepherd. Ahura had asked Yima, son of Vivanghat, to be the teacher of his law. Yima felt that he had not the skill and that he had not had the instruction to enable him to do so. But when Ahura asked Yima to make his world thrive, he received an enthusiastic response. Yima gladly accepted a golden ring and a poniard as symbols of authority, and at once began his beneficent rule.

After three hundred winters there was no more room for flocks and herds, for men and their red blazing fires, and for dogs and birds, those friends of men. Warned by Ahura, Yima pressed the soil with his ring and bored it with his poniard, saying to the genius of the earth, "O Spenta Armaiti, stretch thyself afar, to bear flocks and herds and men." And the earth increased itself by one-third.

After another period of three hundred years there was a similar crisis, with a similar solution—and again after the next three hundred years. Thus, within a thousand years the earth had doubled in size and had become filled with flocks and herds and men, under the sway of the kingly shepherd, Yima.

Ahura knew, however, that fatal winters of frost and ever-mounting snow were about to smite the earth. He and his celestial gods met, therefore, with Yima and the souls of righteous mortals, and, in the presence of all, Ahura gave Yima new instructions. Yima was to build a great foursquare *vara* or enclosure, as long as a riding-ground, into which he was to bring the seeds of men and women, of every kind of cattle, of every kind of tree, of every kind of fruit. But all were to be of the greatest, best and finest sorts; no misshapen individuals or specimens were to be brought thither; nothing was to bear the mark of Angra Mainyu.

Instructed further by Ahura, Yima stamped upon the earth, the earth became clay, and with this clay the vara was made. Snow may beat upon the outer world, but within the vara there is a stream whose banks bear never-failing food, a stream beside which the birds have made their settlements, and there is a dwelling place for men as well: a house with a balcony, a courtyard, and a gallery. The vara has a door and a window, but the whole enclosure has been sealed up with the golden ring. The inhabitants do not lack light; yet they see the stars and the moon and the sun only once a year, and a year seems as a day to them. Every forty years, a male and a female child are born to every human couple. And thus it is for every sort of creature. The law of Mazda is known within the enclosure, for it was brought thither by the heavenly bird Karshiptar. And the men of Yima's vara live the happiest life, for they are the virtuous dead.

LEGENDS OF PERSIAN HEROES

We turn now to the Persian legends and tales which have come down to us principally in the form set by the Persian poet Firdausi, who lived in the tenth century A.D. Firdausi resided at the court of Mahmud of Ghazni, but Firdausi happened to be an antiquarian as well as a poet, an antiquarian with a love for old Iranian matters, though Persia in his day was, of course, under Mohammedan control. Hence, when Firdausi came to write his great romantic epic on the exploits of Rustam, he did not commence with his hero's birth, but, calling his work the *Shah Namah*, or *Book of Kings*, went back even to days before the founding of the fire-worshipers' religion, in order to begin with the best account he could give of Kaiumers, the legendary first king and first law-giver of the Persians.

Kaiumers and Husheng

KAIUMERS dwelt among the mountains, and he and his people wore garments made of the skins of beasts. Yet even in those rude days he established a code of laws and saw to it that there was fair play among his subjects. There was a great sorrow in Kaiumers' life; his son, Saiamuk, had been slain by the demon-son of an old opponent of the king.

But Saiamuk had left a son, HUSHENG, to comfort the grandfather and to wipe out the old defeat. Animals as well as men were obedient to Husheng, so that when he marched against the daevas his army was joined by wolves, tigers, panthers, and birds of prey. The enemy could not stand against him, nor could the daevas flee for long without being run down by Husheng's terrible allies.

Husheng was the first to bring fire from stone. This he did by chance, for he hurled a stone at a monster and missed, but happened instead to strike a rock upon the mountainside, with the result that sparks flew out, causing a fire which swept across the whole plain, swallowing up the monster in its course.

Husheng identified fire, which he could now kindle at will, with the light from heaven. He therefore instituted the Religion of the Fire-worshipers. But he saw, too, that fire had mundane uses, and in time he was able to teach his people to bake and also to work as blacksmiths at the forge. Nor did his contributions end here, for it was he who first guided streamlets into the fields to irrigate them.

TAHUMERS, the son of Husheng, continued his father's work, and in his days falcons were trained to assist the huntsmen, wool was spun, and garments and carpets were woven. He was called the Binder of Demons, for, having defeated an army of daevas in battle, he took many of their number prisoners. On condition that he would spare their lives, the captives promised to teach him a wonderful art. Then, to the king's great joy, the daevas brought books and pens and ink and instructed him in their full use.

Jemshid and Zohak

The story of JEMSHID, the next in the royal line, is made up of contrasting brilliance and gloom, with one moment of soft and tender light.

The monarch began by continuing the civilizing work of his ancestors. Coats of mail were made in his time, as well as garments of silk. His servants built palaces of brick and constructed vessels which moved upon sea and river. And he invented for himself a jewelled throne upon which at his word of command he could instantly be transported by daevas whithersoever he would. So he reigned for seven hundred years, during which time not one of his subjects suffered death or even was afflicted with disease.

But in the end Jemshid came to believe that his subjects' happiness proceeded from himself alone, and he uttered words which heaven could not tolerate. Then his earthly splendor faded and the tongues of men grew bold against him.

While Jemshid had been falling into the sin of presumption, terrible things had been occurring in the Arabian royal house. Tricked by IBLIS, an evil spirit, the Arabian prince, ZOHAK, had killed his father and ascended the throne. To distract the new king's mind and to get him completely in his power, Iblis day by day provided for Zohak more and more delicate dishes, such as up to that time had never been known. In return, Iblis asked only that a mere whim of his might be gratified. It was his wish to kiss the naked shoulder of the monarch. Zohak made no objection, Iblis bestowed the kiss and instantly vanished, but from Zohak's shoulder sprang up two black serpents, which writhed about, seeking food.

The serpents could not be detached or charmed away from Zohak, and eventually it was learned that if the monarch was to live, each snake would have to be fed daily with the brains of a man.

A hysterical fear of the king now began to spread in all directions, so that the neighboring Persian nobles in time came to the assistance of the Arab troops, even at the expense of Jemshid and their own land of Persia. Jemshid tried to stem the current, but at last despaired and became an exile and a lonely wanderer.

Having escaped Zohak's spies, Jemshid at length found himself in Zabulistan. Now the king of Zabulistan had a daughter, at that time fifteen years of age. She had great beauty and charm but was even more remarkable for her courage, judgment, and discretion. She could fight against heroes in the field, and contribute her share to the discussions of her father's council. The nurse of this princess was another remarkable woman, a Kabul sorceress, who had long ago told her charge that her destiny was to meet and to wed the great Jemshid.

Jemshid, weary and dispirited, chanced to sit down by the door of the palace garden, under the shade of a tree. One of the princess's slave-girls, coming out of the door upon an errand, was so struck by Jemshid's beauty and melancholy that the question "Who art thou?" suddenly escaped from her lips. Jemshid replied that he had once been in possession of great wealth but that his good fortune was now far behind him, as was his native land. And just as the slave-girl had asked a question without intending to, he now involuntarily expressed a wish for a few cups of wine. The girl returned to her mistress to speak the traveler's praises. Thinking, doubtless, of her nurse's prophecy, and guessing the identity of the stranger, the princess said: "He asks only for wine, but I will give him both wine and music, and all my heart."

Straightway she invited Jemshid into the garden. Fearing for his ultimate safety, he hesitated, but when he looked into her face he was unable to resist what his eyes saw there. She took him by the hand and led him to a cool spot near the basin of a fountain, where carpets had earlier been spread for her. Handmaidens washed the traveler's feet, and then the princess called for music and food and wine. Jemshid ate very little, but readily accepted several cups of wine. When the princess gave a half-hint of her disapproval, she learned that Jemshid was no slave of wine: he drank to forget that he had enemies. And again the princess thought of her nurse's prophecy and felt sure in her heart that the man who sat facing her was indeed Jemshid.

Two doves, a male and a female, happened to alight on the garden wall at a spot not far from the fountain. Their billing and cooing brought a blush to the cheek of the princess, who immediately had her bow and arrows brought to her. "Which of them shall I hit?" she asked, but Jemshid gently took the bow from her hand and, selecting a well-feathered arrow, asked, "If I hit the female, shall she whom I most admire in this company be mine?" The damsel assented, Jemshid drew the string, and the arrow pierced the raised wings of the female dove and pinned them together. The startled male bird flew away, but soon returned to the spot where its mate had fallen. The maidens were still exclaiming over Jemshid's strength and dexterity, for the story went that no man in that kingdom could so much as bend the bow he had handled; but now the princess took the bow again, saying, "The male bird has returned; if my aim is successful shall I have for my husband the man I choose?"

But now the Kabul nurse appeared and in a moment confirmed the damsel's conjecture. A picture of Jemshid was brought from the palace, and, after glancing at it, the princess put it into Jemshid's hand. Tears welled up in Jemshid's eyes, but he denied himself and said that he was not the man who had sat for the portrait, and that he wept only out of sympathy. But just as the princess had made him disregard his fear of entering the garden, she now made him thrust aside his fear of divulging his identity. He uttered his name and told her of his wanderings. Then the princess led him to her own quarters and they were married, but without the knowledge of her father, the king.

The king, who now saw very little of his daughter, in time came to know, through his servants, that the princess was with child. One may readily imagine what his feelings were. But the Kabul nurse defended her charge, reminding the king that no dishonor attached to being the father by marriage of Jemshid; and the princess herself reminded her father that he had long ago promised her she might bestow her heart upon the man of her choice.

The king then declared that he was satisfied, but actually all that pleased him was the opportunity he envisaged of gaining the favor of Zohak by sending him Jemshid as a captive.

Jemshid distrusted the king's professions of friendship and slipped away, but by doing so he only prolonged his trials, for in distant India he was taken in his sleep by a party of his enemies. So at last he fell into the hands of Zohak. The tyrant ordered that Jemshid be bound between two boards. Then with a saw the body of Jemshid was divided, lengthwise, into equal halves.

The princess, hearing of this, lost all interest in her life and began to waste away for grief. At last, impatient, she took poison and so died.

Feridun

Not long after, Zohak had a terrible dream, which signified, as his wise men reluctantly told him, that a certain youth named FERIDUN would cause his death. Now Zohak's very fear was one cause of his undoing. He ordered that all men of the family out of which his enemy was to come, should be slain. Feridun, only two months old, was luckily brought into a place of safety, but his father was done to death. At the age of sixteen, Feridun learned from his mother why Zohak had destroyed his father; and from that time on he could not rest until he had slain the evil-doer.

Meanwhile, Zohak, brooding over the coming of Feridun, had become so unnerved that a bold blacksmith named GAVAH defied him to his face and with his whole family about him departed from the court without being punished. To be sure, Gavah's provocation had been strong enough: it had fallen to the lot of two of his sons to be killed to feed the serpents, a horror which Gavah would not endure.

The wronged multitudes now gathered around Gavah's banner—his leather apron fixed upon a spear. Feridun was found, and Gavah thanked Heaven for his good fortune. Now the leathern banner was adorned with gold and jewels. It became a sacred symbol of justice; and in later years all good kings were to do it honor.

Zohak madly led his army off toward India, his reasons being—according to one of the sisters of Jemshid, who had been his prisoners—first, that he expected Feridun to come from that direction and hoped to overpower him; and, second, that if he failed to meet Feridun, he might subdue all India, the home of sorcery, and thus obtain the aid of a great magician to cast a spell upon Feridun whenever he should actually appear. However, Zohak's absence enabled Feridun and Gavah to sack the king's treasury and to draw more people around them.

Now Feridun with his army began to move toward the king, and Zohak at first intended to face about and meet him with his loyal forces. But were they still loyal? He soon perceived that they were not. Going by night, alone, therefore, to spy upon the camp of his enemies, he saw Feridun laughing and talking with one of the beautiful sisters of Jemshid as if he had not a care in the world. This was more than Zohak could bear. He rushed in upon Feridun; but the youth heard him in time, seized his great mace, and struck him a blow upon the temples which crushed the bone. He was about to strike a second blow, which would have killed the tyrant instantly, when a supernatural voice whispered: "His punishment must be prolonged." So Feridun bound him with heavy chains and left him within a deep mountain cave to die a lingering death, alone.

The White-Headed Zal

SAM, one of Feridun's chiefs, who long survived his king, had a son, ZAL, whose hair was white, even from infancy. In other respects the child was without blemish, but the people felt there was something ominous about poor Zal's white hair—that he was a daeva's son and that he should be removed from the sight of men. At last Sam, with heavy heart, was persuaded to abandon the child. He left him upon the mountain Alberz to be devoured by beasts of prey.

The little white-haired child, crying upon the hard rock of the mountain, was discovered by the simurgh, who swooped down, and, instead of harming him, carried him off to his aerie and brought him up with his own nestlings.

One night, years later, Sam dreamed that his son was still alive. Hoping that the dream was true, he sent his people to the mountain, but in vain. In a second dream he was told that although he had been cruel to Zal,

Heaven had shielded the boy and blessed him. Now Sam went himself to the mountain and prayed that the boy might be restored to him, if only he were his own son and not the offspring of a daeva.

The simurgh now explained to Zal that he must return to his human father. But before he parted from the youth he gave him a feather from his wing, with these words: "When you are troubled or in danger, put this feather on the fire, and I will instantly appear to ensure your safety. Never forget me." Nor did he leave the lad without presenting him to his father and predicting that Zal would be worthy of the throne and diadem.

Zal was well received at court, and in time was left by his father in charge of Zabulistan. There he governed well, but, discontented with his lack of knowledge of the world, he refused to remain long in Zabul, and visited several other places, Kabul among them.

The chief of Kabul paid annual tribute to Sam, but because he was descended from the family of Zohak, Zal knew that he should keep at a distance from him, lest he incur the disapproval of his father and the king of Persia. Yet Zal ached to see RUDABEH, the chieftain's daughter, who was, he was told, all fragrance, as fair as the moon or as polished ivory, stately and tall, yet with dark ringlets extending to her slender feet, a maiden whose soft eyes, whose mere presence, made men think of heaven and love.

Within the city, Rudabeh had heard one of her father's emissaries describe Zal to her mother in the warmest terms. Zal's strangeness—his white hair and his peculiar upbringing—served rather to increase than to quell Rudabeh's desire to see the young hero whose tents were pitched so near her dwelling.

Perceiving that their mistress's interest in Zal was serious in its nature, Rudabeh's attendants strayed out of the city, their apparent intention being merely to gather roses, but they followed a stream which flowed past Zal's halting place. Zal, having discovered whose handmaidens these were, also followed the stream, taking with him only one servant, a lad to carry his bow. A bird sprang up from the water. Zal shot it upon the wing, and it fell to the earth, not far from the rose-gatherers. The servant, sent to get the bird, returned with something very different—a message that Rudabeh might be Zal's, if he proved to be her equal in rank. And soon those who had come to gather roses returned also with very different things—precious gems, and honorary robes, and two bright rings for the fingers of their mistress.

There was a beautiful rural retreat which the Kabul princess was fond of visiting, and to this favorite little palace she now retired. Informed of this, Zal approached the retreat soon after the sun had gone down. A sweet voice reached him from a balcony, thanking him for being willing to come so far on foot. Zal looked up and saw the bright face of the princess. His reply to her greeting must have pleased Rudabeh, for she now let her long tresses flow down from the balcony; and after she had tied the upper part of them to a ring in order to protect herself from the anticipated strain, Zal climbed up to Rudabeh's level by means of them.

Then these two were able to talk together all the night, with no one the wiser for it. Yet had anyone seen them—Rudabeh in her sweetness and beauty and Zal in his youthful majesty—he could only have felt that they were born to be man and wife. But the young lovers themselves knew that the views of their elders on matters of state might prevent their union.

After this there were stormy days, during which it looked as though Rudabeh would surely not become the bride of Zal, and might not even remain alive, so intent was the king of Persia upon rooting out all descendants of Zohak, the serpent-king.

Zal confessed to his father his love for Rudabeh; and when Sam, disturbed, consulted the astrologers, they told him that if the lovers were permitted to wed, the issue would be a son who would become a famous conqueror. At last the brave and charming mother of Rudabeh came to Sam with many magnificent presents, and begged him to use his influence with the king of Persia to prevent an attack upon Kabul. Zal was sent to the king, with a letter from Sam. The king, upon reading the letter—and Zal's heart, too—relented, and agreed to make peace with the ruler of Kabulistan. He also consulted astrologers, as Sam had done, and heard in his turn that the child of Zal and Rudabeh would be a hero of matchless valor. At last, to everyone's joy, the lovers were married at that beautiful summer palace where first they had met.

A new danger arose when Rudabeh was advanced in her pregnancy. She fell ill, and grew constantly worse. At last Zal took the feather of the Simurgh and placed it upon the fire, as his foster father had instructed him. There was a moment of darkness, but this was immediately dispelled when the simurgh appeared. Like the astrologers, the simurgh predicted that a wonderful child was about to be born, but not in the usual manner. Under the simurgh's directions, Rudabeh was drugged with wine, her side was opened, the child was drawn through the wound, and the incision was closed up and rubbed with an unknown herb and another feather from the Simurgh's wing.

The child, RUSTAM, astonished and overjoyed his parents. There was no other boy like him. Some even maintain that in his third year he rode on horseback, that in his fifth he ate as much as a man, and that in his eighth he was as powerful as any hero of the time.

Sohrab and Rustam

Many are the exploits told of RUSTAM, who, when he had reached manhood, came to be called the champion of Persia—his killing of a raging elephant with a single blow, his capture of the foal Rakush (whose sire was a daeva and whose dam had killed several persons who attempted to seize her young one), and his various encounters with his heroic foe, AFRASIYAB, prince of Turan, who, like Rustam himself, owed a part of his fame to a closely linked series of seven great labors. But his greatest—and most unhappy—victory is the most famed of all.

As Rustam's mind was almost completely taken up with thought of battle and deeds of valor, he seldom let his glance fall upon women. But once, when Rustam was on a hunting excursion, he awoke from a short sleep to discover that his horse, RAKUSH, had been stolen from him. The hoofprints of Rakush led to Samengan, not far off. In great wrath, Rustam protested to the ruler of the small principality. The king promised to make every effort to find Rakush, showed Rustam all signs of respect, and prepared a magnificent feast and entertainment for his heroic guest.

During the night, Rustam was awakened by the light of a lamp which had been brought close to his pillow; and by this light he was enabled to see the beautiful TAHMINEH, daughter of his host. Tahmineh declared that men had not heretofore had any opportunity to look upon her face, but that now she had come to Rustam to make a confession. She had employed men to steal Rakush for a time so that she might obtain a foal of his breed. And there was a further confession. She herself, having long ago been captured by stories of Rustam's prodigious deeds, wanted to be mother of a child by Rakush's master.

Rustam, far from displeased, asked for the princess's hand in marriage;

and the king, almost equally pleased, gave his consent, and at once commenced preparations for the ceremony.

Rustam, true to his warrior's nature, passed only one night with his bride. Before leaving Tahmineh, he said: "If Heaven should bless you with a daughter, place this amulet in her hair; if a son, bind it upon his arm." And, mounted upon Rakush, Rustam went away to his own country.

In due time, SOHRAB was born. But his mother, fearing to lose the son as she had already lost the father, sent word to Rustam that the child was a daughter. At first the hero felt disappointment, but then he was able to let the whole matter drop out of his mind.

As Sohrab developed, he proved to be a brave, strong youth, very much like his father in temperament. At the age of ten, he was told whose child he was. As length he conceived the romantic plan of joining with Afrasiyab, conquering Persia, and then presenting the kingdom to Rustam.

Upon the horse that had been sired by Rakush, Sohrab rode to Afrasiyab. Afrasiyab received his new ally gladly, but his plans, naturally, were very different from Sohrab's. He explained to his chief warriors that Sohrab and Rustam, unmindful of each other's identity, must be brought together in single combat. The chances were good that Sohrab, being the younger, would overcome his father. Later, Sohrab could be dispatched by stratagem. And then the crown of Persia would be nearly within reach.

Afrasiyab now commenced his march toward Persia. The singlehanded deeds of Sohrab in the early stages of this campaign were amazing, and word soon reached Rustam that he would have to reckon with a new foeman of importance, a foeman such as Sam had been in his youth. This mention of Sam made Rustam ponder, but after all, at least so it seemed to him, he had no good reason to doubt Tahmineh's word that her child was a daughter.

Though speed had been urged upon Rustam, the aging warrior seemed reluctant to set out; and instead he spent seven days, and even an eighth day, in feasting, in drinking wine, and in listening to music.

Like the seasoned warrior that he was, Rustam did not underestimate his youthful opponent, but put on a disguise (when he had reached the field) and went out to spy upon his enemy and observe his motions.

In the morning, Sohrab looked upon the Persian tents and asked questions about the banners floating over them. He hoped that a certain green pavilion was his father's (for his mother had described his father's tent to him), but the false friend beside him said, "Rustam's tent may be in some degree similar to that, but it appears that Rustam has not yet arrived from Zabulistan."

Sohrab stood before the Persian camp and dared the king to come forth to oppose him. But there was no one save Rustam to take up the challenge; though on that particular day Rustam had resolved not to fight and would have surrendered the honor to another.

The two heroes withdrew to a considerable distance from the camps.

Sohrab said, "Thou must die."

Rustam asked the youth why he was boasting, reminding him that he was but a child, after all, and asserting that he himself was a man who had slain heroes and daevas and the wild beasts of the earth.

"Perhaps you are Rustam?"

"No, only the servant of Rustam."

When their spears were splintered and useless, the heroes fought with swords; then, when these weapons began to look more like saws than anything else, they fought with clubs. Even their horses were near exhaustion, so prolonged was the strife.

After a breathing-space, Sohrab called, "Let us try it with bow and arrow!" They did so, but both survived. They then took to wrestling, but neither was able to throw the other, though before they parted Sohrab struck Rustam a shrewd blow upon the head with his mace.

At last Rustam said, "Night is falling; we will begin again tomorrow."

Each hero then made a dash into his enemy's camp to spread damage and confusion; but Rustam, remembering his unprotected king, returned to his own lines and called out, "A truce for tonight, or face me again!" Sohrab accordingly rode off.

Rustam told his friends that he had never battled against anyone like the youth; and Sohrab asked his false friends if his opponent had not been Rustam indeed, but they answered, "No, this is not the champion of Persia, though his horse does look very much like Rakush."

When the two faced each other again, the next morning, an instinctive feeling of affection rose in Sohrab's breast, and he went so far as to say that he would value his opponent's friendship, and again he asked his name.

But Rustam was already tightening his wrestler's belt and making ready for the struggle.

Sohrab's initial reluctance did not carry over into the battle. He raised Rustam into the air, dashed him down upon his back, and leapt upon his breast like a tiger, his dagger ready for the neck of his foe.

But Rustam called out, "In Persia, we do not strike off the head of an opponent until after the second fall!" Sohrab believed him and allowed him to return to his tent.

Back in his own camp again, Sohrab was told he had been unwise, but the youth declared that he was confident he could throw his antagonist on the next day also.

Rustam spent all night in prayer.

When the fight was renewed, Rustam made a great effort and got Sohrab under him, but fearing that he could not keep him there he plunged his dagger into the boy's side.

Sohrab groaned and said, "I came to find my father and instead have lost my life. But if you could, like a fish, seek the depths of the ocean, or, like a star, the depths of the sky, my father would still be revenged on you."

"What is your father's name?"

"Rustam; and my mother's father is the king of Samengan."

Darkness fell upon Rustam and he sank to the ground, but when he came to himself again he asked for proof—"For I am Rustam."

"Ungird my mail," said Sohrab, "and see upon my arm the amulet which my mother bound upon it."

Then Rustam would have slain himself had not his dying son dissuaded him.

When the Iranians saw Rakush without his rider, they assumed that Rustam was dead, and sent a horseman to the place of the struggle. This man found Rustam still alive but heard him say, "I have done that which has made me weary of life. In my old age, I have slain my son."

And later, when Sohrab's corpse was placed on its bier, those standing nearest to Rustam heard him mutter, "Right would it be were I to cut off both my hands, and sit forever in dust and darkness."

Myths and Legends of India

THE group of Aryans who swept into the land of India, long ages ago, were "cousins" of the Iranians, whose ancient religion has been briefly described in the preceding chapter. One finds in the earliest Indian literature deities who go back to the time when the ancestors of Persians and Indians were still one people: Yama, god of the dead, for one, identical with the Iranian Yima, and, for another, Mitra, counterpart of the Persian Mithra.

But the ways parted, and the people of India—despite times when they were invaded and partly conquered—were to develop their own culture; and their literature was to evolve in comparative isolation during three thousand years and more.

The mythology of India is actually the lore of the ancient religion of India. The earliest Indian religious writings are the *Vedas* or *Books of Knowledge,* written between 2000 and 1000 B. C. One of these, the *Rigveda,* or *Veda of Verses,* is particularly rich in tales of the gods. The gods of the *Rigveda* were for the most part personifications of the forces of nature, although the concept of the gods as being concerned with moral and ethical matters is also present.

Several hundred years after the so-called Vedic Age, the *Brahmanas* and the *Upanishads* were written. These are philosophic works in which the old gods were considerably modified and were transformed into gods who were representative of various aspects of the relationship of the outer world to the inner self of man. From these writings and beliefs, modified through the years, has come the religion known as Hinduism, the leading religion of contemporary India.

It was between 200 B. C. and 200 A. D. that the two great poems of India, the *Mahabharata* and the *Ramayana,* were written. In these two famous works are recorded the stories and legends of India's early heroes. From this same period comes the greatest of dramatic works of India, *Sakuntala,* written by the poet Kalidasa.

The accounts of the myths and legends of India given below present the most vivid and concrete material and episodes selected from the vast records of Indian mythology which in general tended in the direction of complexity and nebulosity and rhetoric and paradox, and from Indian epic, which on the whole was marked by dreaminess, slow-motion, with unbridled employment of descriptive and moral passages and inclusion of non-essential episodes.

DEITIES OF THE VEDAS

To the poets who composed the *Rigveda,* the universe seemed to contain three domains: heaven, air, and earth. Heaven was thought of as the home of light, as the realm of sun and stars, and as the true dwelling-place of the gods. Heaven was also a divine father, DYAUS PITAR. The middle realm was the area of lightning, rain, and wind. Because it contained water, this realm was often called a sea (like the sea Vourukasha of Persian myth); yet the clouds of thunderstorms were called lowing cows, and the rain from them was said to be milk, which had been given to nourish the earth. Though their true home was in the highest realm, the gods did not hold in scorn the earth, the third domain. Indeed, two of the most wonderful among them, AGNI, (fire) and SOMA (the sacred intoxicating drink), spent much of their time among the sons of men.

A very important though not especially colorful deity of the sky was VARUNA, the upholder of *rita,* or regularity and order, both physical and moral. It was believed that Varuna saw all things, far and near, and that he could perceive whether truth or falsehood dwelt within a man. He was a hater and punisher of falsehood, but when men were penitent, he was quick to forgive them and to free them from the fetters of sin. In post-Vedic days, an increasing interest in Prajapati, a creative god, forced Varuna out of most of his original realm, and he became at last only the god of the sea.

There were at least five solar deities. MITRA was the Sun as Friend. SURYA, the Sun itself, was the eye of the gods. He was a form of Agni. Riding across the sky in his car, which was drawn by seven steeds, he banished disease and horrible dreams. SAVITRI, the Stimulator or Quickener, yellow-haired, golden-armed, was a god who bestowed immortality upon other gods, as well as length of days upon mere men. As the setting sun he conducted departed spirits to the dwelling-place of the righteous. PUSHAN, the Prosperer, also conducted the dead upon the far path, but he was more concerned with affairs on earth, as is clearly indicated by the fact that his car was said to be drawn by goats. He guarded roads and he also protected cattle, guiding them with a goad which he always carried. VISHNU was known for his three strides (in earth, air, and heaven—or, perhaps, it may be conjectured, from the eastern horizon to a point over head, then down to the western horizon, and then by an unknown path to the east again). He was far from the most famous solar deity in Vedic times, but his character as a god helpful to humanity was to undergo a tremendous development, and he was destined to become one of the two great gods of modern Hinduism.

She who day after day awoke all intelligences was USHAS, the shining one, the bountiful goddess of dawn. She threw colorful garments round her like a dancing girl, opened heaven's gates, and rode forth on her bright car, drawn by ruddy steeds or kine. She was sometimes called the wife of Surya, but sometimes was regarded as the wife of Agni, as the sacrificial fire was kindled at the very moment when she made her welcome appearance. Her brothers were the ASVINS, twin gods of the half-light, perhaps the morning and the evening star. They were famous charioteers; at the yoking of their car, Ushas was born. They were friends of men, restorers of men's sight and youth, rescuers from shipwreck and other perils and distresses. Their name means "the two horsemen," and it is difficult to doubt that they and the famous Greek horsemen Castor and Pollux had a common origin in the Indo-European period.

RATRI, immortal and magnificent goddess of night, was not a sovereign of blackness, but a true sister of Ushas and the Asvins, a daughter of Heaven, like them, who drove away darkness with the shining of her eyes, the stars.

A nymph called APSARAS was said to make her home in the celestial waters. She was the devoted wife of the GANDHARVA, who stood on the vault of heaven and guarded the precious soma. Later on, many Apsarases were thought of as dwelling on earth, amid trees, where they played their lutes and cymbals and danced unseen. And there came to be many Gandharvas, but though they were the lovers of the Apsarases, they spent much of their time in the skies and became celestial singers. That is why even today a mirage may be called "the city of the Gandharvas."

Aerial adversaries of the gods were the ASURAS and the PANIS, the latter being foes of Indra primarily. (*Asura* beautifully illustrates how a word may have two very different histories in separate areas, for, as we have already observed, in the form of *Ahura* it serves as part of the name of the chief Zoroastrian god. In exchange, so to speak, the *daevas* or fiends of the *Avesta* become *devas,* gods, in the Vedas.) The Panis, "niggards," seem to have been given their name because they were thought of as withholding heavenly treasures.

INDRA was the great deity of the air. A tremendous drinker of soma, he was, to be sure, at times unpredictable and violent, but he could be depended on to fight on the side of the Aryans in battle, and it was he who again and again slew the re-born demon of drought (VRITRA, the Obstructor), broke the cloud-castles of men's enemies, pierced the mountain behind which the cloud-cows had been held, and delivered over the cows (the rain clouds) to his friends.

In the conflict with Vritra, Indra was often accompanied by the MARUTS or RUDRAS, storm-gods. These were the sons of RUDRA, a beautiful but terrifying deity. Indeed, although Rudra was said to know a thousand remedies and to be the greatest of physicians, his arrows or lightning shafts were greatly feared, it was out of fear that he was called SIVA, "auspicious", and he was to become, in later Hindu religion, Siva the Destroyer.

Lesser deities of the region of air were a wind-god, VAYU, or VATA, and a god of rain, PARJANYA.

Greatest of the gods of earth was AGNI, Fire. Born in heaven as sunlight, in the aerial waters as lightning, and on earth as fire, Agni had three dwellings and a triple nature, facts which are said to underlie certain other subsequent Indian groups of three, even including the later triad of BRAHMA, the Creator; VISHNU, the Preserver; and SIVA, the Destroyer.

As the sacred drink soma was a necessary part of the ritual of the *Rigveda,* SOMA was the second most important god of earth. He was said to give life, even endless life, to the gods and to certain men. He was sometimes thought of as a bowman and the best of charioteers, but he can hardly be regarded as an anthropomorphic god, since the poets who wrote of him were usually thinking of the plant and its juice from which the intoxicating soma (or "mead" or "drop") was made. Soma was naturally called the king of plants and the lord of the wood. In time Soma—because of the color of the draught? or because the moon is drop-shaped? or because the waning moon was thought of as being quaffed by the gods?—came to be mystically identified with the moon.

Just as the Asuras and the Panis annoyed and hindered the gods, the prowling, hungry RAKSHAS stood between men and their best interests. Sometimes these Rakshas had the shapes of men, sometimes of animals, but they were almost invariably deformed, and if not of one strange color, then of another.

The following entries give a more detailed account of the attributes and functions of the principal Vedic gods.

Dyaus

DYAUS, the god of the bright sky, or the universal father, represented the sky or the heavens; he was an abstract, rather than a personal god. He was regarded both as creator and as being created; with Prithivi, his wife or consort, representing or personifying the earth, he was the original parent of all the gods and of all human beings. He is the Hindu equivalent of the Greek god of gods, Zeus. The name by which he was invoked, Dyaus Pitar, is merely Zeus Pater, Zeus the Father, or, in the Roman system, Jupiter.

Prithivi

PRITHIVI, the goddess of the earth was the wife of Dyaus. As the mother, or Mother Earth, titles by which she was known, she seems to correspond to the Greek Ge or Gaea. Her symbolic father was King PRITHU—whose name is said to be the source of her own—who in a period of great famine allowed her to live only when she promised that she would again cause or permit the earth to bear fruit and food, or would do so herself. With Dyaus, she was honored by seven hymns in the *Rigveda.*

Varuna

VARUNA, the all-seeing or all-enveloping one, was a god of the sea and of the waters. He was a personification of the sky, especially the night sky. He was described as a god of the highest moral grandeur. He measured out the earth and made paths for the sun, the stars, and the rivers. He controlled the winds, sent refreshing rain, and he gave fire to mankind. With his thousand eyes he was believed to see all and know all; the secrets of men were not secret to him. He judged sinners, who could not escape him no matter where they went, severely, but not unjustly. His great powers made him the guardian of the universe. He was, in some ways, human, that is, he ate and drank. As a sea-god he corresponds somewhat to the Greek Poseidon and the Roman Neptune; as a god of bodies of water other than sea and ocean, he may be the Hindu equivalent of the classical minor sea divinities, and he may be connected with the Greek Uranus.

Surya

SURYA represented the sun in his rising and setting. He was the son of Dyaus, or of Aditi, a Hindu goddess, or of Ushas, the Vedic goddess of the dawn, who was also referred to as Surya's wife. With Agni and Indra, Surya was one of the trinity of Vedic gods, and was celebrated in six hymns. His chariot was drawn by seven red horses. He was a far and all-seeing god, like Varuna, and he had flaming red hair, like Indra. As the god of the sun or as the god who lived in the sun, Surya is the Hindu equivalent of the Greek Helios.

Savitri

SAVITRI (or Savitar) was the inciter or the enlivener. He was identified with Surya, the sun, and with Vashti. He was another personification of the sun, and as the sun he had golden eyes, a gold tongue, and gold hands. According to legend, Savitri cut off his hand at a sacrifice and was given by the priests one of gold in its place. He was addressed ecstatically in the *Rigveda* as the splendor of the sky, the wide-seeing, the far-shining, the shining wanderer, the golden-eyed, golden-handed, life-bestowing, well-guarding, exhilarating, and affluent Savitri. He was an all-powerful god, as were many of the Hindu gods.

Indra

INDRA was a Hindu god of the firmament and of rain and battle, as well as a sun-god. He was the son of Dyaus and Prithivi, that is, of Heaven and Earth. He was represented with four arms and four hands. He carried lances and thunderbolts, a hook and a net to conquer his foes. He could take on any shape that he chose. He had a chariot of gold, drawn by thousands of horses. He rode on a white animal, either an elephant or a horse. He conquered Vritra, a monster serpent, and many other enemies, aided by the Maruts, deities of the storm and wind, and by Vishnu and Agni. He shattered the clouds with his bolts, and he released the pent-up waters. Originally, the king or chief of the Hindu gods and the twin brother of Agni, he later came to occupy a much lower position in rank and importance. His rule was not eternal, having a definite time limit imposed—a hundred divine years—after which period he could be deposed in favor of another god or even by a great, but human hero. As the thrower of thunderbolts, Indra recalls the Greek Zeus.

Agni

AGNI, one of the chief Vedic gods and the youngest, was the god of fire, as his name, a form of the Latin *ignis,* indicates. He was the twin brother of Indra. He was the Hindu equivalent of the Greek Hephaestus and the Roman Vulcan. He personified fire in three forms: the sun, lightning, and fire as used in sacrificial ceremonies. Stories of the circumstances of his birth and parentage are varied and confusing. He was the son of Dyaus and Prithivi, that is, of Heaven and Earth; or of the sky, or the clouds or the dawns; or he was born of mortals, or in heaven, or in the heavenly waters. He was generated or born as a result of the rubbing together of two sticks, after which act he burst forth from the wood in flames. When aroused by the wind he rushed among the trees as though he were a wild bull. His shining chariot was drawn by red horses; his hair was gold and his limbs were red. Physically, he was out of the ordinary, as he had two faces, three legs, seven tongues, and as many arms. He carried a bow and arrows. He enjoyed hiding from the other gods, in water, in tall grass, or in a tree, and in making them search for him. With Indra, he was one of the guardians of the world. He resembled his fellow gods, in being all-powerful. Like many other gods, Agni was both good and bad, both reasonable and viciously irrational; he was a friendly god and an angry one; he healed and he killed; he protected the home and made it comfortable to live in, and he destroyed the home and killed those who lived in it. He appealed to the imaginations of the poet-priests, who found a thousand ways of speaking of him. His flames were like the roaring waves of the sea; among the trees those flames could bellow like a bull; his steeds made black furrows and the track of his car was black; his banners were clouds of smoke. Yet at every dawn, when he was kindled by the friction of the priest's fire sticks, he was the youngest and most ingratiating of the gods; and when he was so kindled he would, like a bird of rapid flight, immediately dart upward toward the other gods. Again, when a guest in men's dwellings, "the lord of the house," he could give to his worshipers a hundred boons, but chiefly prosperity, domestic happiness, children.

Soma

SOMA was both the name of a sacred plant from which an intoxicating juice was drained and the name of the god or the personified deification of the juice of the plant. Soma, the Indian equivalent of the Bacchus of the Greeks and Romans, had all the attributes of a supreme deity. He was associated with Agni, a triple god. Like many other Hindu divinities, Soma was an all-powerful deity. Many legends tell how Soma, the juice, was brought to the earth. It was believed that Varuna, the god of the sea, placed it on the top of a faraway mountain or on a high point in heaven. Another account says that an eagle or a falcon brought it there for Indra, the four-handed god, or that a daughter of the sun brought it from a secluded spot where it was under the care of the rain-god. Soma's power was the ability to cure all ailments; its gifts to those who drink it were inspiration, vitality, and immortal life. When going on dangerous military adventures, Indra drank it without restraint. In the kingdom of Yama, the chief of the dead, all those who sipped it became immortal. It enabled Indra to conquer his enemy, Vritra, the snake of darkness. Like Vishnu, Indra, and Varuna, Soma supported the heavens and the earth. Soma was celebrated, both as god and plant, in many hymns in the *Rigveda,* where it is hailed as the drink of the gods and of those who worship the gods.

Ushas

USHAS was the goddess of the dawn and of wisdom. She was invoked as a beautiful daughter of heaven. She was the universal life, both physical and spiritual. Her name means both "to awake" and "to know"; hence, as goddess of the dawn, as the first in all the world to awake, she corresponds to the Greek Eos, and as one who knows, she is the Hindu equivalent of the Greek Athene. She sent men out to their daily tasks with renewed strength, and when she awakened she roused her children and her worshippers. She was represented as ever young, beautiful, immortal, and was born anew each day. She had a hundred chariots harnessed to red horses. The recipient of as many as eleven Vedic hymns, she was hailed enthusiastically as diffuser of light, as auspicious Ushas, as the mighty, as the giver of light who beholds all things from on high, and as the mother of morning.

Yama and Yami

YAMA and YAMI, brother and sister, were the first man and the first woman. Yama, the chief lord of the sea, and the king of the lower regions, was the son of Vivaswat, the Hindu sun, and of Saranyu, daughter of Tvashtri, who left her husband after bearing him Yama and Yami. Yama's messengers were two monstrous dogs, and sometimes an owl or a pigeon. He rode a buffalo. In paradise, where he ruled with Varuna, Yama played the flute, the music of which was only one of the countless joys in store for the happy dead. Under the shade of heavenly trees they listened to his magic melody and drank the juice of the Soma plant that would make them, with the gods, immortal. As a judge of the dead he handed out rewards or punishments as they were deserved. The good went to SWARGA, the Hindu heaven of Indra, and the bad went to NARAKA, the Hindu hell. Yama was represented as green, with red robes; he carried a club and a noose, which he used to draw out the soul from the body. Yami, his twin, was the queen of the lower world, as he was the king. According to one of the Vedic hymns, she wished to enter into the marriage relationship with Yama but he was not interested. Unmarried women who were tired of living without husbands prayed to him for a month.

Vayu

VAYU (or Vata) was the Vedic god of the winds or the air; he was connected with the four-armed Indra and the children of Heaven and Earth. With Agni, living on the earth, and Surya, living in heaven, he, living in the air, constituted a Vedic trinity of gods; sometimes Indra, instead of Vayu, was a member of this group. Vayu was the father of Hanuman, the monkey chief or god, and Bhima, a Brahman god whose name means "the terrible." He was also described as the father of the Maruts, gods of the storm, deities who went with Indra on his warlike adventures, and as the son-in-law of Tvastri, the Indian Vulcan. He was represented as a fierce god, riding on a deer or being drawn in his chariot by a thousand horses. The Maruts were represented as raging and roaring in the forest wilds and tearing up clouds for rain.

THE BRAHMANIC DEITIES

Brahma, Vishnu, and Siva are the chief gods of the later Hindu religion, forming a Hindu trinity or triad, just as Agni, Vayu, and Surya were the trinity of the earlier Vedic religion. They are not, however, three separate, distinct, independent gods, but are three forms or phases or manifestations of one god, one supreme being. All of them are connected with energy in a different way and are considered individually in order to emphasize their attributes and qualities.

Brahma

BRAHMA, the first god of the Hindu trinity, is a red god. He is four-headed and four-handed. In one hand he holds a copy of the oldest sacred literature of the Hindus, a copy of the Vedas; in the second, a spoon or sceptre; in the third, a drinking vessel; and in the fourth, a string of beads. He had five heads in the beginning but Siva, displeased with his bold conduct, cut one off. Brahma's vehicle, or *vahanna,* is a goose or a swan in which he rides. He is represented pictorially with his four heads and as many crowns and hands, and richly garbed. Seated by his side is Saraswati, dressed with equal elegance, but with only one head and crown. As the first god of the trinity, Brahma represents and creates energy.

SARASWATI (or VACH), the goddess of poetry, wisdom, and eloquence, was the wife of Brahma, and the daughter of Kama, the god of love. She is identified with Viraj, who was supposed to be the female half or part of the two halves into which Brahma divided his body. Saraswati was also a teacher of worship and of the ways of holiness and wisdom.

Vishnu

VISHNU, the second god of the Hindu trinity, is a blue god. He occupies a comparatively unimportant position in the Vedic system, but is given second place in the later Brahmanic order of deities. His wife, LAKSHMI, was the goddess of wealth and beauty. His *vahanna,* or vehicle, is Garuda, the king of birds, a creature that is half-man, half-eagle. Like Brahma, he has four hands, in which he holds a shell, or *shankha,* a quoit, or *chakra,* a club, and a lotus flower (the flower from which Brahma was said to have been born). Lakshmi (or Sri), whose supposed birth from the foam of the sea, gives her the name of the Daughter of the Milky Sea, is also represented with a lotus. Vishnu is pictured as sleeping on Ananta, a serpent that lives forever. At the end of the present age of the world, the *Kali Yuga,* Vishnu will remain in that attitude and a lotus stalk will flourish from his navel. The waters of the world will cover everything and on the topmost point of the stalk, high above the water, Brahma will appear to again carry out his periodic task of creating the earth anew.

Vishnu, the second god, preserves energy, as Brahma, the first god creates it. Like other gods, Vishnu has the power to appear in various forms, both animal and human. He visits the earth periodically when it is necessary for him to correct or remove some evil and it is expected that he will return again when he is needed to attack and destroy the forces of evil and injustice. These incarnations, or appearances in bodily form, are known as the *avatars* or the descents of Vishnu, to indicate that he descends from heaven, the world of the gods, to earth, the world of men. There are ten of these physical manifestations. In the first avatar, Vishnu is MATSYA, a fish, who comes to give warning of the approaching flood. In his second avatar, Vishnu is KURMA, a tortoise, and holds Mt. Mandara on his back while the gods churn the ocean to produce a divine drink that confers strength and immortality, the ambrosia or nectar of the Greek gods. In the third avatar, Vishnu is VARAHA, a boar, who saves the earth by raising it with his powerful tusks from the waters in which it has been submerged. As NARASINGHA, the man-lion, he appears in his fourth avatar to tear to pieces a tyrannical demon-king who tried to kill his own son because he insisted on worshipping Vishnu. He is VAMANA, a dwarf who can cover the entire universe in three strides, in the fifth avatar. In the sixth, he is RAMA with the Axe, who overcomes and suppresses the warrior caste, the Kshattriya, the second of the four castes in ancient Hindu society. He is RAMA CHANDRA in the seventh avatar, the hero of the *Ramayana,* who destroys Ravana, a demon, who had stolen Rama's wife, Sita; in this exploit, he was helped by Hanuman, the king of the monkeys. In the eighth avatar, he is either Krishna, who kills Kansa, an evil monarch, or BALA-RAMA, Krishna's twin brother. The eighth avatar is regarded as one of the most important partly because of Krishna's position as one of the best loved of the Hindu gods and as the god of the lower classes. Vishnu is BUDDHA himself in the ninth avatar, and in the tenth, which is still to take place, he *will be* KALKI, riding on a white horse. He will carry a shining sword and will destroy the world with all its wickedness. He will then fall asleep on the waters of the sea; when he awakes he will create Brahma, and the process of creating another world, a new world, will begin again.

Siva

SIVA (or Civa), the third god of the Hindu trinity or the third phase of Brahma's energy, is a white god. He is known by as many as a thousand names, and lives on Mt. Kailasu, in the Himalayas, being called for that reason the Lord of the Mountain. Like other gods in other mythological systems he has a kind side and a cruel one. He is the god of arts and knowledge as well as of dancing and gaiety. He has four hands and three eyes, one of which has the power to kill. He has a trident in one hand and a rope in the other which he uses, with the aid of his wife, BHAVANI or PARVATI, as an instrument to strangle the wicked; he holds various weapons in his remaining hands. His wife, who gave him two sons, is also known under the names of Sati, Durga, Kali, Ambika, Devi, and Uma. Siva has a necklace made of human skulls. He wears serpents in his ears and is wrapped in a tiger or elephant skin. He is generally represented as sitting, lost in thought. From Siva's head (or from Vishnu's too) sprang the sacred river Ganga, the Ganges. Siva cut off one of Brahma's five heads and had considerable difficulty before he was able to dispose of it. His vehicle, a snow-white bull, Nandi, is sacred to him. Siva's weapons are a trident, a thunderbolt, a bow and arrow, a club, an axe, a sword, and a discus. Siva, the third god, destroys energy, as Brahma creates it and as Vishnu preserves it.

Ganesha

GANESHA (or Ganese or Nana-Pati) is the son of Siva and Parvati, or of one or the other of the parents, alone, without the participation of the other, and the brother of Kartikeya. He is the god of wisdom and prudence and of good luck. He is represented as a stout god, in human form, with the head of an elephant, an animal noted for its wisdom. His own head he lost when it was destroyed by a god's angry glance or when Siva chopped it off; and he was given the elephant's head by the other gods as a replacement. Ganesha is also the god who brings success, who removes difficulties; hence he is invoked at the outset of any activity or undertaking. As the wisest of all the gods he is honored as a patron of learning and knowledge, and his name at the opening of a scholarly or literary work will make it a success. As the god of trade and commerce, of worldly prosperity, he is worshipped by those engaged in business and his name appears on the first page of ledgers and account-books. Like Brahma, Vishnu, and Siva, Ganesha has four hands—more in some representations—and he rides on, or is followed by, a rat, another creature that enjoys a reputation for wisdom.

Kartikeya

KARTIKEYA (or Kumara or Skanda) is a son of Siva and Parvati, or of Agni, the god of fire, and the river Ganges, and is Ganesha's brother. He is the Hindu god of war and is represented with six heads. He is mounted on a peacock and carries a bow and arrows. Legend has it that six sparks shot from Siva's eyes and became infants. Parvati hugged them so passionately that the six bodies became one, but the heads remained. Under the later name of Subramanya he is worshipped throughout Southern India.

Kuvera

KUVERA is the god of wealth, as Lakshmi is the goddess. Originally one of the chief gods in the Hindu mythology, he gradually came to occupy a minor place.

Kamadeva

KAMADEVA (or Kama), the Hindu god of love, is a son of Vishnu and Lakshmi. He rides on a dove, and carries arrows of flowers which he shoots from a bow the string of which is made of bees and flowers. He is endowed with the gift of eternal youth and is excessively handsome; as the god of an emotion that cannot be resisted, he rules both men and gods. The cuckoo and the bee, associated with spring, attend him on his travels. The myth associated with Kamadeva tells how Siva killed him by darting at him the rays of his third eye. Siva resented what he regarded as Kamadeva's interference in his personal affairs, when the god of love, who was carrying out orders from the other gods, succeeded in persuading Siva to take another wife after he had lost Parvati.

INDIAN EPIC POETRY

India produced two great epics. The word *great* is used advisedly, for they are great in length as well as in literary value. Each may be compared to a European keep or donjon built in the Dark Ages and constantly increased by the erection of walls, neighboring towers, living quarters, offices, and heterogeneous annexes, each addition a new tribute to the wisdom of the first builders, but also a new screen hiding some part of the original structure. Modern editions of one of these epics, the *Ramayana,* contain over 24,000 couplets; of the other, the *Mahabharata,* over 85,000 couplets! In other words, even the shorter poem is about four times as long as Milton's *Paradise Lost.*

During the past hundred years or so, considerable attention has been given to the problem of determining what the original limits of those legendary narratives were. Restored to their first form, the epics regain unity and proportion, and compare as follows.

The *Mahabharata,* "Great (Epic of the) Bharatas," is the more primitive, the more heroic, and the more successful in presenting large groups of highly differentiated individuals. The *Ramayana,* "Epic of (Prince) Rama," is the more romantic and tender, and the more successful in portraying ideal characters, such as the perfect son, or wife, or brother.

The *Mahabharata* treats of the lives of the Pandavas, descendants of Bharata, five brothers, and their common wife, Draupadi, and of their rivalry with, and final war against, their cousins, Kuru princes. The *Ramayana* tells of Rama's marriage to Sita, of the exile of the newly wedded pair at the very time when Rama should have ascended the throne, of Rama's loss of Sita, of the war he fought to regain her, and of the happy return of the exiles to Rama's kingdom.

In the following pages we first give famous legends from the *Mahabharata;* then episodes of the story of Rama from the *Ramayana;* and, finally, the lovely story of Sakuntala.

LEGENDS FROM THE "MAHABHARATA"

The Rival Cousins

DHRITA-RASHTRA, although he had been blind from his birth, ruled over the ancient kingdom of the Kurus along the upper reaches of the Ganges. He had a hundred sons of his own, and along with these he brought up the five sons of his late brother, PANDU. The five brothers were not only sons of Pandu, but god-born heroes. YUDHISHTHIR, the eldest, was the son of Dharma, or Virtue; BHIMA, of Vayu; ARJUN (the most skillful in fight), of Indra. NAKULA and SAHADEVA, twins, were sons of the Asvins. As these five were worth all the rest put together, a great deal of tension developed at court.

Drona, who was both Brahman and warrior, was the preceptor of all. When the youths had reached a suitable age, Drona proposed that a tournament be held, so that the skill of the princes might be displayed to the people, and Dhrita-rashtra gave his full consent, though depressed by the thought that his blindness would force him to rely on the reporting of others for his information on the contest.

Beside a meadow, white viewing-mansions were erected for the monarch and GANDHARI, his queen, for PRITHA, who was the widow of Pandu, and for other ladies and maidens of the court. The white tents of the nobles were pitched close at hand. And on the other side, stages in a half-circle were built for the men who would soon be crowding in from their looms and anvils and narrow shops.

When the religious ceremonies were over, on the appointed day, the princes strode onto the measured ground, in order of seniority. They seemed more like gods than men, and the spectators were delighted by their skill with various weapons.

A serious moment occurred when mighty Bhima of the Pandavs and DURYODHAN, proudest and eldest of the Kurus, engaged in a mock-fight with maces. Groups in the crowd began to take sides and to call out to the princes as they would have done had the pair been in earnest. But Drona sent his son quickly to part the contestants.

Soon a new tumult of sound arose, and Dhrita-rashtra asked what it meant. Arjun in golden armor was alone on the plain, with his mighty bow in hand. The monarch was pleased, and in his generous way said that Pritha's gallant sons were like sacrificial fires sanctifying the state over which he ruled. Then with rapier and mace but best of all with bow and arrows, Arjun performed feats which men would have declared to be impossible had they not with their own eyes seen them done.

The day was closing and the crowds were beginning to disperse. Suddenly there was another tumult, and like a moving cliff an unknown contender strode into the lists. Pritha knew him, however, for he was actually another son of hers. His father was Surya, the Sun, who had restored to Pritha her virginity before she was wedded to Pandu. The late arrival boasted that he would now duplicate all the marvelous feats performed by the supposedly unrivaled Arjun. And he proceeded to do so. Thus, without knowing that they were brothers, the eldest son and the youngest son of Pritha had earned equal claims to the chief honors of the tournament.

KARNA, for that was the champion's name, would gladly have met Arjun in combat, but he was barred from doing so because he was supposedly the son of a humble chariot-driver. But Duryodhan, glad to find such a powerful helper against the Pandavs, disregarded Karna's humble origin and had him anointed king of Anga.

The Bride's Choice

Later, when the blind monarch recognized Yudhishthir, his nephew, as heir-apparent, Duryodhan and his brothers planned to rid themselves of the Pandavs. At a time when Pritha and her five sons were visiting a distant town, the house which served as their temporary dwelling was set afire. But the Pandavs were not unprepared for this. They escaped through an underground passage and then, for a while, dwelt in the forest.

In time they heard that the princess of Panchala was about to choose her husband according to the ancient custom called *Swayamvara.* In the guise of Brahmans and mingling with Brahmans, the brothers took their way to Panchala.

King Drupad had prepared a fifteen days' feast for the multitudes who came surging in likes waves of the sea. He had also prepared a test for the suitors—the bending of a tremendous bow. Several princes from foreign lands tried to bend the bow, but instead of getting it strung, they were knocked to the ground when the bow rebounded. Karna had taken the bow and was bending it, but with proud and queenly voice the daughter of Drupad said that she, a member of the warrior caste, would not wed a chariot-driver's son. Then to the amazement and delight of the Brahmans, Arjun stepped forward, strung the bow, placed his arrows, and brought the distant target thundering to the ground. Conchshells and trumpets bespoke Arjun's triumph, but at the same time the chagrined warriors began to mutter in a way that caused Bhima and Yudhishthir and the twin brothers to move out toward Arjun to stand by him in case of need. Acting as quickly as she had spoken before in the case of Karna, the princess, DRAUPADI, flung the marriage robe and the bridal garland over Arjun. The people shouted for joy and the Brahmans chanted blessings, but the assembled warriors began to threaten both Draupadi and Arjun. The tiger-waisted Bhima had rapidly uprooted a tree and was ominously shaking it like a mace; and Arjun was standing there with the mighty bow ready.

Among the monarchs, however, was KRISHNA himself. He had recognized the disguised Pandavs. Now he rose and with words that could not be disregarded quelled the rising storm. The warriors gave way, and the marriage of Draupadi and Arjun was celebrated.

When the brothers returned with Draupadi to the humble cottage where they had been living according to the custom of Brahmans, they called out that they had received a great gift. From within the cottage Pritha cheerfully called out, "Enjoy the gift in common." Since in those days a mother's command could not be disregarded, Draupadi became the wife of the five brothers.

Yudhishthir Emperor

Now that the Pandavs had a powerful friend in Drupad, Duryodhan reigned in Hastina-pura on the Ganges; the sons of Pandu cleared forests to the westward and built their own capital, Indra-prastha, on the banks of the Jumna.

At length Yudhishthir was ready to proclaim himself emperor over all the other Indian kings, and accordingly he sent out invitations to them to attend the *Rajasuya,* or imperial sacrifice. One king, who refused, was killed. All others, including Dhritarashtra, accepted and came, bringing tribute.

Yudhishthir, eager that all things should be done in accordance with ancient custom, asked the wise grandsire Bhishma to whom he should first present the *arghya,* an offering due to honored guests. Bhishma replied that it should be given to Krishna. Though the assembled monarchs were pure in lustre, like so many planets, Krishna was like the radiant sun among them. (It will be recalled that by Hindus Krishna is regarded as one of the avatars or incarnations of Vishnu, the Preserver. Thus Bhishma's advice was sound and good.) Sahadeva immediately brought the offering to Krishna.

Proud and angry, the tiger-hearted Sisupala shouted out a list of names which he asseverated should come before Krishna's. Krishna spoke calmly in reply, but his heart was blazing. He told the great assembled company that up to that time he had spared Sisupala because the evil-destined man was descended from a daughter of his own noble race and he had promised to forgive Sisupala for a hundred follies and crimes. But now that number had been overpassed. Sisupala, like a foe, had burnt Krishna's seaport, Dwarka, and in his madness had forced virtuous wives of princes to his will and had even aspired to Krishna's saintly wife, Rukmini. Sisupala laughed and sneered, hinted that Rukmini had preferred him to her lawful husband, and ended by boasting that he was untroubled by Krishna's anger.

It was his last boast. Krishna took into his hands the fatal discus, which sinners dread; and instantly the bright and whirling weapon fell on impious Sisupala and smote his head from his body.

After funeral rites had been performed and Sisupala's son had been conducted to his father's place among the kings, the ceremonies marking Yudhishthir's assumption of the imperial title were resumed and carried through to their conclusion.

As the monarchs departed, each was provided with a suitable escort from among Yudhishthir's relatives or chief servants. Last to go was Krishna, to whom Yudhishthir was actually indebted for the imperial power. He was loath to depart and Yudhishthir was sad because the affairs of his distant kingdom called him away. When Krishna's chariot began to move, Yudhishthir and the members of his household followed after it. The chariot stopped, and Krishna gave a parting blessing and his final advice to the emperor.

"King of men! Guard thy realm with unclosed eyes. Tend thy subjects with a father's love. Be to them like the shower that refreshes the ground, like the tree that provides shelter from blazing heat, like the blue sky that bends in kindness above. Without pride and without passion, rule with virtuous mind!"

The Game of Chance

It need hardly be said that Duryodhan had not been pleased by the Imperial Sacrifice and that he was looking about for some means of humbling Yudhishthir. Now the monarchs of that day had a passion for gambling that was a positive sin, and Yudhishthir was as bad as the worst in this regard, despite his goodness and piety in all other matters.

Yudhishthir, with his mother and brothers and Draupadi, was invited to come to Hastina-pura for a gambling match. When the group had been received at Duryodhan's city, Yudhishthir sat down to play at dice, but he faced not his cousin but one of Duryodhan's friends, Sakuni, prince of Ganhara, who was an expert at false dice.

Yudhishthir lost game after game, but, stung by his losses, was more eager for play as time went on. He grew more and more reckless, placed higher and higher stakes, lost his gold and jewels, his slaves, his wide lands, and finally even the freedom of his brothers and himself and the noble Draupadi.

It would be too painful to tell at length how a menial broke the news to Draupadi and was by the queen sent back to his master in scorn, how Duhsasan, one of the hundred brothers, came next and finding Draupadi in loose attire, instantly dragged her by her raven tresses into the Council Chamber, how the princes threw insulting hints at her—even Karna, because he was Arjun's deadly foe—and how Duryodhan, inflamed with base passion, sought to hold the high-born princess as his slave upon his knee. He soon desisted, however, when threatened by the wrathful Bhima, who in spirit and strength was just as he had ever been, though he was now technically his cousin's slave.

When the jackal's voice and the croaking of the raven were heard above the chanting at the sacrificial fire, the wise and good older people —Dhrita-rashtra, Queen Gandhari, Drona, and the rest—got their first hint that the wild, headstrong princess had offended the gods. The sightless monarch had himself led to Draupadi, to whom he spoke words of love and respect, calling her his dearest daughter and the purest of the Kura ladies, and promising that the Pandavs should be given their freedom, even if they had to go into exile.

At last an agreement was reached. Pritha, the aging mother, was to remain in Hastina-pura, to dwell in the house of the pious-hearted Vidura. The Pandavs were to dwell for twelve years in the forests. The thirteenth year they were to pass in concealment, for if they were discovered within this last year, they would have to live in exile for another twelve years.

The Forest Life of the Pandavs

In the wilderness, Draupadi's mind dwelt on the insults she had endured, and she and the hot-tempered Bhima urged Yudhishthir to break the agreement and attempt to regain his kingdom at an early hour. But here the eldest of the brothers showed himself to be as fine a man of honor as he had earlier shown himself to be a foolish man of honor in the game of dice. Krishna did not forget him, but came to visit him in his adversity.

The great priest Vyasa advised Arjun to obtain heavenly weapons by penance and worship. In time, Arjun obtained the *pasupata* weapon from Siva on earth and celestial arms from Indra in heaven.

Duryodhan intended to come in splendor to laugh at his cousins in their exile. Instead he was caught in a quarrel with Gandharvas and was taken captive, but was freed by the sons of Pandu, who allowed him to return to Hastina-pura unharmed. But the generosity of his cousins only shamed him and made him hate them more than ever.

An ally of Duryodhan's, Jayadratha, king of the Indus country, found an opportunity to carry off Draupadi, but the Pandavs overtook him and punished him, and brought the faithful Draupadi back with them to their forest home.

But most of the days during the twelve years of exile were peaceful ones, which Draupadi and the brothers passed in listening to old tales and legends repeated to them by saints and *rishis* who had sought out Yudhishthir in his quiet dwelling.

Arms and Weapons

The twelve years of forest life being over, the Pandav brothers had next to conceal themselves for one more year, on pain of going into exile for another twelve years. Their plan was this: to disguise themselves and spend twelve months in the service of Virata, king of the Matsyas. Yudhishthir became a courtier; Bhima, a cook; Nakula, a keeper of the king's horses; Sadaheva, a cowherd; Draupadi, a waiting-woman in the service of the princess. The mighty Arjun wore conch bangles and earrings, was mistaken for a eunuch, and was permitted to instruct the members of the royal household in music and dancing. So it went for a year, Duryodhan being unable to find them out.

At the end of that time, Duryodhan laid a plot against Virata which in practice turned out to his own disadvantage. As king of the Kurus he combined with the king of the Trigartas. The Trigartas entered the Matsya kingdom from the south, thereby drawing out Virata with his army. Then the Kurus fell upon the kingdom from the north, like hawks upon their prey, and in brief time had driven off sixty thousand head of cattle. Prince Uttara, who had been left at the palace, was urged to pursue the spoilers, but he complained of the lack of a skillful chariot-driver, as his ancient driver had been slain in a former battle. Let but a chariot-driver be found, and he would cause his foes to ask, "Is this Arjun, famed in war?" Little did he know that the actual Arjun overheard his boast.

Arjun sent Draupadi to the prince to say that he of the conch bangles and earrings was a charioteer who had been trained by Arjun himself. The prince, though in some doubt, resolved to give the dancing instructor a chance to show whether or not he could serve as charioteer. Uttara was not in doubt for long, for the thirteen years had fled, and Arjun could now cast off his disguise and reveal himself as the battle-hungry man he was. Laughing at Uttara's bow and arrows as handsome toys, he drove the chariot to a dark and gloomy *sami* tree, where, he said, worthier weapons could be found.

"Only corpses in their wrappings hang from the branches of this tree," said the prince, "and they appear to have been suspended here for many seasons. Friend, to touch these unclean objects is more than I dare."

But upon being reassured by Arjun, Uttara climbed the tree, while the hero waited below with the impatient chariot. The young prince cut the wrappings, and, lo!, in place of filth and corruption appeared the gleaming weapons of the Pandavs, Arjun's gold-tipped bow, called Gandiva, Bhima's bow, worked with elephants of gold, Yudhishthir's royal weapon, inlaid with golden insects, Nakula's, with golden suns, and Sahadeva's, decked with jewels that sparkled like golden fire-flies. He saw, besides, a thousand arrows for each bow, and each brother's mighty sword in its distinctive scabbard. And it was not long before he heard where the famous brothers and Draupadi were.

Uttara became the chariot-driver, Arjun raised his monkey-standard, well known by Kuru warriors, and took his mighty bow, Gandiva, in his hand. Soon that great bow was speaking after its thirteen years of silence, but Arjun instructed the prince not to bring the chariot within actual bow-shot of Drona, Bhishma, Karna, and the rest, but to drive on to where Duryodhan and another group were with the stolen cattle. Then Arjun's arrows like countless locusts began to whistle in earnest through the air, Kuru warriors fled or fell where they stood, and the rescued cattle began a stampede toward their old grazing grounds.

Virata, returning with joy to his royal city, saw the restored herds of cattle, saw Prince Uttara safe and sound, saw the Pandav brothers and Draupadi attired like themselves. He offered his daughter to Arjun, but Arjun answered that he might not take as bride a girl toward whom he felt as if she were his own daughter; and he suggested, instead, that the beauteous child be given to Abhimanyu, his son by fair Subhadra, Krishna's sister. This, accordingly, was done.

The Two Councils

To the wealthy city of the Matsyas, which had been decked with flags and cloth of gold for the marriage celebration, came all the friends of the god-like sons of Pandu. On the day after the wedding, the princes gathered in the council chamber, where Krishna reminded them that Yudhishthir and his brothers and Draupadi had completed all the conditions of the exile imposed upon them by the proud Duryodhan, and asked if it were not time for Yudhishthir to reassert his claim to the kingdom of Indra-prastha. Opinion was divided, but at last all agreed that Krishna should travel to the council hall at Hastina to open negotiations.

After certain days, then, Krishna stood in that hall and with a voice like rolling thunder urged mighty Dhrita-rashtra to restore the Pandav brothers to full sonship, allowing them to divide and share the two kingdoms with Duryodhan and his brothers and mighty Karna. Bhishma spoke and agreed, Drona spoke and agreed, Vidura spoke and agreed, the sightless parent, Dhrita-rashtra, spoke and agreed. Last spoke Duryodhan: "There shall not be given to them so much ground as can be covered by the point of a needle!"

The Great War

All efforts toward a peaceful solution having fallen through, Northern India prepared for war. Duryodhan and his allies gathered perhaps a hundred thousand men, who were placed under the command of the grand old fighter Bhishma. Yudhishthir and his allies were able to gather seventy thousand, by conservative estimate; and these were put under the joint-command of Krishna and Arjun.

When Arjun saw his old friends drawn up in battle array opposite him, and knew in his heart that—with the exception of Duryodhan and Karna—they were his friends still, he could not lift his bow against them. Then, in that memorable discourse known as the *Bhagavat-gita,* Krishna explained to him that for every man, regardless of his caste, the zealous performance of his duty is his most important work. The one Supreme Deity may range devoted friends under opposing masters. Thus Arjun's loyalty to Yudhishthir would force him to attempt to slay Bhishma, and Bhishma's loyalty to Duryodhan would force him to attempt to slay Arjun; and yet the two fighters might love each other no less than in the peaceful old days when Arjun was only a youth, growing up in his uncle's court. Arjun accepted Krishna's greater wisdom, bowed to the stern will of the Deity, and the war began.

For ten days, on one of which even Bhima was wounded and almost lost, Bhishma's generalship put the Pandavs on the defensive. Yet all the while Bhishma was urging Duryodhan to put a stop to the war, maintaining that the Pandavs had justice on their side and would win in the end.

At last Bhishma was slain. In accordance with a vow he had made, he refused to defend himself against an attack made by slight Sikhandin, a transformed warrior who had been born a girl. But in so refusing, he laid himself open to the lances and arrows of Bhima and Arjun, as Krishna had planned. The stainless palmtree standard fell, and down fell the ancient Bhishma—yet he did not fall quite to the earth, for he was supported by the many arrows which Arjun had poured into him. Lying on this strange bed, he once more begged Duryodhan to soften his heart and end the war. At the very last, Karna, who had been a rival of his, in a way, came gently and stood beside him. Then with dying breath Bhishma told the hero that he was Pritha's son and Arjun's half-brother, that the chariot driver was not his father, for the Sun, during Pritha's maidenhood, had inspired his birth. But even in this last effort to stop the fratricidal war, Bhishma was unsuccessful, for new hatred against the Pandavs, rather than affection for them, stirred in Karna's heart.

In place of Bhishma, Drona, the Brahman chief who had once been preceptor of all the Kuru and Pandav princes, took over the leadership of the Kuru forces.

During one of the five days of Drona's command, the young bridegroom Abhimanyu, son of Arjun and fair Subhadra, made a glorious sally against the Kurus. Elephants, battle steeds, and warriors fell before him. He wounded Duryodhan and Salya and Duhsasan (who long ago had dared to insult Draupadi) and Duhsasan's son. But at last Jayadratha and six more car-borne warriors ringed him round, so that when starlight fell, Abhimanyu slumbered lifeless upon the field.

Arjun, who had been all day in another part of the battle, was informed of his son's death by sad Yudhishthir. Grief and a sense of irreparable loss filled Arjun's heart, just as they had filled the hearts of Subhadra and Draupadi and the young princess, Abhimanyu's widow. But soon rage welled up in Arjun instead, and he vowed that the morrow should be his own or Jayadratha's last day. And just at the close of that following day, when the Kurus were on the point of believing that Arjun must take his own life or break his vow, Arjun got in an arrow that suddenly dispatched Jayadratha. Bhima slew many brothers of proud Duryodhan. Twice the steeds of Karna were shot by Ghatotkacha, son of Bhima, and twice the humbled Karna had to flee from the battle. But again Karna came into the fray, and this time he slew the son of Bhima, just as the day ended.

After five days the ancient Drona was brought down by an arrow from the bow of one of the younger men in the Pandav ranks, and Karna was then chosen as the leader of the Kuru forces.

Bhishma had commanded for ten days, Drona for five, but Karna's leadership was not to extend beyond two, for the great struggle between Karna and Arjun, long expected, was now about to take place. But even so they did not meet until after Karna had wounded Yudhishthir, driven him from his chariot, and scoffed at him as famed for virtue, not for valor. Shortly thereafter, Arjun's chariot, with Krishna at the reins, came in sight of Karna's, conducted by Salya. The great bowmen began to send their hissing arrows across the space between. Then Gandiva fell silent; the bow-string had parted. Arjun, invoking the honored rules of war, asked for a quiet moment in which to mend his bow. Karna did not heed. Then ill luck struck upon the other side: a wheel of Karna's chariot struck in the soft earth and tilted it dangerously. Salya urged on the horses and Karna put his shoulder to the wheel, but the chariot did not move forward. Then it was Karna's turn to beg for a truce. Arjun laughed aloud, and Krishna gave the answers. "Karna, bold archer, did you seek the path of virtue when Sakuni robbed Yudhishthir of his empire? Did you tread the path of virtue when you heaped insults on Draupadi? Again, did you tread that path when, Yudhishthir's exile being over, I asked that Yudhishthir's empire be returned to him? Were your men obeying the rules of war when seven of them together hunted Abhimanyu? Speak not of rules of honor! Death is here! Arjun is here!"

Karna sent one last arrow against the mailed breast of Arjun, who staggered back, so that the outcome of the battle was in doubt for one more moment. Then the fainting moment passed; Arjun stood erect and, thinking of his lost son, drew his bow Gandiva. The arrow sped like lightning, and the dying Karna fell as a great rock falls.

Soon thereafter Salya was slain by Yudhishthir, and Duryodhan by the tiger-waisted Bhima, who had tracked him down to a dark lake where he had attempted to take shelter. Kripa had advised him to ask for peace, and at last Duryodhan had admitted his own pride and stubbornness, but Duryodhan had also seen that it was too late to ask for friendship or mercy. The Pandavs had endured too many injustices and insults and had lost too many of their dearest and bravest allies and sons.

In conclusion one may speak of Dhrita-rashtra, once father of a hundred sons, now sonless in his old age; one may think of the stately Queen Gandhari uttering her lament on the field of the slain, or of tearful Pritha at last revealing that Karna was her eldest son, her child by Surya; one may tell how Arjun soon helped Yudhishthir to obtain suzerain powers over all neighboring potentates. But the great heroic days of the sons of Pandu were ended.

LEGENDS FROM THE "RAMAYANA"

The men of the *Mahabharata* seem born to fight, and the conflicts in that epic have the narrowness and intensity of a family feud or civil war. The *Ramayana* wants this epic pitch and unity. A reader of the poem is not allowed to forget that the moral problems met by Rama and his brothers and his wife are quite as serious as the war Rama is compelled to engage in. And the hero's loss of his wife and his efforts to regain her give the poem a romantic quality which the *Mahabharata* lacks—but does not need.

The Story of Rama

The young hero was RAMA, eldest of the sons of DASA-RATHA, king of the Kosalas. His wife, SITA, who was miraculously born of a field furrow, was daughter of JANAK, king of the Videhas. Rama had won her by bending—and finally breaking—her father's mighty bow, a bow which, given to Janak by Rudra, had proved too powerful a weapon to be drawn by the arms of anyone among Sita's numerous other suitors.

After the marriage of Rama and Sita, which pleased both Dasa-ratha and Janak well, it occurred to Dasaratha that he might abdicate, giving his throne to Rama, who was intelligent, well educated, and morally flawless. Brahmans, warlike chieftains, and many men of various occupations in town and hamlet were consulted; all agreed that Dasa-ratha had earned the right to enjoy a few unburdened years, and that there could be no finer regent than the princely Rama. Dasa-ratha's city of Ayodhya was decorated, people came crowding in, and all plans for the coronation were going forward smoothly.

But a far different plan had taken shape within the mind of one who dwelt in the inner palace. This was Manthara, the nurse of Kaikeyi, Dasaratha's youthful wife. Now Rama was not the son of Kaikeyi but of Kausalya. So Manthara tried to make Kaikeyi jealous of Queen Kausalya and sought to make her believe that Rama, once established in power, would find some way to harm her own son, BHARAT. There were two younger boys, twins: LAKSHMAN, who waited on Rama with devotion, and SATRUGNA, who waited on Bharat with equal affection. Manthara told Kaikeyi that Rama would not harm the twins, as he did not fear them, but that Bharat was in danger, being in merit and in age too close a rival. And, danger or no danger, the throne would be lost forever to descendants of Kaikeyi. The young queen went off alone to a place of mourning and flung herself down, while Manthara's words stirred like poison in her bosom.

The old king had not forgotten his young consort even in the midst of his preparations for the coronation of the eldest son. He went everywhere seeking her until he found her. Seeing her in tears, he lifted up her head, and vowed to do anything within his kingly power to comfort her. As if this had not been enough, Kaikeyi reminded him of an earlier promise also, of which she had not yet taken advantage, a promise made when she nursed him back to health after he had been wounded in battle. Now he must make good his word or she would end her own life. Then came her request. "Let my Bharat and not Rama be made regent; I would see my son anointed on this day, and Rama banished to the forests for fourteen years."

The king's word might not be broken. Thus Manthara's bitter heart and Kaikeyi's jealousy and lack of trust turned all the joy in the city of Ayodhya into chagrin and the deepest disappointment.

Without a word of complaint, Rama bowed to his father's new wishes; and Sita and Lakshman would not be parted from Rama, but followed him into exile. But had you seen them on the first day, you would have said the whole city was going into exile, to see how many loyal subjects accompanied them as far as the banks of the Tamasa River. But the three slipped away during the night, leaving the citizens to return to their homes. On the third day, the exiles crossed the Ganges, on the fourth they came to a hermitage at the confluence of the Ganges and the Jumna, and on the sixth they came to the hill of Chitra-kuta, where they met the saint Valmiki, who was later to write the history of Rama and Sita. Meanwhile at home the aging Dasaratha, unable to bear the thought of his son's long exile, pined away and died, recalling in his last days how in his youth he had caused the death of an old hermit by killing his son—not deliberately, to be sure, but through failure to exercise sufficient care as an archer.

After the death of the king, Bharat, with others of the court, followed Rama to Chitra-kuta to implore him to return to Ayodhya to reign, but this Rama did not feel free to do. Nor did Queen Kausalya's lament over Sita, when she met her in the dress of an anchorite in the forest, cause Sita to urge Rama to withdraw from his plighted word.

Bharat returned to the palace with Rama's sandals and placed them on the throne in order to show clearly that he was merely viceroy during Rama's absence.

The exiles plunged into deeper forests, but there was to be for Sita one more moment of womanly tenderness, like her meeting with Kausalya, before she departed for the unexplored wildernesses of the south. This occurred when Rama visited the saint Atri, and the ancient wife of the saint dressed Sita richly and adorned her with jewels on the eve of her complete exile.

There was, however, a great saint and explorer to the south of them in the Deccan-Agastya. Him too the wanderers met, and when Lakshman had told their story, the saint welcomed them and encouraged them to build a woodland dwelling in the Forest of Panchaviti, on the banks of the Godavari. Here the exiles lived in harmony and might perhaps have been happy had it not been for the events about to be narrated.

Surpa-nakha, a Raksha princess, ugly as only Rakshas can be, gazed on Rama of the lion-chest and lofty forehead, and wanted him for her own. Sita she scorned as too pale and weak to be a warrior's wife, and Lakshman she regarded as a mere stripling; and she stupidly believed that Rama would not be offended if she offered to do away with both of them. Rama and Lakshman impulsively laughed at her and made jokes at her expense. The result was that she made a rush at Sita to destroy her. Rama sprang to the side of his wife, who had fainted away, and Lakshman wielded his sword like lightning and split the nose and both ears of the Raksha before she knew how it had been done.

Surpa-nakha carried her complaints to her Raksha brothers, RAVANA, the king of Ceylon, and MARICHA. Maricha now took the shape of a deer of such matchless beauty that Sita wished Rama might capture him alive so that he might be tamed, or if that proved impossible, that he might be brought down by arrows so that his skin might in later years in Ayodhya serve as a memento of the exiles' forest days. To capture him alive did prove impossible. Then Rama reached him with his arrows. But as the deer fell he imitated Rama's voice and called to Lakshman to aid him. Lakshman suspected that this was only a trick and wished to adhere to Rama's earlier orders that he remain with Sita to protect her, but Sita yielded to the base suspicion that her husband's brother would be glad to see her a widow so that he might make her his own wife. She proudly declared that she would not long remain alive after

Rama's death. Then indeed Lakshman left her to seek out his elder brother.

Ravana came to Sita in the guise of a hermit and was suitably received. Then he revealed the fact that he was leader of the Rakshas and king of Lanka (Ceylon). As such, he tried to tempt her away from her own lord and husband. When she repulsed him, he seized her as an eagle takes a writhing snake in its talons, bore her aloft in an aerial car, and did not descend until he had reached the towering mountains of Lanka, set in the vast ocean.

After many adventures, Rama and Lakshman wandered into the Nilgiri mountains of southern India, where they befriended SUGRIVA, king of the monkeys, and helped restore him to his rightful throne. HANUMAN, Sugriva's general (but otherwise known as the chief or god of the monkeys), now became Rama's close assistant. Many were sent out to seek Sita, but it was Hanuman who found her in Lanka. Sita, who had remained faithful to her lord, was guarded by terrible Raksha females within a garden of *Asoka* trees. Hanuman managed to get into one of the trees, called to Sita, and dropped down to her a ring which had Rama's name upon it in jeweled letters. In return Sita tossed up to Hanuman a jewel from her brow, a jewel which Rama was soon to see again and instantly to recognize as one which Janak had given to Sita at the time of her marriage.

Preparations for the great war in Ceylon began with Hanuman and a host of monkeys tearing up rocks and trees to make a causeway to the island. Ravana's complete overthrow was a foregone conclusion. Ravana was unwise in disregarding the advice of his brothers KUMBHA-KARNA and BIBHISHAN to make peace with Rama. While Ravana opted for war, his brothers made different personal decisions. His second brother, Kumbha-karna, remained loyal to Ravana in spite of his evil deeds; but the youngest, Bibhishan, renounced his own tribe of Rakshas and went over to the cause of righteousness. In consequence he was able, of course, to give Rama information and advice of the greatest consequence.

The war won and Sita's stainless virtue proved by an ordeal of fire, the reunited lovers were borne home on an aerial car drawn by swans from which they looked down on the causeway (now called Adam's Bridge or Rama's Bridge) built by Hanuman's monkey helpers to bring the troops into Lanka, and then down on India, from south to north, while they recalled their days of exile, not from beginning to end, but from the end to the beginning. And when they reached Ayodhya, where their sorrows had begun, their joy was full, for the exile was over.

Yet the poem as we have it comes to us with a sad epilogue. It is said that in later years the people of Ayodhya did not wish to have as their queen a woman who had dwelt in the household of Ravana, and it is also said that Rama sent her away. She wandered as far as the hermitage of Valmiki and there became the mother of Rama's twin sons, Lava and Kusa. Later the sons came to court and their recital of Valmiki's epic concerning the early exile of their parents touched Rama's heart and made him long for Sita's return. Sita came, but her heart was broken, and she could not take up the old life again. She called upon the Earth to take her back, and the Earth, who had given the true and loyal Sita birth, took her weary child into her bosom. Rama had her sons, who were destined later to found new kingdoms, but Sita herself was gone.

"SAKUNTALA"

Sakuntala, the magnificent play by India's great early poet, Kalidasa, which has been produced from time to time in our own day, tells the story of the beautiful maiden Sakuntala and of King Dushyanta, of their love and marriage, and the birth of their son, the great hero, Bharata. It is from Bharata that the *Mahabharata* takes its name, and it is indeed from the epic that Kalidasa derived the plot of Sakuntala.

The Story of Sakuntala

SAKUNTALA was the daughter of a sage, VISHVAMITRA, and a nymph, MENAKA. As a babe, she was left in a forest, where her only nourishment was provided by birds. There she was found by KANVA, a sage, who brought her up as his own daughter at a hermitage, where he was the chief sage. One day, King DUSHYANTA, who was hunting in the forest, spied her and was attracted to her. He induced her to enter into a Gandharva marriage with him, that is, a marriage made simply by the assent of bride and groom. Before leaving Sakuntala to return to his capital, Dushyanta gave her a ring as his pledge.

When she returned to the hermitage Sakuntala unintentionally offended the irascible sage DURVASAS, who pronounced upon her the curse of being forgotten by her husband. At the entreaty of a friend of Sakuntala, however, Durvasas modified his curse and promised that Dushyanta would remember Sakuntala immediately on seeing the ring which he had given her.

With the blessing of her foster father, Sakuntala then set out to join Dushyanta. However, while on the way, she bathed in a sacred pool and lost the ring. When she presented herself to the king, as foretold in Durvasas' curse, he did not recognize her and disavowed the marriage, although he was sympathetic to Sakuntala, particularly since she told him she was about to have a child. Grief-stricken, Sakuntala withdrew from the presence of the king. Outside the palace, an apparition appeared and bore her away to a sacred grove where their son, BHARATA, was born.

Soon after this a fisherman discovered a valuable ring in a fish which he had caught, and, because this fisherman was suspected of having stolen the ring, he was brought before Dushyanta. On seeing the ring, the king recognized it, thus breaking the curse, and thereupon he remembered Sakuntala. Remorseful at his neglect of his wife, Dushyanta was most anxious to find Sakuntala and to see his son. The god Indra's charioteer appeared and carried him through the heavens to the sacred grove, where Dushyanta and Sakuntala were reunited, their love augmented by the knowledge of the heroic destiny of their son.

Myths and Legends of the Chinese

THE mythology of China goes back in time to the earliest periods of that vast and ancient land. China was the fountainhead of the culture of the Far East, establishing traditions, many of which have continued to the present, but also accepting influences from neighboring areas which fulfilled the mood or need of the Chinese people.

Three great religions—Taoism, Confucianism, and Buddhism—have contributed to the store of Chinese myths and legends.

Taoism basically conceives the movements of the heavens as the cause of the phenomena on earth. Behind the visible system of nature is the *Tao,* or universal cosmic energy. The Tao produced the *yin* and the *yang,* the negative and the positive, the female and the male principles of nature. By their interaction these brought forth heaven and earth, which in turn produced all beings. Hence, humanity is a product of cosmic energy.

Lao-Tze, who lived between 604 and 517 B.C., was the founder of Taoism. After his death he was deified and became the inspiration for a host of miracle stories. It was written that his was an immaculate conception, and that, after being carried in his mother's womb for seventy years, he was born—old and white-haired and already sage.

Confucianism, founded by Confucius, who lived between 551 and 478 B.C., concerns itself, in the main, more with ethical and social teaching than with mythology, although in *The Shu King,* one of the sacred books of Confucianism, legendary tales of China's history are told.

Through its contact with Buddhism, which had been introduced into China from India in 300 B.C., Taoism came to parallel the Buddhist pantheon. Lao-Tze as a divinity was associated with Pan Ku and Yü Huang Shangti in the Taoist trinity patterned after the Three Jewels of Buddhism.

Tao Teh King is the chief of the sacred writings of Taoism. The Buddhist scriptures consist of the *Three Baskets of Wisdom,* the third of which, *Abhidhamma Pitaka,* or Metaphysical Basket contains a detailed account of Buddhist doctrine.

Tou Mu

TOU MU, the goddess of the North Star, was worshipped by both Buddhists and Taoists and was raised to the stars by the latter. By the king of Chou Yu in the north she was the mother of nine sons. With her husband and her family she lives in heaven in a palace around which all the other stars revolve, and her sons have their own palaces nearby. As Tou Mu in the Taoist religion, she corresponds to KUAN YIN in the Buddhist. She is represented as seated on a lotus throne. She has three eyes, and eighteen arms; in her hands she holds a bow, a sword, a spear, a flag, the head of a dragon, the disks of the sun and the moon, and five chariots. She rules over life and death and is worshipped by those who wish to live longer. On the third and twenty-seventh days of each month her followers do not eat meat. Tou Mu is as kind as she is powerful and her heart is full of pity for human suffering.

Mu King

MU KING is the god of the Immortals and the ruler of *yang,* the active, male principle in nature. He lives in a blue and violet palace in heaven, waited on by HSIEN T'UNG, the immortal youth, and YU NU, the Jade Maiden. A list of all the immortals is kept by him. The myth concerning Mu King is that the primitive vapor froze and after a dormant period began to give birth to living things, of which Mu King was the first and the purest. He is the king of the East, of which he is the highest product.

Hsi Wang Mu

HSI WANG MU, the Golden Mother of the Tortoise, was born of the Western Air, as Mu King was of the Eastern Air. She represents *yin,* the passive, female principle in nature, and it is the union of *yang* and *yin* that produces heaven and earth and all the creatures that live on the universe. She was the mother of twenty-four daughters and nine sons.

Yen-lo-Wang

YEN-LO-WANG is the Chinese god of the dead and the king of the hells. With nine other gods connected with him he is one of a band called the Ten Kings. When and how a man dies and the state of his soul after death are matters under his control. In spite of his tremendous power, Yen-lo was once defied by SUN HOU-TZU. Sun, who is known by many names, was a monkey fairy and the king of the monkeys. Two of Wang's messengers trapped Sun when he was lost in a drunken slumber, tied him in chains, and brought him down to the lower regions of their master. When Sun finally came to outside the gates of the regions of the dead and realized what had happened, he snapped his chains, slew the two messengers who were keeping watch over him, and by means of his wonder-working wand gained access to Yen's private office. After uttering fierce threats, which he was well able to carry out, he ordered the ten kings or gods to bring him the registry-book which contained the names of both the living and the dead. He went through the register until he found the page he was seeking—the one with his name and the names of his loyal subjects—and in front of Yen-lo-Wang he tore out the page and boldly declared that from that time on the laws of death did not apply to him. The god of the dead felt compelled to submit to the god of the monkeys, and Sun, in high spirits, returned to the upper world.

Hou Chi

HOU CHI, the founder of the house or dynasty of Chou, was worshipped as a person of divine attributes. He was born of a footprint of God in which his mother, CHIANG YUAN, stepped in order to avoid being childless; as a result she conceived and gave birth to Hou Chi, who is called an associate of God. The myths concerning him tell that he was suckled by sheep and oxen; that he was exposed—to die—in a huge forest but was found and saved by kindly wood-choppers; and that he was placed on ice but was protected by birds covering him with their warm wings. In later life, Hou Chi taught the arts of agriculture to the Chinese people and by them he was deified and worshipped.

The Kings of Heaven

The Four Kings of Heaven live on Mt. Sumeru, the center of the universe; it is a million miles high, and its four slopes are made of gold, silver, agate, and crystal. The four Taoist kings are LI, who is represented as holding a pagoda, or sacred temple, in his hands; MA, who holds a sword; CHAO, who holds two swords; and WEN, who holds a spiked club.

The Four Diamond Kings of Heaven in Chinese Buddhism are four brothers: MO-LI CH'ING (Pure), MO-LI HUNG (Vast), MO-LI HAI (Sea), and MO-LI SHOU (Age). Mo-li Ch'ing, the oldest brother, is twenty-four feet high; he has a magic sword, called Blue Cloud, on the blade of which are engraved written characters representing the elements, earth, water, fire, and wind. He also has a spear and a lovely jade ring. When he waves the sword it gives rise to a black wind which produces thousands of spears that pierce men's bodies and cause them to turn to dust. After the wind comes a fire and the air is thick with thousands of gold snakes, and the blinding smoke is so heavy that nobody can escape. Mo-li Hung carries a pearl umbrella endowed with spiritual powers—the Umbrella of Chaos. When Mo-li Hung opens it, the heavens and the earth are wrapped in total darkness; when he turns it upside down, violent storms and earthquakes follow. Mo-li Hai is represented with a four-stringed guitar; when he plays it, the earth and the elements on it are moved, the entire universe stops to listen, and the camps of the enemy burst into flame. Mo-li Shou carries two whips and a bag made of the skin of a panther in which he keeps a white rat, or a snake, Hua-hu Tiao by name, that has the power to assume the shape of a white man-eating elephant with wings. Whatever form or identity it takes on, the animal is always completely subservient to its master.

All four brothers lost their lives in battle when they came to the aid of the House of Shang. They won at first because of their instruments of magic and because Hua-hu Tiao weakened the enemy forces by eating many of the bravest leaders, but their luck began to turn after the monster made the mistake of attacking and swallowing Yang Chien, a genie and the nephew of Yu Huang, the Pearly Emperor and king or ruler of the first heaven. Yang Chien had a trick or two of his own and as soon as he found himself inside Hua-Hu's body he cut him in two and split his heart. Having the godly power of transforming himself into any shape he desired, he assumed the form and appearance of his slain enemy and returned to his "master," who innocently placed him, as was his custom, in the panther-skin bag. At night, when the four brothers were heavy with wine and food and deep in slumber, Yang Chien came out of his hiding-place and stole Mo-li Hung's magic umbrella, although he failed to secure the other weapons. Later, No-cha, son of Vadjrapani, the god of thunder, broke Mo-li Ch'ing's jade ring. These misfortunes were only the beginning for the Diamond Kings of Heaven. Finally all four of them were killed by Huang T'ien Hua and his long magic spike, appropriately called the Heart-piercer, which had the power of blinding those who saw it as well as killing those whom it struck. Mo-li Ch'ing, the first to die, caught it in his neck. As Mo-li Hung and Mo-li Hai rushed to defend him and to attack Huang, he again hurled his hellish spike and pierced them both to the heart. Mo-li Shou, left alone, saw Huang advancing on him, and quickly thrust his hand into his bag, not knowing that the creature inside was not his own Hua-hu Tiao, as he thought, but the crafty Yang Chien in disguise. As he groped inside the bag, Yang bit off his hand. At the same moment, Huang threw his cruel spear for the last time, and Mo-li Shou, the last of the four brothers and the last of the four Diamond Kings of Heaven, fell dead.

The Metal-bound Casket

King Wû, a wise and beloved ruler, fell ill and seemed about to die. His three brothers, the dukes of the realm, were much concerned over this serious situation, but only one, the duke of Chow, took definite steps to prevent the king's death. He erected a series of altars on an open place and there, with the grand recorder taking down his words in writing, he prayed to his ancestors to spare the king's life. "If he must die," he prayed, "let me die in his place, for I have been lovingly obedient to my father, and am fitted to serve the dwellers of heaven. It may be that I shall serve in heaven better than your great descendant, and it may be that he will serve better on earth."

When he had finished, the duke opened a metal-bound chest and found that the response to his entreaty was favorable—the king would recover and he, the duke, need not die. He then placed the tablet on which his prayer had been recorded in the chest and closed it.

True enough, the king recovered, and he lived for another five years, when he was succeeded by his small son Ching. Because of Ching's youth, the duke of Chow acted as his nephew's adviser. But the other brothers were jealous of the duke's power and spread rumors throughout the hemisphere that he would do Ching no good. When he heard what was taking place, the duke of Chow resolved to leave the kingdom and travel in the east so that Heaven might prove him innocent of the charges.

In the autumn, just as the abundant grain in the fields was ready to be harvested, a heavy storm arose and beat the grain to the earth and uprooted great trees. Terror struck at the hearts of the people and the rulers were at a loss. They came upon the metal-bound chest to examine the holy writings and found the tablet containing the duke of Chow's prayer. When they read that he had offered to die in place of the old king, they realized how false the charges against him were. The young king cried: "We need not now inquire into the meaning of the storm. The duke always has been loyal to the interests of the throne. Now Heaven has moved its terrors to display the virtue of the duke of Chow."

Then Ching went to bring back his adviser. And then, by another, but favorable wind, the grain was raised from the ground and the trees were replaced, and the people had a fruitful year.

Myths and Legends of the Japanese

Two works, filled with myths and legends of *Shinto,* the national religion of Japan, constitute the sacred scriptures of that land. These are the *Kojiki* or Records of Ancient Matters and the *Nihongi* or Chronicles of Japan.

The first of these, *Kojiki,* tells of the Age of the Gods before man came into existence, and describes the creation of the deities and the formation of the islands of Japan. According to Shinto, these islands were the first bodies of land created by the gods, and by design are located in the center of the world. As in the early legends of other religions, the story begins with the conflict of the forces of light and darkness, these ultimately producing the universe and peopling it with many deities. This is represented in the struggle between the Sun-Goddess and her impetuous brother Susa-no-o, the rainstorm. The violence committed by Susa-no-o drives the sun into hiding, but in time she is lured out and her brother banished from heaven to earth. It is noteworthy that the sun is not represented as being male, as in other religions where such nature worship has a parallel, but is female.

The later compilation, *Nihongi,* tells of the emperors of Japan. The first Japanese emperor was, we are told, the direct descendant of the heavenly Sun-Goddess. All emperors of Japan are believed to be direct descendants of this first emperor and thus of the Sun-Goddess. Worship of the sun is symbolized in the national flag of Japan, a rising sun.

Shinto borrows much from other religions and mythologies with which it has coexisted and intermingled, chiefly, Confucianism, Buddhism, and Taoism.

Ama-Terasu

AMA-TERASU is the goddess of the sun and the founder of the royal house of Japan. She was born from the left eye of IZANAGI, the male member of the generative couple in Japanese mythology, IZANAMI being the female part. She was the sister of Susa-no-o, the god of the sea, who was born from Izanagi's nose. After a quarrel with her brother, Ama-Terasu hid herself in a cave and sealed up the entrance, thus depriving the universe of light. Her fellow gods attempted in various ways to persuade her to come out, but without success. Finally, a strangely-garbed goddess more clever than the rest began to go through the steps of a fantastic dance; the laughter and excitement that this aroused was too much for Ama-Terasu's curiosity and she stuck her head out in order to have a look and gradually came out of the cave entirely, so that the world was light again.

Susa-no-o

SUSA-NO-O, like many other divinities, may be placed in more than one godly category. When power was distributed at the beginning, he was given authority over the sea, but was not satisfied with his position and was, at his own request, transferred to the lower world, the home of his mother. This situation makes him god of the underworld, but he is also considered as a god of the moon and of the rainstorm. His offensive conduct to his sister and her hiding from the world as a consequence are the principal myths concerning Susa-no-o and Ama-Terasu. He was naturally violent and belligerent. Before taking up his residence in the nether-world he suggested to his sister that they produce offspring by the novel method of chewing up pieces of gems and swords and then spitting them forth; one of the eight children thus born was the ancestor of the Mikado. Banished for his violent behavior, he partially atoned for it by rescuing (and later marrying) a beautiful maiden from a dragon with eight heads.

Ohonamochi

Ohonamochi, the son of Susa-no-o, is the Japanese earth-god. He is frequently identified with Daikoku, god of wealth, in the sense that the earth is the source of all wealth. His shrine is visited by thousands of his worshippers, and when all the gods assemble to do him honor heaven is temporarily empty. According to another myth, Ohonamochi descended into Yomi, the Japanese equivalent of Hades, and became the husband of Susa-no-o's daughter. Several labors were imposed on him by his father-in-law, but he successfully accomplished them all, thanks to the aid of his wife, with whom he fled from Yomi.

Amida

Amida is an abstract god representing or personifying boundless light. His home is in a remote paradise in the West. He is noted for his wisdom, of which the spot on his forehead is a symbol. He sits with his legs crossed on a lotus-flower. Amida was the chief Buddhist divinity of the Japanese.

Izanagi and Izanami

Izanagi and Izanami are the productive couple in the mythology of the Japanese. After seven generations, they were ordered by their fellow gods to undertake the task of creation. Many islands and the elemental gods were born of their union. Izanami died when she gave birth to the god of fire, and Izanagi cut off his son's head in his grief; from the drops of blood other gods were born. Izanagi searched for his wife in the lower world, but he rushed away in horror when he discovered her body. Upon reaching the upper world he purified himself by bathing in the river. Gods and evil creatures were born from his garments as he threw off his clothing.

Emma-o

Emma-o, a Buddhist deity, rules the regions of hell and exercises the functions of a judge in the underworld.

Inari

Inari is the Japanese goddess, or god, of rice. The fox is sacred to the deity and images of foxes decorate the entrances to her temples. Ukemochi, goddess of cereals and food, is identified with Inari.

Kwannon

Kwannon is the Japanese goddess of mercy and the guardian of the Buddhist faith. Kwannon is also regarded as a god and as the spiritual son of Amida, personifying light and wisdom.

Aizen Myo-o and Dainichi

Aizen Myo-o, the Japanese god of love, was represented as having three eyes and six arms. Dainichi was a Japanese god personifying wisdom and was a member of the Buddhist trinity.

Myths and Legends of the Greeks

It was in Greece that the Ancient World rose to its greatest heights of creativeness. The magnificent achievements of the Greeks in poetry, drama, art and architecture, science, and philosophy have for us today the same freshness of inspiration, the same vitality, the same clarity, the same profound understanding of the essential and beautiful and enduring things that they had for the people of their own day. The religious views of the Greeks, their sense of the intimate reality of their gods and goddesses, the vividness of their accounts of the deeds of their heroes, constitute for us a wealth of myth and legend unparalleled in variety and fascination.

The Greeks, evidently descended from tribes who had come westward from the early home of the Indo-Europeans in south-central Asia, first settled in the land which we know as Greece about 2000 B.C. Separate groups settled in different valleys or in hill country or along the seacoast, and each group felt a very deep attachment to its particular part of Greece, to the locality in which it had made its home. Thus we find different or similar, supplementary or conflicting accounts of the legends and the variations are explained by the fact that individual myths and stories are rooted in the locality in which they originated. Gradually groups merged with neighboring groups, and in time the Greek world included not only the peninsula of Greece but also the many Aegean islands and part of the mainland of Asia Minor. Though so much in the thought and faith of the Greeks was indigenous to their own lands there was a certain amount of contact with Egypt and to a lesser degree with the Babylonian peoples and these influences contributed certain qualities to the characterization of some of the Greek deities and heroes.

The belief of the Greeks—the sense of many gods near at hand—was accepted and a part of the everyday conception of life and the universe through many centuries of Greek life. This early Greek faith was an expression of simple awe and delight, a sense of the presence of the mysterious power and the compelling beauty of nature. Characteristic too was the picturing of the gods as divinely gifted yet ready and eager for frequent association with mortals.

The myths and legends of the Greeks have come down to us from many sources. The two superb epics of Homer, the *Iliad* and the *Odyssey,* written in the ninth century B.C., while dealing respectively with the Trojan War and the wanderings of Odysseus (Ulysses), contain many references to other legends. The *Theogony* of Hesiod, from the eighth century B.C., gives a systematic account of the generations of the gods and of the demi-gods, mortals with a god or goddess as one parent. Many legends are magnificently told in the dramas of Aeschylus, Sophocles, and Euripedes, and important mention of attributes is found in the poetry of Sappho and Pindar. Other Greek writings from early and late periods add to the completeness of our record.

When in the fifth century B.C. the views of Socrates, Plato, Aristotle, and other great philosophers became widely influential, the early polytheistic faith—no longer actively accepted—became more and more a world of exquisite myth and legend to the Greeks, a pagan universe with the qualities of perennial refreshment which still hold their full measure of imaginative replenishment for us today.

In our section on the Greeks, we give first the myths of the Greek deities; then the legends of the heroes. We conclude with a few noted tales from a later period.

The stories of certain famous figures will be found included in the article on one or another primary figure, and can be rapidly located by means of the Index.

It is important to mention here that we use the Greek names for the gods and heroes, even though in some instances the Roman form or equivalent is more widely known. In all instances where there is a Roman equivalent or counterpart, we refer to the Roman name near the beginning or at the end of the entry. In the section on "Myths and Legends of the Romans" we give the deities under their Roman (Latin) names, of course, and point out the characteristics which the Romans assigned to them. The Roman forms of the names came into English literature because Latin was through the centuries so much more generally studied than Greek. The true spirit of the Greek world is best sensed, however, through the use of the Greek forms for the names, and for this reason we use them here.

MYTHS OF THE GREEK DEITIES

The Creation

How did the world begin or originate? How did the gods begin? How did man begin? What are the ages through which the world has passed? The ancient Greeks, thousands of years ago, pondered on these questions as we still do today.

The legendary poet Orpheus is said, in some accounts, to have believed that TIME came first, existing from the very beginning but without a beginning. From Time came CHAOS, a tremendous space containing NIGHT, MIST, and the upper regions of the air, or AETHER. At Time's command, the Mist spun around the airy space with such terrific speed that the mass, taking on the shape of an egg, finally broke into two. EROS (or LOVE), four-headed and double-sexed, came from the center of the egg, and the halves became HEAVEN and EARTH.

According to Homer, OCEANUS, personified as Ocean, a vast flood that encircled all the earth, both land and sea, was the beginning of everything.

According to Hesiod, in the beginning there was not Time (as in Orpheus), but CHAOS, a vast, vacant, undefined, infinite, empty, immeasurable space, a yawning gap, a primal void antedating men and gods and things, before which there is or was—nothing. From Chaos came EREBUS or DARKNESS, and his sisters, NYX or NIGHT, and GAEA, the EARTH. Erebus and Nyx became the parents of a daughter, HEMERA or DAY, and a son, AETHER or AIR. Gaea, goddess of the Earth, gave birth to a son, URANUS, the Heavens.

Many deities who are personifications of primitive ideas are described as the children of Nyx, though some of them are given other parentage in other accounts. Among the offspring of Nyx were: FATE (MOROS) (or the three Fates, the MOERAE); VIOLENT

feet. And according to some versions, from the parts that fell into the sea, a foam arose, creating Aphrodite, the foam-born. (This account of the origin of the Furies differs from that given above in the entry on "The Creation." The entry on "Aphrodite" below gives several versions of her birth.)

After freeing their imprisoned brothers, the Titans dethroned Uranus and elevated the crafty Cronus to the supreme position. Once in possession of complete power, Cronus turned on his single-eyed and hundred-handed brothers and hurled them back into the dark regions from which he had, at Gaea's urging, rescued them.

By her son PONTUS, Gaea was the mother of the primitive sea gods, NEREUS, THAUMAS, and PHORCYS, and the sea goddesses, CETO and EURYBIA. In addition, Gaea was the mother of three giants, TYPHON (by Tartarus), ANTAEUS, and TITYUS.

As the personification of Earth, Gaea was honored and celebrated as the mother of all, the universal mother. In Athens, especially, she was worshipped as the nourisher and nurse of children, and also as the goddess of death who calls all her children back to her and takes them to her bosom. Strange and contradictory as these opposing concepts may seem, the strangeness disappears when we remember that Gaea typified mother earth: as she gave them life, so she took life from them when she called them back to the earth from which they issued. In Delphi, she was celebrated as the primeval prophetess, as the source from which originated the vapors that influenced the seer, and the oracle was in her keeping. In Homer, along with Zeus, Heaven, Hell, and the Sun, she was invoked as a witness to oaths, and a black lamb was sacrificed in her honor.

In the entries which follow immediately, we take up the Titans individually, because of their importance. Then we consider the primitive sea deities and then the giants and monsters who were the lesser offspring of Gaea or of her lesser offspring.

Oceanus, Tethys, and Other Titans

OCEANUS, the oldest of the Titans, was by his sister-wife, TETHYS, the father of the rivers of the world, and the source of all fountains, seas, and streams; the father of three thousand sons, and three thousand daughters, the nymphs known as the OCEANIDS. One of the Oceanids was TYCHE, the goddess of fortune or good luck. Several of the other Oceanids appear in other myths which we shall take up. ACHELOUS, the oldest son of Oceanus, was the god of the river of that name and of a place or region, and of the divinity personifying it. He possessed the godly power of appearing in various forms, sometimes as a bull, a snake, or as a man with the face of a bull. He is important in one of the legends of Heracles.

STYX, the oldest daughter of Oceanus, was goddess of the famous river Styx which encompassed Hades and was crossed by those entering the world of the dead. For swearing falsely by Styx a god was punished by being compelled to lie breathless and speechless for a year and by being forbidden to attend the councils of the gods for nine years.

HYPERION, the primitive god of the sun, and THEA, his sister-wife, were the parents of HELIOS, the sun god; SELENE, the moon goddess; and EOS, goddess of the dawn, who were the deities of light during the dynasty of the Titans. (Because of the importance of the legends concerning Helios and Selene, we give them in a separate entry below.)

COEUS and PHOEBE were also deities of light, and accounts seem to indicate that they represented the light of the end of day before the coming of darkness. Their offspring were two daughters, ASTERIA, or starlight, and LETO, spoken of as "sable-vested" and destined to become, by

Zeus, the mother of Apollo and Artemis.

CREUS, one of the male Titans, represents the primitive power of the sea, and by his wife, EURYBIA, a daughter of Pontus and Gaea, he had three sons: ASTRAEUS, who became the husband of Eos, the dawn, and by her the father of the Winds and Stars; PALLAS, who was the father by Styx of Nike, goddess or personification of Victory, and of Kratos (Power), Bia (Strength), and Zelus (Zeal); and PERSES, who became the husband of ASTERIA and by her the father of HECATE, the strange triple goddess, the power of the underworld, of crossroads, and of witchcraft.

IAPETUS is set somewhat apart from the other Titans since he seems in some way intended to represent the origin of the human race. By CLYMENE (Bright One), one of the Oceanids, he was the father of four sons: ATLAS, MENOETIOS, PROMETHEUS, and EPIMETHEUS, all of whom were associated with the welfare and the struggles of human beings more than with the gods. The legends concerning Prometheus, Epimetheus, and Pandora, the wife of Epimetheus, are given in a separate entry below.

THEMIS represented law, order, and justice; she was a more abstract concept than the other Titans. She continued to preside over justice in the succeeding dynasty of Zeus and was referred to as sitting by the side of Zeus, giving him counsel in the dispensing of divine justice to mankind. She was represented in art as holding a pair of scales and a cornucopia. By Zeus she was the mother of the three HORAE (referred to as Hours or Seasons)—EUNOMIE (Order), DIKE (Justice), and EIRENE (Peace); and the three FATES—CLOTHO (the Spinner), LACHESIS (the Disposer of Lots), and ATROPOS (the Unchangeable, who cut the thread of life at death). Another daughter of Zeus and Themis was Astraea; who lived in the Golden Age, but left the earth because she was unable to stand the growing wickedness of men. She was placed among the stars as the constellation Virgo.

MNEMOSYNE, whose name means Memory, became by Zeus, the mother of the nine MUSES, the goddesses who presided over poetry, song, the arts, and learning. The nine Muses were: CALLIOPE, of epic poetry, represented as holding a tightly rolled parchment; CLIO, of history, pictured with a half-opened roll; MELPOMENE, of tragedy, pictured as veiled and carrying a tragic mask; THALIA, of comedy, holding a comic mask; EUTERPE, of music and lyric poetry, represented with two flutes; ERATO, of love poetry and marriage feasts; TERPSICHORE, of the dance; URANIA, of astronomy, represented with a globe in one hand, a rod in the other; and POLYHYMNIA, of hymns sacred to the gods.

Cronus and Rhea, youngest of the twelve Titans, were pictured as the rulers of the Titan dynasty. Because of the importance of the legends concerning them and because the overthrowing of Cronus by Zeus led to the supremacy of the great gods of Olympus, we give a separate entry to Cronus and Rhea.

Cronus and Rhea

CRONUS was the youngest son of Uranus and Gaea. As we have seen, after unmanning and deposing his father at the instigation of his mother, he became supreme ruler of the world. Cronus is generally considered to represent Time. By his sister-wife, RHEA, he was the father of ZEUS and HERA, later the rulers of the heavens; of POSEIDON and HADES; and of DEMETER and HESTIA, all of them Olympian deities who will be treated individually below.

According to a prophecy of his parents, Cronus would be dethroned by a son destined to be greater than he. In order to forestall this situation, Cronus adopted the strange practice of swallowing all his children at birth. Rhea stood this as long as she could, but she lost patience after Cronus had swallowed five of her offspring. Before giving birth to her sixth child, therefore, she went to Lyctos in Crete where she was delivered of Zeus. Rhea then wrapped up a stone in swaddling clothes and presented it to her husband as their newly born child. The trusting Cronus, having no reason to suspect his hitherto obedient spouse, swallowed the stone and was none the wiser. By this stratagem, Zeus was saved.

Years later, when Zeus was grown up to manhood or godhood, he gave Cronus a potion that made him throw up not only the stone but also Zeus' three sisters and two brothers. In the long struggle that followed, with Zeus and his brothers occupying Mount Olympus in Thessaly, and Cronus and the Titans holding Mount Othrys, Cronus was finally defeated by Zeus' thunderbolts.

Many are the legends that deal with Cronus following his defeat. One version has it that he was thrown into Tartarus as he himself had thrown his conquered enemies, his one-eyed and hundred-handed brothers. Another has it that he and Zeus made up and that Cronus ruled with RHADAMANTHYS, son of Europa, on the Islands of the Blessed.

Still another story tells us that Cronus, after a period of wandering exile at last reached Italy. Here he was received with signs of friendship by the king of the country, Janus, and here he received the name SATURN, by which he was known among the Romans.

As Saturn, Cronus was one of the great deities of the Romans. The account of his worship in Rome may appropriately be included here, since, among the Greeks, the legends told that after Cronus fled from his triumphant son, Zeus, he settled in a western land and ruled there, the land clearly being the Italy of the Romans.

In Rome, Cronus founded a settlement on the Capitoline hill, hence known as the Saturnian hill, at the base of which was erected the Temple of Saturn. He taught the people the art and science of agriculture and was regarded as a king. His reign was called an Age of Gold and his country, a land of plenty. Cronus was honored in Rome by a festival known as the Saturnalia, held from the seventeenth to the twenty-third of December. It was a period of great festivity and rejoicing marked by the exchange of presents and the lighting of candles —features which seem to suggest that it was a forerunner of our Christmas. During the celebration, the courts were closed, violators of the law were exempt from penalty, and slaves assumed the positions of their own masters and were waited on by them. War was outlawed during these seven days and to have begun war would have been regarded as an insult to and a sin against the gods.

In art, Cronus was represented as an elderly man with a mantle drawn back over his head; in his hand he held a scythe or sickle, the traditional representation of Time.

Rhea, wife of Cronus, represented fertility and the fruits of the soil. Her worship gained in importance by her identification with CYBELE, chief goddess of the Phrygians and Lydians in Asia Minor, who was known as the Great Mother. At Crete, the scene of Zeus' birth, Rhea was worshipped as the mother of the gods. In Rome, she was worshipped as OPS, goddess of fertility, sowing, and reaping. She was honored by the Opalia, a celebration held on December 19, the third day of the Saturnalia, held in honor of her husband, Cronus-Saturn. Rhea was also known as Agdistis, Dindymene, and Idaea, from the names of some of the several places where she was worshipped.

The priests of Rhea were called CURETES in Crete and Greece. As Cybele, her priests were the CORYBANTES in Phrygia. The Curetes, kindly-disposed demigods, helped to save the infant Zeus' life by drowning out his cries with the clash of their arms. The Corybantes (also known as GALLI, from the river Gallos in Asia Minor) were eunuch priests who followed Cybele with wild savage dances and intoxicating music on her mountain travels. It was believed that they castrated themselves out of sympathy for and in honor and imitation of ATYS (or Attis), a beautiful shepherd who, driven mad by Cybele, unmanned himself.

The trees sacred to her were the oak and the pine, the latter because it was at the foot of a pine tree that Atys destroyed his manhood.

In art, Rhea was pictured as seated on her throne, with lions on either side, a crown on her head and in her hand a small drum. She rode through the mountains on a lion, an animal sacred to her, or in a lion-drawn chariot.

Helios, Selene, and Eos

HELIOS, the god of the sun, was the son of the Titans Hyperion and Thea, and the brother of SELENE, the goddess of the moon, and of EOS, the goddess of the dawn. He was described as rising in the morning in the east from Oceanus, as traversing the heavens in a chariot, and as sinking in the evening into the west. Many of the attributes of Helios are also those of Apollo, the sun-god of the Olympian dynasty, and some of the legends may refer to either deity. By PERSEIS, an ocean nymph, Helios was the father of ÆETES, the King of Colchis; of CIRCE, the famous or infamous enchantress who turned men into swine; and of PASIPHAE, wife of Minos, King of Crete, who fell in love with her husband's white bull. By CLYMENE, on ocean nymph, he was the father of PHAËTHON, whose unskillful handling of his father's chariot almost set heaven and earth on fire and cost him his life.

In love with Helios was CLYTIE, whose love, however, was not returned. She wasted away watching him and was transformed into a flower, the heliotrope, the very name meaning "to turn towards the sun."

Helios was a god who sees and hears everything, and it was he who revealed the hiding-place of Ares and Aphrodite to Hephaestus, and who told Demeter that Hades had kidnapped her daughter. The islands of Trinacria (Sicily) and Rhodes were sacred to him. On the former, he had seven flocks of sheep and as many of oxen, fifty in each flock, of which he was tremendously proud. In his daily journey it was his great pride and pleasure to look down on his seven hundred animals, but his anger knew no bounds if the total number was increased or lessened. At Rhodes, a yearly festival, the Helia, was held in his honor, and four horses were thrown into the sea as a sacrifice. At Rhodes, also, a famous colossal bronze statue was erected to him. Corinth and Elis were other centers of his worship. The color white was sacred to Helios, and white rams and white horses were sacrificed to him, as well as boars, bulls, goats, lambs, and honey. The cock was especially sacred to him, as was the white poplar tree. Helios was a strong, young, handsome god with gleaming eyes—a feature inherited by his children—curly locks, and rays of light, crown-shaped, around his head. He made his daily trip from east to west in a gold chariot drawn by four snow-white horses whose nostrils emitted light and fire. Helios had twelve roomy palaces—corresponding to the Twelve Signs of the Zodiac—in which he lived in rotation during the course of the year. The Roman counterpart of Helios is SOL.

Selene, the goddess of the moon, was the daughter of the Titans Hyperion and Thea, and the sister of Helios, the god of the sun, and of Eos, goddess of the dawn. By Zeus, she had PANDIA (All-bright) a daughter, who was worshipped with her father at festivals in Athens, and

ERSA (Dew). A lovely woman, Selene wore long wings and a gold diadem which gave out a soft light; she made her journey across the heavens in a chariot drawn by two white horses or mules; in some representations, the animal was a cow, in which case the horns were symbolic of the crescent moon. The days of the new and full moon were set aside for her worship. Selene later became identified with Artemis, Apollo's sister, just as her brother, Helios, became identified with Apollo himself.

To think of Selene is to think of the beautiful legend of the beautiful sleeping youth, ENDYMION, with whom she fell in love as she watched him forever sleeping on Mount Latmus in Caria. Every night she came down from the skies to kiss him. Different legends account in different ways for the perpetual slumber of the handsome shepherd, but the generally accepted belief is that Selene herself put him to sleep so that she might be able to kiss him and hold him in her arms without his knowing it. Other accounts make Endymion the father by Selene of fifty daughters, who represented symbolically the fifty lunar months that elapse between each Olympiad, or Olympic cycle of four years. Selene's counterpart in the Roman system of mythology was called LUNA.

Eos, goddess of the dawn, sister of Helios and Selene, as mentioned above, was the mother by Astraeus of the Winds: ZEPHYRUS, the West Wind; BOREAS, the North Wind; NOTUS, the South Wind. (ENRUS, the East Wind, is generally not mentioned as one of their children.) (The King of the Winds, AEOLUS, and his queen, ENARETE, had been appointed regents over all the Winds, although they were not related to them. Their home was the island of Aeolia.) Eos and Astraeus were also the parents of EOSPHORUS, the Morning Star; HESPERUS, the Evening Star; and PHOSPHORUS (called Lucifer by the Romans), who was also called the Morning Star; and of all the Stars of the heavens.

By TITHONOS, son of Laomedon, king of Troy, she was the mother of MEMNON, later the king of Ethiopia, and AEMATHION. So much did Eos love Tithonos that she begged Zeus to make him immortal. The god assented, but since she had not asked for eternal youth, time made its mark on Tithonos and he lived on and on, feeble both in mind and body. Eos locked him in a chamber, where he babbled on incessantly. Finally, out of pity for him, Eos turned him into a cricket.

Eos appears in the legend of PHAËTHON, her son by Cephalus, as drawing the clouds of night aside for his reckless journey over the heavens. Among the Romans Eos was known as AURORA.

Primitive Sea Deities

As mentioned in our entry on Uranus and Gaea above, Gaea was the mother by Pontus, the sea, of a number of early sea deities. We shall take them up here, along with a few other related figures.

NEREUS, the Old Man of the Sea, was the husband of DORIS, an Oceanid. By her, he was the father, according to different accounts, of fifty or of four times fifty sea-nymphs, the NEREIDS, who had two highly desirable attributes to recommend them: they were lovely to look at, and they were exceedingly friendly to mortals, a quality they derived from their father. Of the fifty or two hundred nymphs, the best known were AMPHITRITE, Poseidon's wife and as such the queen of the sea; GALATEA, whose beloved ACIS was crushed to death by the jealous giant, POLYPHEMUS; and THETIS, wife of Peleus and mother of the great Achilles. Nereus, who was represented with a trident or sceptre and with seaweed leaves for hair, lived with his daughters in a gorgeous cave at the bottom of the Aegean. When time hung heavy, the beautiful maidens came to the surface in order to amuse themselves and to give aid and comfort to sailors in distress. Seats dedicated to their worship were located on islands, coasts, and river mouths. In art, they are always charming creatures, lightly draped or nude, delightful burdens, no doubt, to the dolphins and tritons (see Triton under Poseidon below) who carried them.

THAUMAS (whose name means Wonder) was the husband of ELECTRA (meaning Brightness), one of the Oceanids (*not* the Electra of the Agamemnon story), and was by her the father of IRIS, the beautiful goddess of the rainbow, and also father of the three HARPIES, terrifying winged creatures representing the speed and horror of the storm. The Harpies are mentioned either as two or three—AELLO (Storm) and OCYPETE (Swift-flyer); with PODARGE (Swift-foot) sometimes added.

PROTEUS, sometimes said to be a son of Nereus and Doris, or of Oceanus and Tethys, was another early sea deity, from whose name we get the word "protean," meaning "rapid-changing," because of his frequent swift changes of form and disguise. When Menelaus was returning from the Trojan War, his ship was becalmed, and he and his crew suffered from a lack of food. By a stratagem, they captured Proteus and held him so that, although he changed his form, he could not escape, and was forced to tell them how to get their ship going.

Early Monsters and Giants

Two groups of hideous creatures, the GRAIAE and the GORGONS, were the daughters of Phorcys and Ceto.

The Gorgons, horrible monsters, were three in number, according to Hesiod (Homer mentions only one): STHENO and EURYALE, who were immortal, and MEDUSA, who was mortal. Horrible even in Hell, to see them was to be turned to stone. Their dwelling-place was on the farthest shore of Ocean, and their neighbors, the Hesperides, were the daughters of Night.

The Graiae, the gray-haired women, protected the Gorgons, whom they equalled in ugliness. Like their unattractive sisters, they were also three in number: PEPHREDO, ENYO, and DEINO. Born gray, they possessed only one eye and one tooth among them, which they constantly passed from one to another. Their home, the boundary of the Gorgonian plain at the uttermost end of Libya, was never reached by sun or moon.

Three early giants were among the offspring of Gaea. TYPHON, whose father was Tartarus, was a horrible red-eyed monster with a terrifying voice and the heads of a hundred snakes.

ANTAEUS, son of Poseidon, and a champion wrestler, built a house out of the skulls of his victims. The secret of his power was that each time he was thrown to the ground he arose stronger and more powerful than before, the contact with his Mother Earth being the source of his strength. He finally met his match when the hero Heracles, catching on to his secret, lifted Antaeus high and crushed him to death in the air.

TITYUS, an enormous giant, who covered nine acres as he lay on the ground, attempted to violate Leto, and for this he was slain by the arrows of her children, Apollo and Artemis, and then hurled by Zeus into Tartarus, where his huge, outstretched bulk occupied so vast a space. Tityus was further punished by having two vultures constantly tearing at his liver—regarded by the Greeks as the seat of the passions—which was perpetually renewed as soon as it was devoured.

Other Groups of Primitive Beings

Greek mythology is peopled with certain beings who appear time and again in the stories of the gods, demigods, and heroes.

The NYMPHS were beautiful female divinities of nature. The nymphs who inhabited the mountains were known as OREADES; the nymphs who were associated with the rivers, brooks, and springs were the NAIADS; the wood nymphs were the DRYADS; the tree nymphs were the HAMADRYADS. Other nymphs dwelt in valleys, meadows, lakes, and pools, in the gardens, and among the flocks.

One of the most famous of the nymphs was ECHO. It is said that as an attendant of the gods she kept Hera busy listening to her idle chatter while Zeus was carrying on his various affairs with other nymphs. Hera eventually discovered Echo's artifice and turned on the hapless nymph. She punished her by declaring that henceforth she would never speak again except to repeat the sounds she heard. Sometime later Echo saw the beautiful youth NARCISSUS and fell deeply in love with him, but, of course, she could not speak to him unless she was spoken to. Finally, one day in the forest Narcissus called out, "Is anyone here?" and Echo answered, "Here." Then Narcissus, seeing no one, cried, "Come," and Echo answered, "Come." Narcissus called out, "Why do you shun me?" and Echo answered with the same question. Perplexed, Narcissus then called, "Let us meet here." Echo repeated the words and emerged from the woods and was prepared to throw her arms about Narcissus. But he, repelled by her boldness, rejected her and fled. From that day on Echo hid her shame in the woods and in the caves until she wasted away, until nothing was left of her but her voice. Narcissus, however, was punished for scorning the love of a maiden. He happened to see his own image reflected in a clear pool and became so enamored of it that he could not leave it. He pined away, and was converted into the flower which bears his name.

Another group of creatures were the SATYRS, whose upper bodies were those of men, but whose two legs were shaggy and had the hoofs of goats. Two small horns were seen in their curly hair. The satyrs (who among the Romans were known as Fauns), were rural creatures associated with the fields and woods and pictured as sporting with the nymphs or joining with them in the orgies associated with Dionysus.

The leader of the satyrs was PAN, son of Hermes by one of the nymphs. He was a god of the countryside, the patron of shepherds and goatherds, and the companion and lover of many of the nymphs. He was a wonderful musician, being particularly skilled with the reed pipes, with which he is often pictured—hence the expression "the pipes of Pan." Though looked upon as one of the later gods, his fame and worship spread widely, reaching in later times the point where Pan, whose name means "all," was thought of as the primitive force in all nature.

The CENTAURS had the face and chest of men and the four legs of horses. Unlike the satyrs, they were a savage crew, supposedly the offspring of CENTAURUS, son of Ixion and a cloud, by the Magnesian mares. The best known of the centaurs was CHIRON, son of Cronus and Philyra, a nymph; unlike most of his fellow-centaurs, he was kindly and upright. To him was entrusted the upbringing of Heracles, Jason, Actaeon, Aesculapius, and Achilles. He was noted for his skill in surgery. Heracles accidentally wounded him and his pain was so great that he prayed to Zeus for relief, and he was raised to the sky and became the constellation of the Bowman or Sagittarius.

The centaurs were in time overcome by their rivals, the Lapiths, who were pictured as a primitive tribe of men who learned to build with stone. At the wedding of PIRITHOÜS, king of the Lapiths, who was the son of Ixion by his wife, Dia, to HIPPODAMIA, daughter of the king of Argos, certain of the centaurs, who were invited as guests, became intoxicated and attempted to attack some of the women, wives and sisters of the famous heroes who were also present, and a dreadful conflict resulted in which many of the centaurs were slain.

The SILENI were also half horses and half men, but they differed from the centaurs in that they walked on two legs rather than four.

SCYLLA and CHARYBDIS were two monstrous female creatures inhabiting the two dangerous cliffs on either side of what is now the Straits of Messina, near Sicily. Scylla is said to have had six long necks, each with a terrifying head which she stretched out to threaten passing ships. Charybdis, on the opposite rock, was said to draw in and gorge forth the dark water, creating a continuous whirlpool which was even more dangerous to the sailors than hideous Scylla. These straits were passed by the Argonauts and later by Odysseus. Scylla, it was said, had been once a beautiful maiden, beloved of GLAUCUS, a sea god. Rejected by Scylla, Glaucus appealed to CIRCE, the enchantress, for a love potion, but Circe herself fell in love with Glaucus and, to do away with Scylla, prepared a poison for her. Circe poured this into the waters where Scylla bathed and at once she was transformed into a hideous creature. Charybdis was said to have been a woman who stole the oxen of Heracles and was consequently turned into a whirlpool by Zeus.

The SIRENS were maidens who lived on an island in the sea and by their singing lured sailors to their death. They endeavored to trap the Argonauts with their song and later sought to enchant Odysseus on his voyage. According to some accounts, there were two sirens, AGLAIOPHEMI (Clear-speaker) and THELXIEPEIA (Magic-speaker), but other accounts say there were three, one of whom was said to play the lyre, the second the pipes, and the third to sing, and their names are sometimes given as LEUKOSIA, LIGEIA, and PARTHENOPE. In some later accounts, they are pictured as having the bodies of women, but the underbody feathers and the feet of birds. They are often referred to as daughters of the river god Achelous by one of the Muses, either Terpsichore or Calliope. After their failure to attract the sailors of Odysseus they are said to have thrown themselves into the sea and to have become rocks.

The Gods on Olympus

The twelve so-called Olympian gods were believed by the ancient Greeks to inhabit lofty Olympus, a mountain in Thessaly, ten thousand feet high. Although Olympus is an actual mountain, the myths and legends appear at times to locate it, not high on the earth, but rather in some place in the heavens.

The gods themselves were thought of as having the shape of men but as being larger in size than mortal men. They could assume any shape they wished, and often did. Through their veins flowed, not blood, but a fluid which was known as *ichor.* Instead of food, they existed on *ambrosia,* which was supposedly brought them each day from the shores of Ocean in the West. The partaking of this food conferred immortality. Their drink was *nectar.*

Entrance to Olympus was barred by a gate of clouds, guarded by the Hours or Seasons. Each of the gods lived in his own dwelling, which was made of bright metal. When traveling long distances they used their chariots, swift vehicles drawn by divine steeds. Ordinarily they traveled by means of golden shoes.

For relaxation the gods listened to the music of Apollo and the singing of the Muses. Conversation about the affairs of the heavens and of earth also occupied their time.

In the entries which follow we discuss each of the Oympian gods individually.

Zeus

ZEUS, son of Cronus and Rhea, was the god of gods, the ruling power of air and sky, and the supreme master-god in the mythological hierarchy. The Roman counterpart of Zeus was known as JUPITER or JOVE. Zeus' sister-wife was HERA, goddess of the heavens. By her, he was the father of Ares, Hephaestus, Hebe, and, according to Hesiod, Eileithyia, goddess of childbirth. By LETO, he was the father of Apollo and Artemis. By DIONE, he was the father of Aphrodite. Hermes was his son by MAIA, daughter of Atlas. His sisters were Demeter and Hestia. His brothers were Poseidon and Hades.

Zeus is said to have swallowed his first wife, METIS (meaning Prudence), daughter of Oceanus and Tethys, in order to render null and void a prophecy that he would be conquered by a son born of her. Athene sprang fully grown and armed from her father's forehead.

By THEMIS, one of the Titans, he was the father of the Hours or Seasons and of the Fates.

By EURYNOME, an Oceanid, Zeus was the father of the three fair-cheeked Graces: AGLAIE (Splendor), EUPHROSYNE (Joy), and THALIE (Pleasure).

By DEMETER he was the father of Persephone, and by Mnemosyne, one of the Titans, he was the father of the Muses.

Zeus was also the father of many children by mortal women, to whom he appeared in various guises.

By SEMELE, appearing to her just before her delivery as lightning, he was the father of Dionysus (Bacchus).

To DANAË, he came as a shower of gold, and Perseus was born as a result of their union.

Zeus visited LEDA in the shape of a swan and embraced her on the same night that her husband Tyndareus sought her. As a result she bore Pollux and Helen to Zeus and Castor and Clytemnestra to her husband.

Zeus fell in love with ALCMENE, the wife of Amphitryon, and visited her in the shape of her husband while Amphitryon was away on an expedition. To Alcmene then was born Heracles.

Zeus appeared to EUROPA in the form of a beautiful white bull while she was gathering flowers near the seashore. Europa was delighted with the tameness and beauty of the animal, caressed him, set a wreath of flowers on his head, and mounted on his back. The god then dashed off and carried Europa to Crete, where he revealed himself as a god and embraced Europa. Three sons were born to her as a result: MINOS, RHADAMANTHYS, and SARPEDON.

Zeus changed Io into a cow which Hera drove from Greece. Eventually arriving on the banks of the Nile, she was met by Zeus there. He touched her, and restored her to her original form. She bore him a son named EPAPHUS.

To CALLISTO, daughter of Lycaon, who had served the gods the flesh of a boy and had been angrily transformed into a wolf therefor, Zeus appeared in the form of Artemis, goddess of the hunt, to whom he knew Callisto had dedicated herself. She bore Zeus a son named ARCAS. Artemis, angry at the maiden for having deserted the ranks of the virgins, changed her and her son into a bear and a bear cub. Later Zeus raised Callisto to a constellation, the Great Bear, and her son to the Little Bear.

By ANTIOPE, daughter of the Theban king Nycteus, Zeus was the father of two sons, ZETHUS and AMPHION, whom Antiope, fearing her father's wrath, left on a deserted mountain.

For these mortals and for their children, Hera felt none of the tolerance or friendliness that she exhibited towards the heavenly wives.

Zeus is generally referred to in Greek mythology as the youngest son of Cronus and Rhea, but as the oldest by Homer, according to whom he is the "father of gods and men." His name means "the bright shining light of heaven," hence his position as the light-father, the god of the sky, the wisest, most powerful, and most glorious of all the deities. Born in Crete, or in Arcadia and brought to Crete, he was hidden in a cave on Mt. Dicte in order to escape being swallowed by his father. There he was suckled by a goat, AMALTHEA, and the CURETES, friendly demi-gods, drowned his cries by clashing their brass weapons against their shields. It was believed that Amalthea had a horn which was always filled with whatever food and drink one wished. The Latins called this the CORNUCOPIA (horn of plenty).

The qualities, attributes, and powers of Zeus and the aspects under which he was worshipped are almost innumerable. He was responsible for the changes in nature, bringing storms and tempests as well as blue skies and gentle winds. He called forth the clouds that send down growth-giving rain and he hurled the thunderbolts that killed his enemies or those who aroused his wrath. So great was his position that he was worshipped on the highest mountains, on the peaks of which he reigned as supreme monarch. Mount Olympus in Thessaly, ten thousand feet above the sea, was regarded by the earliest Greeks as his home. Greece worshipped him as Olympian Zeus and the famous Olympian games or the Olympics, the great national festival of Greece and the Greeks, were celebrated in his honor every four years and were used, from 776 B.C., as a means of reckoning time. At the oracle of Dodona he was celebrated as the author of the fertilizing dew, and human beings were sacrificed to him in order to conciliate him at rites on Mount Lycaeus in Arcadia, where he was honored as the Lycaean Zeus. In Attica he personified the powers of nature, and he was honored both as the god of anger and the gracious god.

In his exalted position, Zeus presided over the family and community of the gods and over man and nature. In these capacities he was the ruler or patron of mortal men who all needed his aid and of all family and community life. In his dealings with men, he gave out—from two jars in his palace—both good things and bad, according to their destinies, but the good outweighed the bad on his scales. In misfortune and trouble Zeus was the one that saved, and the third cup at every meal was drunk to him.

As ruler of the world, Zeus was omnipotent, omnipresent, and omniscient. All-powerful, he controlled and regulated the laws of nature and of order in the life of mortals; omnipresent and omniscient, he knew not only the present and the past, but he predicted and revealed the future. He was, in short, the source of all revelation, exercising this great power in many ways. Sometimes he spoke in his own person; at other times, he made his meaning known by signs, such as thunder and lightning or other warnings in the sky; again he used birds—the eagle, for example—or prophetic voices; still again, he spoke through oracles or used other deities to convey his purposes; sometimes he spoke through the mouth of his favorite son, Apollo.

In art, Zeus was represented with a fine noble head of hair, decorated with a wreath of olive leaves—the prized award for victory at the Olympic games—and a fine beard. Divinity and dignity, calmness and benevolence are reflected in every line of the great god's face. The upper part of his body is naked; a mantle of gold envelops the lower part. Golden sandals are on his feet and golden lions are at his side. In his hand he holds his famous aegis, a shield which, when he shook it, caused thunder and lightning and fear and terror in his enemies.

In nature, Zeus was associated with the eagle and the oak, both of which were sacred to him, the eagle because it flies above and beyond ordinary vision, and the oak because it was believed that the wind rustled softly in the branches of an oak when the god was about to speak. Mountain tops, sacred because of their closeness to the source of light, add to the many titles or designations by which he was known, as Zeus Aetnaeus or Zeus Atabyrius, from mountains in Sicily and Rhodes. Yet, at the other extreme, at the shrine of Dodona in Epirus, where he was worshipped as the Dodonian Zeus, the low ground of the place was held to be sacred because its closeness to the earth, the source of everything, made it possible for his followers to experience direct communion with him. So, according to Hesiod, does the son of Cronus live in the pure air of heaven, in the very roots of the earth, and in the hearts of men.

Zeus was terrible in punishment and generous in rewards. Two of the most famous victims of his revenge were PROMETHEUS, one of the demigods, and IXION, king of the Lapithae in Thessaly. For daring to fall in love with Athene and for stealing heavenly fire for the use of man, Zeus punished Prometheus as he had Tityus. For murdering Deioneus, whose daughter, Dia, Ixion had married, Zeus forgave Ixion, purified him from the murder, and went so far as to invite him to join him at the table of the gods in heaven, but he put away all kindly feelings when Ixion in his foolish arrogance attempted to win Hera's love. To punish this poor return for his friendliness, Zeus formed a cloud, NEPHELE, in the likeness of Hera which so deceived Ixion that he became by it (or by her) the father of those strange creatures, half men, half horses, the centaurs. Not satisfied with this comparatively mild punishment, Zeus commanded Hermes to chain Ixion by his hands and feet with serpents to a wheel that turns forever over the hellish flames of Tartarus.

SALMONEOUS was another man who felt the wrath of Zeus. Salmoneous was a bold fellow who asserted himself to be Zeus. He had a kind of kettledrum attached to his chariot which when it moved gave off a noise which Salmoneous said was thunder. To imitate lightning he flung lighted torches against the sky. Zeus was incensed at this impiety and struck him dead with a bolt of actual lightning.

The other side of Zeus' character shows itself in his treatment of some mortal subjects who earned his approval. On one of his earthly visits, when he was of course disguised as a mortal, he came to Phrygia with Hermes, similarly disguised. Not recognized and turned away roughly and rudely by their human subjects, the gods at last found welcome, food, and shelter in the humble cottage of a poor and pious couple, the aged PHILEMON and BAUCIS. Zeus flooded the country but he rewarded the old man and his wife by lifting them to a point high above the raging waters and transforming their hut into a magnificent temple, of which they were made the priest and priestess. He also granted their wish—fulfilled many years later—that they should die at the same moment so that neither one would know the grief of surviving the other; and when death finally came Zeus changed them into two trees, an oak and a linden, that grew and flourished side by side, their branches intertwining.

Hera

HERA was the goddess of women in general, but especially of wives, and she was the patroness or protector of marriage. Although a goddess, she was not above hatred, jealousy, and suspicion, for which Zeus gave her more than sufficient cause. Her jealous quarrels with Zeus and her intense hatred of the various women he loved, and their children, Heracles (Hercules) in particular, are emphasized in the legends and by the poets, though not by Homer, for whom she was the most majestic and the most sublime of all the goddesses.

She was born, a daughter of Cronus and Rhea, on the Ionian island of Samos, but she was brought up in her youth by Oceanus and Tethys, to whom she returned when war broke out between the Titans and the gods. She was both the sister and wife of Zeus, whom she is said to have married on the Islands of the Blessed in the spring, for which reason springtime was sacred to her and was observed by her worshippers. By Zeus, her children were Hephaestus, god of fire; Ares, god of war; Hebe, goddess of youth and wife of Heracles in heaven; and Eileithyia (or Ilithyia), goddess of childbirth.

At first, Hera was simply Zeus' wife, and as such she was inferior to him in position and power and had to obey his commands. It was only later that she became the queen of the heavens, of gods and men, as he was the king. In her lower rank, she was frequently humiliated and punished by her husband. He punished her after a violent quarrel, in which Hephaestus sought to interfere in her behalf, and threw his son out of Olympus, thus, according to some accounts, laming him, although other versions tell us that Hephaestus was born lame. Zeus punished her again when he found out that she was implicated, with Athene and Poseidon, in a plan to put him in chains.

On one occasion he employed gentler means to subdue Hera and bring her to her senses. After an unpleasant scene, Zeus let it be known that he was going to take another wife and had a wooden image made in the form and costume of a bride and carried her in a chariot as in a bridal procession to Mt. Cithaeron, where Hera used to hide herself after domestic quarrels. When it arrived, Hera hurried out to attack her latest and newest rival, but felt rather foolish when she discovered that the other woman was wood, not flesh. She then proved that even a goddess can take a joke by laughing at the trick played on her, forgave Zeus, jumped into the chariot, and returned home with him.

In the contest with Athene and Aphrodite, Hera lost the golden apple which Paris awarded to the goddess of love and beauty (see below). It was because of Paris' decision that Hera was against the Trojans and in favor of the Greeks in the Trojan War. She hated Dionysus and Heracles and other children that Zeus had by mortal wives, and persecuted them wherever they went.

Sacred to her were the peacock, the crow, the cuckoo, in which form Zeus wooed and won her, and the pomegranate (that Persephone ate) as a symbol of married love and productivity. Like Zeus, she sent clouds, storms, thunder and lightning; like him, she was worshipped on mountains and prayed to for rain. Her attendants were the Hours, the lovely goddesses who saw to it that the seasons came round as they should, and Iris, the virgin goddess of the rainbow, who, as a female messenger of the gods, was the counterpart of Hermes.

Hera was worshipped especially at Argos, Sparta, and Mycenae, three cities of which she was particularly fond. Her chief temple, the Heraeum, was three miles from Mycenae. In memory of the time when she was fooled by a dressed-up piece of wood, Hera founded and was honored by two festivals: the Little Daedala, held every seven years, and the great Daedala, held every sixty years.

In art, Hera was a large, majestic, mature woman with a lovely forehead and large, wide-open eyes. On her head she wears a diadem, a royal band or wreath or a crown. Sometimes a veil hangs down from the back of her head, recalling the time when she was Zeus' bride. She is represented as standing, with a scepter in one hand, and a pomegranate in the other, or, seated on her throne, with a crown decorated by figures of the Graces and the Seasons; sometimes Hermes, sometimes Iris, is behind her; sometimes the cuckoo, messenger of spring, when she was married, is perched on the top of her staff. She is always fully draped. The diadem, the bridal veil, the royal wand, and the peacock are her familiar attributes. Among the Romans Hera was known as JUNO.

Poseidon

POSEIDON, the god or lord of the sea and the father of rivers and fountains, was the son of Cronus and Rhea, and thus the brother of Zeus and Hades, and of Hera, Hestia, and Demeter. His rank or rating as ruler of the waves he received by lot at the Council Meeting of the Gods, at which Zeus took the upper world for himself and gave dominion over the lower world to Hades.

Poseidon lived in a golden palace at the bottom of the sea. By his wife and queen, AMPHITRITE, who was a Nereid, one of the daughters of Nereus and Doris, he had three children: TRITON, half-man and half-fish; RHODE (or Rhodos), from whom the Island of Rhodes is named; and BENTHESIKYME, wife of Endius, who brought up EUMOLPUS, Poseidon's son by Chione, because Chione was afraid to acknowledge her motherhood. The parentage of Rhode is variously and confusingly stated, and she is referred to as the daughter of Poseidon and Amphitrite, or Aphrodite, or Helia; or of Helios and Aphrodite, or of Oceanus. On her island, Rhode bore seven sons to Helios.

By GAEA, Poseidon had ANTAEUS, the mighty wrestler who was thrown and killed by Heracles; by MEDUSA, a Gorgon, he had CHRYSAOR, father of Geryon, the three-headed monster, and ECHIDNA, the mother of creatures as ugly as herself. By THOÖSA, a daughter of Phorcys, he was the father of POLYPHEMUS, who was blinded by Odysseus in his one and only eye, an act for which the monarch of the sea kept Homer's hero from his home for twenty years. By AETHRA, daughter of Pitheus, the King of Troezen, he had THESEUS, one of the demi-gods (although in other accounts, Aegeus, King of Athens, is regarded as Theseus' father). Countless other children by many wives, both divine and earthly, are also credited to him.

With Apollo, Poseidon helped to build the walls of Troy for King LAOMEDON. When Laomedon not only refused to make payment of the two horses that had been agreed on, but discharged them with threats and insults, Poseidon punished him by sending a sea-monster to Troy who would have eaten the king's beautiful daughter, HESIONE, if Heracles had not happened along just in time to save her. Poseidon's hatred of the Trojans and his siding with the Greeks in the Trojan War are thus easily understood. Although he favored the Greeks in the Trojan War, being at odds with Zeus on this point, he always hated Odysseus personally for what he did to his man-eating monster of a son, Polyphemus.

Generally speaking, Poseidon was satisfied with his power and his position, but he sometimes resented the attempts of Zeus to lord it over him and he once went so far as to plot with Hera and Athene to lock him up, but Zeus found out about it, punished his wife, and the palace revolution ended.

Poseidon was associated in many ways with horses and was the god of horses as well as of the waves. In his submarine castle, he had horses with bronze hoofs and golden manes who drew his chariot. A horse figured in one of the most important myths concerning Poseidon: his dispute with Athene over the honor of naming the capital of Attica. Becoming tired of the bickering, the gods decreed that the city should be named after the deity who, in their judgment, gave mankind the more useful gift. Poseidon struck the ground with his trident and a horse sprang forth. Athene created the olive-tree, and, the judges voting in her favor, the city was named, in her honor, Athene or Athens. According to another version, water gushed forth as a result of Poseidon's blow.

He also taught man how to ride and manage the animal he invented and was looked upon as the originator and guardian deity of horse races. At the Isthmus of Corinth, horse and chariot races were held in his honor. Poseidon liked horses so much that he assumed the shape of one when he was chasing Demeter, who changed herself into a mare in order to escape from his unwelcome attentions. By her, he was the father of ARION, a horse gifted with the power of speech; and by Medusa he was the father of PEGASUS, the winged horse of the Muses, who produced the fountains of Hippocrene by stamping the ground with his hoof.

Violent and ill-tempered, Poseidon engaged in frequent quarrels and controversies with his brothers and sisters and with other divinities, his difference with Athene being merely an outstanding example. He had similar territorial disputes with Hera over Argos, with Helios over Corinth, with Dionysus over Naxos, with Apollo over Delphi, and with Zeus over Aegina. Like Zeus, he was dignified, or as dignified as his explosive temper allowed him to be, but he lacked the spiritual calmness of the supreme god. His rough ways and rude manners might have been symbolic of the tempestuous element over which he presided.

Sacrificed to him were black and white bulls, wild boars, and rams. His symbol was the familiar trident or three-pronged spear or fork with which he could split rocks, cause or quell storms, and shake the earth, a power which made him the god of earthquakes. The pine-tree and the dolphin and the horse, which were sacred to him, were his attributes in art, as well as the trident. He is represented either singly, or with Amphitrite, with some of his many children, or with various animals of the sea following him or playing around his chariot. Physically, he is shown as a strong and powerful figure, every inch a king. Like Zeus, he had a fine face and a fine head of curly hair, with an equally imposing beard. In Roman mythology, Poseidon's counterpart was NEPTUNE.

Hades and Persephone

HADES, the god of the lower world, which also bears the name of Hades, was the son of Cronus and Rhea, and the brother of Zeus, Hera, Poseidon, Demeter, and Hestia. When the world and the power to rule it was divided by the three brothers, Hades was given sway over the nether regions, mastery of the sky going to Zeus, and of the sea, to Poseidon. He was the husband of PERSEPHONE, Demeter's beautiful daughter by her brother, Zeus. His forcible taking of Persephone from the upper world to his dark kingdom below is the most famous myth concerning this gloomy god. Without saying a word about it to Demeter or asking Persephone how she felt about it, Zeus told Hades, who was lonely in his dark underground kingdom and who was looking for a wife, that he could have Persephone for his queen. One day soon after, while she was picking daffodils near Etna in Sicily or perhaps in the Nysian plain in Asia, the earth suddenly split open and Hades, rolling up in his black car, seized the frightened girl and took her down with him.

The symbol of Hades' power was a staff with two prongs—one less than that of his brother Poseidon—which he used to drive the unwilling shades or spirits into his dark regions. He had a helmet, given to him by the Cyclops, which had the gift of making the wearer invisible; on occasion, he loaned it to other gods and even to mortals, just as Zeus loaned his valuable shield to Athene and Apollo.

Like many gods, he was not always true to his wife; as a result, Persephone found it necessary for her own protection to change MINTHO (or Mintha) a nymph, and daughter of Cocytus, whom he loved, into the mint plant. A hill, near Pylos in the Peloponnesus, where the plant grew, was forever after known as Minthe. Hades himself transformed LEUCE, another nymph who caught his fancy, into a white poplar after she died.

Although not incapable of feeling love, Hades was a grim, fierce, and inexorable god, but not unjust, not a hater or a foe of man, although of all the gods he was the one most hated by both men and gods. In art, Hades bears a strong resemblance to his brothers Zeus and Poseidon. Like them, he has a heavy head of hair and is bearded. Where Zeus is calm, and Poseidon puzzled or perturbed, Hades is gloomy, with his hair covering part of his forehead. Draped, he sits on his throne, holding the key to the infernal regions in his right hand, and his staff in the left. His dog, CERBERUS, an ugly, three-headed animal, sits by his master's right side, comparatively quiet, but listening intently with his right ear down and his left ear up.

The land of Hades was well mapped in mythology. The underworld is divided into two parts, EREBUS, to which the dead come immediately after dying, and TARTARUS, the deeper part. Dividing the underworld from the world of the living are several rivers: ACHERON, the river of woe, across which the dead are ferried by CHARON, to whom they must pay the passage money which was placed on their lips when they died; LETHE, the river of forgetfulness; STYX, by which the gods swear unbreakable oaths; PHLEGETHON, the river of fire; and COCYTUS, the river of lamentations. Before the gate of Hades sits Cerberus, who greets all newcomers, but refuses to allow any to leave. Once in Hades, the dead are judged by MINOS, RHADAMANTHUS, and AEACUS, who allot each either to a place of pain and torment, or to a place of bliss called the Elysian Fields.

The cypress and the narcissus were sacred to Hades, and black sheep were sacrificed at ceremonies to him and his queen. In order to avert evil, the person who was making the sacrifice had to turn away his face.

At first, Hades in person brought the dead from the upper world to the lower, but this duty was later made one of the responsibilities of Hermes. The forbidding side of Hades was naturally emphasized but it was not the only one. As PLUTO, the giver of wealth, he was sometimes shown in a more favorable light to signify that good things—food and corn—come from the lowest depths of the earth and that the bottom of the earth contains treasures as well as the souls of the dead.

Persephone also was represented in a double light. On earth, before Hades, she was a virgin goddess, Demeter's young and beautiful daughter, playing and picking flowers. Under the earth, after Hades, she was the dread queen of the lower world, the dark goddess of death, the grim queen, an unhappy and unwilling wife, a severe and serious lady with a majestic manner and appearance. One may say that there were two Persephones or that Persephone had two aspects. The Persephone who lived on earth with her mother for eight months, who came up with the sprouting seeds, was the grain that feeds men and animals; the Persephone who lived for four months with her husband underground after visiting her mother was the seed planted in the deep earth. In Attica, she was worshipped simply as Core, the Maiden, the Daughter, the explanatory phrase, "of Demeter," being understood. So close was the relation between the two that they were referred to and worshipped as the Mother and the Daughter and as the Two Goddesses. To the Romans, Hades and Persephone were known as PLUTO and PROSERPINA.

Demeter

Demeter, the goddess of corn and fruit, and agriculture in general, and of the peaceful, civilized society that is founded on agriculture, was a daughter of Cronus and Rhea, and the sister of Zeus, Poseidon, Hades, Hera, and Hestia. By Iasion, the god of good crops and the first sower of grain, she was the mother of Plutus, the god of riches (not to be confused with Pluto); by her brother-husband, Zeus, she was the mother of Persephone, and by another brother, Poseidon, of Arion, a noble steed. As a goddess of fertility, Demeter was in many regions associated with Poseidon as the god of fertilizing water, and in Arcadia, Poseidon was regarded not as her brother or husband, but as her father. Demeter's attributes were ears of corn, poppies, a basket of fruit, and a tiny pig. Sacrificed to her were the cow and the sow, both symbolic of prolificness, as well as wine, milk, fruit, and honey. The serpent, which had its home in the earth and renewed its life by periodically shedding its skin, and the torch which Demeter used to light her way when she was searching for Persephone were also associated with her as a goddess of the earth. She was frequently confused or identified with Gaea, or with her own mother, Rhea.

Demeter lived in and through her daughter Persephone, and the two were so inseparable that one cannot be mentioned without the other. After Hades had carried Persephone off to the underworld to be his wife, Demeter wandered all over the world for nine days searching for her beloved daughter, but without success, until Helios, the sun, told her what had happened. Furious at Zeus for allowing her daughter, and his, to be thus married against her wishes, she quit Olympus and decided to pay a visit to the earth to see how she would be received and treated by mortals. While Demeter was carrying on her search for Persephone, her duties were completely neglected and as a result the land became barren and produced nothing. In the course of her travels, she finally came to Eleusis in Attica, where, disguised as an old woman, Deo, the seeker, she was welcomed by King Celeus and his wife, Metanira. As a reward for their honest kindness she sought to confer the gift of immortality on their new-born son, Demophoön, by burning his mortal parts, but did not succeed because she was interrupted while the process was going on by his mother's startled scream, as a result of which the baby died in the flames. She made up for this loss as far as possible by teaching agriculture and all its benefits to another son, Triptolemus (which means "three-times ploughed"), who became her favorite. She also gave him seeds of wheat and a chariot drawn by dragons and serpents. In his carriage, Triptolemus covered the earth and, acting under Demeter's instructions, brought to men the lessons of law and order, the blessings of agriculture and civilization, of living permanently in one place, and of settling down and marrying. In this way, through her pupil who spoke for her, Demeter became, in places where Greeks gathered, the goddess of peaceful living in settled communities, of civil order and of marriage and the family circle, as well as an agricultural or earth goddess.

Of all the people she met in the palace of Celeus and Metanira, although they were all kind and did their best to cheer her, only one by her jests was able to make the worried goddess smile in spite of herself, and to show any interest in food. This was Iambe, a Thracian slave, the queen's maid and a daughter of Pan and Echo, whose name is commemorated in *iambic* verse and meter.

Having discharged her debt of gratitude to her mortal friends, but still smarting at Zeus' high-handed treatment, Demeter commanded the earth to refuse to bear food, fruit, or flowers. In order to avert the world-hunger that this would mean, Zeus, realizing that he had made a mistake, sent his messenger Hermes down to the lower world to bring Persephone back to her mother. Hades was perfectly willing to let her go but there was one drawback that interfered with or conditioned her release: Persephone had already eaten part of a pomegranate seed, given her by Hades, which meant that she had become his wife. It was arranged then that she might spend eight months of the year with her mother in Olympus, and the remaining four months with her husband. As this compromise was satisfactory to Demeter, she removed her ban on growth in the earth. In some versions of the story AESCULAPIUS is represented as revealing that Persephone had eaten the fateful pomegranate, and for this Demeter buried him alive under a huge rock, or, as another legend relates it, changed him into an owl.

Others to feel her wrath were STELLIO, a youth whom she changed into a lizard when he made a jesting remark about her eating habits, and ERYSICHTHON, son of Triopas, King of Thessaly, whom she afflicted with a terrible hunger, in which he ate his own flesh, because he chopped down some trees in a grove dedicated to her.

In art, Demeter is always fully dressed; on her head of gold hair is a ribbon or a wreath of corn-ears. She holds a torch and a basket in one hand, and poppies, ears of corn, and a scepter in the other. She is represented as sitting, with her hands concealed under the folds of her dress, or walking, or being drawn in her chariot by horses or dragons. Her golden hair represents the gold ears of ripe corn; the poppies are a reminder of the food Zeus gave her when she was worn out with searching for Persephone and by worry and lack of food and nourishment; the torch, symbolic of the light she kindled from the flames of Mount Etna, also recalls her trying experience.

Demeter was worshipped by an elaborate festival lasting for eleven days, held in Athens and Eleusis, from which city it is called the *Eleusinian Mysteries,* a series of secret performances, known only to those who were privileged to participate in them. Such persons were sworn to secrecy, and the anger of the gods would fall on those who revealed what had passed. Another festival, the Thesmophoria, lasting five days, was held in November in many parts of Greece, but was celebrated with special splendor in Athens. It honored Demeter as the goddess of agriculture and as the founder of the institution of marriage, and only married women of spotless reputation were allowed to participate in it. Demeter was worshipped as the goddess of fair children. In Roman mythology, Demeter is called CERES.

Hestia

HESTIA, goddess of the hearth, was the first born of Rhea by Cronus, and the sister of Zeus, Hera, Poseidon, Hades, and Demeter. Hestia was a virgin by choice, as she was wooed by Apollo and Poseidon, but she swore by the head of Zeus to live forever in the unmarried state. As a symbol of domesticity, she was honored, by the command of Zeus, by a hearth consecrated to her not only in every private home but also in the public town-hall of every capital city in Greece, as well as in the temples of the gods. All sacrifices began and ended with honors paid to Hestia, and she was mentioned first in all prayers, before the name of any other god. She was honored especially by a sacred fire that was always kept burning. Colonists, bound for a new destination, took some of the fire for the public hearth of the colony to be established.

In art, Hestia is draped and wears a veil over her head; her hair is unornamented and unadorned, which is not usual for a goddess; her right hand is on her hip; her left, with the fingers pointing upward, holds, or formerly held, a scepter. With Athene and Artemis, she was one of the trinity of virgin goddesses. If her character be not as clearly outlined as that of other divinities it may be because she was little more than the female counterpart of Hephaestus, the god of fire. The Greek Hestia is the same as the Roman VESTA.

Apollo

APOLLO, the sun-god, god of music and poetry, and one of the great divinities of the Greeks, was a son of Zeus and of LETO, and the twin brother of Artemis. Leto, known by the Romans as LATONA, was a daughter of Coeus and Phoebe, both Titans. Apollo was born on the island of Delos, originally a floating island until Zeus considerately chained it to the bottom of the sea so that Leto might be a little more comfortable while giving birth to Apollo and Artemis.

Apollo was a many-sided god and was worshipped variously under different qualities and capacities. He was a god who punishes, hence his bow and arrows which cause sudden death and plague.

With his darts he killed all of Niobe's sons. NIOBE, the mother of many children by Amphion, had set herself above Leto, who had borne only two children. Leto, much vexed, complained to Apollo and Artemis, whereupon Apollo killed Niobe's sons, and Artemis killed her daughters.

Apollo was the god of prophecy, a power that he exercised in many oracles, especially the famous one at Delphi, which is constantly mentioned; hence he was also known as the Pythian Apollo from the old name of Delphi, Pytho. In addition to having this gift, he also had the power of transmitting it to men and to other gods.

He was the god of music and was even credited with the invention of the lyre and the flute. His playing was a frequent source of delight to his fellow gods. Apollo was very proud of his musical ability; he was in fact so sensitive on the point that he took drastic measures against those who dared to question it. MARSYAS, a Phrygian satyr, challenged the god to a contest, the terms being that the winner was to do what he wanted with the loser. Apollo played the cithern, and Marsyas, the flute. The Muses were the judges. Apollo won, tied Marsyas to a tree, skinned him alive—which is described as a just punishment for the satyr's impertinence—and then changed him into the river that bears his name. In another contest, between PAN, playing the pipes, and Apollo, the lyre, MIDAS—the foolish Midas of the Golden Touch—preferred Pan's music and awarded him the prize, an exhibition of bad taste for which the offended Apollo punished him by changing his ears into those of an ass.

Apollo was also the god who protected flocks and cattle. In this capacity he took care of the flocks of King ADMETUS for nine years, a task to which he was assigned by Zeus for snatching the infant AESCULAPIUS from the hands of Hades. While Apollo was guarding his flocks, Admetus went to seek the hand of ALCESTIS. Alcestis' father set Admetus the task of yoking a wild boar and a lion to his chariot, a deed which he accomplished with Apollo's aid. Apollo also arranged with the Fates to defer Admetus' death if anyone would die in his place. When that time came, Alcestis offered to die in Admetus' stead. As she lay in her tomb, the hero Heracles happened by and fought with Death, forcing him to relinquish Alcestis, who was then restored to Admetus.

Apollo was also the god of towns and communities; any town or colony founded by the Greeks was established only after consultation with Apollo's oracle and with his approval.

Apollo was the god of light and youth; his other name, PHOEBUS, means bright and light, and is used either alone or in the form Phoebus

Apollo. In this connection, Apollo was identified with the sun and was in fact the god of the sun through his identification with HELIOS, although this belief belongs to the later Greeks.

As the god who helped men, as well as punished them when they deserved it or when they displeased him, as the god who made it possible for healing plants to grow and thrive, he was the god of medicine. By virtue of his breath-taking skill with bow and arrow he was regarded as the god of archery. As the god of shepherds, he was not averse to making love to pretty nymphs and shepherdesses. By CYRENE, a Thessalian nymph, daughter of Peneus, he was the father of ARISTAEUS, who was the cause of the death of Eurydice, wife of Orpheus (see below).

With DAPHNE, a nymph, another daughter of Peneus, he was less successful. Daphne was chaste and wished to remain so. Thus when she saw that she could not escape Apollo's eager attentions and that he would not take no for an answer, she was changed, at her own request, into a laurel or bay-tree.

Apollo also loved DRYOPE, a shepherdess, who was a playmate of the hamadryads. Apollo appeared to her and her friends in the form of a tortoise, with which they began to play. Dryope placed the tortoise in her bosom and the god changed himself into a serpent, whereupon the nymphs fled in fright. Dryope bore Apollo a son, AMPHISSUS, who built a temple to his father. When Dryope appeared there the hamadryads spirited her away and caused a poplar to grow in her stead. Two wardens who informed on the nymphs were transformed into fir trees.

One of the most pathetic legends concerning Apollo is concerned with CORONIS, whose infidelity to Apollo was revealed to him by a raven, a beautiful white bird. In a jealous fury he killed Coronis. Later, when his anger cooled, overcome by sorrow, he turned his resentment against the unfortunate bird, cursed him for a tattle-tale, plucked out his feathers, sent him back to Hades, and made him coal-black. Just before Coronis' death Apollo saved the son whom Coronis was about to bear. He gave the boy, Aesculapius, to Chiron to raise, and his foster-father taught him the use of herbs and potions so that Aesculapius became the great physician.

One of those to whom Apollo was attracted was CASSANDRA, daughter of Priam, King of Troy. In return for her favors she asked from Apollo the gift of prophecy, which the god was glad to grant. But when Cassandra refused to give herself to him, Apollo, unable to withdraw his gift, made it useless to her by providing that those who heard her predictions would not believe them.

Apollo was a great friend of HYACINTHUS, a beautiful youth. One day the two were throwing the discus and Apollo made a great cast which accidentally struck Hyacinthus in the forehead. Apollo rushed to aid the injured lad, but it was too late. Apollo cried out that he wished he could die with his friend, and just then from the blood-stained grass sprang the flower which we know today as the hyacinth. On the petals of the flowers Apollo inscribed the word "Ai," the Greek exclamation of grief.

The wolf, the dolphin, the swan, the hawk, the crow, the raven, and the snake, because of its supposed curative powers, were sacred to him; among plants and trees, the laurel was sacred to him in honor of Daphne, and the palm-tree, because he was born under the shade of one on Delos. In art, Apollo was a tall, athletic, handsome youth; he has long hair, topped by a laurel crown, but no beard; he holds a bow or a lyre in his right hand, and a quiver of arrows on his shoulder; he is nude, except for a cloak which is tied around his neck and covers part of his left arm. As Phoebus Apollo, the sun or the god of the sun, rays of light shoot from his head.

Apollo was regarded as the most influential of all the Greek gods in the effect he had upon the people; without the worship they gave him, the Greek people, it has been said, would never have become what they did. Apollo occupied such a superior position that it is believed that he was originally, like Zeus, his father, the supreme god, the one god; that he had his origin in some section of Greece where Zeus was not known, and that he was much later reduced or made secondary, if even in a slight degree, to Zeus by becoming his son. As the highest type of masculine beauty, Apollo was widely worshipped by both Greeks and Romans and by both he was known as Apollo.

Artemis

ARTEMIS, the moon goddess, goddess of hunting and chastity, was a daughter of Zeus and Leto and was born on the Island of Delos with her twin brother, Apollo, the sun-god and the god of music and poetry. She had many attributes in common with Apollo. Like him, she carried a bow and arrows, and her darts, like his, brought sudden death to those whom they struck.

Like many of the Greek divinities, she represented and exercised qualities that are antagonistic to one another; hence she brought evil and suffering to mortals and she also cured their ailments and helped them to solve their problems. In the great Trojan War she was, with her brother, on the side of the Trojans, and her arrows as well as his caused consternation among the Greeks.

Artemis was also the goddess of wild life, of childbirth, and of children after they are born, and of animals. She was the protector of all young creatures, animal as well as human, and was the goddess of flocks, as Apollo was the god. A great huntress, she was the goddess of the chase. As a virgin goddess, like Hestia and Athene, never marrying, she knew neither the joys nor the sorrows of love. Yet, as the goddess of the moon, she acquired many of the qualities of SELENE.

For a while, ORION, son of Poseidon, and a mighty hunter, dwelt with her, but this displeased her brother, Apollo. One day, while Orion was swimming in the sea, Apollo challenged her skill with the bow and arrow and doubted her ability to hit a black thing bobbing on the sea. Artemis took aim and hit the object squarely. Of course, the object was Orion's head and Apollo had tricked her into killing him. Bewailing her error, Artemis placed Orion among the stars. Another version attributes Orion's death to Artemis' shooting him in jealousy over Eos' love for him.

Artemis is connected with another hunter, ACTAEON, grandson of Cadmus of Thebes, whom she changed into a stag because he had seen her bathing. He paid dearly for his look, being immediately torn to pieces by his fifty dogs.

One of Artemis' hunting companions was the nymph ARETHUSA. One hot day coming upon a river, Arethusa stripped off her garments and plunged into the waters to refresh herself. While swimming about idly she felt something stir beneath her and heard a strange voice. It was the river god, ALPHEUS. Terrified, she sprang to the shore pursued by Alpheus. After fleeing for many miles, with Alpheus close behind her, she felt her strength about to give way. Desperately she prayed to Artemis for aid and was immediately changed into a fountain. Undaunted, Alpheus resumed his aqueous form and sought to mingle his waters with hers. She fled under the earth and through the sea, emerging on the isle of Ortygia in Syracuse as a bubbling stream, still pursued by Alpheus.

In art, Artemis was represented as goddess and huntress. As goddess of the moon, she is dressed in a long robe reaching to her feet; her head is covered by a veil, and the crescent of the moon surmounts her forehead. As a huntress, she wears a short mantle covering her breast; her legs, up to the knees, are bare; sandals or hunting shoes are on her feet; she holds a bow or a spear; across her shoulders is slung a quiver of arrows. Sometimes she is with a dog; sometimes she leads or carries a hind; at other times hinds draw her in a chariot. She is always beautiful—tall, slender, and swift-footed. Her hair is tied up in a knot, or is loose; sometimes a few stray locks manage to escape and hang down or wave in the wind. The Roman counterpart of Artemis was DIANA.

Athene

ATHENE, also called PALLAS ATHENE, or Pallas alone, was the goddess of wisdom and one of the great deities of the Greeks. She was a daughter of Zeus and, in a way, of his first wife, Metis, who was one of the many daughters of Oceanus and Tethys. Before her birth, when Metis was in the first month of her pregnancy, Zeus swallowed the mother because it had been predicted that she would give birth to a child destined to be greater and stronger than himself. At the proper time, with an ear-splitting war shout, fully armed, Athene sprang from his head. She immediately took her seat on her father's right side in the Great Council of the Gods. In the war then going on between the gods and the giants, Athene helped Zeus and Heracles, who was sent for at her suggestion, not only by giving them sound advice on military strategy but by taking part in the action. She buried ENCELADUS, the hundred-armed son of Tartarus and Gaea, under Mt. Etna.

Athene was the preserver of the state, Athens and Attica, especially, having been under her divine protection. She combined in herself the best qualities of her parents in perfect balance. Inheriting the power and valor of her father, and the prudence and wisdom of her mother, whose name means wise counsel, she was qualified to preside over all the intellectual phases of life. She was both a goddess of war and of peace and of the arts and trades connected with peace. As the former, she protected the state from its enemies and hence was usually represented as wearing armor. It later became the custom to associate her with the ways of peace, but her belligerent attributes dominated all others in earlier conceptions of her. Like Zeus, she could send storms and rough weather; she was the mistress, as Zeus was the master, of thunder and lightning and she hurled thunderbolts to enforce her will and frighten her foes. Zeus permitted her to carry the aegis, a shield with the Gorgon's head. She invented the plough and the rake, and created the olive-tree, services that made her the protector of agriculture.

Teaching was one of the important peaceful activities of Athene. She taught mortals how to tame horses and yoke oxen; she taught ERICTHONIUS how to fasten his horses to his chariot, and BELLEROPHON, who ate his heart out, how to tame the winged steed, PEGASUS. At Lindus in Rhodes, she showed DANAÜS, father of fifty daughters, how to build a fifty-oared ship; she gave similar instructions to ARGUS (or Argos), builder of the *Argo,* the ship that carried Jason and his comrades to Colchis in quest of the Golden Fleece, and she actually supervised its construction. For these performances she was regarded and worshipped as the inventor and protector of the arts or sciences of ship-building and horse-taming. She also invented the flute, the trumpet, the spindle, the distaff, and the famous Pyrrhic War-Dance, which she was the first to perform in the ceremonies following the celebration of the victory of the gods in the war with the giants, a victory to which she contributed. The flute, which, in other accounts, is credited to Apollo, she threw away in disgust when she noticed that playing on it distorted her features and made the gods laugh. It was this same flute that, picked up by the Phrygian satyr, MARSYAS, gave forth sweet sounds of its own accord because the lips of a goddess had touched it, and led to the contest in which Marsyas was defeated and flayed to death by Apollo.

One of the most famous myths concerning Athene tells of her contest with ARACHNE, a Lydian maiden, whose father, Idmon of Colophon, was a famous dyer in purple. Arachne excelled in the art of weaving and was proud of it. As Athene was known to be deeply interested in work for women, so much so that all forms of household art and activity were described as the "works of Athene," and as she was an expert weaver herself, Arachne proposed a test of skill between them. She produced a piece of cloth in which she had woven the loves of the gods. Athene, angered in the first place at the challenge, at the choice of subject, and chiefly at the fact that she could find no fault in the work—it being flawless—tore it to shreds and threw the pieces in Arachne's face. The unhappy girl, burning with shame and humiliation, hanged herself. Then, probably realizing that she had gone too far in what was really a slight matter, Athene cut down the rope and brought Arachne back to life, but punished her for daring to compete with a goddess by changing her into a spider and the rope into a cobweb which Arachne was condemned to spin through endless ages.

Athene also meted out a hard fate to TIRESIAS, a young Theban—the same Tiresias who many years later, as an old man and a great seer, tells Oedipus that he himself was the murderer he was seeking—was stricken blind by Athene because he accidentally happened to see the goddess bathing. Moved by the tears of his mother, Chariclo, and by her plea that her seven-year-old son be made to see again, Athene regretted her impulsive action but it was beyond her power to restore the sight she had destroyed. In order to compensate Tiresias to the extent that she could do so, she gave him three gifts: she made him a soothsayer, and he became one of the greatest in all antiquity; she endowed him with the power to understand the language of birds; and she gave him a gold staff which took the place of his eyes and helped him to walk as though he were not blind.

In the Trojan War, Athene was on the side of the Greeks until Ajax violated Priam's daughter, Cassandra. She then killed Ajax and disrupted the retiring Greek fleet by sending violent storms.

Odysseus was Athene's hero, as he was Homer's, and she made no attempt to conceal the fact that he was one of her favorites. It was through her good-will and assistance that he finally—after twenty years of hardship—reached home safely in spite of Poseidon's hate and all his efforts to prevent it. In addition to her partiality for Odysseus, Athene was also the good friend and helper of Jason, Perseus, Bellerophon, Hercules, and Diomedes, and it was fitting that she should be so in her capacity of goddess of war, as all these heroes were brave soldiers and fighters.

As one of the twelve gods who sat as judges at the court of Areopagus, where Ares was acquitted—of having killed the violator of his daughter—Athene had the privilege of casting the deciding vote in the case of a tie, a privilege she exercised when the judges could not agree, at the trial of Orestes for the murder of Aegisthus and Clytemnestra.

In art, Athene was a beautiful, majestic, blue-eyed woman, wearing a sleeveless tunic, over which a cloak is thrown. She holds a golden lance, point up, in her right hand; her helmet is decorated with griffins—peculiar creatures with the head and wings of an eagle and the body of a lion—heads of rams, horses, and sphinxes. In rites and ceremonies, bulls, rams, and cows were sacrificed to the goddess. Sacred to her were the owl and the serpent, typifying wisdom, the oak, symbolizing strength and power, and her own creation, the olive-tree. It was the latter that won for Athene the control of Attica in her struggle with Poseidon, in which CECROPS, acting as judge, decided that her tree would be of greater benefit to mankind than the horse that the sea-god produced by striking the earth with his three-pronged spear. Cecrops' daughters, AGRAULOS, PANDROSUS, and HERSE, representing, respectively, pure, clean air, dew, and rain, were Athene's first priestesses, and the sacred olive-tree stood in the Pandroseion, the temple of Pandrosus on the Acropolis of Athens, where the daughter of Cecrops was honored equally with the goddess. In her honor the Parthenon was built in Athens; it takes its name from the Greek word for virgin. At Rome, Athene was worshipped as MINERVA.

Aphrodite

APHRODITE, the goddess of love and beauty, was, according to one version, a daughter of Zeus and Dione, perhaps, but not certainly, the Oceanid of that name. According to another version, she was born of the foam of the sea—the meaning of her name—that gathered around the limbs of the mutilated Uranus, and first approached land at the island of Cythera, and from there went to the island of Cyprus. The unfaithful wife of the homely Hephaestus, she was in love with at least four other gods: Ares (with whom she was caught), Hermes, Poseidon, and Dionysus, and at least two mortals, ANCHISES and ADONIS, both noted for their beauty.

By Anchises, she was the mother of the Roman hero, AENEAS. From the blood of Adonis, killed by a wild boar, sprang the anemone; another rendering, equally poetic, has it that the anemone sprang from the tears Aphrodite shed for the beautiful boy. Refusing to be consoled and refusing to give him up, she created a difficult situation for the gods which was not improved by the fact that Persephone, wife of Hades and queen of the lower world, had also fallen in love with Adonis since his arrival in her domain. The always-resourceful Zeus settled the problem by decreeing that Adonis spend six months with Aphrodite in the upper world and six months with Persephone in the lower regions. This arrangement, probably the best that Zeus could do, appears to have been satisfactory to the two goddesses, who had no choice but to submit to the will of the all-powerful god of gods.

Aphrodite was awarded the prize of the golden apple by Paris, who may have been swayed by the prize *she* offered—the fairest woman in the world for wife. Aphrodite's beauty was so great that it led to her being summoned to Olympus, to which she was conducted by the Horae, or Hours. In addition to her own beauty, of which she was proud, Aphrodite loved and recognized beauty in others, and to others she granted beauty and irresistible charm. Her magic girdle made its wearer, male or female, the object of passionate love and desire. At Mount Olympus, Aphrodite's arrival produced mixed feelings and aroused all the gods and goddesses, the former to love and admiration; and the latter to hate and jealousy.

By Hermes, Zeus' special messenger and ambassador, she became the mother of HERMAPHRODITUS, a youth as beautiful as herself and as handsome as his father.

By Ares, or one of the other gods to whom she was kind, but not by her husband, she had EROS, the god of love; his brother, ANTEROS, the god of unrequited love who punished those who did not return the love they inspired in others; and HARMONIA, later the wife of Cadmus; and other children.

In Greek mythology and legend, Aphrodite as the goddess of love was far more important than her son Eros. Eros frequently accompanied Aphrodite, and in his own right he was worshipped especially among the Thespians and the Boeotians. His parents were sometimes said to be Zephyrus, the West Wind, and Iris, the Rainbow, expressing the mood of spring, the season of love. The young god Eros must be clearly distinguished from the primitive conception of Eros or Love as a primary force in the creation of the universe, mentioned in the entry on the Creation, above. Eros is pictured as carrying a bow and a quiver of arrows, and is very closely identified with the Roman CUPID. Eros was attended by Anteros; HYMEN, the god of Marriage; and HIMEROS, Longing. The most famous legend of the god of love is the story of Cupid and Psyche, which we give under Cupid in the section on Roman mythology.

By a mortal, BUTES, one of the companions of Jason on the Argonautic expedition, and a priest of Athene, Aphrodite was the mother of ERYX. Butes was the only Argonaut who, unable to resist the song of the Sirens, jumped overboard, but Aphrodite saved him as he was floundering in the sea, and brought him, none the worse for his ducking, to Lilybaeum, a town on the western coast of Sicily. Eryx (for whom, in other accounts, Poseidon is made responsible) was the legendary king of the mountain of the same name in the northwestern part of Sicily. A champion boxer who challenged and defeated all who crossed his path, he finally met his match when he was knocked out and killed by Heracles in a quarrel about a bull that had escaped from Heracles and had found its way to or had been taken by Eryx. Eryx was buried on the top of the mountain that bore his name, and a famous temple to Aphrodite, said to have been built by him, stood near the spot.

The myrtle, the rose, the apple, and the poppy were sacred to her as goddess of love; among animals, the swan, and the dolphin were sacred to her as goddess of the sea, and the ram, the hare, the sparrow, the he-goat, the dove, and the swallow—amorous animals—were dedicated to the love aspect of the goddess. The sparrow, the dove, the swan, and the swallow frequently pulled her chariot or acted as her messengers. Also sacred to Aphrodite was the month of April, a month dear to lovers. She was worshipped widely at Paphos, Amathus, and Idalion, all in Cyprus, at the Island of Cythera, at Corinth, and at Eryx in Sicily.

In art, she was represented with her son, Eros. She is always beautiful, but she is beautiful in different ways, depending not only on the skill of the artist but on the conception behind his work. As Aphrodite Urania—the sky—she was both worshipped and represented as the goddess of the sky and as the goddess of pure love on a high level; as Aphrodite Pandemos—all the people—she was the goddess of marriage and family life, but later degenerated into a goddess of lust. She is depicted as rising from the foam (*aphros*) of the sea, or stepping from her bath; in earlier representations, she is clothed; she appears in later conceptions in various degrees of nudity. The divine features characteristic of early work gradually disappear, their places being taken by representations of human physical beauty. The goddess of love and beauty, of the sky, of storm and lightning, the goddess of victory and the sea, of groves and gardens, the goddess of spring and its treasures becomes a beautiful woman. The Roman counterpart of Aphrodite was VENUS.

Hermes

HERMES, the messenger and herald of the gods, was the son of Zeus and of Maia, a Naiad who was the oldest and loveliest daughter of Atlas. He was born on Mt. Cyllene in Arcadia. As the herald of the gods, he was required to speak frequently in public and to do a great deal of travelling; he therefore became the god of eloquence and speech and the god of roads who protects travellers like himself. The conception of him as the god of roads was only one sign of his friendly feeling for mortals. Piles of stone named after him were erected in his honor at crossroads to which every passer-by added a stone, and quadrangular stone pillars, called *hermae,* with his head at the stop, were common in Athens, being set up in the streets and open spaces and in front of doors, and serving as milestones for travellers on country roads.

Hermes was the god of prudence and cunning, not only in any legitimate aspects those qualities may have, but also in their less favorable suggestions; that is, Hermes was the god of fraud, perjury, and theft. He was the god of commerce and good luck. As the father of gymnastic science, he was the patron and guardian of gymnastic games and athletic contests, all gymnasiums in Greece being under his special protection.

In many places, Hermes was worshipped as the god of crops, the god of mining, and the god who helps those who dig in the earth for buried treasure. In Arcadia, he was regarded as a god who bestows the blessing of fertility on both soil and animals. He was the god of sleep and dreams (as well as MORPHEUS, who played a minor role).

In addition to his many godships, Hermes was one of the most active, most energetic of the gods, and he held many positions of trust and executed many of Zeus' most important missions. Many inventions were credited to his account, among them the lyre (although some authorities say this honor belongs to Apollo); the syrinx, also known as Pan's Pipes; numbers; the alphabet; the science of astronomy; the art of fighting; weights and measures; and sacrifices. For the last accomplishment, he was regarded as the protector of sacrificial animals and was therefore worshipped by shepherds.

Hermes was a precocious infant and he certainly lost no time in beginning his career of thievery and general mischief. Born in the morning, he climbed out of his crib, took a long walk, and invented the lyre by or before noon of the same day by killing a tortoise that crossed his path and using its shell; in the evening, before it got too dark, he stole fifty of Apollo's best oxen, caused them to walk backwards so that they could not be traced and hid them in a cave. He slaughtered two of the animals, cooked and ate part of the flesh, burned the rest, and nailed their skins to a rock. Then, the stories tell us, he returned home and lay down quietly in his cradle, where he was found, with his eyes closed, when Apollo came to make a complaint to Maia. Realizing that he could expect no justice from a doting mother, Apollo appealed to Zeus, who compelled his youngster to return the cattle. However, when he heard Hermes play the lyre Apollo was so delighted that he told the infant he could keep the oxen and the two gods became good friends.

Hermes was said to have stolen Hephaestus' tools, Zeus' scepter, Poseidon's trident, Ares' sword, and—a Herculean task—Aphrodite's girdle. Because of this ability, Hermes was employed as an ambassador by Zeus and the other gods on so many important and difficult assignments. He led Priam to Achilles when the old and feeble warrior-king of Troy wanted to fetch the body of his son, Hector. He took the three goddesses, Hera, Aphrodite, and Athene, to Paris when that Trojan hero had to choose the loveliest woman of the three. His were the unpleasant duties of tying Ixion to the forever-revolving wheel as Ixion's punishment for trying to make love to Zeus' queen, and of chaining Prometheus, the fire-stealer, to Mount Caucasus because he would not tell Zeus which child would threaten his father's supremacy. He saved Dionysus at birth from the flames and led him to Semele's sister, Ino, the daughter of Cadmus, and of Harmonia of the fatal necklace. He told Odysseus how to resist the magic charms of Circe, and he told Calypso, daughter of Atlas, that she would have to give Odysseus up, no matter how much she loved him. He rescued Io, changed into a cow by Zeus in order to save her from the jealous anger of Hera. With his wonderful music, he put Io's keeper, Argus, the hundred-eyed giant, to sleep and then cut off his head. To him were entrusted all the arrangements for Heracles to enter the humiliating service of Omphale, the widow queen. He conducted the shades or ghosts of the dead from the upper to the lower world, a duty so important that it was formerly done by Hades himself.

A friendly god, guiding the living as well as the dead, Hermes spent much of his time with shepherds, whose patron god he was, and with nymphs and shepherdesses, by whom he was the father of countless children, including PAN and DAPHNIS, believed to be the inventor or originator of pastoral poetry. Many of his children were, with their mothers, nameless.

By CHIONE, daughter of Daedalion, who killed himself over grief at her untimely death, he was the father of AUTOLYCUS, the prince of thieves. Chione was killed by Artemis for venturing to suggest that her own beauty might be mentioned in the same breath with that of the goddess.

By Aphrodite, the fickle goddess of love and beauty, he had a son, HERMAPHRODITUS, born on Mt. Ida, who united in his name (Hermes and Aphrodite) and his body, the names of his parents and the beauty, masculine and feminine, of both. SALMACIS, the lovely nymph of the fountain of Salmacis, fell in love with Hermaphroditus one day when he, still a young lad, was bathing in her spring. Seizing him, she held him so tight that he could not get away, even if he wanted to. As Hermaphroditus did not respond to her caresses, she prayed to the gods that she might be united to him and be allowed to keep him with her forever. The gods granted her plea, joined the boy and the maid together, and created a being combining and uniting in one body the physical characteristics of both sexes.

The number four was sacred to Hermes as he was born in the fourth month, which was named after him in Argos, and in Athens he was honored by sacrifices on the fourth day of every month. Incense, hone, cakes, lambs, pigs, and goats were sacrificed to him at his festivals, known as the Hermaea. Arcadia, his birthplace, was the oldest center of his worship but it was not confined there, spreading to Athens and finally to all Greece. The palm-tree, various kinds of fish, and the tortoise, a reminder of his first day's activity, were also sacred to him.

In art, he was an exceedingly handsome beardless youth, wearing a broad-brimmed hat, carrying a golden staff (given to him by Apollo in exchange for the lyre), and, highly appropriate for a messenger of the gods, with winged sandals on his feet. Except for his hat and sandals, he is nude. He is also represented as a shepherd with his flock, as the god of gain or profit, holding a purse in his hand, as a thief, as the patron of physical culture with a curved blade in his hand, with a lyre as the patron of music, and, as an older man, with a beard. His attributes—hat, staff, sandals—are well-known today because of the many popular uses to which they are put. The *petasus,* the hat used for travelling purposes, had two wings on it, one on either side. The wings attached to his ankles, known as the *talaria,* took him over land, sea, and air with the speed of wind. In his hand he holds a staff or wand, the famous *caduceus,* with serpents wound around it. This he later gave to Aesculapius, the god of medicine, and it is familiar to us today from its use as a symbol of the medical profession. The Roman counterpart of Hermes was MERCURY.

Ares

ARES, the god of war, was one of the sons of Zeus and Hera. So belligerent was he and so violent was his temper—inherited from his mother—that he was detested by his parents and by his fellow-gods, and especially by Zeus and Athene, who hated him for his blood-lust. For a war god, Ares made a surprisingly poor showing in the contests in which he participated. When he was wounded before Troy by Diomedes, the son of Tydeus, his cry of pain, like that of ten thousand warriors, made both Greeks and Trojans tremble. In the battle of the gods, Athene, who had helped Diomedes, caught him in the neck with a huge rock, his stunned body, as he fell, covering seven hundred feet. He was conquered in single combat by Heracles, who had killed his son, Cycnus. OTUS and EPHIALTES, usually known as the Aloadae, after their supposed father, ALOEUS, overcame him and kept him a prisoner in a bronze jar for a year and a month. These brothers were remarkable youngsters in size, strength, and daring. At the age of nine they declared war on the Olympian gods and almost succeeded in their attempt to storm heaven by piling Mount Ossa on Olympus and Mount Pelion on Ossa, which they would have accomplished if Apollo had not killed them.

Ares killed HALIRRHOTHIUS, son of Poseidon, for attempting to violate ALCIPPE, his daughter by Agraulus. This contest and the case growing out of it are two of the very few victories that can be chalked up to Ares' credit. Poseidon brought charges against Ares and haled him before the gods, who were in session on a hill in Athens. They delivered a verdict in favor of Ares, from which the court was henceforth called the Areopagus (Hill of Ares).

By trickery, Ares killed the beautiful youth, ADONIS, who was the beloved of Aphrodite. Jealous of Adonis and aware of his fondness for hunting, Ares transformed himself into a boar and was soon followed by the youth, as he knew he would be. Turning suddenly he ran upon Adonis and killed him.

Ares loved and was loved, more or less, by Aphrodite. Once when he was with Aphrodite he was caught by Hephaestus. Ares had placed the youth ALECTRYON as a guard and, vexed at the boy's neglect of his task, changed him into a cock. By Aphrodite he was the father of EROS, the god of love and of the suffering caused by the pangs of love; of ANTEROS, the god of slighted love; and HARMONIA, wife of Cadmus. By ERIS, his sister, goddess of Discord, he was the father of DEIMOS (Fear) and PHOBOS (Terror). Eris was also the mother, by Zeus, of ATE, personification of blind rage and folly. By PELOPIA, Ares was the father of CYCNUS, and by PYRENE, he had another son of the same name; both sons were slain by Heracles and both of them, as well as Cycnus, son of Poseidon and Calyce, and Cycnus, son of the Ligurian king, Sthenelus, were transformed into swans.

The attributes of Ares are a spear and a burning torch. In art, he was young and strikingly handsome, with curly locks and a powerful frame. Sometimes he is bearded and wears armor; sometimes, beardless, with a helmet on his head. He is with Aphrodite and their son, Eros, who is playing with his father's implements of war, or sitting at his father's feet and looking up at him with wonder and admiration. Also with him is his companion ENYO, goddess of war and daughter of Phorcys and Ceto. There is little agreement on the rank and dignity of Ares in relation to the other divinities. Ares is referred to both as one of the great Olympian gods and as a figure of no great importance in mythology, who does not play a very glorious role in the episodes in which he takes part. He was not always a gentleman; he was easy to beat, and when he did win he used fraud. His own colleagues had no use for him, avoided him whenever possible—except Aphrodite—and were always glad to help his enemies. In Roman mythology, the counterpart of Ares was MARS.

Hephaestus

HEPHAESTUS, the god of fire and the chief workman of the gods, was the son of Zeus and Hera. Born lame and ugly, he was twice thrown from heaven or Olympus, once by his mother in shame and anger at his deformity, and once by his father because, in a quarrel between his parents, he sided with his mother. The first time, Hephaestus fell into the ocean where he was received with great kindness by the nymphs EURYNOME and THETIS. With them, he lived in secrecy for nine years in a subterranean cave, making many beautiful works of art and lovely ornaments for them to show his gratitude for their goodness in taking care of him. The second time, Hephaestus fell on the island of Lemnos, one of the largest islands in the Aegean Sea, where he again had the good fortune to be kindly treated by the Sintians, the earliest inhabitants of the island. Some idea of the distance involved in this enforced journey may be gathered from the fact that although he was hurled from heaven early in the morning it was not until late in the evening, as the sun sank, that Hephaestus dropped in on the surprised but hospitable Sintians.

During his period of residence with the nymphs in their underground hideaway he also made a golden chair or throne which he sent to his mother as a gift. The remarkable feature about this seat was that it held fast by invisible chains the person sitting in it, and Hephaestus was the only one who could set the person free. With the queen of the heavens fastened to the seat and unable to rise, it was of course vitally necessary to recall Hephaestus to the region from which he had been so unceremoniously ejected. Ares was sent to fetch him, but even the god of war was frightened by the fire-torch in his brother's hand, and it took the art of Dionysus to bring Hephaestus back to Olympus by making him drunk. It was on this occasion that the god of fire incurred his father's wrath and suffered his second expulsion from the abode of the gods.

In spite of his physical unattractiveness, Hephaestus had three wives, and beautiful wives they were: CHARIS, AGLAIA, and Aphrodite. Charis was the personification of grace and beauty. Aglaia, representing brilliance, was the youngest of the Graces or Charites. Aphrodite was unfaithful to him, preferring the company of other gods, especially Ares. With the help of Apollo, or of Helios (versions of the story differ), Hephaestus discovered the rendezvous of the lovers, threw an invisible net around them, and brought them before the assembled gods. The hearty laughter of the gods at the embarrassment of the guilty pair was one of the rare occasions when the majestic dwellers on Mount Olympus were moved to laughter.

Hephaestus fathered many children, among whom the most important were ERECHTHEUS, ERICHTHONIUS, CACUS, and CAECULUS. Erechtheus, in his babyhood, enjoyed the protection of Athene, who hid him in a casket as she did not want the gods to know that she was taking care of the child. AGRAULOS, HERSE, and PANDROSUS, the three daughters of Cecrops, the first king of Attica, were put in charge of the box and were given strict instructions by Athene not to lift the cover of the box. But their curiosity overcame them and they raised the lid; the sight that met their eyes—Erechtheus in the shape of a serpent—

drove them mad and they hurled themselves into the sea.

Erichthonius was distinguished as being the first to use a chariot with four horses, for which feat he was placed among the stars as Auriga, the charioteer. Cacus, an enormous giant, lived in Latium on Mount Aventine, and plundered the surrounding territory with impunity. Emboldened by his success, he stole some cattle belonging to Heracles, a rash act for which he paid with his life.

Caeculus, who, like Cacus, lived by plunder, was credited with having built Praeneste, one of the most ancient towns of Latium.

As the master workman of the gods, Hephaestus had shops and forges at Lemnos, Lipara, Hiera, and Sicily, in addition to his splendid palace at Olympus, which contained a fully equipped workshop, anvils, and twenty bellows, which operated spontaneously at his order. Among the specimens of his skill as a craftsman may be mentioned all the palaces of the Olympian gods, the thunder-causing and fear-inspiring shield of Zeus, the armor of Achilles and Aeneas, the scepter of Agamemnon, the fire-breathing bulls of Æetes, king of Colchis, the crown of Ariadne, and the beautiful but fatal necklace of Harmonia, the wife of Cadmus. For himself, he made two beautiful gold maidens gifted with the power of movement to help him in his lameness and to support him when he walked. Perhaps the most important and far-reaching contribution made by Hephaestus was his invention of PANDORA, the first woman on earth, whom he made out of clay at the command of Zeus in order to plague mankind.

In art, Hephaestus was represented as a strong man, bearded, with the hammer and tongs of a smith, an oval cap, and an undershirt covering his left shoulder, the right arm and shoulder being exposed; the left leg is shorter than the right. At Lemnos, sacred to him since his landing on the island and his hospitable reception there, he was honored by a yearly festival lasting for nine days, during which period all fires were put out while atonement and purification rites were performed; at the end of the ninth day, new fires were lit to signify the beginning of a new life. Smiths, smelters, and metal-workers honored him at an annual feast; animals were sacrificed to him, songs and hymns were sung, torches were kindled, and torch-races were held in his honor.

Hephaestus' parentage and lameness are two interesting points in dispute. According to Homer, the god of fire was the son of the king and queen of the heavens, but later legends make him fatherless, stating that Hera gave birth to him herself in order to show that she could get along without his co-operation, just as Zeus had given birth to Athene. Earlier legends make Hephaestus lame at birth, but later ones make his second fall responsible for his handicap. More important than the cause or origin of his physical defect is the defect itself, since ugliness and deformity of any kind were abhorrent to the Greeks, known for their love of physical beauty and perfection, qualities which their gods and goddesses possessed to a superlative degree. In Roman mythology, the corresponding deity was called VULCAN.

Hebe

HEBE, a daughter of Zeus and Hera, was the goddess of youth. On Olympus she served the gods their nectar, attended the chariot of Hera, and attended the convalescing of Ares. When Heracles came to Olympus to live, Hebe was given to him in marriage.

After her marriage Hebe was succeeded as cupbearer to the gods by GANYMEDE, a Trojan prince who had been seized by Zeus in the shape of an eagle and brought to Olympus.

Dionysus (Bacchus)

DIONYSUS, also known as BACCHUS, was the god of wine. He was born in Thebes, the son of Zeus and SEM-

ELE, the daughter of Cadmus. The circumstances of his birth were quite out of the ordinary. Urged and tricked by her jealous rival, Hera, who pretended feeling of friendship for her, the trusting Semele begged Zeus to appear before her in all the dazzling glory of a god. Unwilling to go back on his promise to grant any request she made, Zeus did as she wished, although he knew what the result would be, since no mortal could live after seeing him thus. He visited Semele as the god of thunder, and she was immediately consumed by his lightning, but not before Zeus snatched from her their child, who was three months away from being born. Zeus saved Dionysus from the flames and sewed him up in his thigh, where he kept him until it was time for him to be born properly. In his infancy, the god was taken care of by his aunt, INO, and later by the nymphs of Mount Nysa in Thrace. Hera punished Ino by causing her husband to go mad, but the nymphs were rewarded by being transformed into stars, known as the Hyades.

When Dionysus grew up, Hera drove him mad, in which condition he travelled through many parts of the earth: Egypt, Syria, Asia, India. Where he was received with hospitality he responded in kind and taught people the elements of civilization and how to cultivate the vine; where he was not accorded the respect due him and not recognized as a god entitled to worship, he visited horrible punishments upon the inhabitants, usually madness.

MIDAS, king of Phrygia, is the best example of Dionysus' friendship. For treating with respect and courtesy the teacher and companion to Dionysus, the aged SILENUS, King Midas was rewarded by being granted his request that everything he touch be turned into gold. When the foolish monarch found that his food turned into gold in his mouth and his daughter in his arms, he begged Dionysus to revoke the gift, which the god very obligingly did by instructing Midas to bathe in the river Pactolus in Lydia, which ever after ran gold.

Those who incurred his wrath were not only sent into a frenzy but in that state harmed or killed themselves and those they loved or were attacked by their loved ones. For showing scant respect to the god and for refusing to participate in his worship, LYCURGUS, king of the Edones, was driven mad, in which condition he killed his own son, DRYAS, whom he mistook for a vine, and chopped off his own leg under the same mistaken impression. PENTHEUS, grandson of Cadmus, king of Thebes, was punished for the same reason; his palace was destroyed, and he was torn to pieces by his mother and his sisters, who in a wild Dionysian (or Bacchic) frenzy took him for a wild beast. By ARIADNE, the cast-off loved one of Theseus, whom he found heart-broken on the island of Naxos, Dionysus was the father of THOAS, who later became king of Lemnos.

Among animals, the ram, the dolphin, the serpent, the tiger, the lion, the lynx, the ox, the goat, the panther, and the ass were sacred to him, but he lost all control at and could not stand the sight of an owl. In nature, the vine, ivy, laurel, asphodel, and rose were sacred to him. In art, he appeared variously as an infant, being taken care of by his nurses, the Nysa nymphs, or as a young man with a crown of ivy leaves and holding a two-handled drinking cup. The body is masculine but it has something of the softness and the roundness of a woman. Sometimes he is represented as being older, wearing a long beard and wrapped in long Lydian robes; sometimes he is alone, and at other times he is with companions on whom he rests or leans idly, with no trace or suggestion of worry. Usually nude, he is sometimes partially covered by the skin of a fawn or panther.

When he returned to Thebes after his travels, he forced the women of the city to leave their homes and to take part in celebrating his wild festivals on Mount Parnassus or Mount Cithaeron, both sacred to him and the latter famous as the death place of Actaeon and Pentheus. At Argos, where he was denied worship, he revenged himself by making the women mad until the city recognized his godship and set up temples in his honor. His female followers, known under many names as Bacchae, Lenae, Maenads, Thyiads, Clodones, Bassarids, and Mimallones, ran wild on the mountains, singing, shouting, screaming in intoxicated fury, tearing animals to pieces, and carrying serpents, swords, and cymbals in their hands; their disheveled appearance, their bloodshot eyes, and the snakes twisting and writhing in their hair did little to add to their attractiveness. His male adherents, the satyrs, horned, goat-footed, and pug-nosed, with pointed ears, were no worse than their female counterparts.

The last and perhaps the greatest feat associated with Dionysus concerns his journey from Icaria to Naxos on a ship manned by Tyrrhenian pirates, who put him in chains while he slept; as the vessel sped along the god awoke and realized from the conversation that his captors were sailing in the direction of Asia, with the intention of selling him there as a slave. He immediately changed the sails and oars into snakes and caused ivy to grow around the ship; his chains fell from him and he became a lion, surrounded by hungry panthers, and the air was pierced on all sides by the sound of flutes. Feeling that they had heard and seen more than enough, the sailors, mad with fright, threw themselves into the sea and were changed into dolphins. It is only fair to record that ACOETES, the captain of the crew, was saved by Dionysus from the general destruction, as he tried in vain to persuade his mutinous men to recognize his authority. With all rebellious groups and individuals brought under control and ready to toe the mark and with his godship universally recognized, it is also pleasing to remember that Dionysus did not forget his mother. Like a good son, he left his high home on Mount Olympus, visited Semele in Hades, secured her release and took her back to Olympus, where, with him, she was worshipped as THYONE. The Romans preferred to use the name Bacchus for the god of wine.

LEGENDS OF THE GREEK DEMI-GODS AND HEROES

Prometheus, Epimetheus, and Pandora

PROMETHEUS and EPIMETHEUS were two of the sons of Iapetus, one of the Titans, and Clymene, an Oceanid, their brothers being ATLAS and MENOETIOS. The name Prometheus means "forethought," while Epimetheus means "afterthought." Hence Prometheus was thought of in Greek mythology as a wise being and to him was credited the bringing of knowledge to mankind. Epimetheus, on the other hand, was thought to be deficient in wisdom, one who acted on impulse.

Prometheus was regarded as being especially concerned with man. It was told that after the gods had created man and the other living beings, Prometheus and Epimetheus were imposed the task of distributing powers and qualities among them. Epimetheus asked to be allowed to do this alone and Prometheus assented. But when he reviewed his brother's handiwork he found that Epimetheus had given the animals ample protection against the elements but had left man naked and helpless. To remedy the situation Prometheus stole fire from the gods and gave it to man.

Another myth tells that early in his existence man lived in a state of bliss. It was always spring and the climate mild, so Zeus withheld fire from man, but then came Prometheus, representing in this case man's inquisitive, inventive nature, and introduced fire and the uses of fire. From that time on man became a prey to the cares of the everyday world.

Prometheus had another encounter with Zeus over man when Prometheus asked the god of the heavens to choose between the parts of an ox which he had slain. In one pile Prometheus had placed the flesh and entrails in the hide; in another had hidden the animal's bones in its fat. Zeus chose the bones and fat and so, it was said, it became customary for man to burn only fat and bones as sacrifices for the gods, while he kept the meat for himself.

These encounters with Prometheus caused Zeus to look with disfavor on this son of the Titans and he plotted to take his revenge on him. Until then there had been no women on earth, so Zeus directed Hephaestus to mold a female human being out of earth and water, and he ordered the other gods to give her some of their attributes as gifts, and she was named PANDORA, which means "the gift of all." Before being taken to the earth she was given a box which she was warned never to open. Zeus had Hermes conduct Pandora to the home of Prometheus, but he refused to accept her. Then Hermes took her to the home of Epimetheus. Although his brother, Prometheus, had warned him not to accept any gifts from Zeus, Epimetheus was so impressed with Pandora's charms that he took her as his wife. After a while Pandora's curiosity about the contents of her box got the better of her and she raised the lid. Out flew, in the shape of terrible demons, all the evils which henceforth were to plague mankind. Startled, Pandora closed the box in time to prevent the escape of Hope, which was thus saved to remain a comfort to man.

Zeus had still a score to settle with Prometheus for his continued defiance of the gods and defense of man. He had Prometheus taken to a mountain in the Caucasus, and there bound with chains. Zeus then sent an eagle who each day ate out Prometheus' liver, which was renewed each night. Prometheus was in time released from this agony by Heracles.

Prometheus was said to have been the husband of CLYMENE, or HESIONE, or ASIA, or Pandora. His only child was his son, DEUCALION.

Deucalion married PYRRHA, the daughter of Epimetheus and Pandora, and became ruler of Phthia. It was said that men the world over became so brazen and wicked that Zeus was determined to destroy them. Deucalion and Pyrrha, however, on the advice of Prometheus, built themselves an ark and stocked it well with provisions. Then Zeus sent down a tremendous rain that flooded the land to the heights of the mountains, leaving only the top of Mount Parnassus dry. In nine days and nine nights the ark of Deucalion drifted until it landed on Parnassus. When the rain ceased Deucalion set forth on the mountain and sacrificed to Zeus, who sent Hermes to ask Deucalion what his desire was. Deucalion replied that he wished the earth to be replenished with men. Zeus then directed the pair to cast stones behind them, and the stones which Deucalion cast became men, and those which Pyrrha cast became women.

Deucalion and Pyrrha were the parents of HELLEN, one of the primitive ancestors of all the Greeks, after whom they were known as the *Hellenes,* and from whom the word "Hellenic" comes. Hellen was the father of DOROS, AEOLUS, and XATHOS; Xathos had two sons, ACHAEUS and ION. From these names we derive some of the familiar names for the Greeks, such as *Dorians* and *Achaeans,* as well as such adjectives as "Doric" and "Ionic". It will readily be seen that these primitive heroic figures are of geographic significance. Among their descendants are the famous heroes of

Greek legend whom we shall take up in the group of entries which follows.

Orion, Atlas, The Pleiades, and the Hyades

ORION, a mighty hunter, was the son of Poseidon and EURYALE. Poseidon was said to have given him the power to walk through or on the sea. Orion fell in love with MEROPE, whose father, OENOPION, agreed to their marriage, and, as a token of his intentions cleared the land of wild beasts. But one night Orion attempted to violate Merope, whereupon Oenopion blinded him and cast him upon the sea. Orion managed to make his way to Lemnos where he came upon Hephaestus. The god took pity on him and had him escorted to the Sun-god, who restored his sight. Orion then returned to the land of Oenopion to seek revenge on the king, but the people concealed Oenopion and Orion was forced to withdraw. He went to Crete where he lived with Artemis who, tricked by Apollo, killed him (see the entry on Apollo for details of this event). Orion was placed among the stars where he appears as a giant with a girdle, his sword, a lion's skin, and a club. His dog, Sirius (the dog star) follows him, and the Pleiades fly before him.

ATLAS, a brother of Prometheus, was the father of CALYPSO, of the PLEIADES, and the HYADES. Being one of the Titans, he was one of those deposed by Zeus in his war against the Titans, and was condemned to stand at the western extremity of the earth and hold up the heavens with his shoulders and hands. Ancient mythology was not consistent with regard to Atlas, some versions describing him as a king to whom the garden of the HESPERIDES, his daughters, belonged. A prophecy of Thetis had declared that a son of Zeus would come to plunder the trees which bore the golden apples. Therefore, when the hero PERSEUS announced himself as a son of the god, Atlas attempted to cast him out, but Perseus displayed the head of Medusa, turning Atlas into the North African mountains which bear his name. In another account it is Heracles, also a son of Zeus, who steals the golden apples.

The Pleiades were the seven daughters of Atlas and PLEIONE, an Oceanid. They were: MAIA, ELECTRA (not the Electra of the Agamemnon story), and TAYGETE, each of whom bore a child to ZEUS; Alcyone (not the Alcyone who was Ceux's wife); CELAENO, mother of a child by Poseidon; STEROPE, mother of a child by Ares; and MEROPE, wife of Sisyphus. Orion became enamored of them and pursued them but they prayed to Zeus for aid and he changed them into a constellation.

The Hyades were daughters of Atlas and AETHRA, although some accounts describe them as nymphs of Dodona. Zeus entrusted the infant Dionysus to their care, and as a reward the great god placed them among the stars.

Cecrops and His Descendants

CECROPS, the first king of Attica, was an aboriginal being, that is, one existing from the origin or the very beginning of things; as such he is represented as half man, half snake. Many remarkable accomplishments were credited to him. He founded Athens, the citadel of which was named Cecropia after him; he divided Attica into twelve communities and made the crude inhabitants familiar with the fundamental elements of civilization. He put an end to bloody sacrifices, drew up laws of property, and instructed his subjects in the proper way of worshipping the gods, especially Zeus and Athene. He was responsible for introducing the institution of marriage and for dividing the country into political groups. During his administration the famous contest took place between Poseidon and Athene for possession of Attica, a contest decided by Cecrops in favor of the goddess on the ground that her contribution, the olive tree, was of greater value than the horse that sprang from the earth when Poseidon struck it with his trident.

By AGRAULOS, Cecrops had a daughter of the same name, two other daughters, HERSE and PANDROSUS, and a son, ERYSICHTHON, who died childless. His wife was the daughter of ACTAEUS, the first king of Athens.

Agraulos (or Aglauros), the daughter, was changed into a stone by Hermes because she tried to interfere with his love for Herse by preventing him from entering her sister's home. According to another legend, in which she is something more than a busybody, Agraulos threw herself down from the Acropolis in response to the oracle that had decreed that Athens would not be conquered if one of her subjects sacrificed life for love of country. She was honored by a festival, the Agraulia, held at Athens, as Pandrosos, the first priestess of Athene, was honored along with the goddess, in her own shrine, the Pandroseum. Her name, meaning the "all-bedewing" or the "all-refreshing," indicates her function as a deity of the fertilizing dew and the reason for her being invoked in time of drought.

Cecrops was succeeded as king of Athens by ERICHTHONIUS (or Erechtheus). His son, PANDION, was the father by Zeuxippe of two daughters, PROCNE and PHILOMELA. Procne married TEREUS and by him had a son named ITYS. One day, Procne, anxious to see her sister, Philomela, asked Tereus to fetch her from Athens. Tereus agreed, but on the way he violated Philomela. To prevent her from telling of the incident, he cut out her tongue and placed her under guard. However, Philomela managed to inform her sister of what had happened by weaving a message into a garment which she conveyed to Procne. Procne read the message with horror and determined to take revenge on her husband. She secured the release of Philomela and then killed her son Itys, cut up his flesh and served it to Tereus. The sisters then fled, pursued by Tereus. Just as they were about to be overtaken by him, they prayed that they might be changed into birds, and their prayer was answered. Philomela was transformed into a swallow and Procne into a nightingale (some versions reverse the transformations). Tereus was changed into an ugly hawk.

A brother of Procne and Philomela, ERECHTHEUS, was the father, by Praxithea, of a daughter, PROCRIS. Procris fell in love with CEPHALUS, a grandson of Aeolus, and they were married. For a while they shared a great happiness, but then Cephalus, egged on perhaps by Eos, determined to test his wife's fidelity. He told Procris that he was leaving on a long journey, but he soon returned home in the guise of a stranger. He made ardent love to Procris, who at first refused him, but eventually yielded. Cephalus then revealed himself and upbraided her. Procris, shamed, fled, but soon returned. In time Procris began to suspect him of infidelity, since he often left home on hunting expeditions. She followed him on one hunt and hid herself in the bush. Hearing him call, "Come, Nephele, come"—Nephele was a cloud, and Cephalus merely wished it to shield him from the heat of the sun—Procris rushed forth to confront her husband. Confused and astonished, he hurled his javelin at her and killed her.

A later descendant of Cecrops—actually the uncle of Theseus—was NISUS, king of Megara. He had a purple lock of hair on his head, and it was said that Nisus would live as long as this lock remained uncut. But his daughter, SCYLLA (not to be confused with the sea-monster of the same name), had fallen in love with King MINOS of Crete, who at that time was besieging Megara. In her attempt to gain Minos' favor, she cut off her father's lock while he was sleeping and he died immediately, giving the Cretans an opportunity to take the city. When Minos heard of Scylla's deed he was repelled by her disloyalty and tied her to the stern of his vessel and dragged her through the water until she drowned. According to another version of this legend, Nisus, transformed into an eagle, continually pursued Scylla, who was changed into a bird.

Perseus

PERSEUS, one of the great Greek heroes, was the son of Zeus and DANAË, and the grandson of ACRISIUS, king of Argos. An oracle having predicted that Acrisius would meet death at the hands of his daughter's son, he locked Danaë up in a brass or stone room. But Zeus, mindful of the saying that love laughs at locks, came down through the roof and fell into her lap in the form of a shower of gold.

After the birth of Perseus, the frightened grandfather put his daughter and her son into a wooden box and hurled it into the sea. But Zeus watched over the chest and caused it to be carried safely to the Isle of Seriphos in the Aegean Sea. Here, the mother and child were found by a poor but honest fisherman, DICTYS, who carried them to POLYDECTES, the king of the island, by whom they were received and treated with kindness and hospitality until Polydectes began to fall in love with the mother and to find Perseus in the way. In order to get rid of him, Polydectes commissioned Perseus to fetch him the horrible head of Medusa, one of the Gorgons. Aided by Hermes and Athene, Perseus went to the Graiae, the gray women, whom he robbed of the only eye and tooth they possessed among them. Having the ugly creatures at this disadvantage, he compelled them to furnish him with some vitally needed equipment for his undertaking. This material consisted of winged sandals to give him magic speed, a bag or large wallet, and the helmet of Hades to render him invisible. Later, Hermes gave him a sword-shaped sickle, and Athene, a mirror. Thus equipped, the Argive hero mounted into the air and in less time than it takes to tell it he arrived at the dwelling place of the Gorgons—who were asleep when he called—on the shores of Oceanus near Tartarus. Turning his face away and looking at her through the mirror—as the sight of her features would have turned him into stone—he cut off Medusa's head, his hand being guided by friendly Athene. Thrusting the bloody head into his bag, he again rose into the air and flew away with the other Gorgons in hot pursuit but managed to escape, thanks to his sandals and helmet.

Arriving at Ethiopia, he found ANDROMEDA, daughter of CEPHEUS and CASSOPEIA, the king and queen, chained to a rock and on the point of being sacrificed to a hideous sea-monster. Seeing that not a moment was to be lost, he slew the monster, then married Andromeda. But Andromeda's uncle, PHINEUS, who, having been previously engaged to Andromeda, felt that he had a prior claim and plotted to kill Perseus. But the latter displayed the Gorgon's head and turned Phineus to stone. Perseus also made use of the Gorgon's head on Polydectes and his friends, who were persecuting his mother and Dictys, on Atlas (who became a mountain), and on many others who incurred his wrath. Then having no further use for the gifts of the Graiae, he presented them to Hermes, who, in his turn, gave them back to their original owners. Medusa's head he gave to Athene, who placed it in the middle of her breastplate.

Taking part in the public funeral games held at Larissa in Thessaly in honor of the dead king of that country, he accidentally killed Acrisius, his grandfather, with a discus, thus fulfilling, as Greek characters always do, the decree of the oracle. He rewarded Dictys' early kindness to him and his later kindness to his mother by establishing the faithful fisherman on the throne of Seriphos. By Andromeda, he had a daughter, GORGOPHONE. His oldest son, PERSES, is looked upon as the ancestor of all Persians; of his other sons, ALCAEUS was the father of Amphitryon, king of Tiryns; STHENELUS, of EURYSTHEUS, king of Mycenae, who imposed the famous twelve labors on Heracles; and ELECTRYON, also king of Mycenae, of ALCMENE, who by Zeus himself became the mother of Heracles.

In Argolis, Perseus built the towns of Persepolis, and Mycenae; he was worshipped with godly honors at Athens, at Seriphos where he landed, and at many other places. Eventually his name was given to one of the great constellations, as was that of Andromeda, his wife, and of her father and mother, Cepheus and Cassiopeia.

Cadmus

CADMUS was the son of AGENOR, king of Phoenicia, and of TELEPHASSA. He was the brother of EUROPA, who was carried off by Zeus, disguised as a bull, and of PHOENIX and CILIX. After Europa's kidnapping, Agenor commanded his sons to search for her and not to think of returning unless they found her. Discouraged by their vain efforts, Phoenix and Cilix finally settled in the countries named after them, Phoenicia and Cilicia. Telephassa went with Cadmus as far as Thrace, where she died.

After burying her, Cadmus consulted the oracle at Delphi and was commanded to give up the search and to follow a cow that he would meet and to found a city on the spot that she chose as a resting place. Acting on these instructions, Cadmus met a cow in Phocis, and, following her to Boeotia, where she sank down fatigued, built Cadmea, later the citadel of the future Thebes. Planning to sacrifice the animal to Athene, he sent some of his comrades to a nearby well, sacred to Ares, for water. All of them were killed by a dragon, Ares' own son, guarding the spring. Still protected by the goddess, Cadmus slew the dragon and sowed its teeth in the ground. Armed giants immediately sprang up and would have destroyed Cadmus had he not thrown a huge rock among them. In the fast and furious fight that followed, the warriors destroyed themselves, only five escaping with their lives. These five, known as the Sparti, the "sown men," helped to build Cadmea and became the ancestors of the five oldest and noblest Theban families.

Cadmus married HARMONIA, daughter of Ares and Aphrodite. The wedding, a grand affair, was attended by all the Olympian gods, who gave handsome presents to the happy couple, and vocal entertainment was provided by the Muses. Cadmus gave his bride a wonderful necklace, made by Hephaestus, and a richly embroidered, pleated dress, woven by no less a seamstress than Athene. By Harmonia, Cadmus had four daughters, AUTONOË, INO, AGAVE, and SEMELE, and a son, POLYDORUS. Autonoë was the wife of Aristaeus and the mother of Actaeon; Agave married Echion, one of the Sparti, and bore him a son, PENTHEUS. Ino, wife of Athamas, the king of Orchomenus in Boeotia, was the mother of two sons, Learchus and Melicertes. During a Bacchic orgy his mother and aunts mistook Pentheus for a wild beast and tore him to pieces. Semele, tricked by Hera into making a request that caused her death, was the mother of Dionysus by Zeus (for details of this episode, see the entry under Dionysus). Polydorus, king of Thebes, was the father of Labdacus and the great-grandfather of the unhappy Oedipus.

Weighed down by the misfortunes that fell on their children, victims of Hera's hate, Cadmus and his wife left Thebes and sought peace in Illyria, a country so named by Cadmus in honor of another son, ILLYRIUS, who was born there. Chosen king by the people, Cadmus later resigned his throne to Illyrius. Finally, feeling that they had had enough, Cadmus and Harmonia asked Zeus to end their lives. They were transformed into serpents and Zeus carried them to Elysium. Cadmus was credited with having civilized the Boeotians and with introducing and teaching to them an alphabet consisting of sixteen letters.

It is interesting to note that many of the members of Cadmus' family have names which are identified with well-known places and peoples. EPAPHUS, the son of Io and Zeus, married MEMPHIS, the daughter of the Nile, and they had a daughter named LIBYA (the Greek name for Africa). Libya in turn was the grandmother of Cadmus, Europa, and BELOS. The latter was the father of DANAÜS (the Greeks were often called the Danaäns) and ÆGYPTUS.

Heracles

HERACLES, the most famous of all the heroes in Greek mythology, was born in Thebes the son of Zeus by ALCMENE, who was the wife of AMPHITRYON. While that warrior was busy fighting the Teleboi, Zeus visited Alcmene in the likeness of her husband, the result being that she gave birth to twins, IPHICLES by Amphitryon, and Heracles by Zeus. (Heracles is more generally referred to by the name which the Romans used, HERCULES.)

Heracles symbolized physical strength and unflinching courage. He accomplished many marvelous deeds, beginning a few seconds after he was born.

Hera, who hated Heracles even before he was born as she did all the children of Zeus' mortal wives, sent two serpents to destroy both Heracles and Iphicles a few minutes after they first saw the light, but Heracles alone strangled them in his crib. As an infant and in his young manhood Heracles studied under some of the finest teachers of his day. Amphitryon, his stepfather, but long regarded as his father, taught him how to drive a chariot. AUTOLYCUS (better known as a thief) taught him the art of wrestling. From EURYTUS, one of the greatest archers of all time, he learned how to use the bow and arrow. CASTOR taught him horsemanship and the use of military weapons, and POLLUX, a master boxer, the use of his fists. CHIRON, a centaur, taught him the various branches of science. RHADAMANTHUS, later one of the three judges of the dead in the underworld, taught him wisdom and virtue. From EUMOLPUS, a son of Poseidon and Chione, he learned the arts of song and music. According to other versions of the story it was a wandering minstrel, LINUS, a son of Apollo, who taught him to play the lyre or the lute. When the master reproved or corrected the pupil, Heracles, forgetting the lessons of the judge, lost his temper and killed Linus with the lute or the lyre. Another account makes Apollo kill Linus because he challenged him to a musical contest.

After this display of a lack of self-control, Amphitryon decided that it was not safe to keep Heracles at home and sent him to Mount Cithaeron to tend his flocks, at which place and in which occupation he remained until he was eighteen. During this period he made what is known as the Choice of Heracles. Two women, Pleasure and Virtue, both tall, dark, and beautiful, suddenly appeared before him as he was wondering what course of life to adopt. Pleasure promised him ease and enjoyment; Virtue, hard work and glory. The hero unhesitatingly accepted Virtue's offer. Before returning to his native city, Heracles hunted down and killed the huge and hungry lion of Cithaeron that had been destroying the flocks of Amphitryon and of THESPIUS (or Thestius), the king of Thespiae. As a reward for saving his cattle, Thespius entertained the brave youth royally and offered him his fifty daughters. After slaying the lion, the hero wore its skin as a covering for his body; from the head and mouth he shaped a helmet that he wore on his own head. Arrived at Thebes, he freed his city of the yearly tribute it had been forced to pay for twenty years to ERGINUS, the king of Orchomenus in Boeotia—the tribute being in the form of a hundred oxen a year. Heracles, fresh from killing the Cithaeronian lion, met Erginus' ambassadors on their way to collect the animals. Either ignorant of or with no respect for diplomatic immunity, he cut off their ears and noses, tied their hands behind them, and sent them back to the king. Their report of the treatment accorded them so enraged Erginus that he immediately gathered his forces and marched on Thebes without bothering about the formality of a declaration of war. In the battle that followed, he and hundreds of his men with him were slain by Heracles; as further punishment, he ordered the Orchomenians to pay an annual tribute of two hundred oxen. In this bloody conflict, Heracles lost his stepfather, but gained a wife and many presents from the gods. The Theban king, CREON, grateful to Heracles for having cut his taxes, gave him his daughter, MEGARA, as a wife, a gift that Heracles later returned. Hermes' gift was a sword; from Apollo came a bow and arrows; Hephaestus gave him a bronze club and a gold suit of armor, and Athene presented him with a peplus, a loose outer garment, richly embroidered with battle scenes, deeds of great heroes, historical events, and the images of famous men, to be draped over the clothing and wrapped around the entire body.

The joy and triumph of Heracles did not last too long and congratulations and good wishes were soon turned to grief and curses, for Hera sent him a fit of madness, under the influence of which he slew his own three children by Megara and two of his brother's children. To punish himself for this deed Heracles went into voluntary exile. At Delphi the oracle told him that he had to be purified, and that this could be done only by a terrible penance. The oracle advised him to proceed to his cousin EURYSTHEUS (son of Nicippe and Sthenelus), king of Mycenae (or Tiryns), and serve him for twelve years and perform twelve tasks to be imposed by him.

Although physically weak, Eurystheus proved to be a hard taskmaster, capable of imposing on anyone unfortunate enough to be in his power tasks designed to break the heart and spirit of the stoutest hero. The twelve labors that Eurystheus imposed and that Heracles carried out triumphantly are known as THE TWELVE LABORS OF HERACLES. We now take them up in turn.

The Nemean Lion. A savage lion, offspring of Typhon, a hundred-headed monster, and Echidna, half-woman and half-serpent, lived in Nemea, a valley in Argolis. Eurystheus commanded Heracles to bring him the skin of this ferocious animal. Without a word, the hero hurried away to carry out his instructions. When he found that his club and arrows were of no avail, Heracles strangled the beast with his own hands and returned to town carrying the dead lion on his shoulders. Eurystheus was so frightened at this exhibition of strength that he told Heracles to relate his deeds to him from a distance, outside the city gates.

The Lernean Hydra. The hydra, another child of Typhon and Echidna, was a poisonous water-snake living near the well of Amymone, so named after one of the fifty daughters of Danaüs. Brought up by Hera, for reasons of her own, it ravaged the district of Lerna, near Argos. Its foul breath was fatal to those who ventured too close, and it had nine heads, the middle one of which was immortal. As soon as Heracles cut off one head with a swipe of his club, two new ones, larger and uglier, grew in its place, which made the struggle difficult and discouraging for the hero. Heracles also had to contend with a huge crab, sent by Hera, that kept biting him. He finally overcame the monster, aided by his faithful companion, and nephew, IOLAUS. As fast as Heracles lopped off the heads, Iolaus burned the stumps with a torch, thus preventing the growth of the duplicate heads. Head number nine—the immortal one—Heracles buried under a huge rock.

The Arcadian Stag. This creature, with golden antlers and bronze feet, was sacred to Artemis, having been dedicated to her by Taygete, a nymph and one of the Pleiades, in gratitude for having been rescued from Zeus, who was pursuing her. Heracles was required in this labor to capture the animal and to bring it back alive to Eurystheus at Mycenae. Heracles chased the stag in vain for a whole year before wounding it with one of his arrows. While carrying it to Eurystheus, he met Artemis, who was enraged at him for wounding an animal sacred to her, but when he explained the situation to her and convinced her that he was not exactly a free agent, she forgave him and allowed him to continue his journey.

The Erymanthian Boar. The terms of this exploit are similar to those connected with the Arcadian stag. Heracles, commanded to take it alive and to bring it to Mycenae, chased it through deep snows, exhausted it, and then caught it in a net. The sight of the animal threw Eurystheus into such a fit of fear that he hid himself in a tub under the ground and repeated, with much more emphasis, his definite instructions to Heracles that in the future he exhibit the proofs of his prowess outside the city gates.

The Augean Stables. The fifth labor was not as dangerous perhaps as the first four tasks but it had its own difficulties. Eurystheus ordered Heracles to do a thorough cleaning job—in one day—of the stables of AUGEAS, king of the Epeans in Elis. In order to fully realize the unpleasant nature of this task, one must bear in mind the fact that Augeas had three thousand oxen and that the stables had not been cleaned for thirty years. Heracles carried out his part of the performance by turning the rivers Alpheus and Peneus into the stable yards and stalls. Both Augeas and Eurystheus cheated Heracles in connection with this assignment. Augeas had promised Heracles that he would give him three hundred oxen as a reward for cleaning his stables but refused to abide by the agreement—made in the presence of his son, PHYLEUS—on the grounds that Heracles was under obligation to Eurystheus, while that tricky taskmaster, always looking for a chance to throw out one of Heracles' labors so that another might be added, used the same argument in reverse, claiming that Heracles had disqualified himself by entering into negotiations on the side with Augeas. For testifying against him, that is, for telling the truth, Phyleus was banished by his father. Heracles later invaded Augeas' kingdom and killed him and all his other sons.

The Stymphalian Birds. These creatures lived near Lake Stymphalis in Arcadia. Reared by Ares, they were man-eating monsters, always hungry, with brass beaks, wings, and claws, and with feathers that served as arrows which they shot out on the slightest provocation or without any provocation at all. Heracles' task was either to kill them or drive them from their nests. By means of a brass rattle—Athene's gift—he frightened the birds and shot them with his own arrows as they flew away.

The Cretan Bull. As in the cases of the stag and the boar, Heracles was instructed to bring the bull back alive. MINOS, king of Crete, and son of Zeus and Europa, asked Poseidon to send him a bull for sacrificial purposes. The god of the sea responded by causing a beautiful snow-white bull to rise from the waves. Minos, attracted by the beauty of the animal, decided to keep it for his own herd and substituted another in its place. Poseidon punished him for trying to fool a god by driving the bull mad and by causing Minos' wife, PASIPHAE, to fall in love with the brute and bear him a son, the monstrous MINOTAUR. Heracles bested the bull, threw him over his shoulders, and carried him home to Mycenae, where he set him free. The bull enjoyed a brief spell of liberty, wandering through Greece and devastating the country until it met its end in Marathon, where it was killed by the hero, Theseus.

The Wild Mares of Diomedes. DIOMEDES (not the Greek hero of the same name), son of Ares and Cyrene, and king of the Bistones in Thrace, had a stable of mares to whom he fed human flesh. Heracles captured the horses without much difficulty and was taking them to Mycenae when he was attacked by Diomedes and his Thracian followers. During the fight that followed, Heracles, unable to defend himself and look after the animals at the same time, turned them over to the care of his friend, ABDERUS, but the wild beasts tore him to pieces and ate him. He defeated the Bistones, killed the king, and threw his body to the mares, which immediately became tame after eating their master's flesh. They were now easy to manage and Heracles had no difficulty in bringing them to Eurystheus, who set them free. They were soon destroyed on Mount Olympus by beasts which were as wild as they had once been.

Hippolyte's Girdle. HIPPOLYTE, daughter of Ares and Otrera, was queen of the Amazons, a race of heroic women, whose name comes from the fact that they cut off their right breasts so that they might better draw their bows (*a*—without, *mazos*—breast). Hippolyte had a girdle, her father's gift and a symbol of her power, that ADMETE, daughter of Eurystheus, was eager to own. In order to please her, and without involving himself in any way, Eurystheus ordered Heracles to fetch it. After traveling through Europe and Asia, Heracles finally arrived at the court of the Amazonian queen, probably with no very clear idea of how he was going to carry out his delicate mission. To his great surprise and relief, Hippolyte received him with signs of friendship and told him that she would be only too glad to let him have the girdle for the asking. But this pleasant solution did not fall in with Hera's plans. The goddess spread a false report among the Amazons that Heracles was carrying off their queen. They rushed to defend her, and Heracles, thinking that Hippolyte had played him false, slew her. On the way back to Mycenae, Heracles stopped off at Troy and saved the life of HESIONE by rescuing her from the sea-monster sent by Poseidon. For this deed, one of his many *extra* labors and apparently thrown in by the hero for good measure, Hesione's father, LAOMEDON, king of Troy, promised Heracles two divine horses that had been given to him by Zeus in return for the loss of his son, the beautiful GANYMEDE. Laomedon refused, as he always did, to keep his word, and Heracles later attacked Troy, killed the king, and gave Hesione to his good friend, TELAMON, to whom she bore a son, TEUCER, the famous archer and one of the great Greek heroes before Troy.

The Oxen of Geryon. GERYON, a monster with three heads and three bodies and enormous wings, was a son of Chrysaor and Callirrhoe, an Oceanid. He lived on the fabled island of Erythia in the far west, the *red* island, so called because it lay under the rays of the setting sun. His magnificent oxen, also red—which Heracles was commanded to capture—were guarded by a giant, EURYTION, and a two-headed dog, ORTHRUS, son of Typhon and Echidna. After passing through many countries, Heracles at last reached the island and killed the giant and the dog. Later, hurrying off with the oxen, he was pursued by Geryon, whom he finally slew with his arrows after a fierce contest. Before arriving at his destination, Heracles traveled through Gaul, Italy, Illyricum, and Thrace. The oxen, after being delivered to Eurystheus, were sacrificed by him to Hera.

The Golden Apples. These apples were in the keeping of the HESPERIDES, the daughters of Atlas and Hesperis. They had been given by Gaea to Hera as a wedding present. The eleventh labor of Heracles was to fetch these apples. Easy as it appears, this labor had one difficult feature: Heracles had no idea where the apples were. After covering a good deal of ground he found NEREUS, the Old Man of the Sea, and forced him to reveal where the apples were hidden. On his way to get them, he passed through Libya (where he killed ANTAEUS, the champion wrestler), Egypt (where he slew BUSIRIS, and all his sons, whose custom it was to sacrifice a stranger every year to Zeus), and Ethiopia (where he killed EMATHION, who had usurped the Ethiopian throne of his handsome brother, MEMNON). His thirst for adventure still unsatisfied, he freed PROMETHEUS from his chains and, following his advice, sent ATLAS to bring him the golden apples. In order to carry out this assignment, Atlas had to transfer the heavens from his own shoulders to those of Heracles, who agreed to hold the heavy weight while he was away. Returning with the coveted fruit, the tricky Atlas refused to take up the burden that belonged to him, telling Heracles that he would take the apples for him to Eurystheus. Heracles, as sly as Atlas when the situation demanded it, agreed to the proposal and asked him to hold the heavens for just a minute while he arranged a pad for the convenience of his head and back. As the change was being made, Heracles picked up the apples and hurried away. When he reached Mycenae, Eurystheus gave him the apples as a gift, the first gracious sign exhibited by the taskmaster. According to another version of the eleventh labor, Heracles slew LADON, a hundred-headed dragon, who stood guard over the apples with the Hesperides.

Cerberus. The twelfth and last labor of Heracles was the most difficult. It was to bring CERBERUS, the three-headed watchdog of Hades, from his home in the lower regions to the upper world. Conducted by Hermes and Athene, whose friendship for him served somewhat to counteract the deadly opposition of Hera, Heracles made the trip down without any mishap. Hades, the prince of darkness, allowed him to take the dog on the condition that he do so with his bare hands, without using any weapons of war. The hero grabbed the growling dog in his powerful arms, tied him up, took him to Eurystheus for a good look, and then brought him back to the lower world. As in his other adventures, Heracles accomplished extra tasks while carrying out one duty. During the short time that he spent in Hades, he rescued Theseus, the would-be kidnapper of Persephone, and Ascalaphus, who had been turned into an owl for having revealed that Persephone had eaten a part of the pomegranate seed.

After the Twelve Labors, Heracles returned to Thebes to continue his career of heroism and violence. He gave his wife, Megara, in marriage to Iolaus, feeling that the gods would not approve of his living with a woman whose children he had murdered. He rescued ALCESTIS, the loving wife of ADMETUS, from death by snatching her from the greedy hands of Hades.

Wishing then to remarry, he heard that EURYTUS, king of Oechalia in Thessaly, and a great archer, was offering his daughter IOLE in marriage to the one who could best him in a shooting contest. Heracles won, but Eurytus refused to give him his daughter, fearing that he might kill their children, as he did Megara's. Shortly after, Eurytus' oxen were stolen by Autolycus, but suspicion fell on Heracles. IPHITUS, who did not see eye to eye with his father and who would have been happy to have Heracles as a brother-in-law, was hunting with him for his father's cattle. But in another fit of madness Heracles threw Iphitus from the walls of Tiryns. As punishment for this crime, the Delphic oracle commanded Heracles to hire himself out for three years for three talents and to pay his wages to Eurytus. In obedience to this decree, Heracles entered the service of OMPHALE, queen of Libya. Here, the matchless hero was degraded by being dressed in soft, silky female garb and by being assigned to such womanish tasks as spinning wool, making the beds, and cleaning. Omphale, on the other hand, wore Heracles' clothing, especially the skin of the Nemean lion, and used the club which was the symbol of his power. In spite of all these humiliations it is reported that Heracles actually fell in love with Omphale but nothing ever came of it.

After serving his time, he sailed to Troy, where he had an old account to settle with King Laomedon, who had refused to give him the two divine horses for having saved his daughter's life. Arriving at the city, he stormed it with eighteen ships, and killed King Laomedon with all his sons, except PODARCES, as Priam was known in his youth. Returning from Troy, he encountered a storm sent by Hera and had a hard battle on the Island of Cos with EURYTION, the son of Poseidon, and his sons. Wounded and compelled to seek safety in flight, he finally won with the timely aid of Zeus. Later, in the battle between the giants and the gods, Heracles, summoned by Athene, gave vital aid, without which the giants could not have been conquered. Still later, he slew CYCNUS, son of Ares and Pelopia, and another CYCNUS, son of Ares and Pyrene. Then returning to the kingdom of Eurytus he slew the king and took Iole captive.

Later, in Calydon he won the hand of DEIANEIRA, after having vanquished ACHELOUS, the river god, who had turned himself into a bull. While traveling with Deianeira, he killed NESSUS the centaur for attempting to violate her while she was one of his ferry passengers. In a long-drawn-out fight he killed THEIODAMAS, king of the dryopes, and took his son, HYLAS (not to be confused with his own son, Hyllus) with him on the expedition of the Argonauts.

His last act of violence, which can in no degree be held against him, was to hurl his attendant, Lichas, into the sea for bringing him, innocently, the poisoned robe sent by Deianeira, who had become jealous of his love for Iole. Lichas did not know that the cloak was poisoned. As soon as Heracles put it on, pain shot through him and his body burned. Mad with anguish, he tried vainly to tear off the fatal garment but all he could do was to rip off pieces of his own flesh, in which horrible state he hurled his unhappy attendant into the foaming sea below, where Lichas was transformed into a cliff. Deianeira, in despair, hanged herself. PHILOCTETES, or his father, POEAS, set fire to the funeral pile as directed by the hero with his last breath.

A great friend of Heracles was CEYX, the son of Eosphorus, the Morning Star, whose wedding to ALCYONE, a daughter of Aeolus, the king of Thessaly, the hero attended. It was the fate of this pair to be turned into birds. According to one legend, they called each other Zeus and Hera, a practice which so annoyed the real Zeus that he transformed them into winged creatures. Another version tells that Ceyx was shipwrecked while going to consult an oracle, and his wife, finding his body on the shore, cast herself into the sea. Out of pity the gods changed them into birds called the Halcyons (from the name Alcyone). It was said that the Halcyon sits on her eggs for seven days and for seven more she feeds her young on the surface of the sea, which remains calm—and these days are termed "Halcyon days."

After his death, Heracles was carried up to heaven as a son of Zeus and made one of the immortals. Hera, who hated him throughout his life, at last became reconciled to him, and he married her daughter, Hebe, the goddess of eternal youth and the cup-filler of the gods. By her he had two sons, ALEXIARES, who turned away curses, and ANIKETOS, who could not be conquered; their names suggest that they were perhaps little more than personifications of traits or qualities for which their father was famous.

When Heracles died, his nephew Iolaus was the first to pay the necessary sacrifices to his memory. When Iolaus himself died he obtained special permission from Hades, the overlord of hell, to return to earth for a short period, to help the Heraclidae—Heracles' descendants—who were being persecuted by Eurystheus. The loyal Iolaus killed the tyrant and then, true to his word, returned to the lower world, satisfied that he had discharged the ties of true friendship. The ghost or shade of Heracles, as dark as night, roamed the lower world; true to his nature he was ever and always ready to let his arrows fly. The hero himself lived forever with the immortals as Hebe's happy husband.

Theseus

THESEUS, the great hero of Attica and Athens, compares very favorably with Heracles, the great Theban hero. He was the son of AEGEUS, king of Athens, and AETHRA, who was the daughter of Pittheus, king of Troezen in Argolis, where Theseus was born and reared, and where he was educated by his grandfather. Before departing for Athens, Aegeus deposited his sword and sandals under a large heavy rock, instructing Aethra, when the infant was able to lift the stone by his own strength, to send him with the tokens to his father at Athens. When he was sixteen, Theseus raised the stone without the slightest difficulty and began his journey to his father's court, carrying with him the necessary articles of identification. Eager to distinguish himself as Heracles had done and with that hero definitely in mind as example and incentive, Theseus decided to travel by land so that he might have an opportunity to meet and defeat robbers and thus become a hero. At Epidaurus, he met PERIPHATES, monster son of Hephaestus, who used to slay unwary travellers with an iron club, for which reason he was called CORYNETES, the club-bearer. Theseus killed him in a brief contest and added the club to his own equipment with the thought, no doubt, that it might come in handy.

On the Corinthian Isthmus, he encountered SINIS, a robber, son of Poseidon, who was known as the pine-bender because he used to tear passers-by to pieces by tying them to the tops of pine trees, bending the branches down, and then suddenly letting them fly up. With a sense of poetic justice, Theseus disposed of Sinis by his own method.

At Crommyon, near the city of Megara, he slew PHAEA, the wild sow. At the boundary between Megara and Attica, he met and killed another robber, SCIRON, who robbed travellers on the top of the Scironian rock which he called his home and then forced them to wash his feet; while they were carrying out this enforced labor he kicked them into the sea, where they were eaten by a huge tortoise lying in wait at the bottom of the rock. In Eleusis, he met the tyrant CERCYON. A champion wrestler, Cercyon threw and killed all who crossed his path, until Theseus killed him, just as Heracles killed Antaeus, by lifting him off the ground. Also at Eleusis, in Attica, Theseus met the brigand DAMASTES.

This monster, better known to us as PROCRUSTES, which means "stretcher," used to lay his guests on a bed specially provided for their convenience; if the guests were shorter than the bed, he stretched and pulled their limbs until they were the length of the bed; if they were too long, he cut off just enough of their limbs to make them accommodate the bed or the bed accommodate them. Theseus wrote finis to the career of this monster.

After ridding the world of these various undesirables, Theseus was purified of bloodshed by the PHYTALIDAE—descendants of Phytalus, an Eleusinian hero—who enjoyed that privilege by ancient custom. Arrived at Thebes, Theseus found that his father had married MEDEA, the sorceress who had been the wife of Jason. Through her magic powers she recognized him as Aegeus' son and as a threat to her security, and almost succeeded in getting Aegeus to poison him, until the father himself recognized the son by the sword he was using as a knife for his meat. Medea, foiled, escaped through the air with MEDUS, her son by Aegeus, as she had done once before when fleeing from Corinth after killing Jason's children—and her own. PALLAS, brother of Aegeus, whose throne he had usurped, and father of fifty giant sons who hoped to inherit their uncle's throne at their father's death, rushed to Athens when informed what had happened and declared war on his dethroned brother. Theseus, warned of their approach in the nick of time by the herald, LEOS, killed his uncle and all his cousins and restored his father to power.

At that time Athens was being forced to pay tribute to MINOS, king of Crete. Every year seven maidens and seven youths were sent to Minos, who fed them to the MINOTAUR, a monster which was half human and half bull. The Minotaur was the offspring of Minos' wife, PASIPHAE, and a beautiful bull. Contrary to what might have been expected Minos did not have the Minotaur slain, but rather had the architect DAEDALUS build a place from which it could not escape. Daedalus built the Labyrinth, a maze of intricate passageways from which he could not find the exit. Daedalus later incurred the wrath of Minos and, to escape from Crete, he made wings of feathers and wax for himself and his son, ICARUS. They soared successfully into the air, but Icarus flew too high and the heat of the sun melted the wax on his wings, causing him to plunge into the sea. Daedalus landed safely in Sicily.

It was in the Labyrinth that the Athenian youths were placed. Anxious to relieve Athens of the onerous annual tribute, Theseus offered to go as one of the fourteen young Athenians. The ship on which they were to sail had black sails, and Theseus arranged to signal their successful return by hoisting white sails instead. Once in Crete the intended victims were displayed before Minos. His daughter, ARIADNE, was among the spectators and she immediately fell in love with Theseus. Surreptitiously she supplied him with a thread by which he could trace and retrace his steps in the Labyrinth. He made his way to the Minotaur, who was asleep. Theseus attacked him with his bare hands and killed him. Once outside, he fled with the other Athenians to their ship, taking Ariadne with him. En route back to Athens they put in at the island of Naxos and here Theseus left Ariadne. Just why he did this is variously accounted for. One tale says that Ariadne was seasick and he left her on Naxos to recover; then when he returned to the island he learned she had died. Another legend says that Theseus actually deserted her.

When the Athenian vessel sailed near the Athenian coast Theseus forgot to hoist the white sails as prearranged, and his father, Aegeus, despairing of Theseus' life, took his own life by throwing himself into the sea, henceforth called the Aegean.

Theseus then succeeded his father on the throne. Under Theseus' influence the government was turned over to the people, and the city grew from nothing but a provincial town to one of the great cities of the ancient world. However, the affairs of state did not prevent Theseus from pursuing his adventures in many lands. He participated in the Calydonian Boar Hunt and in the Argonautic search for the Golden Fleece. He accompanied Heracles to the land of the Amazons and married ANTIOPE, sister of HIPPOLYTE, queen of the Amazons, and herself queen after her sister's death at the hands of Heracles. By Antiope he was the father of HIPPOLYTUS. Some accounts say that he married Hippolyte, not Antiope; perhaps he married both of them.

At one time Theseus wanted to marry HELEN, later the cause of the Trojan War but then a very young girl. He kidnapped her from Sparta, aided by his friend, PIRITHOÜS, and took her to Aphidna, one of the twelve towns established by Cecrops, and placed her in charge of his mother. He also tried to kidnap PERSEPHONE, not for himself but for Pirithous who, aiming higher than his friend, wanted to wed the queen of hell. For this rash act, they were punished by Hades, Persephone's husband, by being chained to a rock on which they were forced to sit, presumably forever. There they remained for a long time until Heracles descended to the lower world to fetch Cerberus, the hound of hell, for Eurystheus. The hero could not help Pirithoüs, who had acted on his own, but he released Theseus from his torment because he had endangered his life and liberty out of friendship.

In later years Theseus married PHAEDRA, Ariadne's sister. By her, he had two sons, ACAMAS and DEMOPHOÖN. Phaedra nursed a guilty love for her stepson, Hippolytus, and she slandered him to his father when he rejected her advances. Theseus asked Poseidon to punish him, a favor the god of the sea granted by sending a bull to frighten Hippolytus' horses, as a result of which he was thrown from his chariot and killed. Torn by grief and conscience, Phaedra took her own life.

Acamas was brought up with his brother by ELEPHENOR, king of the Abantes in Euboa. With Diomedes, he was sent as an ambassador to Troy to negotiate with Priam to send Helen back peacefully. He was one of the heroes hidden in the Wooden Horse and he played an important part in the fall of Troy. With Demophoön he restored his father to power in Attica. He died in Cyprus after leading a colony there from Athens.

Demophoön is credited with having stolen the Palladium—an image of great antiquity on which the safety of Troy was believed to depend—from Diomedes who, with Odysseus, had stolen it from the citadel in Troy and carried it to Argos. Betrothed to PHYLLIS, daughter of King Sithon of Thrace, Demophoön was the innocent cause of her death. He was late in arriving for the wedding, and the sensitive Phyllis, thinking that she was forgotten and that he did not wish to marry her, hanged herself and was changed into an almond tree.

Eventually Theseus was exiled from Athens. Deprived of his throne by the invasion of Attica by CASTOR and POLLUX, who were avenging the abduction of their sister, Helen, and by an insurrection, Theseus thought it best to strike out for new parts. He left his two sons, Acamas and Demophoön, with Elephenor, who had brought them up after Phaedra's suicide, and went, alone, to the Island of Scyros. There, instead of finding the refuge he sought, he was treacherously murdered by LYCOMEDES, king of the Dolopians, who threw him from a rock into the sea. According to legend, the dead hero was seen, fully armed, leading his men, at the famous Battle of Marathon (490 B.C.), between the Athenians and the Persians. His bones, or bones believed to be his, were brought in 476 B.C. to Athens from Scyros, the scene of his murder, by Cimon at the command of the Delphic oracle. At Athens they were buried in a magnificent temple, known as the Theseum. A great festival, the Theseia, marked by athletic contests and feasting and drinking, honored him on the eighth day of October, and in addition the eighth day of every month was dedicated to him. Poets and artists outdid each other in praising him, and public buildings were ornamented with representations of the deeds that won him fame. In art, he is a handsome youth, with a powerful frame, and beardless. He resembles his prototype, Heracles, whose strength he suggests, but he is smaller. He is armed with a sword in early conceptions, but with the club and lion's skin of Heracles in later ones as the idea of his similarity to the Theban hero took root.

Amphion and Zethus

AMPHION and ZETHUS, two Theban heroes, were the twin sons of ANTIOPE, daughter of the river-god Asopus, and Zeus. Exposed at birth on Mount Cithaeron, they were discovered and brought up by shepherds, among whom they spent their early years. Reaching manhood and aware of their godly origin, they marched into Thebes, which was ruled by LYCUS, their mother's husband, but not their father. Learning that Lycus had divorced Antiope, and that she was being humiliated and mistreated by his new wife, DIRCE, the brothers captured the city, killed (or deposed) Lycus, and killed Dirce by tying her to the horns of a wild bull, which dragged her to death. The fountain into which her body was thrown was forever after known as the fountain of Dirce. Once in command of Thebes, the twins decided to fortify it against invasion by building a wall. Zethus, the stronger of the two, sweated and toiled in carrying huge rocks from one place to another, but Amphion, whose skill on the lyre was second only to that of Orpheus, had merely to pluck the strings of his instrument, and the stones, of their own free will, picked themselves up and rolled into their proper places.

Amphion married NIOBE, daughter of the unwise and unfortunate TANTALUS, and by her he had seven sons and seven daughters. Justifiably proud of her large family, Niobe was so foolish as to sneer at Leto, who was the mother of only two children, Apollo and Artemis. The gods punished her arrogance by having Apollo kill all the sons and Artemis all the daughters. Amphion killed himself in despair, and the widowed and childless Niobe wept unceasingly until even the gods took pity and turned her into stone.

Zethus married (according to different accounts) either THEBE, a nymph, after whom Thebes is named, or AEDON, daughter of Pandareos, who stole Zeus' golden dog. By Aedon, he had one son, ITYLUS. Envious of her sister-in-law's better showing, as Niobe had been scornful of Leto, Aedon planned to kill Niobe's eldest son, but she slew her own son, ITYLUS, by mistake. Zeus finally terminated her grief by changing her into a nightingale, whose mournful but musical notes represent a mother's cries for the loss of a child.

Amphion and Zethus, the Boeotian Dioscuri, recall those other twins, CASTOR and POLLUX, whom they in many ways resemble. Like them, they rode white steeds, with whom they appear, bringing aid, in time of trouble, and their brotherly love was as strong and appealing. They present striking character contrasts, Amphion being a great musician devoted to his art, a second Orpheus, and of a gentle and thoughtful nature, with Zethus, physically stronger, preferring the rougher and more active life of a hunter and a herdsman. When he died, Amphion was buried at Thebes in the same grave as his brother.

Sisyphus and Bellerophon

SISYPHUS, king of Corinth and the son of Aeolus, was one of the craftiest personages in ancient legend, although by trying to outwit the gods, he was assigned an intolerable fate. He came in conflict with Zeus when the great god abducted AEGINA. Sisyphus informed her father, ASOPUS, who the ravisher was, whereupon Zeus sent Death to end Sisyphus' life. But the wily Sisyphus outwitted Death and even bound him up, and while Death was so contained no mortal died on earth. Hades, however, soon rescued Death and brought Sisyphus to the underworld. Here he was set the task of rolling a tremendous stone up a hill, an endless job, since every time it reached the top it rolled down again.

Sisyphus was the husband of Merope, daughter of Atlas, and by her the father of GLAUCUS, who also drew upon himself the dislike of the gods, by feeding his steeds human flesh. For this practice the gods arranged to have him thrown from his chariot, whereupon his flesh-eating horses tore him to pieces and ate him.

BELLEROPHON was Glaucus' son, although he was also thought to be the offspring of Poseidon by Eurynome. Desiring to ride the winged horse PEGASUS, he received from the gods a gold bridle with which he tamed the animal and made him his own. A fine handsome youth, Bellerophon was loved by ANTEIA, wife of King Proetus of Argos. Because the youth rejected her, she falsely told Proetus that he had attempted to ravish her, whereupon the king sent him to his father-in-law, king of Lycia, with a certain sealed tablet upon which were inscribed the deadly characters which were to cause his death.

In Lycia, the king, after reading the tablet, sent him off to slay the hitherto unconquerable CHIMAERA, a monster with the fore part of a lion, the middle of a goat, and the hind part of a serpent, and breathing fire. Riding Pegasus, he easily slew the hideous creature. Bellerophon was next ordered to fight the Solymians, which he did successfully. Then he fought the Amazons, and while returning was ambushed by the bravest men of Lycia, all of whom he slew. The king now saw that Bellerophon was of the race of the gods and gave him his daughter and half of his kingdom.

Later Bellerophon tried to ascend to Olympus, a deed which incensed Zeus, who caused Pegasus to throw her rider to Earth. Here he wandered alone and melancholy until he died.

Castor and Pollux

CASTOR and POLLUX, two celebrated heroes who are always mentioned together, were the twin sons of Leda and brothers of the lovely Helen. Castor, famous for his ability to tame horses, was mortal, his father having been TYNDAREUS, while Pollux, a great pugilist, was immortal, his father having been the great god Zeus. They were as famous for their mutual love as for their strength and bravery. The wonderful life they led is associated with many great events. They took part in the expedition against Athens in which they rescued Helen, who had been kidnapped by Theseus. In the expedition of the Argonauts, Pollux engaged in a boxing match with ANYCUS, king of the Bebryces, in which he not only knocked him out but killed him. In the great battle against their cousins, IDAS and LYNCEUS, Castor, being mortal, was slain by Idas, but Pollux slew Lynceus. Zeus himself destroyed Idas with a bolt of lightning. Pollux begged Zeus to allow him to die with his brother, a request that the god granted, also allowing them to live alternately one day in hell and one in heaven. According to another version, Zeus rewarded their brotherly love by placing them in the sky as the Heavenly Twins, the Gemini, the morning and the evening stars. Poseidon, for the same reason, gave them control over the winds and the waves, for which power they were worshipped by sailors as their patron saints. Castor and Pollux were worshipped at Athens, Sparta, and Olympia. During the Argonautic expedition, they founded the town of Dioscurias, in Colchis, so called because of their common name, the Dioscuri, meaning "the sons of Zeus." In art, they are young horsemen, wearing egg-shaped, star-crowned helmets, and carrying long spears; they are usually shown with their beautiful white steeds, XANTHUS and CYLLARUS.

Orpheus and Eurydice

ORPHEUS, a legendary and mythical pre-Homeric poet, was born on the banks of the river Hebrus, the son of Oeagrus, the king of Thrace, and Calliope, the muse of epic poetry. So great was his skill on the golden lyre, Apollo's gift to him, that he moved not only gods and mortals, not only savage beasts who became tame at hearing his music, but even the forces and elements of nature, such as mountains, rocks, and trees, which uprooted themselves so that they could follow him and his music. In Hades, the fiendish tortures of the sufferers were halted so that all—victims and avengers alike—might listen to his sweet sounds: the forever-turning wheel of Ixion stood still, the forever-rolling stone of Sisyphus stopped in its downward course, the never-ending thirst of Tantalus was assuaged, the vultures ceased pecking at Tityus' liver, and the Furies halted their hellish persecutions of the unfortunate souls entrusted to their care. In the Argonautic expedition, of which he was a member, his magic music saved his companions from the Sirens, whose melodies, almost as beautiful as his own, led men to their destruction.

The most famous legend concerning Orpheus, and one of the most appealing and pathetic in all mythology, concerns his love for EURYDICE, a lovely nymph whom he married after returning from his voyage with the Argonauts. While running away from the unwelcome attentions of ARISTAEUS, the god of bees and bee-keeping, Eurydice stepped on a snake, from whose bite she died; she was avenged by her sister-nymphs, who destroyed all Aristaeus' bees. The heart-broken husband begged Zeus for permission to visit Hades, the underworld, in an attempt to persuade Hades, the god of the underworld, and his queen, Persephone, to release Eurydice. The ravishing music of Orpheus, the reckless courage of the player in invading the region of the damned, the uncontrollable grief of the lover, and the passionate love of the husband were a combination that the rulers of the underworld could not resist. They agreed to restore Eurydice to life and to her husband's arms, but on one condition: he must not look back as she followed behind him. Joyfully, Orpheus accepted the terms and began the long journey back; almost successful, he was torn by love, fear, eagerness, doubt, and as he neared the land of the living, he turned his head to see if his wife was really following him. As he did so, Eurydice uttered a cry and vanished from his sight, to return, forever, to Hades.

As this part of the myth is beautiful and pathetic, so is the sequel equally painful and horrible. Returning to the upper world, Orpheus managed to live or to exist, without food or drink, by the banks of the river Strymon or on the Haemus and Rhodope mountain ranges. Not caring for life or for what happened to him, he was finally torn to pieces by the Maenads, followers of Dionysus, for being indifferent to their charms. The Muses, in pity at his sad fate, gathered his mangled limbs and buried them at Libethra, a town at the foot of Mount Olympus. His head and his lyre, thrown by the enraged Maenads into the Hebrus, floated down to the sea, the head still crying out the name of his beloved Eurydice, and the lyre still playing. They finally reached Lesbos, famed as the birthplace of Sappho and were buried at the town of Antissa. At the pleading of Apollo and the Muses, the lyre was later placed by Zeus among the stars as the constellation Lyra. The Greeks regarded Orpheus as the greatest, the most celebrated, and the oldest poet, who lived long before the days of Homer.

Jason and the Golden Fleece

JASON, the famous leader of the Argonauts, whose name is forever associated with the Golden Fleece, was the son of Aeson, the lawful king of Iolcus in Thessaly, and Alcimede. In order to save him from the attacks of PELIAS, his father's half-brother, Jason was sent away to Mt. Pelion to be brought up by the wise and just centaur, CHIRON, with whom he remained until he was twenty years old. He then returned home to confront his uncle with a demand that he restore his father to his throne. In order to gain time and to get rid of him by assigning what he thought was an impossible task, the crafty Pelias commissioned Jason to bring to him the Golden Fleece.

The story of the Golden Fleece starts many years before Jason. INO, daughter of Cadmus and wife of ATHAMAS, a Grecian king, was resolved to do away with her husband's son, PHRIXOS, by a previous wife, NEPHELE. Ino persuaded the women to parch the seed-corn before planting it so that there would be a famine. Athamas then sent to the oracle at Delphi to find a way of averting the famine, but Ino bribed the messengers to say that Apollo had ordered the sacrifice of young Phrixos to Zeus. Athamas reluctantly prepared to carry out this order, but Nephele snatched away her son—and a daughter, HELLE—and placed them on a golden-fleeced ram which she had obtained from Hermes. The ram carried them over sea and land, but as they were passing over the straits between Europe and Asia, Helle fell from the ram and drowned. These straits were henceforth known as the Hellespont, the Sea of Helle. Phrixos, however, landed safely at Colchis, the land of King Æetes, son of Helios. Æetes gave Phrixos to one of his daughters. Phrixos then sacrificed the golden-fleeced ram to Zeus and gave the fleece to Æetes, who put it under the guard of fire-breathing bulls and a dragon that never slept.

When Jason was ordered to bring the Golden Fleece to Pelias, he gathered around him the bravest heroes of the land to sail with him. His company included HERACLES, CASTOR and POLLUX, ORPHEUS, THESEUS, NESTOR, PELEUS, and many others. Jason ordered a special vessel to be built by ARGUS, after whom the ship was named the *Argo;* and the company of heroes were thus called the ARGONAUTS.

The voyage to Colchis was fraught with danger. The SIRENS lured some of the company to leap into the sea. They had an encounter with the HARPIES, who had been preventing an old seer, PHINEUS, from partaking of food. Phineus begged the Argonauts to help him and two of the heroes drove off the loathsome creatures. In return Phineus gave them instructions for passing through the Symplegades, the Clashing Islands, which ground to bits any object caught between them. Following Phineus' instructions, as they approached the Symplegades, they released a dove, which flew safely through. Then Jason waited for the favorable moment, and, urging his men to ply their oars with full strength, he saw his vessel pass safely through.

Once in Colchis, Jason laid his request before Æetes, who agreed to let him have the Golden Fleece, on condition that he would carry out some seemingly impossible tasks. These included taming the savage bulls, killing the dragon, sowing his dangerous teeth in the ground, and killing the fully armed soldiers that would immediately spring from the teeth. Jason, fully aware of the difficulties involved, accepted the terms imposed and met them, aided by the magic skill of Æetes' daughter, MEDEA. He fled with the fleece and with Medea, whom he married, to Iolcus.

Years later, after a long period of happiness, Jason grew tired of Medea and left her in order to marry GLAUCE, daughter of CREON, king of Corinth. Medea's revenge, a terrible combination of fury, femininity, and ferocity, is one of the great stories of mythology and of world literature. She sent her rival a beautiful poisoned garment which burned her to death as soon as it touched her shoulders; then she killed her two sons by Jason, killed Creon, and burned his palace and Jason's to the ground. Finally, taunting her grief-crazed husband, she rose in the air and escaped to Athens in a chariot drawn by winged dragons. There she lived with and may have even married king Aegeus. As for the hero of the Argonautic expedition, he killed himself, according to one story, or was killed, according to another, by a piece of wood which fell on him as he was sleeping under his famous ship, the *Argo*.

Meleager and Atalanta

MELEAGER, the son of OENEUS, king of Calydon, and ALTHAEA, and brother of Heracles' wife, Deianeira, and half-brother of Tydeus, is one of the greatest and most attractive figures in Greek legend. He was with Jason on the Argonautic expedition, but his greatest, and last, adventure was his leadership of the Calydonian Boar Hunt.

The innocent cause of this celebrated expedition was king Oeneus. While he was sacrificing to the gods, Oeneus unintentionally omitted to pay honor to Artemis. Taking this slight as a deliberate insult, the goddess sent a savage boar to ravage the country. Meleager then called on many heroes from all parts of Greece to help him in killing the wild beast. Among those who answered his call for volunteers were: AMPHIARAUS, from Argos, one of the Argonauts and later one of the Seven against Thebes; THESEUS, the great Athenian hero; IDAS and LYNCEUS, brothers from Messene, as brave and as devoted as their cousins, Castor and Pollux; PIRITHOUS, of Thessaly; JASON, the hero of the Golden Fleece; ADMETUS, of Pherae, also an Argonaut, and husband of Alcestis; PELEUS, of Thessaly, husband of Thetis and father of Achilles; ANCAEUS, of Arcadia; TELAMON, father of Teucer and Ajax; and NESTOR, whom we usually think of as a very old man but who was a young fighter at the time of the boar hunt.

Also in the expedition was one woman, ATALANTA, daughter of Iasus and Clymene, and a remarkable huntress. When she was born, her father, disappointed that she was not a boy, left her in the mountains to die of exposure. But she was suckled by a bear and brought up by hunters, who taught her their art. So skilled was she with the bow and arrows that when two centaurs pursued her with the intent of ravishing her, she calmly waited until they were within shooting range and dispatched them with two arrows.

Jason, Nestor, and Telamon began the attack on the infuriated boar, but to no purpose. Atalanta was the first to draw blood, although the wound she caused was a slight one. Meleager hailed it with great glee and praised her skill and bravery. Attracted by his shouts, Peleus, Amphiaraus, Theseus, Jason, and Ancaeus continued to hurl their spears at the beast, who rushed on Ancaeus and killed him. Finally, Meleager gave the boar his deathblow and was praised and congratulated by his comrades as the glorious hunter. But, instead of accepting their plaudits, Meleager picked up the skin and the head of the dead animal—the prizes of victory—and handed them to Atalanta, partly because he was in love with her and partly because his gallantry made him feel that she was entitled to the honor as she had inflicted the first wound.

Angered and humiliated at having to play a role subordinate to a girl, even a beautiful girl, two brothers of Queen Althaea, PLEXIPPUS and TOXEUS, braggarts and cowards, laid rough hands on Atalanta and sought to rob her of the boar's hide. Meleager in a rage forgot that they were his uncles and ran his spear through them. In this manner he unwittingly brought about his own end. When she learned what had happened, Meleager's mother, Althaea, was torn by powerful conflicting emotions: pride and joy in her son's achievement in ridding Calydon of the threat to its security, grief and sorrow at the death of her brothers, and a mad desire for revenge when she found out that they had been killed by her own son. Then she remembered a prediction of the Fates, made when Meleager was only seven days old, that he would die as soon as a piece of wood then burning in the fire was consumed by the flames. At that time Althaea had snatched the burning wood from the hearth, put out the flame, and hidden the wood. Now, angry, bitter, confused, not in a position to realize what she was doing, and not knowing whether she was primarily a mother or a sister, she rushed to the hiding place and brought out the scorched piece of wood. Again and again she almost hurled it on the fire; again and again she pulled back her hand. At last she summoned the courage or the cruelty to throw the block on the flaming pile. It burned for a few minutes and went out; as the flame died, Meleager felt a sharp pain and breathed his last, unaware of the cause of his death. As life left him, he called for Atalanta and for his mother. Too late, Althaea repented and hanged herself, an act in which she was followed by Meleager's wife, CLEOPATRA (who is not to be confused with Antony's Cleopatra). His sisters wept for him so violently that Artemis, moved by pity, changed them into guinea-hens.

Meleager was as brave, after death, in the lower world, as he was on the battlefield; when Heracles came down to Hades, all the ghosts trembled at the sight of him and fled—all except Meleager.

In art, the conqueror of the Calydonian boar is represented as a beautiful youth, nude; in his left hand he holds a spear with the point up, or two spears with the points facing down; his right hand he holds behind him. On the right side or the left his dog looks up to him, affectionately.

Atalanta continued her exploits after the death of Meleager. At the funeral games of Jason's uncle Pelias, she bested the hero Peleus. Later, she was reconciled with her father, who was determined to find a husband for her. Atalanta was reluctant to marry but agreed only on condition that her suitors were to run a race with her. Whoever beat her in the race she would marry. So fleet of foot was she that she outraced all suitors until one MELANION (or HIPPOMENES) appeared. He obtained three wonderful golden apples from Aphrodite, and as he raced with Atalanta he dropped them one by one. Each time Atalanta (some say that she was compelled by Aphrodite) stooped to pick one up, she lost time in the race, so that Melanion won and married her. She bore him a son, PARTHENOPAEUS, who was one of the Seven against Thebes. Later, for profaning a temple of Zeus or Aphrodite, Atalanta and her husband were transformed into lions.

Oedipus and His Children

OEDIPUS, one of the most tragic figures in Greek mythology and in world literature, was the son of LAIUS, king of Thebes, and JOCASTA; and the husband of his mother and by her the father of two sons, ETEOCLES and POLYNEICES, and two daughters, AN-

TIGONE and ISMENE. Laius, son of LABDACUS—whence Oedipus and his children were called Labdacidae—received a warning from Apollo that he would be killed by his own son. Therefore, when Oedipus was born, Laius gave orders that a spike be driven through his feet and that he be exposed to die on Mount Cithaeron. The name Oedipus was appropriate, for it means "swollen feet." The infant was found by a kind-hearted shepherd who took him to his master, POLYBUS, the king of Corinth. Being childless, Polybus and his wife, MEROPE, decided to adopt the castaway, and they brought him up with love and tenderness as though he were their own son. Grown up, Oedipus heard taunts that led him to doubt his parentage. Hurrying to Delphi to find out the truth from the oracle, he did not have his doubts cleared up but he was told that it was his destiny to kill his father and marry his mother. Believing that this horrible prediction referred to Polybus and Merope, Oedipus resolved to keep away from Corinth forever. In his horror-stricken anxiety to avoid carrying out the destiny in store for him, he ran *into*—not *away from*—the fate he was seeking to escape. Fleeing in the opposite direction, he met on the road between Delphi and Daulis an old man whom, of course, he did not know and had never seen. The meeting took place at a point where three roads met, and in a quarrel caused by Oedipus' refusal to step aside, Oedipus killed the older man, along with his attendants, of whom one managed to escape with his life. The stranger—none other than Laius himself, Oedipus' real father—had been on his way to consult the oracle at Delphi, from whom the son had just come.

Oedipus continued on his journey, unaware that he had already fulfilled half of the oracle's decree. In Thebes, he solved the Riddle of the SPHINX. The Sphinx was a monster with the face of a woman, the breast, feet, and tail of a lion, and the wings of a bird, who had been sent by Hera to afflict Thebes. She sat on a hill and asked this riddle: "Who is it that walks first on four feet, then on two feet, and then on three feet?" Until someone solved this riddle the Sphinx would plague Thebes. Oedipus gave the correct answer—man—and received in return, as CREON had promised to the one who should rid the city of the plague, the kingship of Thebes and the hand of its queen, Jocasta, now a widow. He mounted the throne and married his mother, thus bringing to pass the second half of oracle's prophecy.

When famine later struck Thebes the oracle declared that the city could expect no relief until it discovered and expelled the murderer of King Laius. Then unfolded one of the greatest stories ever told, in which Oedipus set about the task of finding out who had killed his predecessor, only to learn finally, from the reluctant confession of TIRESIAS, the blind seer, that Polybus and Merope were his foster-parents, that Laius and Jocasta were his real parents, and that he had slain his own father and had married his own mother. Jocasta hanged herself and Oedipus put out his own eyes.

Then, blind and mutilated, Oedipus went into exile and left Thebes, accompanied by his daughter, Antigone, one of the noblest examples of Grecian womanhood. He found refuge in Attica, and at Colonus, near Athens, he disappeared from earth and the sight of men.

Pelops and His Sons

PELOPS, the king of Pisa in Elis, was the grandson of Zeus, and the son of TANTALUS and DIONE, who was the daughter of Atlas. His father was, according to different accounts, king of Lydia or Phrygia or Argos or Corinth. Pelops was the husband of HIPPODAMIA, the daughter of OENOMAUS, the king of Pisa; in marrying Hippodamia he also won her father's throne. By her, he had six sons, and two daughters; by AXIOCHE, a nymph, he had another son—his favorite—CHRYSIPPUS.

On one occasion, Pelops was cut up into little pieces by his father, Tantalus, and boiled. Tantalus, moved either by scientific curiosity or by a strange sense of humor, wondered whether the gods, whom he invited to a feast, would be able to distinguish between human flesh and animal. When the steaming dish was set before his guests, all the gods recognized it for what it was, pushed their plates away, and left the table—all except Demeter, who, still dazed at the loss of her daughter, ate a part of the shoulder without realizing what she was doing. At this point, Hermes, commanded by his fellow gods, assembled Pelops' limbs, made a careful check to be sure that he had picked up everything, put them into a cauldron, and went through a magic formula designed to restore life. When it was completed, Clotho, the spinning Fate, pulled Pelops out of the cauldron, as good as new except for a missing shoulder, a deficiency which was no sooner noticed than it was remedied by Demeter who, feeling herself responsible, gave him a beautiful shoulder made of ivory. In addition to being ornamental, the new shoulder was also useful, as it had the power by its touch of curing all diseases and wounds. The ivory shoulder was forever after inherited by all Pelops' descendants, the PELOPIDAE, and no doubt served as a mark of identification. For his contribution to the feast, Tantalus was punished in Hades by being afflicted with a terrible thirst and a fierce hunger and by being placed in the middle of a lake, the waters of which always drew back as he attempted to drink, and surrounded by delicious fruit trees whose branches were brushed aside as he stretched his eager hands to pluck the food. Furthermore, a huge rock, suspended over his head, always threatened to crush him. The situation of Tantalus, who was once a favorite of the gods, is remembered whenever we use the verb, *to tantalize.*

Another Pelops legend deals with his racing contest, his victory, and his marriage. Oenomaus had learned from an oracle that it was his fate to be killed by his son-in-law. Naturally desirous of avoiding this unpleasant situation, he required that all those who sought the hand and heart of his daughter, Hippodamia, oppose him in a chariot race. The ground to be covered was from Pisa to Poseidon's altar on the Corinthian isthmus. Many had tried and had lost their lives. The prize was Hippodamia—if the rash suitor won; if he failed, he was put to death. As Oenomaus' horses were faster than the wind and as his driving skill was extraordinary, any contender was at a disadvantage. Pelops, with his wife-to-be by his side, was even given a head start. Although provided with a golden chariot and exceedingly fleet horses—the gifts of Poseidon—he bribed MYRTILUS, in the king's employ, to remove a bolt from his master's chariot. Pelops promised Myrtilus half of Oenomaus' kingdom should he win. The race had no sooner begun than Oenomaus' chariot broke down; he was thrown out on his head and killed, uttering with his last breath a curse on Myrtilus that was only too soon to be carried out. Pelops won the race, the hand of Hippodamia, and the kingship of his late lamented father-in-law. Once in power on the throne, Pelops forgot or pretended to forget his promise. When Myrtilus, who was a son of Hermes, came for his half of the kingdom, Pelops took him for a ride along the coast and threw him over a convenient cliff. As the dying Myrtilus sank into the sea he, in his turn, uttered a curse on Pelops and all his tribe for countless ages to come. Pelops returned to Pisa with his bride and soon made himself powerful in

Olympia, where he expanded the Olympian games to a glory that they had never known. But the curse of Myrtilus—the famous curse on the House of Pelops—worked itself out to a horrible end, all the calamities that fell on the Pelopidae being attributed to it.

A third legend deals with Pelops and the bad feeling between ATREUS and THYESTES, two of his sons by Hippodamia, and Chrysippus, who was the apple of his eye. Hippodamia and her sons, hating Chrysippus, murdered him and threw his body into a well. Pelops, who knew what was going on, had good reason to suspect Atreus and Thyestes and banished them forever from his kingdom. Hippodamia, afraid that her part in the affair would be found out, fled to Argolis, and never came back. When she died, however, Pelops transported her remains to Olympia and gave her decent burial.

After his own death, Pelops was honored as a great hero and his name had such magic that it was constantly on the lips of poets and was associated by them with his numerous descendants and with the many cities they inhabited. The name of the southern peninsula of Greece, the Peloponnesus —the island of Pelops—is a memorial to him.

The Seven against Thebes

The Seven against Thebes is the name given to the war against ETEOCLES, one of Oedipus' two sons. The cause of the expedition was Eteocles' failure to keep his promise to rule for a year and at its end to turn over his authority, also for a year, to his younger brother, POLYNEICES. In this way, the government of Thebes was to be carried on by each brother ruling for a year and retiring for a like period. In order to defeat his father's curse that each brother should kill the other, Polyneices left the city of Thebes. When Eteocles refused to let him have the throne for his year, Polyneices appealed to ADRASTUS, king of Argos for help.

Adrastus was the son of Talaus, and of Lysimache, and father of ARGIA and DEIPYLE. According to the legend, Polyneices appeared before Adrastus with a shield on which was painted a lion. At the same time TYDEUS appeared with a shield on which was painted a boar. Coming out to greet them, Adrastus recognized that their unconventional garb was in keeping with the terms of an oracle that had commanded him to marry his daughters to a lion and a boar. In obedience to this decree, Adrastus gave his daughter Argia to Polyneices, and Deipyle to Tydeus, and promised his all-out aid in restoring them to their thrones. In this way Adrastus became the leader of the Seven against Thebes.

Tydeus was the son of Oeneus, king of Calydon, and Periboea. Compelled to leave home because of his connection with the murder of his uncle, Melas, he had sought and found refuge at Argos. The others who joined the expedition were AMPHIARAUS, CAPANEUS, PARTHENOPAEUS, and HIPPOMEDON.

Amphiaraus, hero and prophet as well as soldier, was the son of Oecles and Hypermnestra, and father by Eriphyle of Alcamaeon and Amphilocus. His father was the companion of Heracles and fell with him in the battle against Laomedon of Troy; his mother was the only one of the husband-killing daughters of Danaüs who spared her own husband, Lynceus. Endowed with heroic strength and wisdom and the gift of vision, he enjoyed the favor of Zeus and Apollo, and was sometimes regarded as a son of the latter god. He had been on the hunt of the Calydonian boar with Meleager. He joined the expedition against Thebes with intense regret and much against his will, seeing, as he did, that it was bound to fail, that he and his comrades would be killed, and that Adrastus, whose motives were not of the highest, would be the only one to return alive. He was forced to enter the campaign by his wife, ERIPHYLE, the sister of Adrastus. Eriphyle, bribed by Polyneices' gift of the beautiful (but fatal) necklace of Harmonia, insisted that he do so, although her husband had told her that it would mean his death.

Capaneus of Argos, the son of Hipponous, was the husband of Evadne and the father of Sthenelus, Diomedes' charioteer.

Parthenopaeus was the son of Atalanta and Melanion (or Hippomenes).

The expedition set off for Thebes stopping first at Nemea. While there a serpent killed the king's child, OPHELTES, and the warriors crushed the snake and buried the child. Amphiaraus claimed that this was an ill omen for the expedition.

Arrived at the walls of Thebes, the Seven sent Tydeus into Thebes as an ambassador in the hope that it might be possible to reach a peaceful settlement and thus avoid bloodshed. When he arrived in Thebes he found the Theban chiefs feasting with King Eteocles. As they were in no mood to listen to diplomacy, Tydeus challenged them to single combat and proceeded to defeat each one. The Thebans then ambushed him with fifty soldiers, but, aided by Athene, who always looked on him with favor, he killed all of them, except MAEON, whom he allowed to escape.

The Seven then attacked the city and a fierce battle raged, with the forces of Adrastus suffering severe losses and being forced to fall back. Both sides agreed that Eteocles and Polyneices should meet in single combat. They did, and both perished, thus fulfilling their father's curse. ANTIGONE, sister of the slain men, buried Polyneices in defiant disobedience of the order of CREON, the new king of Thebes, that the body should remain exposed, an act of loyalty for which she paid with her life by committing suicide in the underground prison into which she was cast by the command of Creon.

The battle was then resumed, with further losses by the Seven. Tydeus killed Melanippus but was also mortally wounded by him. As he lay on the ground dying, Athene came to him, prepared to administer a remedy that would restore his life and make him immortal. However, the good intentions of the goddess were spoiled by a trick of Amphiaraus, who had a deep hatred for Tydeus. He cut off the head of Melanippus, just slain by Tydeus, and placed it before him. In a wild fury, Tydeus broke open the skull of his enemy and sucked out his brain. Disgusted and sickened by this awful act, Athene turned away from her former favorite and left him to his fate. Grateful to him for having spared his life when he might have taken it, Maeon buried the body of Tydeus.

Hippomedon distinguished himself by the fury of his attack after the death of Tydeus. He was wounded by Lycus, whose javelin pierced his helmet. Although in a weak condition from loss of blood, he continued to fight with reckless courage, and aided by Alcon of Sicyonia, killed Mopsus, Polites, Eryx, and many other famous Thebans. He cut off the hand of Leontius when he found him plundering the dead bodies. Tisiphone, one of the Furies, induced him to leave the battlefield by causing him to believe that Adrastus had been captured, but the benefit to the Thebans was of slight duration. As soon as he discovered the fraud, Hippomedon returned to the fray, all the more eager, if possible, to renew the fighting. He drove his foes into the river, followed them, and proceeded to execute tremendous slaughter. Finally, resisted by the river itself, which was not friendly to him, he was thrown on shore, overpowered by a large force of Thebans, and slain, in spite of Hera's pleading for his life with Zeus.

Parthenopaeus met his death on the Theban wall while the city was being stormed, brought down by a rock thrown by Periclymenus, son of Poseidon and Chloris, who was a daughter of the blind seer, Tiresias.

Amphiaraus fought with great courage and skill but no matter what he did he could not avoid his fate. Just as he was on the point of being speared by Periclymenus, Zeus split the earth open with a thunderbolt and commanded it to swallow Amphiaraus so that he might make him immortal.

Capaneus was slain when, mounting the walls of Thebes, he foolishly boasted that not even lightning could frighten him. As he spoke, Zeus struck him dead with one of his bolts. The grief-stricken Evadne, his wife, threw herself on his funeral pyre and perished with him in the flames.

Of all those who took part in the war Adrastus was the only one who was not killed, as Amphiaraus had predicted. He escaped, thanks to the swiftness of his black horse, ARION, a gift of Heracles.

The disastrous adventure of the Seven against Thebes had a sequel, when, ten years later, the children of the Seven resolved to avenge the fate of their fathers. They precipitated the war known as the War of the Epigoni (the Greek word meaning "descendants"). The Argive leader was ALCMAEON, son of Amphiaraus. Other Argives who participated were AEGIALEUS, son of Adrastus; PROMACHUS, son of Parthenopaeus; DIOMEDES, son of Tydeus; STHENELOS, son of Capaneus; and AMPHILOCUS, another son of Amphiaraus. The Argives were successful and they set their own king on the throne. Aegialeus was killed, however, and news of the loss caused his father, Adrastus, to die of grief.

Ten years earlier, before leaving Argos for Thebes, Amphiaraus had uttered a terrible curse on his wife, and had commanded his young sons to avenge his death by killing her. After his victory at Thebes, Alcmaeon carried out the curse, but was punished for his crime by madness. After being purified and partially cured, he married, first, ALPHESIBOEA (or Arsinoë), daughter of Phegeus, king of Psophis in Arcadia, and then, completely cured, he married CALLIRRHOE, daughter of Achelous. By her, he had two sons, Acarnan and Amphoterus. He was later robbed and killed by Phegeus' sons, Agenor and Pronous, when he was bringing to his wife the necklace of Harmonia. The two sons of Alcmaeon then killed the two sons of Phegeus and then Phegeus himself, and his wife. Settling at Epirus, they established a kingdom, called after the older brother, Acarnania.

The Trojan War

The greatest war in classical mythology was the ten-year conflict between the Greeks and the Trojans. Legend has it that the cause of the war rested with the gods. Zeus, believing the earth to be overstocked with people, decided that some way must be found to rid the earth of some of its inhabitants. The best plan seemed to be to cause a war to be fought between Greece and Troy.

Troy at that time was one of the great cities of the world. It had been founded by ILOS, son of TROS and CALLIRRHOE. One time, Ilos, having been victorious in a wrestling match, was given a spotted cow as a gift, and was told by an oracle to build a city where the cow would lie down. Ilos followed the cow until she rested on a hill, where he built the city. He called it Ilium, after himself. It was as Ilium that the Greeks knew the city, but the name preferred by the inhabitants of the city was Troy, after Tros, Ilos' father.

When the city was built, Ilos asked Zeus to send a sign of his favor. The next day Ilos found an image of Pallas Athene which the great god had evidently sent down from the heavens. This statue was treasured in the city as a PALLADIUM, or safeguard. It was believed that as long as the Palladium remained in the city, Troy could not fall.

To return now to the war plans of Zeus. He directed Eris, Discord, to proceed to the banquet of the gods at the marriage of Peleus and Thetis and there to cast down a golden apple inscribed, "To the Fairest." The goddesses Hera, Aphrodite, and Athene each put in her claim, and Zeus appointed a judge to decide the dispute. The judge was PARIS, a son of Priam and Hecuba, king and queen of Troy. Each goddess attempted to influence Paris' vote. Hera offered him wealth and power; Athena, wisdom and glory in war; and Aphrodite, the most attractive woman in the world for his wife. Paris realized that his was an unenviable position, for no matter how he decided he would bring down upon himself, and probably upon Troy, the wrath of two of the goddesses. Finally, with the goddesses assembled on Mount Ida, he cast his vote in favor of Aphrodite, and gave her the golden apple.

In return for the prize, Aphrodite agreed to give Paris as his wife the beautiful HELEN, daughter of Zeus and Leda, even though Helen at that time was married to MENELAUS, the son of Atreus and Aerope, and had a daughter by him, HERMIONE. The goddess directed Paris to build a ship and sail to Sparta with AENEAS, her son by Anchises, as his companion.

At Sparta Paris was treated most hospitably by Menelaus, who was, of course, unaware of the plot. Menelaus then having sailed for Crete, Paris and Helen, influenced by Aphrodite, fell in love, and, taking much of Menelaus' wealth with them, set off for Troy, where they were married.

On his return, Menelaus, discovering what had occurred, consulted with his brother, Agamemnon, and determined to war against the Trojans. The great heroes of Greece joined him in the expedition. We take up now the most outstanding of these heroes individually.

ACHILLES, the bravest and handsomest of all the Greeks, was the son of PELEUS, a mortal, king of the Myrmidons in Thessaly, and of THETIS, a sea-goddess. Presented by his mother with a choice between glory and a short life and infamy and a long one, he deliberately chose the former, and he knew from the beginning that he would not return alive from the Trojan War, in which he led fifty ships against Troy.

Many of the legends concerning him are connected with his mother's well-meaning but unsuccessful attempts to help him. It was Thetis who attempted to make him immortal by subjecting him to a nightly process of baking, who dipped him in the River Styx to make him invulnerable. The first effort failed because it was interrupted before completion by the entrance of Peleus; the second, because Thetis forgot in her anxiety that her hand was covering the heel by which she was holding him.

Achilles is one of the most attractive of mythological characters, having more than his share of admirable qualities. He was superlatively handsome; his strength was so great that he could kill wild animals with his bare hands; on the field of battle his appearance alone—to say nothing of his terrible courage—paralyzed his foes with fear. He loved his parents and his friends, and his loyalty knew no limit. He loved fighting for the sake of fighting, but he was generous to beaten enemies. In his less admirable qualities he was thoroughly human: he was unspeakably violent in his anger, heartless in his revenge, hysterical in his grief.

By Deidamia, one of the daughters of Lycomedes, king of Scyros, he was the father of NEOPTOLEMUS, a worthy son of a worthy father, and one of the heroes of the war.

The soldiers of Achilles were the MYRMIDONS, creatures who had been changed from ants into men by Zeus at the request of AEACUS, Achilles' grandfather. The legend tells that at Hera's instigation a pestilence was wiping out the population of the island of Aegina. Aeacus prayed to Zeus for aid and while praying noticed a colony of ants. He entreated the gods to make of the ants men to fill his city. That night Aeacus dreamed that his prayer was answered, and, to be sure, the next morning he espied a multitude approaching his palace who proclaimed themselves as his faithful servitors. The men were named Myrmidons, for the Greek word for ant, *myrmex*.

AGAMEMNON, the king of Mycenae and the commander-in-chief of the Greek forces against Troy, was the son of ATREUS and AEROPE, who was thrown into the sea by her husband because of her adulterous relations with his brother, THYESTES. Agamemnon was the husband of CLYTEMNESTRA. His contribution to the war effort was a hundred ships, fully equipped and staffed, and a loan of sixty ships to the Arcadians. A brave fighter, he was of a proud and passionate nature, but a tendency to be easily discouraged was his chief weakness.

AJAX was the son of Telamon, king of Salamis. He led twelve ships against Troy, and was a close second to Achilles in strength and courage.

AJAX THE LESSER, so called because of his smallness and in order to distinguish him from the other Ajax, was also known as the Locrian Ajax, in allusion to his father, Oileus, king of the Locrians. What he lacked in height he more than made up for by his contribution to the struggle, bringing, as he did, forty ships against Troy. He was one of the bravest and swiftest of the Greeks, and his spear was a mighty weapon.

NESTOR, the king of Pylos, was one of the twelve sons of Neleus and Chloris, and the only son who was not slain by Heracles when he invaded Pylos. As a young man, he had distinguished himself by defeating both the Arcadians and the Eleans, by taking a major part in the battle of the Lapithae against the Centaurs, and by his activity in the Calydonian hunt and the Argonautic expedition. Nestor, like Priam, was an old man by the time of the Trojan War, but he gave a good account of himself in the battle against Troy not only in an advisory capacity but in actual combat. With his sons, ANTILOCHUS and THRASYMEDES, he sailed against Troy with ninety ships. Having ruled over three generations of his people, Nestor was venerated for his justice, his knowledge of war, his wisdom, and his power; in the latter qualities he was regarded as equal to the immortal gods. He was so eloquent that language sweeter than honey flowed from his lips. Homer praises him with such enthusiasm—he is elder statesman in the *Iliad*—that the poet was suspected of being a citizen of Pylos. The reputation Nestor earned in his day, giving him the title of the Pylian Sage, has come down to the present, his name being used as a synonym for a wise old man.

PROTESILAUS was the son of Iphiculus and Astyoche, rulers of Phylace in Thessaly, and brother of Podarces, who took his place. He led many Thessalian warriors against Troy.

PHILOCTETES, the most famous archer in the Trojan War, was the son of Poeas and the friend and armor-bearer of the great Heracles. One of his most celebrated deeds was setting fire to the funeral pile on Mount Oeta, on which the suffering Heracles perished, a deed Heracles rewarded by leaving him his bow and poisoned arrows. On the way to Troy, he commanded seven ships.

IDOMENEUS, the king of Crete, was the son of Deucalion, and the grandson of Minos, one of the judges of the dead in Hades, and of Pasiphae, who fell in love with a bull. As leader of the Cretans against Troy, he had eighty ships.

PATROCLUS, Achilles' dearest friend,

was the son of Menoetius of Pous and Sthenele, and the grandson of Actor and Aegina. The deep friendship between these two heroes provides the frequently grim mythology of the Greeks with one of its most pleasing touches.

DIOMEDES was the son of Tydeus, the king of Calydon, who was one of the Seven against Thebes, and of Deipyle. Like Idomeneus, he was in command of eighty ships in the Trojan War.

PALAMEDES was the son of Nauplius, the king of Euboea, and Clymene, and the brother of Oeax. Palamedes was regarded by the Greeks as the inventor of lighthouses, weights and measures, the game of checkers, and dice. To the original sixteen-letter alphabet of Cadmus he was believed to have added four letters, theta, xi, phi, and chi.

TEUCER, another great archer, was the son of Telamon of Salamis, and of Hesione, daughter of Laomedon, the king of Troy who cheated Poseidon, Apollo, and Heracles.

MACHAON and PODALIRIUS were the sons of Aesculapius, the god of medicine, and Epione, whose name means "the soother." They led the Thessalian troops from Tricca in thirty ships. Inheriting their father's skill, they were to act as physicians and surgeons to the Greek soldiers.

Only ODYSSEUS, the king of Ithaca, was reluctant to join in the war against Troy, feigning madness. But Palamedes suspected him of artifice and, to test him, placed Odysseus' son, TELEMACHUS, before a plough. Odysseus saved his son by turning the plough aside, revealing himself to be quite sane. He then had to agree to participate in the war.

The Greeks assembled at Aulis to sacrifice to the gods before setting out. There the prophet CALCHAS announced that the war would last ten years, and also predicted that the first Greek to land on Trojan soil would be killed. The fleet of a thousand ships was ready to set sail from Aulis but Agamemnon, having boasted of his skill as a hunter, offended Artemis, who sent a severe storm which detained them. Calchas read the signs and predicted that only the sacrifice of IPHIGENIA, Agamemnon's daughter, would assuage Artemis. Agamemnon ruefully consented and the girl was made ready for the sacrifice, but just as they were about to offer her, Artemis relented and carried Iphigenia to Tauris.

The Trojan heroes who were to attempt to resist the attack on their city were worthy opponents of the Greeks in every respect.

The titular leader of the Trojans was PRIAM, the king and son of Laomedon, but he was an old man when the war began so he turned the generalship of his armies over to HECTOR, his oldest son and husband of ANDROMACHE; he was the chief hero of the Trojans as Achilles was of the Greeks. Hector had a great and deserved reputation for bravery.

PARIS, the second son of Priam and Hecuba, had been exposed at birth on Mount Ida because of Hecuba's dream that she had given birth to a firebrand, the flames of which enveloped the entire city of Troy. On Ida he was suckled by a she-bear in his early infancy and later brought up by a shepherd who found him and reared him with his own children. The name Paris was given to him by the shepherd. He was also called Alexander, which means "defender of men," because of his bravery as a shepherd in championing both man and beast. Paris married OENONE, a daughter of the river-god, Cebren, whom he deserted for Helen. For his responsibility in starting the war he was hated by the Trojans.

Other sons of Priam and Hecuba who participated in the war were DEIPHOBUS, TROILUS, and POLYDORUS.

Among the other Trojan heroes were:

ANTENOR, the son of Aesyetes and Cleomestra, and one of the wisest of the Trojans; AENEAS, the son of Anchises and Aphrodite, of whom more will be told in the section on Roman mythology, since he was the hero of Virgil's AENEID; SARPEDON, a Lycian prince and the son of Zeus and Europa; GLAUCUS, also a Lycian prince, the son of Hippolochus and the grandson of that Glaucus who was torn to pieces by his own horses; RHESUS, the son of the Thracian king, Eioneus, and the Muse, Terpsichore; MEMNON, the son of Priam's brother, Tithonus, and Eos. Also fighting on the side of the Trojans was a great heroine, PENTHESILEA, queen of the Amazons, who was the daughter of Ares and Otrera.

Before reaching the shores of Troy the Greeks put in at the tiny island of Tenedos to make the necessary sacrifices, and here Philoctetes was bitten in the foot by a snake. So offensive was the stench of his wound and so horrible were his cries of agony that his comrades, at the urging of Odysseus, left him alone on the island. Here he suffered and limped for ten years—the war meanwhile proceeding without him.

Here too the first quarrel between Achilles and Agamemnon took place, but it was made up and the fleet passed on to Troy.

When the Greek forces landed on the shores of Troy the first of their number to land was Protesilaus, and, according to the prediction of Calchas, he was the first to die. His comrades paid this brave hero deep homage, and Hermes brought him back from the dead so that he might see once more his grieving wife, LAODAMIA. When he returned to the underworld, she killed herself.

Odysseus took revenge on Palamedes, who had revealed he was a malingerer, by planting a forged letter, supposedly from Priam, in his bed. Upon the discovery of the letter, and Odysseus' charge that he was a traitor, the angered Greeks stoned Palamedes to death.

The tides of war ebbed and flowed for nine years, first one side then the other gaining the advantage. Then the hard feelings between Achilles and Agamemnon flared up again, this time over CHRYSEIS, a daughter of a priest of Apollo, whom the Greeks had captured and given to Agamemnon. Agamemnon refused to return her to her father, whereupon Apollo sent a pestilence among the Greeks, during which many of the armies were stricken and died. Achilles then called a council of war, where Calchas declared that the pestilence would stop only when Chryseis was given back to her father. Agamemnon agreed, but insisted that some other maiden be given in her stead. Agamemnon then sent a herald to take from Achilles the maiden who had been allotted to him. At this point, Achilles' mother, Thetis, intervened with Zeus and made him promise victory to the Trojans for the shabby way in which Achilles' comrades had treated him. Achilles then sat in his tent and sulked.

It was only when the Greek cause was in serious danger of being lost that Patroclus succeeded in persuading his bosom friend to lend him his weapons and his suit of armor and to let him lead his Myrmidons into battle. Thus equipped, Patroclus drove the Trojans back, but he lost his life in doing so, as he was killed by Hector. Antilochus, Achilles' best friend next to Patroclus, was selected by his comrades for the unpleasant duty of breaking the news of Patroclus' death to Achilles.

Burning for revenge, Achilles took the field again. Reconciled with Agamemnon, he sought out Hector. Brave as Hector was, his great courage failed him for a moment and he fled at the sight of his foe and ran around the city three times with Achilles in pursuit. Even Zeus felt sorry for him, but when the scales of fate decided against him, no force could alter that which must be. Achilles, finally catching up with Hector, brought him down with a well-aimed spear. So great was his fury that he dragged Hector's dead body behind his chariot three times around the city walls, which was one of the few unheroic acts performed by Homer's hero.

Always a favorite with the gods, Hector was aided by them in life and protected by them in death. Aphrodite sprinkled his corpse with ambrosia to save it from decay and Apollo saved it from being mangled as it was dragged over the rough stones. When his rage was somewhat appeased, Achilles, moved by the prayers of the aged Priam, gave the grief-stricken father his son's body. Hector was buried with great pomp and ceremony at Troy and there he was in days to come worshipped by the citizens, who came to offer sacrifices at his grave. As a soldier, Hector was a great hero; as a man, he was a good son, a loving husband, and a devoted father. Not without reason was he loved by immortal gods and mortal poets.

Penthesilea joined the Trojans after Hector's death, and her women, all trained fighters, were a great source of trouble to the Greek heroes. Achilles had to slay her but he hated to do it as she was young, beautiful, and brave. As he mourned over the dying queen, mortally wounded by his arrow, the soldier and the conqueror became the man and the lover. His grief was misinterpreted and ridiculed by THERSITES, a coarse and vulgar Greek, and a foul jest sprang from his lips which so infuriated Achilles that he killed Thersites with a blow of his fist. Diomedes, a kinsman of the ungallant Greek, threw her body into the river Scamander, but Achilles rescued it and buried it tenderly on the banks of the Xanthus.

Memnon joined the conflict at this point, killing Antilochus when that Greek warrior threw himself in front of his father, Nestor, just as Memnon was about to kill him. Antilochus' death was avenged by Achilles in a fierce contest in which the issue was long in doubt. While the heroes were struggling, with victory seeming to favor first one and then the other, Zeus weighed their fates in his scales and noted that the side containing Memnon's fate sank. Moved by the pity that frequently stirred him, the god of gods made him immortal in order to lessen his mother's grief. A flock of birds—Memnonides they are called—flew out of his funeral pile and fought over his ashes; every year his grave on the Hellespont was visited by them and great was their grief. Even Zeus' well-meant kindness seems not to have been completely successful: the mother still wept for the son, and the early morning dewdrops which she shed every day were supposed to be the teardrops of Eos.

Achilles then chased the Trojans back to their city, and as he was forcing his way in he was killed by an arrow aimed at his one unprotected spot, his heel (hence the expression "the heel of Achilles" to refer to a vulnerable spot). The arrow was shot by Paris, guided by Apollo. Ajax carried the body of Achilles to the ships while Odysseus fought off the Trojans. Then Thetis proposed that Achilles' armor go to the one who had done the most to save his corpse, and Ajax and Odysseus contended for it. When Odysseus was declared the victor, Ajax, in great shame and anger, lost his senses and mistook a flock of sheep for his enemies and killed them. Upon coming to his senses, he killed himself in mortification at his mistake. From his blood, according to legend, grew the purple lily bearing on its petals the first two letters of his name. He never got over his resentment of Odysseus, cherishing the feeling even in the lower regions.

At this point Odysseus captured HELENUS, also a son of Priam, but hardly a Trojan hero. Endowed with prophetic power, Helenus told the Greeks that they could never take

Troy unless they had the help of the bow and arrows of Heracles, which were in the possession of Philoctetes, who had been left behind on the island. Odysseus and Diomedes went to bring him and his precious weapons back. After a certain amount of necessary and understandable persuasion, Philoctetes having resented his forced inactivity, he agreed to accompany them. Arrived at Troy, he did his duty nobly and to him fell the honor of killing Paris. His wound was cured by Aesculapius, or by his sons, Machaon and Podalirius.

As Paris was dying, he fled to Oenone, his long-forgotten wife, for aid, but she refused her assistance, feeling that, no longer being his wife, she did not wish to be his nurse. Repenting after he died, she committed suicide.

Helenus, the Trojan traitor, revealed that not only would the Greeks need Heracles' bow and arrows, but also Neoptolemus, the son of Achilles. The youth was accordingly brought to the city by Odysseus.

The Greeks had learned of the existence of the Palladium and were determined to gain possession of it, a deed that Diomedes accomplished.

Certain now of victory, the Greeks had only to find the means of getting their army into the city. Odysseus (or Athene) conceived of a monstrous ruse—they would build a tremendous wooden figure of a horse, hollow inside, in which they would place a contingent of soldiers. Meanwhile, to mislead the Trojans, the remainder of the Greeks would sail out of sight, but remain nearby.

The trick worked as planned. One morning the Trojans awoke to find the large horse before their gates. What to do with it? The majority, taking it as a sign that the Greeks had given up, were for drawing it into the city. Among the dissenters was CASSANDRA, Priam's daughter, who had been given the power of prophecy by Apollo but was afflicted with the curse of never being believed. Another dissenter was LAOCOÖN, who proclaimed that he feared the Greeks bearing gifts, but then two serpents appeared and crushed Laocoön and his two sons to death, the people taking this as a sign that the gods viewed Laocoön's objections with disfavor. Accordingly, singing and dancing, they hauled the wooden horse into the city, thinking peace had come. In the middle of the night the Greeks emerged from the horse, and, aided by the return of the men who had sailed, they wrought terrible havoc in the city. Neoptolemus slew Priam while he was fleeing the city with Hecuba. Menelaus killed Deiphobus. Odysseus killed Astyanax, the son of Hector. Antenor was spared because he had advised the Trojans to return Helen to the Greeks. So ended the ten-year war against Troy.

Numerous legends are concerned with the aftermath of the war—dealing with the Greek heroes who returned home, or attempted to return home.

Helen, the beautiful cause of all the trouble, regained the love and confidence of her first husband, Menelaus. Even before the end of the conflict she had shown her love for him by secretly admitting him to the room of Deiphobus, her husband after the death of Paris, where Menelaus killed him after cutting off his nose and ears.

Although Menelaus, with Helen and Nestor, was one of the first to leave Troy, he wandered about the shores of the Mediterranean for eight years before he finally arrived home. Menelaus spent the rest of his life at Sparta and lived in great happiness and wealth with Helen. Their magnificent palace dazzled the eyes with its brilliant light, which rivalled the sun and the moon. As the husband of a daughter of Zeus, Menelaus never died; with Helen, he was, after a timeless period, carried off by the gods and entered Elysium, the happy land—alive.

Agamemnon returned home safely from the war with the beautiful but unfortunate Cassandra, who fell to him as his prize. Meanwhile, however, his wife Clytemnestra had fallen in love with AEGISTHUS, and the couple murdered him at the banquet celebrating his return. However, Agamemnon's children, ELECTRA and ORESTES, avenged their father's death by killing Clytemnestra and her lover. Orestes later married HERMIONE, daughter of Helen and Menelaus.

Neoptolemus received Andromache, Hector's widow, as his prize, and by her he had a son, MOLOSSUS, who is said to have given his name to the country or region of Molossia. By Lanassa, a granddaughter of Heracles, he had a son to whom the later kings of Epirus traced back their descent. Neoptolemus died at Delphi and was annually worshipped as a hero with appropriate sacrifices by the Delphians (although, according to another legend, he was killed by them at the command of Pythia, the priestess of Apollo at Delphi).

Ajax the Lesser, on the night of the taking of Troy, attempted to violate Cassandra, and for this he was punished by Athene. While returning from the Trojan War he was shipwrecked, but managed to swim safely to shore. However, he made the mistake of boasting that he had escaped without the help of the gods, something that always incensed them. Poseidon therefore split the rock on which he stood and Ajax was drowned. He was worshipped as a hero by the Locrians, who always honored him by leaving a vacant place in his name in drawing up the line of battle. With the greater Ajax and with the other famous heroes, he was supposed to go on living in the island of Leuce, happy in the companionship of the one and only Achilles.

Idomeneus lost his own son in consequence of a rash promise he had made to Poseidon to sacrifice the first person he met on landing, if the god would grant him a safe return from the Trojan War, and deliver him from a storm that sprang up while he was on his way home. As he touched shore his son ran out to greet him. Bound by his vow, the father had no choice but to offer up his son's life. The plague that followed was attributed by the Cretans to this act, and Idomeneus was deposed and banished. He found refuge in Calabria in Italy and later in Asia, where he was believed to have died and been buried. At Cnosus, the capital of king Minos, he was worshipped as a hero, along with his nephew, Meriones, who had sailed with him against Troy.

Diomedes, returning to his home in Argos after the war, found his wife Aegiale living in adultery with Hippolytus. Leaving Argos, he went to Aetolia, and to Daunia, in Italy, where he married Euippe, the daughter of king Daunus. According to different stories, he died in Daunia or in Argos, or elsewhere, and was buried on one of the islands of the Adriatic, named after him the Diomedian Islands. His companions, grieving at his loss, were changed into birds. Forever after, the story tells us, they always flew in the direction of Greek ships and away from Roman ones.

Teucer, returning from the war, was banished by his father, who held him responsible for the death of his step-brother, Ajax. Acting on the advice of Apollo, he made a new home for himself in Cyprus, where he soon rose to power and founded the town of Salamis. By Eune, daughter of Cyprus, he was the father of Asteria.

Podalirius, after the fall of Troy, stayed with the prophet Calchas until he died. He then settled at Syrnos in Caria. He had a hero's shrine in Apulia, next to the one honoring Calchas.

The Wanderings of Odysseus

The wanderings of ODYSSEUS (who was known to the Romans as Ulysses) after the Trojan War are as extensively detailed as the war itself, and they form the subject of Homer's great second epic, *The Odyssey.*

On his homeward journey, which was to last ten years, Odysseus first stopped at the city of Ismarus, where, after a brief encounter with the inhabitants, he sailed again and was borne by a storm to the land of the LOTOPHAGI, the Lotus-eaters. Here his men partook of the lotus, which caused them to lose all thought of returning home. Odysseus had to drag them back to the ships and tie them to the benches.

He then set sail with a dozen comrades for Sicily, where he had an exciting adventure with the Cyclops POLYPHEMUS in his cave. The horrible giant ate six of Odysseus' companions and kept the other six and Odysseus himself prisoners in his cave. The hero saved his life by making the monster drunk and blinding him in his one eye with a burning pole; he and his followers then escaped by holding on to the under side of the sheep as they were allowed to pass out of the cave. The wily Odysseus had told Polyphemus that his name was Nobody; when the giant cried out in his agony for his fellows to help him they asked him who was hurting him, to which he roared "Nobody is hurting me." As a result they left him alone to nurse his wound.

Odysseus' next stop was at the island of AEOLUS, king of the winds, who gave him a bag of winds to carry him and his companions home, but some of the sailors opened the bag, letting the winds out, and the vessel was driven back to the point it had so recently left. Annoyed at not having his instructions followed, Aeolus refused further help to Odysseus and told him that he must shift for himself.

After visiting several other places, Odysseus finally reached the island of Aeaea, the home of CIRCE, a sorceress who specialized in turning men into swine. The hero sent his men to explore the island and all of them, with the exception of EURYLOCHUS, were transformed into swine by Circe. Aided by Hermes, whose friendship for him somewhat counteracted the hatred of Poseidon, Odysseus confronted Circe without fear of falling a victim to her power, and forced her to release his companions and to change them back to men. Once she knew that she was defeated and that her magic was useless, Circe was perfectly willing to be friendly, and even affectionate. It was by her advice that Odysseus sailed across the river Oceanus and landed in the country of the Cimmerians. He went to Hades and had a long talk with the blind prophet, TIRESIAS, who told him how to get home.

From Hades, Odysseus returned to Aeaea and was further advised by Circe, now his friend, who gave him a wind that would carry him and his crew to the island of the SIRENS, those lovely sea-maidens who sing songs that men cannot resist. Knowing the danger, Odysseus put wax pellets in the ears of his companions and had himself tied to the mast of the ship so that he could enjoy the ravishing melodies of the enchanting maidens without being able to yield to them and throw himself into the sea. Having escaped this peril, Odysseus and his band met another in sailing between the twin monsters, SCYLLA and CHARYBDIS, the former of whom caught and made a meal of six of his party.

Landing at Thrinacia, his companions disregarded the advice of Tiresias the seer, and killed some of the black oxen of Helios. For this impious act, Zeus punished them when they again ventured on the sea by hurling a bolt of lightning at their ship, and all were drowned, except Odysseus, who managed to save himself through the resourcefulness that was one of his outstanding qualities and of which he was a symbol.

Ten days later, he reached the island of Ogygia, the home of the nymph CALYPSO, daughter of Atlas. She gave him a grand reception and was so eager to marry him, or for him to marry her, that she promised to make him immortal and forever young. Although Odysseus refused her offers, he stayed with Calypso for eight years, but he really wanted to get home as he was beginning to feel lonesome for his wife, PENELOPE. Athene spoke to Zeus about this, and the king of gods, decreeing that Calypso must surrender Odysseus, sent Hermes to Calypso with the message. Having no choice but to obey the royal command, Calypso helped Odysseus to build a raft that carried him away from her and the island forever.

Eighteen days later he was in sight of Scheria, the island of the Phaeacians, but before he was able to land, a storm sent by his old enemy, Poseidon, threw him off the raft and he was in danger of drowning. Aided by LEUCOTHEA, a marine goddess, and by Athene, always his friend, he reached the shore, buoyed up by Leucothea's scarf. Exhausted by the buffeting he had received, Odysseus sank to the ground and fell fast asleep. He was awakened by gentle female voices and opened his eyes to see NAUSICAÄ, the beautiful daughter of King ALCINOUS and Queen ARETE, and her attendant maidens. She brought him to her father's palace where he was treated kindly. Demodocus, the king's minstrel, sang of the fall of Troy so movingly that the hero was stirred to tears and told the story of his wanderings when he was questioned. Without delay, the humane monarch provided a ship for the homesick hero, who had now been away from Ithaca long enough for many changes to have taken place. His father, LAERTES, old and weak from grief, had retired into the country; ANTICLEA, his mother, had died of sorrow and disappointment at never seeing him again. His son, TELEMACHUS, an infant when Odysseus had left on the expedition against Troy, was a young man when the father finally returned home, and Penelope, wife and mother, had had her hands full looking after the house, bringing up a child, taking care of an old father-in-law, managing servants, and keeping a hundred hungry, unruly, and undignified suitors at arm's length. She put off the suitors by insisting that she would not choose one of them until she had finished a large garment that she was making as a gift for her old father-in-law, Laertes. Actually, however, each night she unwove what she had done during the day.

When Odysseus landed at Ithaca, Athene changed him into an ugly old beggar so that he would not be recognized before it was time for the hero to declare himself, but his faithful dog, ARGUS, knew his master, and his joy at seeing him again was so great that it killed him. Odysseus was received with kindness by EUMAEUS, a swineherd who had given long and loyal service to the house of Odysseus, and he stayed with him to await developments.

Telemachus now returned from Sparta and Pylos, where he had been tracking down information concerning his father; to him Odysseus revealed his identity. Between them, father and son devised a plan to dispose of the suitors without delay. Penelope had promised that she would accept as a husband the suitor who could draw the great bow of Odysseus—a feat that only he could accomplish. When all the suitors had their try and failed, Odysseus shot an arrow from the bow, and then shot all the suitors. Odysseus revealed himself to his wife and paid a visit of affection and respect to his aged father. The relatives of the slain suitors demanded reprisals and took up arms against Odysseus, but Athene, disguised as MENTOR, the wise friend of Odysseus and the teacher of Telemachus in his father's absence, stepped in, reconciled the warring groups, and stopped the bloodshed. Odysseus was thus restored to his wife and son.

LATER GREEK LEGENDS

Pyramus and Thisbe

PYRAMUS and THISBE were a youth and a maiden who lived in ancient Babylon. They loved each other, but their parents forbade them to marry. Their only means of communication was through the chink of a wall. Here every day they met, Pyramus on one side, Thisbe on the other, and spoke words of love until night fell.

Unable to endure their separation any longer, they resolved to meet one night and run away. At the appointed time Thisbe appeared at the meeting place. Suddenly a lioness, with blood dripping from her jaws, appeared. Frightened, Thisbe fled, but in doing so she dropped her cloak. The lioness snatched it and tore it to shreds with her fangs, then ran off into the woods.

When Pyramus appeared a short time later he noticed Thisbe's torn, bloodstained cloak, and the animal's footprints. It was clear to him that Thisbe had been killed. Blaming himself for her supposed death, he plunged a sword into his heart. Blood spurted from his wound and stained the mulberries on the nearby tree all red.

Then Thisbe, not wishing to disappoint her lover, fearfully returned to the spot. Finding Pyramus still alive she embraced him and kissed his cold lips. He opened his eyes briefly and then died. Realizing why he had died, she resolved to be as brave as he and plunged the sword into her heart. It is said that the fruit of the mulberry tree is red from the blood of the lovers.

Hero and Leander

LEANDER was a youth who lived in Abydos, a town on the Asian shore of the straits which separate Europe and Asia. Across the straits lived his beloved, HERO, a priestess of Aphrodite. Each night Leander swam across the straits to Hero, guided by a torch which she held high. But one night a severe storm arose and the torch was extinguished. Leander lost his strength in the rough waters and was drowned. Hero, finding his body washed up on the shore, killed herself.

Pygmalion and Galatea

PYGMALION, a sculptor of Cyprus, resolved to live only through his art and never to marry. But once he molded a figure of a woman that was so beautiful that he fell in love with it. He asked Aphrodite that she might find for him a living woman as beautiful as his statue. But the goddess, knowing that he really desired the statue, breathed life into her form. Almost mad with joy, Pygmalion embraced his now-living creation, whom he named GALATEA, and married her.

Ibycus

IBYCUS, a poet, was en route to Corinth, when he was attacked and fatally wounded by thieves. Before he died he called upon a flock of cranes which were flying overhead to avenge him. News of Ibycus' death shocked the populace, who loved his songs, and they resolved to punish the murderers. At the theater in Corinth a play was being performed in which the Furies were so realistically and frighteningly portrayed that when the cranes flew over, the murderers, panic-stricken, thought they were the Furies themselves come for vengeance and revealed themselves as the guilty ones.

Daphnis and Chloe

Daphnis and Chloe were the shepherd and shepherdess whose love story is told in the pastoral romance by Longus, written in the fourth or fifth century A.D. From this story then the name Daphnis has come to represent a shepherd in love, and the name Chloe, his shepherdess.

Myths of the Etruscans

In NORTHERN ITALY, between the Tiber and Po rivers, there flourished during the years 900–500 B.C. a group of people whom the later Romans called Etruscans, and the Greeks the Tyrrhenians. Where the Etruscans came from is not known with certainty, but it is believed that Lydia in Asia Minor was their original homeland.

The civilization which they established in Italy was a rich one. They exploited the iron mines of the region and produced fine objects in bronze. They were also skilled in pottery work, the beauty of which is admired to this day. It is said that they introduced the chariot into Italy. In agriculture, they were the first in Italy to cultivate the vine and the olive tree, and it is believed that they made extensive use of irrigation.

In their religion the Etruscans showed no such lively use of the imagination as did the Greeks. In fact, theirs was a somber and melancholy religion. Its object seemed to be to learn the will of the supernatural powers by means of the thunder, the lightning, and similar phenomena. It was believed that there were two orders of gods: a superior one, veiled and nameless, and an inferior order of six male and six female deities, called the Consentes. The chief deities were Tinia, Cupra, Menrva, Usil, and Losna.

When commerce with the Greeks was established, the Etruscans found much to admire in the religion of their neighbors to the east, and Greek mythology made great progress in Etruria. The deities and legends of the Greeks virtually replaced those of the original Etruscan system. It was through the Etruscans that much of Greek mythology was introduced into Roman culture.

Tinia

TINIA (or Tina) was the chief Etruscan god, corresponding to the Greek Zeus and the Roman Jupiter. Originally, Tinia was regarded as heaven itself, considered or taken as a whole. A special temple was dedicated to Tinia in every Etruscan city. He was also worshipped as SUMMANUS, the supreme god or the thundering god, which does not mean that he was the one and only god, a belief that was no part of the Etruscan religion, but merely that he was the head of the gods in an assembly or senate of equal gods. He was, in other words, the first among his peers. Gates bearing his name, as well as temples, honored him in Etruscan cities.

Cupra

CUPRA, a goddess personifying light or day, corresponds to the Greek Hera and the Roman Juno. Like Tinia, she was honored by temples in every Etruscan city and by city gates that were named after her. The other names by which she was known or referred to, Thalna or Thana, suggest that they are nothing more than variants of Tinia, and tend to reduce her to a female counterpart of the chief god.

Menrva

MENRVA (or Menrfa) was the third heavenly deity of the Etruscans. She corresponds to the Greek Athene and to the Roman Minerva. Indeed, the name of the Roman goddess was derived from Menrva. Like Cupra and Tinia, she was honored by temples and gates in every Etruscan city. Her connection with Minerva is indicated by the fact that she was shown, as were her Greek and Roman counterparts, on vases and mirrors as being armed and carrying a shield. She personified the half light of the morning and evening.

Usil and Losna

USIL and LOSNA, were the Sun and the Moon. Usil corresponds to the Apollo—the Aplu of the Etruscans—and was represented as a young boy with bow and arrows. Losna's symbol was the crescent, and she was the equivalent of the Diana of the Romans. Usil and Losna appear to have been objects of worship, rather than gods.

Three Elemental Gods of the Earth

SETHIANS was the god of fire, the Etruscan equivalent of the Hephaestus of the Greeks and the Vulcan of the Romans. NETHUNS, the god of water, corresponds closely to Neptune, the Roman trident-bearing god of the sea. PHUPHLANS was the god of the earth and the treasures of the earth. He corresponds to the Greek Dionysus. Phuphlans was also known and worshipped under the names of VORTUMNUS or VOLTURNUS. The temple of his feminine counterpart, VOLTURNA, was honored by Etruscan princes and dignitaries by being used as their central meeting place to consider affairs of state. Phuphlans was regarded as the special divinity of Pupluna, an ancient Etruscan town, known to the Romans as Populonia.

Three Native Etruscan Deities

TURAN corresponds to the Aphrodite of the Greeks and the Venus of the Romans. THESAN is the equivalent of the Greek Eos and the Roman Aurora, goddesses of the dawn. TURMS is equivalent to the Greek Hermes and the Roman Mercury. His name, it is suggested, was simply the Etruscan form of the Greek name Hermes. These three gods do not seem to have been worshipped by the Etruscans to any great extent; although they play a part in the mythology of their people, they seem not to have been included in the real religion of the people. Of the three, Turan is the most often, and Thesan the least often, mentioned.

The Gods of the Lower World

MANTUS and MANIA, to whom human subjects were occasionally sacrificed, were the king and queen of the Etruscan underworld. As such they correspond to the Roman Pluto and Proserpina (the Greek Hades and Persephone). Mantus is represented as an old man, with a crown on his head and wings on his shoulders. Sometimes he holds in his hand a torch, and a fistful of large nails to indicate, perhaps, that his decrees are final and cannot be changed or avoided, once pronounced. The same idea is illustrated in the representations of the Greek and Roman deities of Necessity.

CHARUN, a demon, was associated intimately with Mantus and Mania as the more-than-willing agent who carries out the decrees of his king and queen. Half man and half animal, he was cruel and monstrously ugly. He was an old man with flaming eyes and a wild appearance, having the ears and the tusks of a savage brute. His features are thick and black and he wears wings. Snakes are twisted around his head or on his arm, making him an ideal companion for Strife and Discord. He holds a huge hammer in his hand—or a sword—so poised as to suggest that he is about to strike some unfortunate victim a death-blow. Death, in any form, he enjoys exceedingly; either when it is a result of man's violence or when it comes in the course of nature. He also holds the horses on which the departed souls make their journey to the lower regions. He orders them to mount their steeds and either leads or drives the animals with their riders into the gloomy empire of the dead. In that realm he happily torments his victims, striking them with his sword and hammer as they bend before him and beg for mercy. He is surrounded by assistant furies and demons, both male and female, who carry out his cruel orders as willingly as he does those of Mantus and Mania. In representations of the nether regions, Charun is usually the outstanding figure. His name, but not his character, is identical with that of the Greek ferryman of Hades, Charon.

VANTH, or Death, was a genie or spirit. He is seen standing at the door of an open grave or urging the speedy slaughter of a prisoner or encouraging bloodshed in some form. He is one of the spirits or genii bearing names—Charun's creatures being nameless—and he is as familiar with and as pleased at death, violence, and destruction as Charun himself.

KULMU was the Etruscan god of the tombs. He holds the fatal shears that cut the thread of life in one hand and in the other a funeral torch. He opens the door of the tomb so that a new visitor may enter.

NATHUNS was a male fury. He is distinguished by tusk-like fangs and hair that stands on end. He holds serpents in each hand and shakes and swings them violently over the spirits in order to arouse them to the equivalent of Bacchic frenzy.

Myths and Legends of the Romans

THE greatness of Rome lay most of all in the capacity of the Romans for organizing the political and social aspects of life, systematizing them into law, and carrying their sense of order and plan widely over the known world of their day.

The Romans were essentially a more practical, less imaginative people than the Greeks. We find that their architecture and sculpture, their literature and drama derives very largely from Greek sources, which they copied or adapted to suit their temperaments and times.

The beliefs of the Romans took the form of a more organized religion than that of the Greeks. Their deities were for the most part equivalents of individual Greek deities to whom new names were given. But in Rome the forms and formalities which attended their worship, the assigning of special days to certain deities or to aspects of their influence, were as important as the deities themselves.

Certain qualities of the Roman gods which differ from those of corresponding gods of the Greeks come from the influence of the Etruscans who lived in the Italian peninsula before the Romans, and we have indicated in our section on the "Myths and Legends of the Etruscans" specific instances of this influence.

The legends of Roman heroes are, many of them—such as Romulus and Remus—wholly indigenous to Rome, although the story of Aeneas derives from the Greek accounts of Troy.

The Roman sense of the importance and influence of personifications of abstract virtues is particularly notable. Although the Greeks also personified some qualities as deities their conceptions were usually very concrete. The Romans gave homage to the abstract quality itself in many instances, as will be seen in the latter part of the following section, which deals with Roman personifications.

The relation between the names of the Roman and the Greek deities is discussed in our introduction to the section on "Myths and Legends of the Greeks." In the entries here in the Roman section we use the Roman names by which the gods are most commonly known, and mention any variant names.

ROMAN DEITIES

Coelus and Terra

COELUS, personifying or representing heaven, was the son and husband of Terra and the Roman equivalent of the Greek Uranus. With his wife, he belongs to the first dynasty of the supreme gods.

TERRA (or TELLUS) corresponds to the Greek Gaea. She was the mother and the wife of Coelus. A daughter of Chaos and the goddess of marriage and fertility, she was always invoked, with Jupiter, in the most solemn oaths as Mother Earth (*tellus mater*) and as the common grave of all things. The Romans regarded her as one of the deities of the lower world. As the goddess of fruitfulness, she was honored at festivals held in January, after the winter sowing of seed, and in April by a feast at which cows with calf were sacrificed to her. The Romans also worshipped TELLUMO, as the male counterpart of Terra.

Saturn and Ops

SATURN (or Saturnus) is the Roman equivalent of the Greek Cronus. He was the husband of Ops and the father of Jupiter, Juno, Neptune, and Pluto. He was originally one of the NUMINA, the pre-Greek gods. His reign was associated with the wonderful Golden Age. He was honored by a festival, the Saturnalia, during which people exchanged presents, schools and courts were closed, war was outlawed, and criminals were not punished.

OPS (or CYBELE), the wife of Saturn, was the Roman goddess of plenty and fertility corresponding to the Greek Rhea. Her names, related to *opulens* and *copia,* indicate her nature, and her position as the protector of agriculture.

Sol and Luna

SOL, the early Roman god of the sun, and LUNA, goddess of the moon, are the Roman equivalents of the Greek Helios and Selene. Later many of their attributes were assigned to Apollo and Diana.

Jupiter

JUPITER was to the Romans what Zeus was to the Greeks. He was also known as JOVE, a name which originally meant simply "god." Often called Joves Pater (Father Jove), this term was contracted to Jupiter. He summed up in himself and was the complete essence of all divine power and the object of a worship accorded to none of the other deities, who were secondary to him. The Capitol in Rome was the main center of his worship; there he was celebrated as the Ideal Head of the State, as the Increaser and Preserver of all the strength and might of Rome, and as Jupiter Optimus Maximus, "Jupiter the Best and the Greatest." At this temple his companions were Fides, personifying faith and loyalty, and Victoria, victory. At other Roman temples, he was worshipped as Jupiter Pluvius, the god of rain; as Jupiter Capitolinus, he presided over the great Roman games, and, as Jupiter Latiaris, over important holiday festivals. In other capacities, he figured as Jupiter Lucetius, the god or bringer of light; as Jupiter Fulgurator and Fulminator, the Flasher of Lightning; and as Jupiter Tonans, the god of storms and thunder. He was also worshipped under countless other names and at countless shrines, temples, and statues erected in his honor.

Juno

JUNO was the Roman equivalent of the Greek Hera. As the wife of Jupiter, the king of the heavens, she was the queen of the heavens and was so worshipped at Rome. She was the guardian angel of women from the second they were born and throughout life until they died. As Juno Virginalis and Matrona, she protected virgins and matrons. As Juno Natalis, women honored her and offered her sacrifices on their birthdays. Her great festival, the Matronalia, was celebrated by all women on the first day of March. As Juno Juga or Jugalis she was keenly interested in seeing that women married and she presided over their marriages. The month of June, originally known as Junonius, was for that reason supposed to be the best month for marrying. As Juno Lucina, women in childbirth called on her for help. As Juno Moneta, with a temple on the Capitoline Hill, where the mint was located, she took care of money. Sacred to Juno were geese, because they are prolific and domesticated, and ravens, because they fly high in the heavens.

Neptune

NEPTUNE, the god of the sea, is the Roman equivalent of the Greek Poseidon. He was the husband of SALACIA, the goddess of salt water, who was the Roman counterpart of Amphitrite. His festival, the Neptunalia, was celebrated in July with games and water sports. The first horse, Scyphius, was invented by him in Thessaly.

Pluto

PLUTO, the prince of the underworld, is the Roman equivalent of Hades. He was called many other names, such as DIS, ORCUS, and TARTARUS. As monarch of the lower world, Pluto was the giver of wealth, and the giver of the blessings that come from the earth.

Ceres and Proserpina

CERES, ancient Roman goddess of agriculture, corresponds to the Greek Demeter. Festivals and games were held in her honor in April to celebrate the founding of her temple, and in August to celebrate the happy reunion of Ceres with her daughter PROSERPINA, who was the Roman equivalent of Persephone. The mother and daughter were known and worshipped as "The Mother and the Daughter" and as "The Two Goddesses."

Vesta

VESTA, the goddess of fire, corresponds to the Greek Hestia. As fire was important in the home, Vesta was also the goddess of the domestic hearth and therefore played an equally important part in the religion of the Romans. Her sanctuary stood in the Forum, between the Capitoline and the Palatine—two of the Seven Hills of Rome. Her fire was kept burning by the Vestal Virgins, her priestesses. If they allowed the fire to go out, or were otherwise remiss in their duties, they were beaten; if they violated their vows of chastity, they were beaten and buried alive. The period of service, fixed by law, was thirty years: for ten years they learned, for ten years they performed what they had learned, and for ten years they taught to the new candidates what they had learned and performed. At the end of their service, they put aside their religious robes and returned to private life. They were even free to marry, if they had any such desire.

Vesta's festival, the Vestalia, was celebrated in June. Because of her association with the hearth, in earlier times used as a place for baking bread, the festival was observed by housewives who asked Vesta to bless their homes, and by millers and bakers who kept it as a holiday. Vesta did not have any statues or images of herself in her temple, because the eternal fire was her living symbol.

Apollo and Diana

APOLLO and DIANA among the Romans correspond to Apollo and Artemis of the Greeks. Diana, like Artemis, was the goddess of hunting and chastity. Like the Greeks, the Romans worshipped deities of the sun and moon and later transferred many of the attributes associated with them to deities representing another generation. We have mentioned Sol and Luna above. It will be noted that to the young sun god the Romans assigned all the qualities of his counterpart and used his Greek name, Apollo. Diana was also worshipped under the name NEMORENSIS, in the role of averter of disease.

Janus

JANUS, guardian deity of gates or doors, was always thought of and pictured as having two faces looking in opposite directions, this concept evidently deriving from the fact that gates face both ways. He was thought of as the god of good beginnings. The month of January was named for him.

The name Janus is looked upon as a variant of DIANUS, the male equivalent of Diana; and accordingly, Janus is regarded as an early Roman sun god.

Minerva

MINERVA, the goddess of wisdom and one of the chief Roman deities, corresponds to the Greek Athene. She was regarded as the personification of the faculty of thinking, and it has been pointed out that the root *mens,* meaning "mind," is to be found in her name. With Jupiter and Juno, she had a temple on the Capitol. Her five-day festival, known as the Quinquatrus, took place in March. The fine arts and various practical skills were under her patronage and protection, and talent or genius was believed—by its possessor—to come from her and to be her gift. Minerva was thus the goddess of professional men, of artists, and of artisans. In this capacity she was worshipped by doctors and dyers, by poets and painters, by weavers and carpenters, and by musicians and sculptors.

Venus

VENUS, the Roman goddess of love and beauty, was in the beginning a goddess of the spring, and later became identified with Aphrodite. Her son was Cupid, the equivalent of the Greek Eros. Sacred to Venus was the month of April, because of its association with spring as the season of love, and the myrtle tree, of which she was especially fond; hence she was known as Venus Myrtea, and myrtle groves grew in front of her temple on the Aventine Hill. Caesar advanced her worship because he believed that he was descended from Venus through Ascanius or Iulus, the son of Aeneas, who was the son of Venus. At the Battle of Pharsalia, in which he defeated Pompey, Caesar's battle-cry was Venus Victrix. As Venus Genetrix she was worshipped as the mother of the race of Romans; and as the goddess who turned the hearts of women to chastity she was Venus Verticordia.

Cupid and Psyche

PSYCHE, a young maiden, was the object of widespread admiration for her great beauty, so much so that the worship of Venus, the goddess of beauty, was neglected. The goddess, vexed at this, ordered her son, CUPID, god of love, to cause the young maiden to fall in love with some ugly, reprehensible creature. Instead, Cupid fell in love with her himself. Aided by Apollo, Cupid arranged to have the lovely Psyche brought as his wife to a beautiful palace in a remote place. However, Cupid made himself invisible, and Psyche never saw him, although she was quite content with his love.

After a time Psyche longed to see her two sisters, and Cupid reluctantly agreed to have them brought to the palace. Before their arrival, however, Cupid warned Psyche not to let them persuade her to try to see him. The sisters were quite jealous of Psyche's happiness and convinced her that her husband might well be a serpent and that the only way to find out would be to attempt to see him. They provided her with a lamp and a knife, and that night, while he slept, she sought him out. Instead of a serpent she saw a beautiful being, whom she recognized as the god of love, and, reproaching herself, she fell on her knees. As she did so a drop of oil from the lamp fell on Cupid's shoulder. He awakened and flew away.

Left alone, Psyche wandered through the world in search of Cupid, subjected to numerous torments by Venus. Sent by Venus to Proserpina in Hades to fetch for her some of her beauty in a box, Psyche could not help opening the box, from which there issued dense black fumes which caused her to fall into a deep sleep. In this state she was found by Cupid and returned to consciousness. He took her then to the palace of Jupiter to interest the god in her favor. Jupiter endowed Psyche with immortality and, insisting that Venus be reconciled to her, the pair were married.

Mercury

MERCURY, the Roman god of commerce and gain, was identified by the Romans with the Greek Hermes. He was honored by a festival in May, attended chiefly by merchants, whose god he was. A temple was dedicated to him between the Circus Maximus and the Aventine Hill in 495 B.C. The symbol of Mercury was not the caduceus, as it was of Hermes, but a sacred branch, emblematic of peace.

Mars

MARS, the god of war, corresponds to the Greek Ares. He was the father of Romulus and Remus, the founders of Rome. With Jupiter and Quirinus (as Romulus was known after being deified) he was one of the three gods of Rome to whom Numa, a legendary king, appointed a flamen, a local priest or deity. Mars was worshipped in three capacities: as Mars Gradivus, the war-god; as Mars Silvanus, a rustic divinity, who presided over agriculture; and as Mars Quirinus, the guardian and protector of the state. As Mars Ultor, the Avenger, he punished the enemies of Rome.

Sacred to him were the wolf, the dog, the raven, the horse, the woodpecker, and the crowing cock. March, the first month of the Roman year, takes its name from him. His great festival took place the first three weeks in March during which his priests—the Salii—marched around the city, dancing war dances, singing, shouting, and beating on sacred shields which were believed to have dropped on Rome from heaven during the reign of Numa. Mars' consort was NERIA, or NERIENE, that is, the negative of the Greek Eirene, or Peace. Mars is naturally represented as an armed warrior. He is driven in his chariot by a demented woman, with Discordia running in front of him. His horses are Fright and Terror, and he is surrounded by Clamor, Fear, Anger, and other personifications appropriate to war.

The female counterpart of Mars was BELLONA, goddess of war, corresponding to the Greek goddess, Enyo. She was the sister or the wife of Mars, whose side she never left. She eagerly prepared his chariot for war, and appeared in battle disheveled, with a torch in one hand and a whip in the other, with which she further stimulated her own fury and that of the already maddened participants. Her degenerate priests, the Bellonarii, dressed in black, honored her at sacrifices by screaming, shouting, and wounding themselves in the arms and legs. Bellona's temple, built by Appius Claudius Caecus outside the city walls, was used for meetings of the Senate when it was negotiating with ambassadors from foreign countries, and to receive Roman generals returning from a victory.

Vulcan

VULCAN, the Roman god of fire and of furnaces, also called MULCIBER, the hammer god, corresponds to the Greek Hephaestus. The oldest festival in his honor, that of the Furnalia, celebrated him as the god of furnaces. His greatest festival was known as the Vulcanalia. His worship goes back to the time of Titus Tatius, King of the Sabines, who erected temples to him, to Vesta, goddess of fire, and to Romulus.

Bacchus

BACCHUS, so called by both Greeks and Romans, was the god of wine and the equivalent of the Greek Dionysus. The Romans sometimes called him LIBER.

Genius

GENIUS was a generative deity. Every man was believed to have his own Genius and every woman her own Juno (Juno in this sense being the female counterpart of Genius, with possibly some relationship between the names)—in other words, spirits who had given them being and were their special protectors. A man swore by his Genius and implored other persons by their Genius. The expression *Genius Loci,* or the Genius of the Place, referred to the spirit identified with or serving as guardian of a particular locality or even a specific spot.

Faunus and Flora

FAUNUS was a rural deity who was identified with the Greek Pan. The grandson of Saturn, he was believed to be a prophetic god. His name was taken to name the Fauns, minor deities who were the equivalent of the Greek Satyrs. Faunus had a feminine counterpart in FAUNA, one of the names of the Earth.

FLORA was the goddess of flowers, whose festival, the Floralia, was celebrated at the end of April and the beginning of May. It was said that Flora was the bride of the West Wind, whose gentle breath called the flowers into being.

Pomona and Vertumnus

POMONA, the goddess who presided over fruit trees, was much sought after by the male deities, the most ardent among them being VERTUMNUS, a god of the seasons. But Pomona shunned them all until Vertumnus, in the guise of an old woman, won her confidence and expatiated on wedded bliss, particularly with Vertumnus. Pomona was convinced, and when the old woman revealed herself as the handsome Vertumnus, Pomona yielded, and they were wed.

Lares and Penates

Every Roman family had its own domestic gods. The LAR (plural LARES) was a household god that was regarded as the owl of the ancestors who watched over their descendants. The PENATES (from *Penus*, or pantry, where they were worshipped) looked after the welfare and property of the family.

Terminus

TERMINUS was the Roman god of boundaries and frontiers. His worship was begun by Pompilius Numa, second legendary king of Rome, who ordered the citizens to put up stones (*termini*) dedicated to Jupiter in order to mark the boundaries of their estates. Festivals known as the Terminalia were held annually on these estates in February. The ceremonies were attended by all who lived in the neighborhood: men, women, children, and servants. The first step was to make the hole ready for the stone; this was done by watering it with the blood of an animal; honey, wine, incense, and products of the field were sprinkled over the hole, and the selected victim—a sheep, goat, or other animal—was sacrificed. The stone, smeared with oil and decorated with flowers and ribbons, was then placed on the burning bones and set into the earth. Any one who would dare to pull up the stone was considered cursed, and one might kill him without fear of punishment and without having his death on his conscience. A shrine of Terminus stood in the temple of Jupiter in the Capitol. According to the legend, when Tarquin planned to remove it, along with shrines to other deities, in order to make room for a temple dedicated to Jupiter, Juno, and Minerva, all the gods assented except JUVENTAS, goddess of eternal youth, who corresponds to the Greek Hebe, and Terminus. Their objection was taken to mean that Rome would never grow old and that her boundaries would never be pushed back.

ROMAN PERSONIFICATIONS

The Romans, more so than the Greeks, personified abstract qualities and attitudes. Some of their personifications were counterparts of the Greek personifications but a good number were of their own invention.

Pax

PAX, the goddess of Peace, was the Roman counterpart of the Greek Irene. She was honored by a magnificent temple at Rome. She is represented as a young woman holding a cornucopia on her left arm, and an olive branch or Mercury's staff in her right hand. She is sometimes represented in the act of setting fire to a stack of arms. She also has ears of corn on her head and in her hand.

Concordia

CONCORDIA, as her name indicates, was Concord or Harmony. Several Roman temples honored her memory. She was shown as a matronly woman, holding the horn of plenty in her left hand, and in her right, an olive branch or a broad, flat dish used by the Romans for ordinary drinking and for offering libations to the gods. She was invoked with Janus, Pax, and SALUS, the goddess of Health, at a family festival, marked by the exchange of presents, known as the Caristia and held in March.

Libertas

LIBERTAS was the personification of Liberty. Many temples were dedicated to her in Rome. She is represented as a matron, wearing a felt cap, the symbol of liberty, sometimes with a laurel wreath on her head, and a cap in her hand.

Fides

FIDES was the Roman goddess of Fidelity and honor in keeping and observing one's word or oath. She is shown as a matron wearing a wreath of olive or laurel leaves and a white robe. She carries ears of corn and a basket of fruit. Her attributes are a turtle-dove and clasped hands. As Fides Publica, symbolizing the Honor of the People, she had a temple on the Capitol built for her by Pompilius Numa, a legendary King of Rome. At her sacrificial rites, held on October first, the flamines, the priests who blew on the fire and kept it alive, rode to her temple in a covered chariot with their right hands also covered by white ribbon. The covered vehicle signified that no precaution was too great when honor was being protected; the concealing of the right hand, regarded as the seat of honor, indicated that it had to be kept clean and pure.

Pietas

PIETAS was the Roman goddess or personification of dutiful love and domestic affection. At Rome she was held in the highest esteem. She is represented as a matron sprinkling incense on an altar or taking care of an old parent. She is surrounded by her symbols, children and a stork.

Fortuna

FORTUNA, the Roman equivalent of the Greek Tyche, was the goddess of good luck. She was worshipped at numerous shrines under numerous titles, each one connected with an important situation in life which she influenced and in which her good will was highly desirable, if not essential. As Fortuna Primagenia she determined the destiny of the child when it was born; as Fortuna Publica, she had the welfare of the state under her guidance. As Fortuna Caesaris, she protected the emperor, and she guarded private family life as Fortuna Privata. Under appropriate designations, she was worshipped by the different social classes. She took care of children as Fortuna Liberum, and of unmarried girls as Fortuna Virginalis. Women invoked her as Fortuna Muliebris. As Fortuna Virilis she brought happiness to women in marriage. Boys and young men, the first time they shaved, dedicated the cut hair to Fortuna Barbata. She was the leader as Fortuna Dux, and she gave victory as Fortuna Victrix. In the harbor at Rome, she was worshipped, with PORTUNUS, the god of ports, as Fortuna Tranquilla, the goddess who insured safe and prosperous voyages. Of course, fortune has two sides, so the Romans recognized Fortuna Bona, good fortune, and her sister, Fortuna Mala, bad or evil fortune.

Honos and Virtus

HONOS and VIRTUS, the personifications of honor and bravery in war, were honored by many temples in Rome. Honos is shown holding a cornucopia in his left hand, and a spear in his right; he wears a wreath on his head and his chest is exposed. Virtus, symbolizing manly valor and the type of courage displayed on the field of battle, is dressed in a short tunic; she wears a helmet on her head and a helmet is under her right foot; her right breast is exposed; her left hand holds a spear and her right, a sword.

Victoria

VICTORIA, the goddess or the personification of Victory, was the Roman equivalent of the Greek Nike.

Discordia

DISCORDIA is the Roman counterpart of the Greek Eris, the goddess of Strife, and had the same attributes, which are fully discussed in the passages devoted to Eris in the Greek section of this book.

Necessitas

NECESSITAS was the Roman goddess or personification of Necessity. She was a powerful deity who could not be resisted by men or even by the gods themselves. She holds bronze nails in her bronze hands with which she fastens the unalterable decrees of destiny. She is surrounded by chains and hammers. The Greeks gave the name ANANKE to their personification of Necessity, whom they regarded as a male figure and honored in Athenian temples.

LEGENDS OF ROMAN HEROES

Aeneas

AENEAS, the hero of Virgil's *Aeneid,* was the son of ANCHISES, a high member of the royal house of Troy, and of Venus, the goddess of love. He was born on Mt. Ida and was brought up until he was five by the mountain nymphs. He was the husband of CREUSA, daughter of Priam and Hecuba, king and queen of Troy, and by her the father of ASCANIUS (who is also called IULUS).

In spite of his position as a member of the junior branch of the royal house of Troy and his kinship, by marriage, to Priam, he was not over-anxious to enlist in the Trojan War, and he did not take part in it until Achilles attacked him on Mt. Ida and stole his cattle. He then gathered his Dardanian forces and led them against the Greeks. Aphrodite favored him, saving his life, with the help of Apollo, when he was attacked by Diomedes, and Poseidon performed a similar service by tearing him away when he was having difficulties on the battlefield with Achilles. There are many stories of his escape from Troy which differ in details and agree only on the point that he did escape. According to one legend, he fought and hacked his way through the enemy lines to reach the safety of Mt. Ida. Another tells us that the Greeks spared his life because he urged that Helen be returned to her husband. A third legend, the most familiar, relates that he escaped when Troy fell in flames, carrying his old father on his back, holding his son by the hand, and followed, in the rear, by the faithful Creusa, and finally found refuge on Mt. Ida. From there, after a short rest period, he gathered what was left of the Trojans and sailed with them, in twenty ships, to Crete, by way of Thrace and Delos, in the belief that he was carrying out the wishes and instructions of Apollo. Finding out by a dream that the god meant Italy, he corrected his mistake and finally reached Sicily, the island at Italy's foot.

In the course of his long travels on his way toward Italy, he was driven by a storm to the coast of North Africa near the famed city of Carthage. There he aroused the violent love of Carthage's queen and founder, DIDO (or ELISSA). Dido was, according to legend, the daughter of Matgenos (or Belus), King of Tyre, sister of the greedy PYGMALION, and wife of her uncle, Sychaeus. Pygmalion had murdered his sister's husband in order to obtain his wealth, but Dido had fled to Africa, taking with her all the possessions of her dead husband. When Aeneas reached her shores and told her the story of his adventures, the widowed queen, still struggling to be true to her husband's memory, nevertheless fell passionately in love with him. As for the warrior, he returned Dido's love, or at least allowed her to declare and express her love for him. When the prince and the queen were brought together, it was the work of Venus and Juno; when Aeneas left Carthage and deserted Dido, unchivalrous as his treatment appeared to be, it was at the command of Jupiter, whose orders he had to carry out, regardless of his personal wishes. Dido pleaded with her lover not to abandon her, but her cries and her curses did not move him. As his vessel sailed out of the harbor, ending her brief romantic interlude, she hurled herself on a funeral pile and was consumed by the roaring flames. In other versions of the story, earlier than Virgil, Dido stabbed herself and then leaped into the fire in order to escape an unwelcome marriage with Iarbas, a barbarian king, whose suit she had rejected.

After leaving Africa, Aeneas, accompanied by his faithful friend, ACHATES, paid a visit to the underworld to see his dead father, on the advice of the Sibyl of Cumae. After a long and frightening journey through the infernal regions, Aeneas found his father, who showed him who their future descendants would be—all great Romans—and the wonderful deeds they would accomplish. Before parting from his son, Anchises instructed him how to establish his home in Italy and how to endure the hardships ahead of him.

Aeneas then sailed to Italy and cast anchor in the mouth of the Tiber. The place, Latium, was ruled by LATINUS, son of Faunus, and a great-grandson of the god Saturn. A daughter, LAVINIA, was Latinus' only child, and her hand was sought by TURNUS, king of the neighboring Rutulians. However, it had been predicted that the husband of Lavinia should come from a foreign land and that from this union a race would be born that would rule the world.

When Aeneas arrived in Latium, Latinus felt that Aeneas was the one who would fulfill the prediction. But at this point the goddess Juno intervened and sent the Fury Alecto to stir up a war. She persuaded Turnus to march against Latium, and also stirred up the people of Latium against Aeneas and his small band of Trojans. Juno then opened the two gates of the temple of Janus, a sign of war. Turnus then became the leader of the combined Rutulian and Latin forces, assisted by the cruel MEZENTIUS, an Etruscan, and CAMELA, a virgin huntress who was skilled in the art of war.

Aeneas, aided by an army of Etruscans who joined him to defeat the monstrous Mezentius, led his forces in a series of bloody and horrible battles against the enemy, and personally killed Turnus. With victory, Aeneas married Lavinia and together they founded the Roman race.

Romulus and Remus

The Romans invented a line of Roman rulers who were supposed to have reigned in the long ago. The first of the legendary kings was ROMULUS, twin brother of REMUS, offspring of Mars and Rhea Silvia. The brothers were cast adrift in a basket as infants by their grand-uncle Amulius, but were found by wolves, who suckled them and raised them. When they grew up they organized a warlike band of shepherds and founded a city, named by Romulus Rome, after himself, on the spot where they had been exposed and brought up. A quarrel broke out between the brothers over the interpretation of an omen that had appeared over the city, and Romulus struck Remus down, killing him. Romulus then became Rome's first king.

Romulus encouraged outcasts, robbers, and others who had done dangerous deeds to come to the city so that he might have men of daring with him. But there was a dearth of women in the city and, fearing that the population might not replenish itself because of this, Romulus attempted to induce women to come to Rome voluntarily. But the city had a bad name, and Romulus was unsuccessful in this. He then saw that he would have to use other means. He invited the neighboring Sabines to attend a Roman festival, and while they were the guests of the Romans, the followers of Romulus drove off the men and made the women their brides. Although Romulus sent word to the Sabines that the women would be wedded to the Romans and be treated with respect as their wives, the Sabines resolved to make war on their neighbors. Just as the battle was about to start, the Sabine women rushed between the opposing armies and begged that they not fight. They said that no matter who won, they, the women, would be the losers—they would lose their husbands, or brothers, or both. A truce was arranged and from then on the Sabines and Romans lived as one people.

Romulus ruled for many years, while the city grew in strength and size. Once, in the course of a battle between the Etruscans and the Romans, a cloud appeared and hid Romulus from sight. When the cloud disappeared, Romulus, too, was gone, having been made immortal and raised to the heavens. From then on the Romans worshipped him under the name QUIRINUS.

Numa

After Romulus, the throne of Rome was occupied by NUMA, the husband of EGERIA, a nymph, who would meet him each night by a clear spring and give him counsel. When a plague visited the city, Numa prayed for a sign, and a shield fell from the sky. Numa was told that as long as the shield remained in Rome, the Romans would be prosperous. Numa then had eleven other shields made just like the first so that no one could steal away the one sacred shield. The plague soon left the city.

Numa was remembered as the great law-giver, for he established the religion of the Romans, fixed its rites, built many temples, made the calendar, and brought Jupiter down to earth to tell men how to charm away the thunder and lightning. When Numa died he was buried in one stone coffin and his sacred books in another.

Tarquin the Proud

One of the later kings of Rome was TARQUIN THE PROUD. To him came one day an old woman, who offered to sell him nine books which would enable him to foretell the future. Her price, she said, was half the king's fortune. Tarquin scoffed at this as being too high. Then the woman cast three books into the fire and again asked the same price for the remaining six books. Once more Tarquin refused to buy them, whereupon the woman burned three more books. Her price for the remaining three was still half the king's fortune. Although his advisers scoffed, Tarquin, after considering for a long time, agreed to the woman's terms. He paid her and placed the books in the temple of Jupiter, where for a thousand years they were consulted on every occasion when the welfare of the state was involved. The books were called the Sibylline Books, after the woman who brought them, who was a Sibyl.

Myths and Legends of the Celts

Centuries before the beginning of the Christian era the Celts settled in Western Europe, especially in Gaul (later to become France) and in Britain and Ireland. The Britons or Brythons were the early Celtic people of Britain, and it is from them that the name Britain comes. The Romans under Caesar and others fought their way into Gaul and Britain and when the next wave of migrations brought the Teutons into Europe, the Celts were gradually forced westward, those in Gaul retaining Brittany, those in Britain gathering in Wales and parts of Cornwall and of Scotland, those in Ireland remaining undisturbed.

Not a great deal is known about the beliefs of the earliest Celts. The teachings of their priest-leaders, the Druids, were not permitted to be written down. Only bits of sacred verse recorded by later writers and fragments of ancient Celtic monuments give some clue to these Celtic beginnings.

The centuries toward the start of the Christian era saw the formation of a great wealth of mythical stories and legends, some originating in Ireland, some in Wales, some in Brittany. These myths and legends from different regions in some instances have much in common, in other instances are wholly independent and with no equivalents or counterparts. Chief among the sources of our knowledge of Irish mythology are such great manuscripts as *The Book of Leinster* and *The Book of the Dun Cow.* For Welsh legend, the great record is the *Mabinogion.*

In presenting the great myths and legends of the Celtic peoples we divide them regionally when this is necessary as is particularly the case in the accounts of the deities. The legends of the heroes belong clearly to one Celtic people or another. The great stories of Cuchulain, of Deirdre, and of Finn, belong to the Celts of Ireland. The superb cycle of tales of King Arthur and his knights belongs primarily to the Celts of Wales and Cornwall.

We give here many of the famous stories of the Celtic world, and many which are not so widely known as their interest warrants. Here is an extraordinarily rich and varied treasure.

DEITIES OF THE IRISH CELTS

The People of Dana

The gods of the Irish Celts were known collectively as the Tuatha de Danaan—the people of the goddess Dana. This race of gods were the offspring of Dana, the universal mother, who represented Earth, by her husband Bilé, god of the underworld.

The people of Dana were not the first divine inhabitants of Ireland, having been preceded by the Partholans and the race of Nemed. The Partholans emerged from the dark abyss of time to dwell in Ireland, which then was a tiny place set in the ocean. However, during their stay the land grew in size. The reign of the Partholans did not go unchallenged, for they had to fight with the forces of evil and darkness, the FOMORS, who had the form of hideous misshapen monsters. The best known of the Fomors was BALOR, a creature with two eyes, only one of which provided him with sight. The so-called "eye of Balor" had magic power and was the equivalent of the evil eye in the mythology of other peoples. So heavy was the lid of Balor's good eye that it took the strength of four men to lift it.

Although the Partholans bested the Fomors, their rule of Ireland was ended by a mysterious epidemic which wiped them out completely on May First of a certain year. May First was called Beltaine, a day sacred to Bilé.

The Partholans were succeeded by the race of NEMED, under whose reign Ireland also grew in size. They too defeated the Fomors, but, like the Partholans, they were wiped out by a plague.

The next inhabitants of Ireland were a race of human beings, the FIRBOLGS, who came from either Greece or Spain. They were of the race of DOMNU, and her son INDECH was their king. A dark people, small in stature, they were to constitute the servile class of the Irish people.

On another May First a dense cloud appeared on the coast of Ireland and from it stepped the Tuatha de Danaan, the great gods of the Irish Celts, who had come from the sky or from some faraway place on the earth.

The chief of the people of Dana was NUADA, son of Dana, and the supreme god.

After Nuada the greatest of the gods was DAGDA, whose name means "good god." He was the god of the earth, and as he played his harp the seasons came in order. By his wife, BOANN, Dagda was the father of Brigit, Angus, Mider, Ogma, and Bodb the Red.

BRIGIT was the goddess of fire and the hearth, and of poetry. ANGUS, the Celtic god of love, played sweet music on his golden harp, and his kisses became birds which hovered protectingly over lovers. MIDER was a god of the underworld, whose wife, ETAIN, was carried off by Angus, and whose daughter, BLATHNAT, was later taken as part of the spoils by the heroes of King Conchobar. OGMA was god of eloquence and literature and it was said that he invented the Ogam alphabet which was used in sacred writings. BODB THE RED later succeeded his father as king of the gods. CAMULUS was the war god of the Danaans, a deity who delighted in battle and slaughter.

LER was the god of the sea, who was to have an unfortunate experience with his children by his first wife Aebh, as we shall see below. One of Ler's sons was MANANNAN, who was the patron of merchants and sailors. Manannan had a sword which never failed to slay, a boat which propelled itself wherever its owner wished, a horse which was swifter than the wind, and magic armor which no weapon could pierce. He endowed the gods with a mantle which made them invisible and he fed them from pigs which renewed themselves as soon as they were eaten. At his Feast of Age, those gods who ate never grew old.

GOIBNU was the smith of the people of Dana and he forged their weapons. He also had the formula for a magic drink which made the gods invisible.

DIANCECHT, whose name means "swift in power," was the god of medicine. He had a Spring of Health in which the gods wounded in battle were healed.

LUGH, Diancecht's grandson, was the sun god of the Irish Celts. His weapon was a rod-sling which worshippers sometimes saw in the sky as a rainbow. He also had a magic spear which fought of its own accord.

When the people of Dana landed in Ireland they were not unopposed. The

Firbolgs would not unwillingly relinquish their hold of the island. At Leinster the two forces met, but a truce was declared so that each side could make for itself the weapons of the other. Then on Midsummer's Day the battle was fought at Magtured by groups of equal numbers or by warriors in single combat. The slaughter on both sides was terrible. The Firbolgs, however, suffered the greater loss and asked for a compromise, which was granted. They asked for a fifth of the land of Ireland and chose Connaught as their dwelling place.

In the course of the fighting Nuada lost his hand, and Diancecht made a silver hand to replace it. Henceforth Nuada was known as Nuada Argetlam, Nuada of the Silver Hand. But good as the hand was, it was regarded as a blemish, and no king could rule who was in any way blemished. Consequently Nuada was deposed.

To conciliate their neighbors, the Fomors, the gods made an alliance with them and asked BRESS, son of the Fomor king, to rule them. Bress assented, but soon he began to oppress his divine subjects. He levied burdensome taxes, took their cattle, put them to work, and withheld food from them so that they grew weak. Finally the gods could stand their king no longer. One of their number, the bard CAIRPRE, went to the king and wrote a sharp satire on his reign. When Bress heard the poem his face became mottled in anger, and this was taken as a blemish, and he was deposed. Nuada, whose hand had been magically restored, returned to the throne.

It was inevitable that war with the Fomors would follow. Command of the gods was given to Lugh. The battle, called the Magtura of the North, was a furious one and many gods were killed. Nuada was killed by Balor, and in turn, Lugh blinded the one-eyed Fomor. Nuada's son Bodb the Red succeeded him as king.

Although the people of Dana were victorious a prophecy was made that their reign would soon come to an end. This prediction came true when the MILESIANS, followers of MILE, son of Bilé, landed and settled in Ireland. The Milesians, who had come from Spain, were regarded as the first Gaelic settlers in Ireland. The gods then retired temporarily beneath the earth. Later some of them, including Manannan, went to lands beyond the sea. Others sought new homes in the hills and these were henceforth known as the AES SIDHE, the People of the Hills. (See also the section on "Fairy Lore of Europe and the Orient.")

The Children of Ler

While the gods dwelt in the hills Ler's first wife died and he married her sister, AOIFE, by whom he was childless. Brooding over her condition, and jealous of the great love that Ler had for his children—a daughter, FINOLA (Fionuala), the Maid of the Fair Shoulder, a son, HUGH, and twin sons, FIACHRA and CONN—and in fear that he loved them more than he did her, Aoife grew to hate Finola and her brothers and planned to destroy them. She ran away with the children to a lonely site by Lake Darva and tried to bribe or threaten her servants to murder them. When they not only refused to carry out her evil orders but denounced her, she decided to commit the crime herself. At the last moment, however, courage failed her, and she ordered them to bathe in the lake. As they were playing in the water she cast a spell on them, transforming them into beautiful white swans. She also doomed them to spend nine hundred years in this state, three hundred years on Lake Darva, the scene of their transformation, three hundred years on the Sea of Moyle (between Erin and Alba, or Ireland and Scotland), and the last three hundred years on the Atlantic, by Erris and Inishglory. At the end of this period they would be delivered from their spell when they heard the sound of the first bell ringing for mass, and when a man of the North married a woman of the South. For nine hundred years the children of Ler suffered, their miserable condition being eased only by the fact that they still had the mentality of gods, without feeling any grief at their change, and they had the gifts of speech and of singing beautiful songs.

The wicked stepmother did not go unpunished, but her evil could not be undone. When she returned home, she foolishly told Ler that his children had fallen into Lake Darva and had been drowned. Not believing her, the stunned father went to the lake to see if he could find their bodies for burial. Instead he saw and heard four swans swimming and talking. They greeted him with cries of sorrow, telling him what had happened, and begging him to change them back into gods. This Ler could not do, although he was the god of the sea, and even his friend, Bodb the Red, could not help him, although he was the king of the gods. All that Bodb could do was to summon Aoife to appear before him and to tell him, under oath, what form or shape on or under or above the earth she most feared and detested and would most hate to be transformed into. When Aoife answered, Bodb executed poetic justice by changing her into a shrieking demon of the air.

Ler's children spent their first three centuries at Lake Darva, being visited by gods and men who came to hear them talk and sing and to feast with them. The second three hundred years were less happy because of the cold winds and the stormy sea and because their terrible loneliness was broken only once, when they were visited by a committee of the ancient gods and two sons of Bodb, who came to tell them what had been going on in Ireland during their absence. The last period of exile brought their suffering to an end. They heard the sound of a Christian bell ringing, at which they were at first filled with fear. Later they returned and spoke to the hermit in charge of the chapel and told him what they had gone through in the past nine hundred years. He taught them the lessons of the true faith, which they accepted.

At this point, when their troubles seemed to be over, the kindly hermit and the swans were interrupted by LAIRGNEN, the Man of the North. He had come to ask the hermit for the swans, which he wished to give as a present to DEOCA, the Woman of the South, whom he was about to marry. When the hermit refused, Lairgnen took them from him by force and rushed off to his bride-to-be. As soon as she saw them, a horrible transformation took place. The feathers dropped from the swans and four old —very old—people, three old, white-haired shrunken men and an old woman, stood before the engaged couple. Lairgnen, although a brave Connacht chief, ran away in terror, apparently forgetting his obligations to Deoca.

Finola and her brothers did not long survive their last change. They embraced Christianity, were baptised by the hermit, who had followed them, were buried in a single grave, and their souls went to heaven.

DEITIES OF THE OTHER CELTIC PEOPLES

The gods of the other Celtic peoples—the Welsh, the Scotch, the Bretons—cannot be presented so systematically as those in the Irish Celtic pattern. Some of their gods were variants of the Irish gods, while others were independent inventions. We give the chief gods of the other Celts here.

Don

DON was the British goddess of fertility; she corresponds to Dana, the earth-mother of the Irish Celts.

Nudd

NUDD (or LUDD), a son of Don, was the British god of the sun. He is the equivalent of the Irish Nuada Argetlam. His shrine, according to tradition, was at Luggate, an old London gate built and named for him in 66 B.C. Nudd's wife was MORRIGU, goddess of war. She loved the excitement of battle, and she flew over battlefields disguised as a raven. Their son was GWYNN, originally a god of the underworld and lord of elves and fairies, but later also a hunter. At night he gathered up the souls of the dead who had fallen in the field of battle and carried them to the underworld, where he ruled over them. As his adventures and activities took place in nocturnal hours, his appropriate companion was the owl.

Math

MATH, a brother of Don, was a benevolent ruler of the underworld.

Gwydion

GWYDION, another son of Don, was the druid of the gods and a teacher of all that is useful and good. He was a friend of mankind and a fighter against the underworld powers. In this he was aided by his brothers AMAETHON, the god of agriculture, and GOVANNON, the god of smiths and the British counterpart of the Irish Goibnu. Govannon brewed the powerful ale that the gods loved, forged their powerful weapons for them, and won fame as a magic architect. The brothers reclaimed a vast stretch of waste territory, a labor that had been regarded as one that neither man nor god could possibly accomplish.

Llew Llaw Gyffes

Gwydion married his sister, the beautiful ARIANROD, called the Silver Circle, and they became parents of twin sons, DYLAN, who represented the power of darkness, and LLEW LLAW GYFFES, a god of the sun and the British equivalent of Lugh. Dylan early went to live in the sea and was called the Son of the Wave. He was killed by his uncle, Govannon, and when he died it was said that the seas wept for him.

Llew Llaw Gyffes was never a favorite of his mother and, in fact, she had refused to give him a name, a serious omission, since one's name and one's soul were looked upon as identical. But Gwydion tricked his wife. He distinguished himself and his son as shoemakers and went to Arianrod to fit her with shoes. While there, the boy shot a wren in the leg. Arianrod admired his marksmanship and praised him, saying, "The lion aimed at it with a steady hand." Gwydion claimed that he had thus named the boy, and he was henceforth known as Llew Llaw Gyffes, which means "the lion with the steady hand." Llew Llaw Gyffes was noted for the great rapidity with which he grew from childhood to maturity, a natural characteristic of the sun. Later he helped his uncles to fight the powers of darkness and evil.

Keridwen, Creirwy, and Gwion

CREIRWY was the goddess of love, the daughter of KERIDWEN, who was goddess of poetry and inspiration and patron of poets. Creirwy was the most beautiful woman in the world, as her brother, AVAGGDU, was the homeliest man. Keridwen owned a magic kettle and a magic liquid that gave the gift of inspiration to anyone who drank it. She sought to endow ugly Avaggdu with the gift in order to make his lot in life easier, but one GWION, ordered by her to stir the potion, drank it himself. In order to escape her just wrath, Gwion was compelled to transform himself many times into many shapes. He thought that he would outwit her by masquerading as a grain of wheat but Keridwen changed herself into a hen and, after chasing Gwion all over, she caught and swallowed him. Keridwen later gave birth to Gwion and threw him into the sea.

Pwyll and Rhiannon

PWYLL and RHIANNON were deities of Annwn, the underworld, but at the same time Pwyll was the prince of the land of Dyfed. Once he chanced to meet Arawn, king of Annwn, and the two entered on a strange compact: each would rule for a time in the other's stead and in the other's person. Pwyll went down to Annwn, where as Arawn, he defeated Arawn's enemy, Heveydd, and extended Arawn's realm. Although much impressed by the beauty of Arawn's wife, he remained faithful to Rhiannon. Arawn meanwhile was also ruling Dyfed well, and when the time came for them to resume their own forms, each was pleased with what the other had done.

Pwyll was a friend of Llyr and an enemy of Don. He liked gloom and hated light. Rhiannon was known as the Great Queen. After Pwyll died, she married Manawyddan, Llyr's son.

Llyr

Llyr, a sea-god, was the British counterpart of the Irish Ler. His city was Llyr-cester, now Leicester. His first wife was Penardun, a daughter of Don. By her he was the father of Manawyddan, a master of magic and a god of Annwn, the Celtic underworld. By Iweridd, Llyr was the father of Branwen and Bran, also deities of Annwn. These three children of Llyr occupy a prominent place in the mythology of the Celts of Wales.

Bran and Branwen

Bran, a giant, was accustomed to holding court in Harlech with Branwen and Manawyddan, and Nissyen and Evnissyen, who were the sons of his mother by her marriage to Eurosswydd. Nissyen was as kind and gentle as he was noble, and he loved peace and harmony and he was happy when he could turn enmity into friendship. Evnissyen, however, was his exact opposite in every respect. He was always looking for trouble or making it; he was sad when peace reigned and when he found trouble his only happiness was to make more trouble. His pugnacious personality was a constant source of grief to Bran and Branwen and ultimately brought about his own death.

Branwen was as beautiful as Bran was brave. She was in fact the most beautiful woman in the world, and was known as "Branwen of the Fair Bosom." The reports of her loveliness spread far and wide, bringing Matholwch (Matholaw), king of Ireland, to Bran's court. He came with thirteen ships of noble followers to ask for Branwen's hand in marriage because he had fallen in love with her beauty and because their union would make both kingdoms, Britain and Ireland, more powerful and better able to fight their enemies. Feasting and entertainment followed, and Bran readily gave his consent to the marriage. The wedding took place in huge tents, no house being large enough to hold Bran, and Branwen became Queen of Ireland.

But the joy of the wedding party did not last long, being interrupted by Evnissyen. Furious at Branwen's being married without his consent, he satisfied his wounded honor by rushing on Matholwch's horses and horribly mutilating them, cutting off their lips, ears, and tails. The Irish king, astonished at this treatment by his new brother-in-law, whom he had not yet met, made ready to leave for Ireland without any unnecessary delay and before Evnissyen could think up any more spiteful schemes.

It fell on Bran to appease his sister's husband and he sent a delegation, headed by Manawyddan, to make peace, to explain that Bran and his nobles were not in any way responsible for the actions of Evnissyen, and to offer gifts by way of atonement and apology. In return for the injuries he had received, Bran gave Matholwch a sound horse for every one that had been crippled, a silver staff as tall as himself, and a gold plate as large as his face. The newly-wedded king accepted the excuses and the presents, but he seemed uncertain as to his footing in the family he had just entered. Noticing his coolness, Bran added another gift, one of the greatest value for a monarch or a fighting man. It was a magic caldron which had the property of restoring to life and fighting fitness a warrior who had been killed in battle. All the king or general had to do was to gather up at the end of the day all those who had fallen on the field and to thrust them into the caldron. On the morrow, the dead soldiers would march out of the huge kettle, as good as new and ready to take up arms with renewed vigor. As the process could be repeated over and over again, the one who controlled the rights to the caldron had decided advantage over his opponent. It was so considerable, indeed, that it outweighed the fact that the alive-again warriors no longer had the power of speech.

Matholwch took his presents with good grace and returned to his kingdom with Branwen, who, a year later, gave him a son, GWERN. Later Matholwch resigned his throne in favor of Gwern, and the men of Britain and the men of Ireland met at the elaborate ceremonies at which the boy monarch was crowned. After the crown was placed on his head, the boy went from one noble to another, to Bran, Manawyddan, Nissyen, and all the others. They kissed and fondled him, uttering words of friendship and congratulation on his new honor. When it came to Evnissyen's turn, he, for no apparent reason, seized his unsuspecting nephew and hurled him into the roaring hearth-fire. The distracted mother sought to throw herself in the flames after her son, being prevented from doing so only by Bran.

Then a great battle took place between the Irish and British forces, led by Bran and Matholwch. The fight dragged on for days, but losses meant little to the Irish, as all their dead soldiers, killed one day, came alive the next after being thrown into and taken out of the caldron. Seeing what he had brought about and realizing his responsibility for a conflict so unequal, the evil Evnissyen attempted to redeem himself by an act that was his nearest approach to decency. In the excitement and confusion of battle, dressed in Irish garb, he played dead on the field. At the end of the day, he was swept, with his supposed comrades, into the caldron. Once safely inside he stretched himself to his full length, and in the superhuman effort he burst both the blazing caldron and his black heart into pieces.

In the great battle that followed, deprived of their wonder-working kettle, all the Irish were killed, and of the men of Britain, only Bran and seven others survived. They were PRYDERI, the son of Pwyll and Rhiannon, GLUNEU, the son of Taran, TALIESIN the Bard, YNAWC, GRUDYEN, the son Muryel, HEILYN, the son of Gwynn the Ancient, and Manawyddan.

Although he escaped with his life, Bran had been wounded in the foot by a poisoned arrow and was suffering the greatest agony. He commanded his seven comrades to cut off his head and take it to London, where it was to be buried with the eyes facing in the direction of France, so that no foreign foe would be able to invade the island as long as his eyes were watching. Pryderi and the others carried out the orders of their leader, and took Branwen with them, but she died of grief on the way, her heart breaking in two as she looked back to Ireland and ahead to Britain and recalled the destruction that she had brought to both islands.

Before his head was chopped off, Bran told his comrades that the journey would take them fourscore and seven years, and that during that time his head would live with them and talk with them as he had done in life, and then someone would open a door facing Cornwall. Then their happy hours would come to an end; then they would remember what had passed, and with remembrance would come sorrow, and his head, uncorrupted for eighty-seven years, would become dumb and require immediate burial. All things turned out as Bran predicted. It was Heilyn who was tempted to open a door facing Cornwall and the consciousness of their past days and the evil that had been done returned to him and his friends and sent them on the journey to London, where they buried the head of Bran. Later legend has it that King Arthur, ages after, dug up Bran's head because he wanted Britain to owe her power to strength and courage, not to magic.

Albiorix, Berecyntia, Borvo, Bussumarus, and Ogmios

ALBIORIX, BERECYNTIA, BORVO, BUSSUMARUS, and OGMIOS were deities of the Celts in France. Albiorix, known as Rigisamos, the king of the world, was the god of war. Berecyntia was the goddess of agriculture and the vine. She seems to be identical with the Irish Celtic goddess Brig. Borvo was the guardian and protector of hot springs. Bussumarus, whose name means "the large-lipped," was later identified by the Romans with their Jupiter. Ogmios was the god of agriculture and eloquence. He is represented as pulling after him men whose ears were tied to his tongue by threads of gold. Ogmios is identical with Ogma, the Irish god of eloquence and poetry.

HEROES OF IRISH LEGEND

Cuchulain

CUCHULAIN is the great hero of Irish legend. Although he lived a brief twenty-seven years, his life was crammed with noble and exciting deeds equal to those of the epic figures of Greece and Rome.

Cuchulain was the son of DECHTIRE, who was the sister of CONCHOBAR, king of Ulster. Dechtire was to marry SUALTIM, but at their wedding, Dechtire swallowed a fly which had flown into her cup of wine. The fly was in reality Lugh, the sun god, who spirited Dechtire and her maidens away to his palace. A year later, the men of Conchobar were impelled to go to the palace, where they found Dechtire, who was about to give birth to a child by Lugh. After the child was born, Dechtire returned to Emain Macha, the palace of Conchobar, and married Sualtim, and the boy was brought up as his son.

At that time Dechtire's son was known as SETANTA. When he was seven years old he killed a great fierce hound, owned by the smith CULAIN, which attacked him as he approached Culain's house. Culain loved the dog, and when he saw that he was dead, he was grief-stricken. Setanta then promised to find another dog as good as the one he had killed and until then he himself would guard Culain's house. CATHBAD THE DRUID pronounced this a fair offer and declared that henceforth the boy would be named Cuchulain, which means "the hound of Culain." The boy demurred saying that he was pleased with the name he had. But Cathbad persisted and predicted that some day all the men in the world would have the name Cuchulain in their mouths. Hearing this, the boy assented.

Not long after this Cuchulain took up arms for the first time, and on his first day as a warrior he brought back the heads of three champions who had slain men of Ulster. This was, of course, a great feat, dimmed only by Cathbad's prediction that he who took arms on that day, though his name would be greater than any other, his span of life would be short.

When Cuchulain was growing up, the women and maidens of Ulster loved him for his bravery and beauty, and while the warriors of Ulster held him in high regard, they were uneasy about the feelings of their women for Cuchulain. They determined to seek out a young maiden for him. They combed the provinces for a wife for Cuchulain but none of their candidates satisfied him. Then Cuchulain himself sought and found a young girl, EMER, the daughter of FORGALL, a wily king. But Forgall was opposed to having Cuchulain as a son-in-law and sent him off to SCATBACH, a female warrior, ostensibly to improve his skill as a fighter. But actually, Forgall hoped that Cuchulain would never survive the dangers of the journey and the fierceness of Scatbach's people. However, Cuchulain confounded Forgall and made his way to Scatbach and forced her to teach him her skill with weapons. On Cuchulain's return Forgall was compelled to give him his daughter's hand and Cuchulain and Emer were married. Cuchulain then became one of the twelve champions of the Red Branch, the warriors of Conchobar.

BRICCRIU, of the poisoned tongue, a lord of Ulster and a mischief-maker, on one occasion gave a grand feast for Conchobar to which he invited all the great heroes of the Red Branch. For Briccriu the feast was nothing more than an opportunity to get the nobles to quarreling among themselves as to who was the undisputed champion of the land of Erin. After much discussion and excitement, the choice narrowed down to three candidates: Cuchulain, CONALL OF THE VICTORIES, son of Amorgin, and LAERY THE TRIUMPHANT. It was agreed that the question of the championship must be decided by a horrible monster, a giant known as Terror (or The Terrible), who lived at the bottom of a lake. Terror, summoned from his watery home, demanded that the claimants for the title submit to a test of courage devised by himself. Any one of the trio, he said, might have the pleasure of cutting off his head today, provided that the one who took up the challenge would grant Terror the same pleasure tomorrow. Both Laery and Conall, brave as they were, and unafraid of blood, begged to be excused from Terror's test. But Cuchulain accepted willingly. He grasped his sword, uttered a magic charm over it, and chopped off the demon's head. But Terror rose from the ground, undisturbed, picked up his head and his axe and dived into the lake. Early the next day he returned, none the worse for his experience, with his head on his shoulders, and eager to swing his axe. Cuchulain could not help wincing slightly, but without a word he placed his head on the chopping block. Three times the lake-dwelling giant went through the motions of bringing the axe down on his impatient and uncomfortable victim, and then let the blunt end fall on the block, being careful to avoid the hero's head. At his command, Cuchulain rose from the ground, unharmed, to be greeted as the Champion of Ireland.

Briccriu also stirred up trouble among the warriors' wives, striving to make each one jealous of the other by whispering to each one that she ought to have the right of entering the noble hall before the others. An ugly quarrel took place, which was just as Briccriu would have it. Conall and Laery made holes in the wall for their wives to go through, but Cuchulain simply removed one side of the house which made it easy for Emer to enter first. Although the dispute was a result of his own planning, Briccriu demanded that Cuchulain make good the damage he had done.

On another occasion, Briccriu again used a feast as an occasion for causing bloodshed. The feast was given by a wealthy Leinster lord, MESRODA, son of Datho. The main dish of the meal was Mesroda's prize boar, an enormous creature, and the guests were the powerful lords of Ulster and Connacht and their followers. When the animal was brought to the table, a vital question came up: who, among the distinguished company, was to be awarded the honor of carving the creature? Briccriu suggested that the warriors tell of the brave deeds they had performed and of the enemies they had conquered, the carving of the boar to be awarded as a prize for the best fighter. A battle of words led to a battle of fists and swords and axes. KET, son of Maga, CUSCRID, son of Conor, KELTCHAR (Keltyar) and MOONREMUR, lords of Ulster, Laery, Conall, and many other brave Ulster and Connachtmen participated in the boasting and the bloodshed. When it was all over and the smoke had cleared away it was difficult to see what Briccriu, what anyone, had gained.

Many were the great adventures of the hero Cuchulain, among them his single-handed defense of the frontier of Ulster against the armies of QUEEN MAEVE of Connacht and the rest of Ireland in the war known as the Cattle Raid of Cooley. But the prophecy of Cathbad the Druid that he would live a short life could not be denied. He met his death at the hands of LUGAID, an old enemy. Sorely wounded by Lugaid's spear, Cuchulain tied himself to a pillar stone and challenged his enemies to meet him. However, Cuchulain was too weak to protect himself and Lugaid cut off his head with a mighty blow, although as Cuchulain's sword fell it cut off Lugaid's right hand. In satisfaction his enemies cut off Cuchulain's hand. When news of Cuchulain's death reached Emain there was great crying and lamentation, and he was buried in one grave with Emer, who died of grief over his loss. But it was said that ever after Cuchulain's chariot could be seen going through Emain Macha and he could be heard singing in the hills.

Deirdre

DEIRDRE was the lovely daughter of FEDLIMID, the bard or harper of Conchobar, king of Ulster. When she was born, in her father's house, Conchobar was presiding at a great feast there. Upon seeing her, one of the guests, Cathbad the Druid, predicted that she would grow up to be the most beautiful woman in the world and that her beauty would mean death and tragedy to heroes and to the kingdom of Ulster. In order to avoid these calamities, Conchobar, against the wishes of his warriors, who demanded that she be slain, ordered her to be taken to a secret cave, the location of which was known only to him. It was also part of his plan to make her his wife and queen when she was old enough for such responsibilities. In this cave, hidden from the sight of men, Deirdre was brought up by an old woman, LEVARCHAM, who acted as her nurse and teacher, her only other companions being the birds and beasts of the mountain hills.

Years later, no longer a child, but a beautiful maiden moved by the mystery of love, she told her teacher that she would love and marry a man whose cheeks were as red as blood, whose skin was as white as snow, and whose hair was as black as the plumage of a raven. Meaning no harm and not thinking of the danger that might follow, Levarcham informed her that NAOISE, one of the three sons of Conchobar's brother, Usnach, met all those qualifications. Deirdre persuaded the teacher to introduce Naoise to her, with the inevitable result. Dazzled by her beauty, Naoise, with the help of his brothers, ARDAN and AINLE, carried Deirdre off to Alba (Scotland), where they led a more or less ideal existence, roaming over the country, hunting, fighting battles, and playing chess.

This happy state was finally broken up when Conchobar, who had been planning revenge all the time, succeeded in inducing them, through his messengers, to return to Ulster, under promise that they would not be harmed. This promise he violated as soon as he could safely do so, and had all the brothers treacherously killed. His own men refusing to carry out his orders, he was compelled to engage the services of an outsider, a Norwegian, to slay the brothers. Each brother begged that he be killed first, to escape seeing the death of the other two, a painful situation that was brought to an end when Naoise handed his own sword to the appointed slayer and commanded him to behead them with one blow.

Conchobar's treachery gained him nothing. Shocked at the breaking of his word of honor, his followers left him, transferring their allegiance to his foes. Cathbad, to whom he made the promise, cursed the king and the kingdom of Ulster. Deirdre, in sorrow at the death of her beloved Naoise, and his brothers, in remorse at the trouble she had caused, and in order to escape falling into Conchobar's hands, either as his wife or his captive, killed herself, after delivering a beautiful and pathetic elegy—Deirdre's Lament—over the murdered heroes.

In the mythology of the ancient Celts, this is one of the "three sad stories" of Ireland. Deirdre is the outstanding heroine, the flower, the essence of Gaelic myth and legend.

Finn

FINN MAC COUL—Finn, son of Coul—an Irish and Scotch hero, also known as FINGAL, was born posthumously to his mother, who brought him up in hiding away from his father's enemies, the Clann Morna. Finn had a great reputation for being gentle to women and generous to men. He was an excellent swimmer, runner, and hunter.

Finn was the leader of a band of warriors, known as the Fenians, who wandered about enjoying themselves at hunting, but responding when necessary to the call to defend Ireland against invaders.

Finn had two sons, FERGUS and OSSIAN. Fergus was the Fenian bard and ambassador, while Ossian was a hero who came to be regarded as the equal of Finn. Ossian's mother was SADB, daughter of Bodb the Red, one of the people of Dana.

As a youth Finn gained foreknowledge and magic counsel from having eaten the salmon of knowledge. He then defeated the Clann Morna and turned them into his faithful servants. Then Finn warred against the Fomorian LOCHLANNACH.

Finn came to the aid of the gods Angus, Ler, and Bodb in their fight against the deity Mider and helped to drive him off. At a banquet celebrating the victory a dispute arose as to the relative merits of the pleasures of the table, which Angus championed, and the pleasures of the hunt, which Finn naturally favored. The argument grew heated and Finn declared his two hounds, Bran and Sgrolan, could kill any pig. Later Finn and his Fenians had an opportunity to prove his boast. They and their hounds went after Angus' pigs, which turned out to be as tall as deer and covered with thick, sharp bristles. The Fenians killed the pigs, but at the cost of ten of their number and many hounds. Angus then complained that the Fenians had actually killed his son and others of the people of Dana, who had been disguised as pigs. A war between the two sides over this was only narrowly averted.

One of the best known stories about Finn, which unfortunately does not show him in a favorable light, resulted in his downfall and death. In his old age Finn desired to marry GRAINNE (also known as GRANIA), the beautiful daughter of CORMAC, king of Ireland. But Grainne was already in love with DIARMAIT (or DIARMUID), Finn's nephew, and the couple fled from Finn's reach. Diarmait was a particular favorite of Angus, who gave him a mantle of invisibility which enabled him and Grainne to escape from Finn's clutches many times. Another disadvantage that Finn labored under was the fact that most of the Fenians were not sympathetic to him in this venture, being more inclined to let the young lovers escape.

Diarmait's closest escape came when he and Grainne were hiding from

Finn in the branches of a tree. Finn and his men approached and, while waiting for the heat of the day to pass before resuming the chase, Finn and Ossian sat down under the tree to play a game of chess. Diarmait became absorbed in the game and dropped berries on the pieces to indicate to Ossian which move to make. Finn soon became aware of Diarmait's presence in the tree, but Diarmait was able to escape once again.

Eventually Angus prevailed upon Finn to become reconciled to the marriage of Diarmait and Grainne, but he never forgave his nephew. Finn knew that Diarmait was invulnerable except in the heel, so he arranged to have him step on a poisoned boar thistle, thus causing Diarmait's death. After that Finn's power among the Fenians steadily declined and in time they rebelled against his rule and killed him.

KING ARTHUR AND THE KNIGHTS OF THE ROUND TABLE

Arthur

King Arthur, the greatest name in English romantic literature and one of the great heroes of world romance, is a half legendary, half historical figure. Our first account of him, in two Latin chronicles, presents him modestly as merely a brave and successful leader of the Celtic Britons against the Saxons, a leader or chief in war, who twelve times led the Britons against the Saxons and was twelve times successful. He ends as a hero of romance whose very name calls up the highest qualities of idealism and heroism.

Uther Pendragon and Igerne (or Igraine or Ygerne) were the parents of the great King Arthur. Uther was the legendary chief king of Britain who overcame all the petty kings. Pendragon, meaning "chief leader in battle" or "chief dragon," is a title rather than a name and was given to or assumed by military leaders who exercised kingly powers. Warriors used the dragon on their shields as an emblem of war. Uther Pendragon, aided by Merlin the magician, visited Igerne in the likeness of her husband, Gorlois, duke of Cornwall, and thus was born the greatest British knight of all. According to one legend, she was the mother of three daughters when Uther saw and fell in love with her, and he was compelled to adopt the trick because Igerne was a chaste and devoted wife. According to another version, Uther Pendragon married Igerne when she was Gorlois' widow and Arthur was the lawful child of that union.

When Arthur was fifteen years old, he was elected king by the nobles. He was named to this responsibility when he, of all the knights, was able to withdraw a sword which had been fixed in a stone. After this, Arthur took the field against the Saxons and inflicted a resounding defeat. During one of his many encounters, the sword which Arthur had drawn from the stone was shattered, whereupon Merlin led Arthur to a lake from which rose an arm clothed in white samite holding a sword. A damsel, who was the Lady of the Lake, approached, and Arthur asked whether he might have that sword. She replied that the sword was hers but that Arthur might have it. Arthur rowed out to where the sword was and took it. This was his famous sword Excalibur, which he was to carry for the rest of his life.

Arthur married Guinevere (also spelled Guenevere or Guenever), daughter of King Leodegrance. As a gift Leodegrance gave Arthur a Round Table, with seats for one hundred and fifty knights. One seat was known as the Siege Perilous, which might be occupied only by the knight who was to find the Holy Grail.

The place where Arthur had his court varies in the legends, but the best known to us today is Camelot, where his knights gathered and from which they departed on their various adventures.

Arthur's two great adversaries were LANCELOT and MODRED. Lancelot stole the love of Guinevere (this will be given in detail in the entry under Lancelot) and Modred, Arthur's nephew, was responsible for his death. Arthur's death came after the heroes of the Round Table had taken to fighting among themselves and the noble spirit which had motivated the knights had given way to selfishness.

Modred desired the kingdom for himself and gathered a large force to unseat his uncle. The men of both sides fought hard and nobly, but the slaughter was so great that there remained but a few knights. Of Arthur's men only Sir Lucan and Sir Bedivere were alive. Arthur met Modred and with a mighty thrust of his spear killed him, but not before Modred could retaliate with a sword stroke that smote Arthur severely in the head. His two knights removed Arthur to a chapel not far from the seaside. Then Arthur directed Bedivere to take his sword Excalibur and throw it into the water and tell him what would then happen. When Bedivere threw the sword far into the water, an arm rose out of the water and caught the sword and brandished it three times and withdrew back into the water. When Bedivere related what had happened to Arthur, the king asked him to carry him to the water side. There a barge rode by with fair ladies dressed in black and weeping on it. Bedivere placed Arthur on the raft and it moved away to the vale of AVALON where, Arthur said, his grievous wound would be healed. The legends have it that some day Arthur will return and rule again over England.

Merlin

MERLIN, a famous wizard, magician, and prophet, lived first at the court of King Vortigern and then at King Arthur's court. He was born, if legend can be believed, of the union of a fiend or monster and a helpless, unconscious nun. The attack was part of a plot engineered by Satan, who thought that he could use the son of a demon to ruin and undo the work of the Son of Man, but his hopes were killed by a priest who, certain that the nun was blameless, baptized Merlin as soon as he was born.

Merlin first appeared as Ambrosius, a child without a father, who solved for Vortigern the mystery of why the work that his masons and carpenters did every day in building a fort was destroyed every night. Merlin was only five years old at the time but he knew that the cause of the nightly shattering of the walls was the fierce fighting that took place between a red dragon and a white one, who lived at the bottom of a lake. Acting under his directions, Vortigern began digging and draining operations until the dragons were reached; in the battle that followed, the red dragon was killed, and the white one, who had two heads, disappeared.

Merlin was a friend in need to Uther Pendragon when he helped him to assume the appearance of the Duke Gorlois of Cornwall, so that Igerne, Gorlois' wife, would accept his embraces. For Uther, Merlin made the famous Round Table which he later gave to King Leodegrance, who in turn gave it to Arthur.

At Arthur's court Merlin played an important part, and his magic arts and his advice helped Arthur to conquer his foes and to overcome the forces that opposed him on more than one occasion. In his old age, Merlin fell a victim to the charms of VIVIEN, the seductive enchantress known also as the Lady of the Lake. Vivien, jealous of the great fame of the Knights of the Round Table, came to King Arthur's court for the express purpose of causing trouble by spreading false reports and arousing suspicion and distrust. When her charms failed to attract Arthur, she set out to trap

Merlin, with more encouraging results. However, no sooner did she learn his magic formulas, which was her objective, than she turned them against the old wizard and made him a prisoner in an old oak tree where she left him forever under a spell, the secret of which he had taught her.

Lancelot

LANCELOT (or Launcelot) of the Lake, the son of King Ban of Brittany and Lady Helen, later known as the Lady of Sorrows, lost his parents in early infancy. Betrayed by his own followers, wounded, and in sight of his burning castle, Ban died of a broken heart. While his wife was trying to comfort him and to ease the pain of his last moments, the Lady of the Lake suddenly appeared, seized Lancelot, a babe, and, ignoring the cries of the distracted mother, plunged with him back into the lake from which she had come. Lady Helen entered a convent to spend the rest of her life in sorrow, not knowing that her son would one day become one of the most celebrated knights of the Round Table.

Lancelot was brought up and educated by the Lake Lady in her lake home, hence his title, Lancelot of the Lake. When he was eighteen, Vivien took him to King Arthur's court to be knighted, this occasion marking the first meeting between the young knight, splendid in his white armor, and Queen Guinevere. In addition to becoming one of Arthur's knights, sworn to loyalty, Lancelot also became Guinevere's lover. When he was finally discovered with Guinevere in her apartment he fled with her to his palace, Joyous Gard. He later surrendered Guinevere to Arthur and went on a sea journey in a vain attempt to put her out of his mind. With his son, the peerless Galahad, Perceval, and other knights of the Round Table, he set out in search of the Holy Grail, although he must have known that he could not justly hope to see it in view of his sinful love for Guinevere.

After the death of King Arthur, he attempted to renew his relationship with Guinevere, but she had experienced a change of heart and had become a nun. Lancelot then retired to a religious house, to watch over Arthur's grave, to meditate, to pray, and to ponder on his sins. After six years of purification and penitence, he found peace in death.

Arthur's queen was not the only woman who smiled on Lancelot. ELAINE THE FAIR, the Lily Maid of Astolat, loved him and died for it. He wore her favor on his sleeve in battle and gave her his shield to keep for him, but he could not return her love, that is, he could not be true to her without being false to Guinevere. By another ELAINE, the daughter of King Pelles, whom he was deceived into believing was Guinevere, he was the father of Sir Galahad, a better man and a truer knight than his father.

Tristram and Iseult

TRISTRAM (or Tristrem or Tristan), whose name means "the sad one," was the son of King Rouland of Erminia, and King Mark's sister, Blanchefleur, or of Meliodas, King of Lyonesse, and King Mark's sister, Elizabeth. A great hunter, harpist, linguist, horseman, fencer, and chess-player, Tristram is one of the greatest knightly heroes in the romantic literature of the world.

He killed King Moraunt of Ireland and Sir Morholt, an Irish giant who dared to demand tribute in men and money from KING MARK, but was wounded on each occasion, though not fairly, as his foes used poisoned weapons. Hearing of the magic powers of ISEULT OF IRELAND, he went to that country to be healed of his wounds. When he returned to his uncle's court, cured, he was so enthusiastic about Iseult and painted her in such glowing terms that Mark fell in love with her and decided that he wanted her for his queen.

Tristram then sailed for Ireland

again, not on his own this time but as his uncle's ambassador, to bring Iseult back with him. On the homeward voyage, the inevitable happened: Tristram and Iseult fell hopelessly and madly in love with each other. Nothing could lessen or interfere with their love, not even the marriage of Mark and Iseult. Many times, luck was with the lovers, who were at least as clever and resourceful as the enemies who tried to trap them, but eventually they were discovered together. In order to escape the wrath of Mark, Tristram fled to Brittany and offered his services to the king, HOWEL. Under the mistaken impression that Iseult had forgotten him, he married another Iseult, King Howel's daughter, ISEULT OF THE WHITE HANDS, or Iseult of Brittany, but the marriage never became more than a ceremony, as he did not make her his wife in reality. Tristram soon learned that Mark's Iseult had not forgotten him, but too late. Later, suffering from another wound, he sent for the first Iseult to cure him, but Iseult of the White Hands, jealous, falsely told him that she had refused to come to his aid. Heartbroken, Tristram turned his face to the wall and died. Soon after, Iseult arrived, only to find her lover dead, and she joined him in death. In some versions, Tristram died, not of grief, but by the hand of Mark, who killed him as he sang and played the harp to Iseult of Ireland. In other tellings, Iseult arrived in time to give her lover a moment of happiness before he died.

Geraint and Enid

GERAINT, Prince of Devon, was one of Arthur's bravest knights and a member of the order of the Round Table. Geraint was married to ENID THE FAIR, whose name means "spotless purity," the only child of Earl Yniol. She loved and admired her queen, Guinevere, sentiments that Arthur's wife reciprocated. The growing intimacy between queen and subject was a source of great happiness to Geraint at first, but then, fearful that Guinevere might have a bad effect on his wife, the gentle Enid, he withdrew from the court to his princely estates, giving Arthur the rather flimsy excuse that his land was threatened by robbers and murderers. Foolishly doubting Enid's love and loyalty on a basis no stronger than the friendship and affection that existed between the two women, he made her accompany him on his rides to areas swarming with bandits and criminals. In his anger he sent her on ahead, refusing to speak to her or to allow her to speak to him; in various adventures that followed and in caring for him when he was wounded, she proved her love and his mistake, and husband and wife were reconciled, living happily together with their children until Geraint died a noble death fighting against the pagan foe in the North, fighting for Arthur, his blameless king.

Galahad

GALAHAD, the perfect knight who saw the vision of the Holy Grail, was the son of Lancelot, who could not see the Grail because of his guilty love for Guinevere, and of the Elaine who was the daughter of King Pelles. Galahad, born in a convent, was brought up by nuns in his boyhood, and when he came to Camelot he was knighted by Arthur himself. His strength was as the strength of ten men because of his flawless purity, and it was that purity, his outstanding quality, which made it possible for him to see the Holy Grail, the cup used at the Last Supper, when he went to search for it with his fellow-knights, Sir Bors and Sir Perceval. Galahad uttered a prayer that death might come to him whenever he desired it, a request that was later granted. With his comrades, Galahad carried the Grail to Sarras, a fabulous island city in the Mediterranean. At Sarras he was elected king by the people, whom he ruled wisely and justly for a year. He then prayed that his body might die so that his soul might live eternally. After his death, the Holy Grail was carried up to heaven and no man ever saw it again.

Gawain

GAWAIN, one of the most attractive of Arthur's knights, was the son of King Lot of Orkney, and MORGAN LE FAY, Arthur's sister. He was the brother of AGRAVAIN, who informed on Lancelot and Guinevere; of GAHERIS, accidentally slain by Lancelot; of GARETH, who married LYNETTE or, in some accounts, her sister Lyonors; and of MODRED, traitor to his king and uncle. Gawain was brave, pure, and courteous, always, and under the most trying and difficult circumstances. He acted as Arthur's ambassador at Rome and distinguished himself in battle.

He appeared at his best in his contest with the GREEN KNIGHT. He was brave enough to strike the Green Knight, a frightful foe, with an axe on one New Year's Day and to take a blow from him on the next; strong and chaste enough to resist all the tempting offers of his hostess, not because she was not beautiful, but because she was the wife of his host who (apparently) trusted him, diplomatic enough to refuse the attractive proposals of an attractive lady without being offensive—no easy task—honest enough to return—according to an agreement made with his host—the kisses she gave him in her husband's absence when he returned home after a day's hard work; and human enough, wanting to save his own life, if possible, *not* to return the girdle, which she also gave him as well as the kisses, because it had the power of making him safe from attack. In his honor, in recognition of his fundamental honesty and decency, and with laughing forgiveness for his one human weakness, all the lords and ladies of Arthur's court voted—when they heard Gawain tell his story, somewhat apologetically—to wear green girdles forever after.

Perceval

PERCEVAL, a knight whose father and brothers had been killed in tournaments, was raised by his mother in the isolated forest, where he might never be tempted to become a knight. But one day he chanced to meet five knights in the forest and he determined to ride forth and become a knight, too. His mother, seeing that nothing would stop him, sent him to Arthur's court. Perceval proved himself by conquering a knight who had insulted Queen Guinevere and whom no other knight would challenge. Though rough in his ways, Perceval was a master with a spear and brought down many a wayward knight.

Later Perceval joined the other gallant knights in the search of the Holy Grail. The story of this knight was developed in a German re-telling where his name takes the form Parsifal or Parzival. We tell the story of Parsifal in the section on German myths and legends.

Bors

BORS, a cousin of Lancelot, was associated with Galahad and Perceval in the search for the Holy Grail. Not being flawless in his purity, as Galahad was, he saw the sacred vessel dimly, as through a veil.

Myths and Legends of the Norse and Teutons

As early as the first few centuries before the Christian era the Teutonic peoples spread over a considerable part of central Europe, north of the Rhine and the Danube. Of the same race, religion, and customs, they inhabited what today is the Scandinavian countries—Norway, Sweden, Denmark—and Germany, and developed a set of myths which are to a large degree uniform for the entire area. Lacking the literary culture of the Greeks and Romans, the Northmen transmitted their myths by word of mouth.

When Christianity came to the North, these tales which once had been beliefs largely disappeared from the writings in Germany and Scandinavia. However the Vikings had colonized Iceland to the North; and it was during the next few centuries in Iceland that the pagan faith of the Viking ancestors was preserved.

It was in Iceland that the first written record of these pre-Christian Nordic myths was set down. In the *Elder* or *Poetic Edda* of the tenth century, and the *Younger* or *Prose Edda* of a later period is to be found a detailed account of the cosmogony, mythology, and traditions of the Teutonic and Norse peoples.

Eddic poems can be divided into two groups—the mythological, or stories in which the divinities are the chief personages, and the heroic. We have in these old Norse myths and legends one of the great realms of the world's mythologies.

Many of the Norse and Teutonic deities and heroes are most familiar to us through their use by Richard Wagner in his four great music dramas which comprise the *Ring of the Nibelungs*. Wagner based the course of his narrative and the conception of his characters on the Norse *Volsunga Saga,* rather than upon the Teutonic *Nibelungenlied.* It should be noted, however, that he does not use the Norse names for the gods and heroes, but gives them in their Germanic form.

To Wagner also we owe much of our acquaintance with such figures of later German legend as Parsifal, Lohengrin, and Tannhäuser, whom we take up near the end of this section. The final figure of German legend whom we discuss is Faust, who becomes the central character in a symbolic story of man's destiny, which has become the subject of many great works in literature and music.

In our present section we turn first to the myths of the Norse deities. We use the names of the gods and goddesses, and later the names of the heroes, in their Norse form, in each instance indicating also the Teutonic form and any variants from the form used for the entry headings.

The chief sources of the hero tales are the Norse *Volsunga Saga* and the Teutonic *Nibelungenlied,* both probably written some time between 1100 and 1300. Although there is general similarity between these Norse and Teutonic accounts, there are significant differences in the characterizations of the legendary heroes, heroines, and other persons who appear. Another important fact is that the gods and goddesses who play such a major role in determining the lives and fates of the heroes of the Norse account scarcely appear in the *Nibelungenlied,* which concerns itself primarily with the struggles and conflicts of the heroes themselves.

NORSE AND TEUTONIC DEITIES

The Creation

In the beginning there was nothing but a bottomless deep, known as GINUNGAGAP and a land of mist, called NIFLHEIM. From Niflheim flowed twelve rivers whose waters froze and filled the great deep with ice. In the south was a land of fire, MUSPELHEIM, from which warm winds came and turned the ice into mist. From this mist sprang the frost maidens, YMIR, the first giant, and AUDHUMBLA, a cow whose milk nourished Ymir. Out of the ice came a god who was the father of ODIN, VILI, and VE. They slew Ymir and from his body formed the earth; from his blood, the sea; from his bones, the mountains; from his hair, the trees; from his skull, the heavens; from his brain, the clouds. From his eyebrows they made MIDGARD, which was the place where mankind was to live.

Odin regulated the periods of the day and night by placing the sun and the moon in the heavens. Then out of an ash tree, the gods created man, whom they called ASKE, and out of an alder they made woman, whom they called EMBLA. Odin gave them life and soul, Vili gave them reason and motion, and Ve gave them senses and speech.

Supporting the universe was a great ash tree, YGGDRASIL, whose three roots extended to the abode of the mortals, to the abode of the giants, and to Niflheim. Beside each root was a well from which the tree was watered. Some day, it was believed, the tree would give way and the universe would fall.

The Aesir and Vanir

Collectively considered, the Norse gods formed the AESIR, a group of twelve deities, headed by Odin. These divinities lived in ASGARD in two magnificent mansions, Gladsheim, for the gods, and Vingolf, for the goddesses. The myths tell of an early conflict between two races of gods, the AESIR of whom Odin and Frigga were the leaders, and the VANIR led by Heimdall, Frey, and Freya. Later the two groups reconciled their differences and dwelt together in Asgard.

Odin

ODIN, the greatest of the gods was the god of war, wisdom, poetry, prophecy, and magic. The corresponding figure in Teutonic mythology is Wodan or WOTAN and in Anglo-Saxon, Woden. As the god of war, Odin was lord or ruler of the VALKYRIES, warrior maidens who lived with him at VALHALLA, the hall of dead heroes, where he held his court. His wisdom he derived from drinking at the fountain of MIMIR, the guardian of the fountain in the lower world. Odin had only one eye, having exchanged the other one with Mimir. He had a spear which was called Gungner, and a ring, Draupner. Odin kept in touch with the outside world by means of Hunin and Munin, his ravens, whom he sent out every day from his palace; when they came back they perched on his shoulders and told him what was going on.

From Odin's Anglo-Saxon name we get Woden's Day, or Wednesday.

Odin's wife was FRIGGA (or Frigg), called FRICKA in Teutonic mythology. Everything was known to Frigga and nature was under her control. Frigga was the goddess of love and of the home, and the blessings of marriage were her gifts. FULLA, who was either her maid or her sister, was one of a band of sixteen goddesses who waited on Frigga and who personified her various attributes or qualities.

Odin is represented as a wise old man with a long white beard, or as a war lord with a gold helmet on his head, a spear, made by the Dwarfs, in his right hand, and his breastplate in the left. It was this spear, hurled by Odin, that marked the beginning of the first war of the world.

As god of the wind, Odin rode through the air on his eight-footed horse, Sleipnir. He shared the gift, possessed by many gods, of being able to change himself into any form or shape that he desired. He enjoyed visiting the earth frequently to see how people were behaving and to see how they would treat him, not knowing who he was.

Odin's sons were Thor, Balder, Vithar, Bragi, Bali, Tyr, and Hoder.

Frigga

FRIGGA, wife of Odin, was the queen of the Norse deities, whose interest in mortals was shown in her protection of marriage and the home. (She must not be confused with Freya, the goddess of young love.) See the paragraph on Frigga under ODIN above.

Thor

THOR, the god of thunder, was the son of Odin and Jörd, representing heaven and earth, or of Odin and Fjorgyn, a mountain goddess. He was the husband of Sif, or Jarnsaxa, a giantess with gold hair. Like his father, he found great pleasure in making frequent visits to the earth. He was a friend of mortals and a foe of the giants, although he himself was a giant in every way, physically, in his superhuman strength and in his appetites. With his red beard, symbolic of the lightning, flaming in the wind, he drove to battle in a goat-drawn chariot. When he was in a temper, he growled in his beard and his voice and eyes were horrible things to see and hear. Thor's constant companions were Loki, an evil god, Thjalfi, a peasant noted for his swiftness, and his sister, Roskva.

Thor's home was Bilskirnir, a palace that had no less than five hundred and forty halls. His magic weapons were a hammer, MJOLNIR, which like a boomerang, returned to his hand after being thrown; an axe; iron gloves; and a girdle that gave him strength.

Thor had many other godships in addition to that of thunder: he was the god of productive marriages, of the domestic hearth, and of fire. His day, Thor's day, which gives us our Thursday, was a lucky one for getting married, and was observed by peasants as a holiday.

While other members of the Aesir, the council of the Norse gods, drove to their appointed meeting-place, Thor went on foot, because as the striding god he covered the heavens in three steps. In hand-to-hand combat, Thor killed the giant Hrungnir, whose head and heart were of stone. As Hrungnir died, he fell on Thor, and the gods, with all their strength, were not able to move him, until MAGNI, Thor's three-year-old son, performed the task and released his father. Thor's hammer was the great defense of the gods against the Frost-giants. Thor met his death at the hands of Thiassi, who threw his eyes up to heaven, where they remained fixed and became shining stars.

In war and peace, on land and sea, Thor was worshipped as a god who helped, a god who brought good luck, and his images were carved on doors, seats, houses, and ships for that reason. Thor was a god of the rude peasant as Odin was of brave warriors and noble families, many of whom claimed that they were descended from him. Subordinate only to Odin, he appears to have been worshipped in Iceland and throughout the north to a greater extent than any other god. (In Wagner's operas, the god of thunder is known as DONNER.)

Loki

LOKI, an evil force, was the son of the giant FARBAUTI and of Laufey. His father's chief duty was to ferry dead souls over the waters of the underworld. Loki was a personification of fire in its destructive aspects. His outstanding trait was a vicious cunning. He was physically handsome, but malignant, and his word meant less than nothing. He hated the gods and he wanted to ruin them and overthrow the universe. He committed many murders and was responsible for others committed by his agents or at his advice and suggestion. By ANGURBODA, a giantess, he was the father of three children as vicious and hateful as himself: FENRIS (or Fenriz) the wolf; the SERPENT OF MIDGARD; and HEL, the goddess of the dead. The Serpent was thrown into the sea by Odin and grew so enormously that it was able to wrap itself around the entire world. By his wife SIGYN he had two sons, Nari and Vali. Balder was slain through his trickery, and both FIMAFENGR, Aegir's servant and OTTER, Hreidman's son, were killed by him. As punishment Loki was chained to a rock, with a serpent suspended over him, dropping poison on his head. Sigyn came to help him and caught the poison as it fell. But when she turned to empty the cup, the venom dropped on Loki, causing him to writhe in an agony that shook the earth. Loki finally met his end at the hands of HEIMDALL (who was himself killed in killing Loki) in a contest to recover Freya's necklace, which Loki had stolen. (In Wagner's operas, the god of fire is known as LOGE.)

Balder

BALDER (or Baldur, Baldr), the god of the sun, was the second son of Odin and Frigga. His name means "shining"—he was the shining god—and he was as gentle as he was beautiful. His devoted wife was NANNA, goddess of the moon.

As a result of a dream that he had had foretelling danger to him, Frigga made all things and creatures, animate and inanimate, except the mistletoe, swear a solemn vow that they would never harm him in any way. The mistletoe was not included in the promise because it was regarded as being young and harmless. Loki, the motiveless maker of mischief, learned that the mistletoe was not a party to the promise and, with an evil plan forming in his mind, rushed to secure a twig of it. Since nothing could harm Balder the beautiful, the gods thought it great sport to hurl weapons at him, which were harmless to him. Knowing this, Loki had little difficulty in persuading HODER (or Hodr), the blind god of the winter months, and Balder's brother, to join his fellow-gods in the game. Guided by Loki, the innocent Hoder hurled a mistletoe dart and Balder fell to the ground dead. The astonishment of the gods gave way to uncontrollable grief, in which they were joined by mortals, as both gods and men loved the sungod. Balder's body was placed on a funeral pile on a ship and pushed out to sea. As the torch was applied, Nanna died of a broken heart and her body was burned and buried with that of her husband.

Balder's soul went to Niflheim, the lower world, which was both a place of heavenly bliss for the good and virtuous and a place of punishment and torture for the evil. Odin and Frigga sent a messenger to Hel, the goddess of the underworld and Loki's daughter, begging her to restore Balder back to life. Hel replied that she would return Balder to the upper world if all forms of Nature, dead and alive, would shed tears for him. All the creatures of the earth, loving Balder, wept bitterly, all except a repulsive old hag, a giantess, who cried out vindictively, "Let Hel keep what belongs to Hel," and who turned out to be Loki, in one of the countless shapes he was able to assume. Thus Balder was doomed to remain forever in the lower world.

The hapless Hoder was slain by Bali, a son of Odin, and Loki, after changing himself into a salmon in order to escape the fury of the outraged gods, was trapped by them in a net and kept prisoner until the twilight of the gods.

Frey

FREY (or Freyr, FROH), the god of fruitfulness and the sender of sunshine and rain, was the brother of Freyja, goddess of love. He was a son of Njordhr, who was either a god of fertility or of the sea, and of Sakdi, a daughter of Thjazi the Giant. Frey lived in Elfheim, where the elves made their home. His famous possessions included the Sword of Victory; Skidþladna, a ship that was large enough to carry all the gods on it and yet capable of being folded up and put away into his bag; and Bloodyhoof, a horse that made the earth tremble when its feet touched the ground.

Frey fell madly in love with and married a beautiful giantess, GERDA, daughter of Gymir. Instead of wooing her himself, he sent his servant SKIRNIR to speak for him, who agreed on condition that Frey give him his sword. Frey consented, so, in winning Gerda, Frey lost his sword and when the last great fight came he was conquered. Like Odin, Frey was regarded as the god or patron of seafaring folk. Also like Odin, he was described as the god of rain, sun, and fruit, which makes him Odin under another name. He is variously represented as riding through the air on a wild boar, as in a chariot drawn by a boar, or crossing the sea in a boat.

Freya

FREYA (or Freyja), sister of Frey, was the Norse goddess of love and the art of healing. She was entitled to receive the souls of half the heroes who fell in battle, the other half going to Odin. Freya was also the goddess of marriage, of fruitfulness and fertility, as her brother was the god, and of the dead. The white cats that pulled her chariot were symbolic of prolificness.

She owned and was very proud of a brilliant necklace, BRISINGAMEN, that broke into pieces when she was angry. Brisingamen was forged by four dwarfs, to each of whom the goddess had given herself in order to secure the dazzling trinket. Loki, the mischief-maker, stole it at Odin's demand. Heimdall's attempts to recover it led to his fierce fight with Loki, in which each one killed the other. In order to get the necklace back Freya had to promise that she would stir up serious trouble between two mighty kings. Friday was named for her.

Hel

HEL, the goddess of the dead, was the daughter of Loki and Angurboda, and the sister of Fenris and the Serpent of Midgard. She was all evil, and her associations suggest horror and suffering: her bed was Care, her dish was Hunger, and her knife, Starvation, and her attendants, Delay and Slowness. When she was born, the gods threw her down into Niflheim, a damp, dark, dank region, and made her the queen of nine worlds, in which she divided the dead into different categories. Hel was represented as half black and half blue, and she fed on the brains and marrow of men.

According to some myths, all the dead went to Hel; according to other, later myths, only women and children and those who died of sickness or old age, and men who had not died in battle, were given over to her. Hel was both the name of a place or territory and of the god or goddess who ruled over it. She lived under the roots of Yggdrasil, the sacred ash tree, the world tree. The region over which she presided was so far away that it took

Sleipnir, Odin's horse, using all of his eight legs, nine days and nights to reach it. Hel's realm was surrounded on all sides by the river Gioll.

Fenris

FENRIS (Fenrir, Fenriz), a monster wolf, was one of the offspring of Loki and the giantess Angurboda. He was so huge that he became a problem child to the gods who feared him. They chained him up, but his strength was so great that he broke the first two chains with ease. Finally, the gods, in desperation at the failure of their own efforts, had a magic chain or bond forged by the dwarfs. GLEIPNIR, as the chain was called, was made of the sound of a cat's footsteps, the roots of a mountain, the breath of a fish, a woman's beard, and a bird's spittle. It was powerful enough to hold him until RAGNAROK, the day of judgment or the last day of the gods. On that day, he escaped and swallowed Odin, but was slain by Vithar, Odin's son. It was during his violent struggles to free himself that Fenris bit off Tyr's hand when the god of war thrust it into his mouth in order to distract his attention and allow his fellow gods to bind Fenris. Fenris, rushing to battle after breaking his bonds and before death claimed him, presented an ugly picture, with his lower jaw grazing the ground and his snout scraping the sky.

Bragi and Idun

BRAGI, the god of wisdom, poetry, and eloquence, was one of the chief Aesir. He was the son of Odin and Frigga, and the husband of IDUN (Iduna), the goddess of eternal youth. When Aegir visited the Hall of Odin, Bragi answered all his questions. Idun, who personified spring, had charge of a box containing golden apples; when the gods grew old, they ate the apples and became young again. THIASSI, the god of winter, stole the magic apples and confined the gods in the lower world. Idun managed to escape and recovered the apples, which she gave to the imprisoned gods, who were already beginning to grow old.

One of Bragi's important duties was to welcome the soldier heroes when they entered Valhalla. He is represented as a kind old man, with a long beard, mounted and fully armed.

Heimdall

HEIMDALL was the watchman of BIFROST, the rainbow bridge leading to the underworld. On the lookout for attacks by the giants, he stood guard in Himinbiorg, the heaven-tower of Thor, the thunder-god. The qualities essential for a good watchman—sight and hearing—he possessed in a superlative degree; day or night made no difference to him. So keen was his hearing, and his sight was as sharp, that he could hear grass growing in the ground and wool on the back of a sheep.

Heimdall's heroic equipment consisted of Gulltopr (Goldropf), a horse with a gold mane; Hofud, a magic sword; and Gjallarhorn, a horn that can be heard all over the world. Heimdall's blowing of his horn was the signal for the last great battle that marked the twilight or destruction of the gods. Gulltopr took him to the funeral of Balder, the shining god. Heimdall and Loki were bitter enemies and their constant fighting for possession of Freyja's necklace came to an end only at the final battle that ended everything, when each one killed the other.

Tyr

TYR (also known as ZIU and SAXNOT), the son of Odin, was the god of war and athletic activities. Tyr was a shining or glistening god. His Anglo-Saxon name was Tiw or Tiu, and the day set apart for him, Tiwes daeg, gives us our Tuesday. Tyr's right hand was bitten off in a terrific struggle by Fenris, one of Loki's offspring, a monster wolf. In the last and greatest battle, Tyr killed, and was killed by, GARM, the hell-hound guarding the Gnipa cave. Wrestlers, fighters, runners and other athletes called on Tyr for aid.

Jörd

JÖRD, the goddess of Earth in Old Norse mythology, is the ERDA of Teutonic myths, pictured as deeply imbued with the wisdom of the primitive Earth. By Odin, she was the mother of Thor.

Vithar

VITHAR (or Vidharr) was the strongest god next to Thor. Vithar was as silent as he was strong, and was known as the silent god. At the feasts given to the gods by Aegir, the friendly giant, Vithar was the only god not included in the general abuse and vilification that fell from Loki's nasty tongue. At the Ragnarok, or twilight of the gods, he, son of Odin and Gridh, a giantess, avenged the death of his father by tearing apart the jaws of the wolf Fenris, the eater of the gods. He planted his iron shoe on the monster's lower jaw and forced up the upper jaw, thus wrenching them asunder. He was one of the Aesir and was one of the few to survive the Ragnarok, the other gods, Odin, Tyr, Thor, Loki, Heimdall, and Frey among them, being destroyed.

Ulle

ULLE (or Ullr) was the god of the chase, famous for his skill in archery and noted for his amazing speed on stilts. He was the son of SIF, a giantess with golden hair. As one of the Aesir, the council of the Norse gods, his throne was in Asgard. Ulle possessed a magic ring that mortals swore by, and they called on him when engaging in hand-to-hand fighting. He took Odin's place when the chief god was away.

Mimir

MIMIR was the custodian of the fountain of wisdom in the lower world. He traded some of his precious liquid with his nephew Odin in exchange for one of his eyes, which he kept at the bottom of a well. In the first war in the world, that between the Aesir and the Vanir, Mimir was one of the hostages given by the former to the latter. They chopped off his head because they thought that he was not a satisfactory equivalent for their own hostage. Odin spoke magic words over the head and gave it the power of speech, so that he might still have the benefit of Mimir's wise advice.

Aegir and Ran

AEGIR was the giant of the seashore. Friendly with the gods, he visited them frequently at Asgard, sitting next to Bragi, and listened with eager attention to the stories Bragi told him. Aegir reciprocated by inviting the gods to his home on the island of Hler and brewing wine and ale for them in a huge caldron a mile deep that Thor had stolen from the giant Hymir. The fellowship and harmony that prevailed at these meetings was marred on one occasion by the rude conduct of the uninvited Loki, who pushed his way in and delivered a violent tongue-lashing to the assembled gods.

RAN was a storm giantess and the goddess of the deep. She was Aegir's wife and the mother of nine daughters—the billows. Those who drowned at sea she regarded as rightfully belonging to her and she drew them in a net down to her home under the waves.

Elves, Dwarfs, and Giants

The Norse myths are peopled with innumerable beings, both large and small, good and bad, in addition to great and powerful gods and goddesses.

The ELVES were tiny creatures who had a tendency to tease and to play tricks on mortals, but they were inclined to be peaceful if they were not bothered or mistreated, and they took as much pleasure and delight in serving as in plaguing mankind.

The DWARFS, whose father was IVALDR, lived in the very heart of the hills. All precious gems and metals belonged to them and they were noted for their great skill as workers with jewelry. Hidden treasures were in their keeping, and they would not reveal their hiding place to the hunters until they had been properly appeased by gifts.

At the other end of the ladder were the GIANTS, who stole summer and brought winter in its place. They lived in JOTUNHEIM. Some of the giants were HRUNGNIR, who was killed by Thor; HRESVELGR, living in the far north, who produced winds and tempests by simply moving his wings; and SURTR, a southern giant, who guarded Muspelheim, the fire-land, with his flaming sword.

We give further details on the elves, dwarfs, and giants in the chapter on "Fairy Lore of Europe and the Orient," later in this book.

The NORNS were the three Norse Fates, or the goddesses of fate. Female giants, they brought the wonderful Golden Age to an end. They cast lots over the cradle of every child that was born and placed gifts in the cradle. Their names were URDA, VERDANDI, and SKULD, representing the Past, the Present and the Future. Urda and Verdandi were kindly disposed, but Skuld was cruel and savage. Their tasks were to sew the web of fate, to water the sacred ash, Yggdrasil, and to keep it in good condition by placing fresh earth around it daily. In her fury, Skuld often spoiled the work of her sisters by tearing the web to shreds.

The Norns and Valkyries

The VALKYRIES were the thirteen choosers of the slain, the beautiful military maids of Odin who rode through the air and over the sea. They watched the progress of the battle and selected the heroes who were to fall fighting. After they were dead, the maidens awarded the heroes by kissing them and then led their souls to Valhalla, where the warriors lived happily in an ideal existence, drinking and eating without restraint and fighting over again the battles in which they died and in which they won deathless fame.

LEGENDS OF NORSE AND TEUTONIC HEROES

The Story of the "Volsunga Saga" and the "Nibelungenlied"

The most famous of the Northern hero legends, the story of Sigurd or Siegfried, exists in two forms, one of Norse and one of Teutonic origin. Although the two accounts agree in a great many respects, the names of the characters differ considerably and in a number of instances their personalities are quite different. The great Norse telling of the tale is the *Volsunga Saga,* or Saga of the Volsungs, an Icelandic epic. Its hero is Sigurd the Volsung. The Teutonic version of the same story is the *Nibelungenlied,* or the Lay of the Nibelungs, the hero of which is Siegfried. The principal characters in one work have their counterparts in the other. We tell the story here primarily in terms of Sigurd, the Volsung hero, and give the names of the equivalent Teutonic characters in parenthesis, also pointing out the major differences in incident between the two epics.

SIGURD (SIEGFRIED) was the son of SIGMUND (SIEGMUND) (who was the son of VOLSUNG), and HJORDIS (Sieglinde). Sigurd was born to his mother after Sigmund's death at the hands of HUNDING, who had loved Hjordis. Before he died Sigmund bequeathed to his son-to-be a sword, Gram, which Sigurd was to use often in his adventures. The boy was brought up by a foster-father, REGIN, a blacksmith (or MIME, a dwarf), who taught him well. But Regin was a greedy person and egged Sigurd on to kill FAFNIR, a dragon who sat guard over a hoard of gold. Sigurd slew Fafnir, and ate of his heart, a deed which enabled him to learn the language of the birds, who told him to slay Regin as well, advice which Sigurd took.

Sigurd now had possession of the hoard, which included a magic ring which bore the curse of ANDVARI the dwarf. Not knowing this, Sigurd put the ring on his finger.

Sigurd then came to a great hill where he saw a circle of fire, in the center of which was a beautiful maiden. This was BRYNHILD (BRÜNHILDE), the loveliest of the Valkyries, who, because of her aid to Sigmund (Sigurd's father), had been punished by Odin by being put to sleep in the ring of fire, to be awakened only by a hero who would be brave enough to ride through the flames. This Sigurd did. Sigurd and Brynhild fell in love and plighted their troth, Sigurd giving her the magic ring. But Brynhild knew that they were destined not to come to a happy end.

Sigurd rode on and came to the land of the Nibelungs, where he won great respect for his deeds of valor. There Sigurd was given a magic potion which made him forget his love for Brynhild, and he married GUDRUN (KRIEMHILD). In time he joined with others at the court in urging his wife's brother, GUNNAR (GUNTHER), to seek the hand of Brynhild. Gunnar made two attempts to pierce the ring of fire around the Valkyrie but failed. Sigurd then came to his aid, and, assuming the guise of Gunnar, rode through the flames again and came to Brynhild. They exchanged rings, he thus receiving again the magic ring with the curse. On his return to the land of the Nibelungs, he related what had occurred and gave the ring to Gudrun. In the *Nibelungenlied* Siegfried makes himself invisible by means of the TARNKAPPE, a magic cloak, and prompts Gunther to great feats of strength to win BRUNHILD (*Nibelungenlied* name).

Brynhild came to the court to wed Gunnar, fully aware of the deceit that had been perpetrated on her, but resolved to go through with the marriage. However, at the wedding feast, the magic spell wore off, and Sigurd's love for Brynhild revived. Not until Gudrun, in an angry dispute, reviled Brynhild with the story of Sigurd's ride through the flames in the person of Gunnar, did Brynhild resolve to take her revenge. She incited Gunnar's brother GUTTORM, to slay Sigurd, and while the hero was asleep the deed was done.

In the *Nibelungenlied,* Siegfried is somewhat more artfully done to death. It was known that Siegfried had been made invulnerable by having bathed in the blood of a dragon; only between the shoulders, where a leaf had settled, could he be killed. Brunhild plotted to have Kriemhild make a garment for Siegfried with a cross which would lie on the vulnerable spot. Then HAGEN did the deed while Siegfried stopped by a brook to drink.

In the *Volsunga Saga* Brynhild was overcome with remorse at the death of Sigurd and inflicted a fatal wound on herself, and she was burned on the funeral pile with Sigurd.

Following Sigurd's death Gudrun married ATLI (ETZEL), king of Hunland. Meanwhile the hoard of gold had passed into the hands of Gudrun's brothers, and to obtain it, Atli invited them to his castle, where he slew them. But they had concealed it at the bottom of the Rhine. In revenge Gudrun killed Atli and escaped with SWANHILD, her daughter by Sigurd, to the land of JONAKR, whom she married. Here Swanhild was murdered by JORMUNREK, and once again Gudrun had to avenge a death of a dear one. She called upon her sons by Jonakr to kill Jormunrek, which they did, but were themselves killed in the process by the planning of Odin, the forefather of Volsung and thus of Sigurd.

In the *Nibelungenlied*, Kriemhild ordered her brother Gunther's head cut off; and she herself decapitated Hagen after he refused to tell her where he had hidden the hoard. Then she was killed by HILDEBRAND, one of Etzel's knights.

LEGENDS OF OTHER GERMANIC HEROES

Parsifal

PARSIFAL, the pure knight of the Round Table, came one day to a castle on Montsalvatch. In the splendid banquet hall Parsifal noted that his host seemed to be suffering from a wound and that all the guests seemed to be oppressed by a strange sadness. The doors opened and a procession entered, in which a servant bore a bloody lance, and a maiden bore the Holy Grail, the cup from which Christ had drunk at the Last Supper. The knights present groaned sorely at the sight of the vessel and cast reproachful glances at Parsifal. At a loss to understand the meaning of what had happened, Parsifal retired for the night, and the next day departed from the castle. Just as he was crossing the drawbridge he heard a voice cursing him. Only later did Parsifal learn that the wounded host was AMFORTAS, the guardian of the Holy Grail, who had been struck by the lance when he had left the castle to live a life of pleasure, and that a question from him, Parsifal, as to the cause of Amfortas' suffering would have made it cease.

Parsifal attempted to revisit the castle, but he could no longer find it. Then he returned to Arthur's court, where, at Merlin's bidding, he was about to occupy the Siege Perilous. Just as he was ready to take his place, the witch KUNDRIE appeared and denounced him for having given up the search for the castle of the Grail. Remorseful, Parsifal renewed his search and in time found the castle. There he asked the question, and Amfortas' wound was healed. Kundrie was baptized and Parsifal became the guardian of the Grail.

Lohengrin

LOHENGRIN was the son of Parsifal. The legend associated with him concerns his championing of ELSA, duchess of Brabant. Elsa possessed much wealth and many lands, and for these Count FREDERICK OF TELRAMUND wished to marry her. But Elsa disliked him and would not consent to the marriage. One day, while Elsa was in the forest she had a vision in which the knight Lohengrin appeared and gave her a small silver bell. He told her that if ever she were in difficulty and needed him she should ring the bell. Then Elsa awoke, whereupon a falcon swooped down from the sky and gave her a real bell.

Telramund, not to be done out of Elsa's wealth, trumped up the charge that Elsa had murdered her brother, and she was thrown into prison. King Henry decreed that the case would be decided by a judicial duel. But Elsa had no champion to fight for her. While praying for a knight to come to fight for her, she beat her breast in supplication, thus ringing the bell, which she had tied around her neck. The day of the duel came, and still Elsa had no champion, but then, just as Henry was about to order the proceedings to start, a boat drawn by swans floated down the river, and from this boat stepped Lohengrin to defend Elsa's name and life.

Lohengrin defeated Telramund in the duel. Lohengrin and Elsa fell in love and they were married. However, Lohengrin cautioned Elsa never to ask his name. But in time Elsa's curiosity got the better of her, and she asked Lohengrin his name, whereupon Lohengrin declared that he must leave her. "Love cannot live without faith," he said. Then the swan boat which had brought him appeared and he was drawn away in it, never to appear to Elsa again.

Tannhäuser

TANNHÄUSER, a German knight and singer of songs, was loved by LISAURA, an Italian maiden. Tannhäuser returned her love, but wished to experience the love of some elementary spirit in the form of mortal woman. His philosopher friend HILARIO sent him to Venusberg, the court of VENUS, the goddess of love. Here Tannhäuser enjoyed the favors of Venus and he tarried long there, but he could not forget the world which he had renounced. At length he received the permission of the goddess to return to earth. Here he found that Lisaura had killed herself in grief at his departure. Repentant, he traveled to Rome to Pope Urban, who told him that his sins could not be forgiven. Tannhäuser was bewildered and did not know where to turn. But Venus beckoned to him and he returned to Venusberg, where he remained until the day of judgment.

Faust

JOHANN FAUST, or FAUSTUS, was a magician and astrologer who lived in the sixteenth century in Germany. Following his death a number of legends sprang up about him, centering around his dealings with the devil. He was believed to have sold his soul to the devil for an agreed-upon time in return for renewed youth and knowledge and power. Faust enjoyed the favor of the devil but in time was carried off by him.

Old English Legends

From the legendary characters of England we have selected three well-known figures, Beowulf, Wayland Smith, and Robin Hood. The story of Beowulf dates from some time before 1000 A.D. when the language of England was Anglo-Saxon or Old English. England at that time was oriented toward the Teutonic countries of northern Europe and it is interesting to note that the story of this oldest of English epics actually takes place entirely in Denmark and Sweden, an account from the past by the Anglo-Saxons who settled in England.

Wayland Smith also dates from this period of English history and is, in fact, the English counterpart of a character in the Norse *Edda*.

Robin Hood is the hero of many tales and ballads set in twelfth century England, a time when the country was beginning to assume more of the character of the England of history and tradition.

Beowulf

Beowulf, soldier and king, is the hero of the great Anglo-Saxon or Old English epic, *Beowulf*. The nephew of Hygelac, king of the Geats (Scandinavia), the news came to Beowulf that Hrothgar, king of the Danes, was being terrorized at his palace, Heorot, by a monster who was destroying his men. With a small band of followers, Beowulf decided to cross the sea to Hrothgar's kingdom and to help him in his trouble. Arriving at Heorot, he was received with hospitality by Hrothgar and his queen.

The horrible creature whom Beowulf was to fight was Grendel, who for years had been coming to Hrothgar's hall to satisfy his blood lust by killing and eating the king's warriors, often destroying as many as thirty in one night. When darkness had descended on Heorot Hall, Grendel, true to form, burst through the doors, bent on his evil plans and not expecting to meet opposition. Without unnecessary delay he attacked and ate Hondscio, one of Beowulf's warriors. Then Grendel, who was descended from Cain, made a fatal mistake: he grabbed Beowulf, who was ready for him, and who had in his hand the strength and power of thirty men, which was the equivalent of Grendel's devouring capacity. The palace halls rocked and shook in the terrific battle that followed; it ended only when Grendel, screaming with pain, fled from the hall, leaving his arm behind him, torn out of its socket by the powerful hero. He rushed to his home, a cave under the water, and died.

The next night the castle had another visitor, Grendel's mother or dam, as she was called, no other name being given her. A vile and foul creature, uglier and more horrible than Grendel, she had come to avenge the death of her son. She immediately killed Aschere, the king's confidential adviser, and escaped. Beowulf got ready to follow her to her den, and Unferth, one of Hrothgar's thanes, gave Beowulf his sword, Hruntig. As it turned out, the weapon was useless. But Beowulf killed her with another sword, forged by giants, that he found in the cave. He cut off her head and also the head of Grendel, whose dead body was lying in a corner of the cave. So strong was the blood of these hellish creatures that the sword melted away in his hand, leaving only the hilt.

Returning to Heorot, Beowulf reported his mission accomplished and gave Grendel's head to Hrothgar as a souvenir.

Having delivered the Danes from their enemies, the Geatish warrior was showered with gifts and praise and returned to his home in Scandinavia, where, after the death of his uncle and his uncle's son, he became king. For half a century he ruled in peace and wisdom, gaining the love of his subjects, until the peace of the country was disturbed by a treasure-guarding dragon who went on the warpath when he discovered that he had been robbed. With a handful of companions, WIGLAF among them, Beowulf, now an old man, set out to conquer the fire-breathing beast. When they came face to face with him, all Beowulf's warriors fled for safety, all except Wiglaf, who stayed with his king and kinsmen, helped him to slay the dragon, and was with him at the end. Beowulf's sword again failed him, breaking in the dragon's scaly body, and he finally won by the strength of his bare hands. But in ending the dragon's life, aided by a blow from the faithful Wiglaf, he lost his own. To Wiglaf, before he died, Beowulf gave his ring, his helmet, and his suit of armor.

Thus ended the noble career of the fabulous fighting hero who always met and overcame supernatural forces, who always fought, not for his own glory, but for the sake and safety of others.

Wayland Smith

WAYLAND SMITH (or the Smith, or simply Wayland) was a famous wonder-working smith. He appears in many forms, was known by many names, and his countless stories have many variations. He was the son of a sailor and a mermaid and had a career as interesting as one might expect from such a parentage. He was the king of the elves, and a maker of many wonderful articles, such as a magic feather boat, a garment with wings, victory-winning swords, and a solid gold arm-ring. His brothers married Valkyries, who were compelled by fate to leave them after a period of nine years. Wayland, in spite of all his skill and cleverness, fell into the power of NIDUDR (Nidung), a cruel king of Sweden, who mutilated his feet, threw him into prison, and compelled him to slave for him. Wayland finally revenged himself on his enemy by killing his two sons and raping his daughter, BODHILDA (Bodvilda). The skulls of the boys he set in gold and gave them to the father; to the mother he gave gems fashioned from their eyes; and their teeth, worked into a breast-pin, he presented to the sister. After telling the king what he had done, he flew away to Valhalla on his wings.

Wayland was supposed to have lived for a time in England, and his smithy was believed to have been located at the White Horse, in Ashdown, Berkshire. According to legend, if a rider left his steed at Wayland's forge, with a six-penny fee, and went away for a short time—the smith not wishing to be watched while at work—he would find his animal completely shod when he came back. Wayland is the Norse Volund (or Volundr), the French Gallans, and the German Wieland.

Robin Hood

ROBIN HOOD and his Merry Men were a band of outlaws who lived in Sherwood Forest and delighted in defying law and order. Robin Hood himself was of noble birth; in his youth he had unwittingly killed a man and had fled to the forest. He gathered round him a band which numbered one hundred and forty men. Prominent among them were LITTLE JOHN, WILL SCARLET, ALLAN-A-DALE, and FRIAR TUCK. MAID MARIAN was his beloved.

The Sheriff of Nottingham was in almost continuous pursuit of Robin, but could never bring him to justice. Many of the tales about the popular hero are concerned with the ways in which he outwitted the sheriff. There are many stories, too, of his readiness to come to the assistance of the poor and unfortunate, often robbing the rich to help them.

In later years Robin joined the forces of King Richard, but he missed the free life of the forest and returned to his men. He is said to have died when a prioress, to whom he came with a high fever to be bled, opened an artery instead of a vein and left him to bleed to death.

Legends of the Romance Peoples

FRANCE and Spain, whose people speak languages which are in the group called Romance languages, are the home of tales of love and adventure which are termed "romances" in our modern sense of this word. In the Middle Ages poets travelled about the countryside telling stories of the heroic deeds of knights. Of these, the greatest was the story of Roland, chief of the twelve peers of the emperor Charlemagne. As was the case with many of their narratives, the poets went to actual history for their *Song of Roland,* national epic of France.

In Spain too an actual person was to become the hero of the national epic, *Poema del Cid.* Another legendary figure of Spain whom we take up is the famous Don Juan.

In the entries below we discuss these sources further and then recount the legends themselves.

THE PEERS OF CHARLEMAGNE

Roland

ROLAND was the greatest of the peers or paladins of CHARLEMAGNE, as the Emperor's knights were called. They were *peers* in the sense that they were all equal, and they were known as *paladins* because they were attached to the palace of the king.

In the year 778, Charlemagne, or Charles the Great, the King of the Franks, returned from a military expedition against the Moors in Spain; as his army was marching through the passes of the Pyrenees, its rear-guard was attacked at Roncesvalles by the Basques and completely destroyed. The hero of this historical incident was Roland (or Hrodland), a more or less obscure count, or warden, of the Marches of Brittany. In romance and legend, the real Roland, who is a dim figure, becomes a famous national hero and is described as Charlemagne's nephew, through being the son of Bertha, the Emperor's sister, and Milon, a knight of a distinguished family. The actual expedition of a year is expanded in romantic treatment to a military campaign of seven years. Saracens, the enemy in the *Song,* are substituted for Basques, the enemy of history, and the crushing defeat does not detract from the heroism of the defenders because it is represented as the result of treachery.

Roland, the leader of the peers, was loyal, brave, and noble, but he lacked wisdom and he was proud. When he was attacked by the enemy and when his army was being cut to pieces he refused to blow his horn, OLIVANT, the sound of which would bring aid from the Emperor, because he was too proud to admit that he was in distress and in need of help. When he was finally persuaded by his friend and comrade in arms, OLIVER, to blow it, it was too late. Charlemagne was so far away that he arrived after the destruction had been accomplished, and Roland, already weak from loss of blood, blew such a powerful blast that he burst his temples and died. Although the French were defeated in the battle, they inflicted heavy losses on the Saracens, Roland contributing his share to the slaughter, using his sword DURANDAL as an effective weapon. It was believed that Durandal was once held by Hector of Troy.

In life, Roland's one thought was glory in service to his lord, and he lived and died gloriously as a brave and noble knight. To have blown his horn earlier would have been the better part of wisdom and ordinary common sense, but it would not have been in the spirit of heroic romance. In his dashing manner, his bravery, his impetuosity, his deathless loyalty that made death itself seem a small matter, his love of glory, his desire for fame, and his fighting heart, Charlemagne's nephew was living up to the chivalric ideals that the people of the time wished to find in their leaders, but seldom in actuality did.

Italian romance retold the story of Roland, calling the hero Orlando.

Oliver

OLIVER, the son of Renier, Lord of Genoa, may be called the second hero of the *Song of Roland.* He was one of Charlemagne's peers or paladins and Roland's loyal friend from early boyhood. He was the brother of the maiden AUDE, who was engaged to Roland and who died of grief for the hero who would have married her had he not died in battle.

Roland and Oliver were once selected by lot as opponents in a battle to decide the issue of a conflict between Charlemagne and Lord Guerin de Montglave, his subject. Oliver was drawn to represent the cause of Guerin, and Charlemagne's side was defended by Roland, neither hero knowing the identity of his foe. The battle lasted for hours without sign of victory or defeat. Finally, after five days of fighting, each contestant tore off his opponent's helmet and recognized the other at the same second. They threw down their weapons and embraced, refusing to continue the battle. Roland declared that he was beaten and Oliver that he surrendered. This wholly unexpected turn of events did not settle the dispute which was the origin of the combat, and it therefore became necessary to place the question before a mediation board. Namo, Duke of Bavaria, and also a peer, represented Charlemagne's interests, and Oliver himself was the spokesman for Lord Guerin. As a result of their efforts the king and his subject were reconciled.

Oliver was as brave as Roland but he was wiser and more practical; it was he who begged Roland to blow his horn at the Battle of Roncesvalles, which would have turned the tide of fighting and have saved thousands of lives. The long-drawn-out personal contest between the two friends and heroes gave rise to the expression, as famous as the fighters, a *Roland for an Oliver,* to signify a contest of any kind in which the participants are so evenly matched that one is as good as the other, making it impossible to predict the outcome.

Ganelon

GANELON (Ganalon or Gano) was a peer or paladin of Charlemagne, but he was no hero. Enjoying the complete, but misplaced, confidence of the emperor, he was appointed ambassador to the Saracens in Spain. He made it appear that he had accomplished his mission and that Marsilius, the Saracen king, found agreeable and accepted Charlemagne's terms. As a result, the emperor returned to France with his army. In reality, Ganelon, motivated largely by hatred of his stepson Roland, had not carried out his instructions, but had entered into a secret plot with King Marsilius to betray the rear-guard of Charlemagne's army at Roncesvalles, which would be, as he well knew, under Roland's command. With the Emperor and his main army separated from Roland's small detachment, the French hero and his forces were hopelessly outnumbered by the Saracen troops. Ganelon, his treachery discovered, suffered the fate of a villain and a traitor: tried and found guilty, he was tied to four wild horses and torn to pieces.

Rinaldo

RINALDO (or Renaud), another noble peer of Charlemagne, was a son of Aymon and Aya, the Emperor's sister. He was one of the best knights, perhaps the best after Roland and Oliver. He and his three brothers, ALARDO, RICARDO, and RICCIARDETTO, gave long and loyal service to Charlemagne and they were well rewarded for it with great gifts of land and palaces. From the name he gave his magnificent mountain castle, built of white marble, Rinaldo was known as Rinaldo of Montalban. The most famous myth concerning this paladin tells how he met and conquered the wild horse, BAYARD, who was as famous as the myth in which he appears. The strange thing about Bayard, once the property of Amadis of Gaul, great hero of ancient romance, was that he became loving and gentle as soon as he was thrown to the ground by one who mastered and showed no fear of him. Many knights, seeking name and glory, had been killed or injured by his wild rushes. Rinaldo did not lose his life but he had a hard time before he conquered the ferocious animal and was helped tremendously by the fortunate fact that Bayard caught his foot in the branches of an oak tree. After he was made to know that Rinaldo was his master, Bayard served him well in many stirring adventures. Rinaldo's bitter foe was Ganelon, the traitor. A foe who became a friend was ISOLIER, a Saracen or pagan knight whom he defeated in single combat before overcoming Bayard.

Turpin

TURPIN (or Tilpin) was, like Charlemagne, another historical character who appears, highly romanticized and idealized, in the chivalric literature of the Middle Ages. In history, he was the Archbishop of Rheims; he was mistakenly credited with the authorship of a Latin chronicle on the life and deeds of Charlemagne, and he died about the year 800. In the *Song of Roland* he is one of the paladins, and he gave a good account of himself on the battlefield, not only urging and inspiring the soldiers to fight but slaying several of the pagan foe. He granted absolution to the soldiers and told them that they would enter Paradise because they were giving their lives in a holy cause. His last act, which was too much for his weakened condition, was an attempt to give the dying Roland a drink of water, but he fell to the ground dead before he could carry out this good deed.

Astolpho

ASTOLPHO (or Astolfo) was an English knight who was one of Charlemagne's peers. He was noted for his unfailing courtesy, his good nature under provoking circumstances, and the remarkable ease with which he could be thrown in a tournament, which was not less remarkable than the fact that he never seemed to mind in the slightest degree. As soon as he was unhorsed he would pick himself up, brush off his armor, mount his steed again, and again try—but without success—to cover himself with glory. He owned two highly valuable possessions, given to him by Logestilla, a friendly witch: a magic horn and a magic book. The sound of the horn was so terrible that it struck panic fear into all—men and animals—who sought to attack him. From the book he could learn anything that he desired or needed to know. As a result, Astolpho was never afraid of robbers or murderers, and the secrets of magic were no mysteries to him.

Other Knights of Charlemagne

Other paladins of Charlemagne were NAMO, the Duke of Bavaria; SALOMON, the king of Brittany; MALAGIGI, the Enchanter and Rinaldo's cousin; FLORISMART, Roland's friend; and the celebrated OGIER THE DANE.

When Ogier was over a hundred years old, he was rejuvenated by MORGANA, a fairy, who married him and with whom he lived for more than two hundred years in her castle of forgetfulness. At the end of that period, Ogier turned up at the French court and wanted to marry a widow but Morgana did not approve of the match and made him return to her.

SPANISH LEGENDARY HEROES

El Cid

The CID, or Cid Campeador (meaning "Lord Conqueror"), is the great national hero of Spain. His heroic deeds, both real and legendary, were the inspiration for many Spanish romances. His physical bravery, his gallantry, his qualities of leadership, his supreme military skill, all have been magnified until they take on the features of legend and mythology. A great fighter by nature, he fought both for and against the Christians, and for and against the Moors. The real Cid was Rodrigo (or Ruy) Diaz de Bivar (1040?–1099), a Spanish soldier of fortune. As knight, soldier, hero, he is celebrated not only in the great Spanish epic, *Poema del Cid,* but in hundreds of ballads, chronicles, novels, dramas, and grand opera.

He won his name of "conqueror" by defeating five Moorish kings, bringing to an end the three-hundred-year rule of Spain by the Arabs.

The Cid of the legends killed one Don Gomez, who had insulted his father. Gomez's daughter, XIMENA, appeared at the court of Ferdinand, king of Castile, and denounced the Cid and demanded that he take her life too. She made several trips to the court to repeat her request and learned there of the Cid's heroic exploits. Love overcame her resentment and Ximena became the wife of the Cid.

After they were married the Cid vowed that he would not be worthy of his wife until he had won five battles. In the first of these he was a champion of Ferdinand against Martin Gonzalez, knight of Oregon, with whom Ferdinand was disputing over Calahorra, a frontier town. Mounted on his noble steed BABIECA, the Cid defeated Gonzalez in personal combat. In his second battle the Cid defeated the Moors at Estramadura. After winning three remaining battles, the Cid returned to Ximena. However, the great warrior was not to remain unoccupied for long, for he engaged and defeated a champion of Henry III of Germany, who had complained to the Pope that Ferdinand would not pay tribute to him.

Ferdinand was succeeded on the throne by Sancho, who was murdered under rather suspicious circumstances. Alfonso then became king, but before the Cid would ally himself with him, he wished the new king to acknowledge that he had had no part in Sancho's murder. Indignant, Alfonso banished the Cid from the kingdom. However, the two were later reconciled and the Cid recaptured Valencia from the Moors. During his banishment the Cid had borrowed large sums of money from money lenders, having given as security two locked coffers, which actually contained nothing but sand. After his conquest of Valencia the Cid became master of it and its riches and was able to repay the loan. He returned the money with this message: "Although they can find nothing in the coffers but sand, they will find that the pure gold of my truth lies beneath the sand."

Later the Moors returned, and the Cid had a vision that in thirty days he would die, but would, nevertheless, triumph over the enemy. In making preparations for his death he ordered that his dead body should be strapped on his horse and be led against the enemy. He died in the time predicted and his wishes were carried out. When the moors saw Babieça with the dead body of the Spanish hero strapped to his back, they were terrified and fled, thus fulfilling the Cid's vision.

Don Juan

DON JUAN, the legendary archetype of profligacy, is a character who has his counterpart in the legends of many nations, but the Spanish version of the licentious lover has become a universal figure. The amours of Don Juan carried him over many parts of Europe, but it was in Spain that he met with retribution. After seducing the daughter of the commander of Seville, he killed her father in a duel. According to one version he later visited a statue of his victim in a Franciscan monastery and jeeringly invited it to dine with him. The statue then came to life, seized Don Juan, and dragged him to hell. According to another version, the Franciscan monks, wishing to put an end to Don Juan's career, lured him to the monastery and killed him, attributing his death to the statue.

Myths and Legends of the Slavs

THE SLAVS are the peoples of Eastern Europe who live in what is now Russia, Poland, Bulgaria, Yugoslavia, and Czechoslovakia. Their original home in Europe is believed to have been south-central Russia, to which they had migrated from the East by the beginning of the Christian era. Not long after, they made their way into the Balkans and pushed as far west as the Elbe, but they were forced to withdraw from central Europe by the Germans and Rumanians to the lands which they now occupy. Today Slavs have little more in common than their languages, which belong to the great language family which we call Slavonic; but in their early history they shared a culture and a pagan religion. The myths and legends which we give here were part of this ancient, pre-Christian religion. We have only a scanty and fragmentary knowledge of its nature and what we do know of it is derived in a great measure from the old traditions to which the common people clung even after their conversion to Christianity between the seventh and ninth centuries. Even in very recent times, for example, one could hear a Russian peasant talk of the thunder as the voice of the old thunder god Peroun.

As is true with all peoples who settle a wide area, there were local variants of the Slavic myths and legends. The deities as we describe them here are largely Russian in their attributes, although we point out special qualities ascribed to them by other Slavic peoples and, in a separate section, the deities of the pagan Poles.

Following our discussion of the Slavic deities we tell the stories of several legendary Russian heroes. These date from after the conversion of the Slavs to Christianity, and all but one deal with the critical time in Russia's history when the Russian people were struggling to rid their land of the Tatars and other invaders from the East.

Near neighbors of the Slavs are the Baltic peoples, the Lithuanians and Letts, who speak very similar languages and who in early times shared many traditional beliefs. Though probably related to the Slavs in origin, in their lands bordering the Baltic Sea they developed their own distinctive culture and their own system of deities, which we describe briefly at the end of this section.

MYTHS OF ANCIENT RUSSIAN DEITIES

Svarog

SVAROG was the god of heaven and was regarded as the father of the chief Slavic deities.

Dazhbog

DAZHBOG (Dazbog, Dajdbog) was the god of the sun and of wealth and success. As a sun-god he was called

"Tsar Sun" and he was one of the sons of Svarog.

Domovoy

DOMOVOY, protector of the family, was the god of the house and hearth. He resembled many other gods in his ability to assume various shapes at his pleasure, animal or human. In addition to looking after the welfare of the home and those in it, he also guarded cattle. As a protecting god, he went along with the members of a family when they moved from one place to another. Failure to do this resulted in misfortune through the action of the god of another family seeking to take up his abode in the home of the new arrivals. Domovoy had two sides: he was good and kind and helpful when he was satisfied with the way he was being treated by his worshippers, but he was mean and brought harm to a family when he felt that he was being slighted; in such cases he had to be appeased by evidence of sorrow in the form of gifts of food. A piece of bread sprinkled with salt, carefully wrapped up in white cloth and left for him, in the hall or outside in the courtyard, would chase away his anger and bring back his friendship. Other ways of winning Domovoy's favor were to save some of the evening meal for him, or to put some clean linen in or near his favorite room.

Among the shapes or forms that Domovoy could assume were those of the master of the house in whose home he resided, or some other member of the family, not necessarily alive. In the animal kingdom, he was able to take on the form of dogs, cats, bears, or other beasts. It was possible to see Domovoy, but he was invisible more often than not, and he did not like to be annoyed. In the house of which he was the god, Domovoy sometimes lived in a room behind the stove, in a closet, or in the bathroom, or he might select the courtyard or the stable. When water was being drawn for a bath, a pail of water was provided for his own use. In most cases, this household god was looked on as a bachelor, but sometimes he was said to have a wife and family.

Domovoy was represented as an old man, dressed either in a long robe tied around his waist, or in a red shirt. Although old, he had a thick head of bushy hair, and his eyes gleamed. His entire body was protected by a coat of soft, thick hair.

So much a part of the family was Domovoy that its joys and sorrows were his. When a member of the family died he was overcome with grief and sobbed and howled at night. There was nothing that Domovoy would not do for a master who pleased him, even to the extent of stealing from other people in order to increase his master's wealth. If he was not treated with the respect and honor that he deserved, or if any member of the family circle offended him by cursing or by using foul language, Domovoy would destroy the cattle or leave the house in fury, thus depriving the inmates of his protection. When this happened, it was believed that both the humans and the animals would become sick, waste away, and die.

Jessis

JESSIS, one of the old gods of Slavic mythology, was worshipped above all other deities. He was the source of material success and prosperity, and he rewarded those who honored him by keeping them from harm and protecting them from their foes.

Stribog, Vesna, and Morana

STRIBOG, the god of storms and of cold and frost of the early Slavs, was an unfriendly god and an enemy of man. The winds were his grandsons. VESNA was the goddess of spring, and MORANA, the goddess of death and winter.

Baba

BABA (Baba Yaga, Baba Jaga) was a horrible old witch in Slavonic mythology and folklore. Represented as an ogress, she was noted for her cannibalistic habits. Hideous, bony, long-nosed, with hair disheveled, she rode through the air on an iron mortar propelled by a pestle. According to some versions, Sun, Day, and Night were her servants. She had a magic cudgel which turned living beings into stone.

Cernobog and Byelun

CERNOBOG (Zcernoboch), the Black God, who contrasts with Byelun, the White God, was the Slavic god of evil. He was regarded by his worshippers as the source of all misfortune and distress. Prayers were addressed to him at festive occasions in the hope that they would persuade him to hold back the bad luck that he sent.

BYELUN, the White God, was a bright-shining god. He guided people who lost their way on dark roads and he helped them to get out of the woods. He rewarded those who worshipped him by throwing showers of gold on them. It was said that "the woods are dark without Byelun," and that a man who became rich and successful had found favor with Byelun. He was represented as an old man with a long, flowing white beard, and was dressed in a white gown. He rested or concealed himself during the night and allowed his worshippers to see him only in the day time.

Svarazic

SVARAZIC, one of the sons of Svarog, was a god worshipped by the Elbe Slavs, although it is not perfectly clear of what he was the god. Statues made by his worshippers represent him wearing armor and helmet; frequently seated on a rock, his right hand grasps a double-edged battle ax, his left resting on his shield decorated with the head and horns of a black bull. Nearby, grazing, is his black steed, with saddle and trappings; above him, flying over a mountain-top, is an eagle with outspread wings. These statues, or idols, made of gold, with the name of the god inscribed on them, were supposed to strike terror into those who saw them. The Elbe Slavs also worshipped a god Svarozic who was the god of fire and was in all probability identical with him.

Peroun

PEROUN (Perun), the god of thunder, was the chief deity in the mythology of the eastern and southern Slavs. He rode through the air in his fiery chariot and hurled his lightning bolts at those who displeased or offended him. The elements of nature were subject to his will and he was known as the "lord of the harvest." He was honored by a huge wooden statue with a face of silver and a beard of gold. At Novgorod, in front of his statue, a fire was kept continually burning, and any priest who was so careless as to let it go out was punished by death.

Siva

SIVA (Ziva) was a female divinity worshipped as the goddess of life. She was represented, usually seated, with an ornamental headdress, suggestive of the sun's rays; dressed in a flowing gown, her shoulders and chest are bare. Her left hand holds a sheaf of wheat, her right hand, an apple-like fruit.

Veles

VELES, the god of flocks, was so revered by Russians that it was a custom to swear by him—a most solemn oath—when entering into a treaty. In this connection, his name was often coupled with that of Peroun, the god of thunder. At harvest time in south Russia, the people "pleated the beard of Veles" by binding the last handful of ears of corn into a knot, a custom that was also known as "leaving a handful of ears for Veles."

Bouyan and Raj

BOUYAN was the paradise of Slavic mythology. It was an island and a holy city. It was spoken as the home of the sun and of various personifications of different phases of nature. On it lived many animals, an old serpent, older than all others of its kind, and a beautiful maid, called ZARYA. It was noted for its river, the waters of which had the power to cure all pain and sickness. The source of the river was Alatuir, a magic stone on the island. The city of Bouyan, underneath the river, was the dwelling-place of the dead.

RAJ was another paradise that appears in the mythology of the early Slavs, or it may be the same as Bouyan. An ideal place, it figured in folklore as a playground for children whose happy souls play and shout among the trees and forever pick golden fruit. It was always warm, and birds and other animals made it their home in the winter. Raj was also a storehouse where were kept all kinds of seed and samples of everything that people need and use on earth.

The Heavenly Bodies in Slavic Mythology

According to early chronicles, all Slavic peoples worshipped the sun, the moon, and the stars. Travellers brought back stories indicating the existence of sun and moon worship on the part of the Slavs, some of them either giving up, or not accepting, Christianity in favor of a religious system centered on worship of the heavenly bodies.

The Slavs believed that the moon was the home both of the souls of the dead and of sinners whose souls were transported to it as a punishment for their evil deeds. The moon was likewise held to be closely connected with the realm of the lower animals and with plant life and growth. In Slavic mythology, the stars play a large part in man's life. It was believed that there were as many men living on the earth as there were stars twinkling in the sky, that is, enough stars were made to go around for all. When a man was born, a star—his own—was given to him: when it was time for him to go, the star fell to earth, and as it did so the man's physical life came to an end; released from his body, the soul rose to heaven.

The ancient Slavs may have worshipped sun-gods who were represented by idols or statues, but it is believed to be certain that the pagan Russians had a solar deity. In addition to the sun, the moon, and the stars, fire and water and trees and mountains were worshipped by pagan Czechs.

ANCIENT POLISH DEITIES

In the mythology of the pagan Poles, the following deities were worshipped: YESZA, god of gods; LYADA, god of war; DZYDZILELYA, goddess of love; NYJA, god of the underworld; DZEWANA, goddess of the hunt; and MARZYANA, goddess of fertility. PODOGA was the pagan Polish god of the air, and ZYWIE, the goddess of life, corresponding to the Russian Siva.

LEGENDARY HEROES OF RUSSIA

Ilya Murometz

For thirty years ILYA of Murom, son of Ivan, had the use of neither his legs nor his arms. But one day, when he had been left alone in his cottage, Christ and two of his apostles came and restored life to his limbs. They gave him great strength and predicted that he would defend the Christian faith and destroy all infidel hosts and warriors.

Ilya then set forth with his steed, CLOUDFALL, and came upon a pavilion wherein was a bed of heroic proportions. Here Ilya slept for three days and three nights until SVYATOGOR, a hero who stood higher than the trees, awakened him. Svyatogor bore with him a casket of crystal, out of which stepped his beautiful wife. She made them food and drink and presently Svyatogor fell into a deep sleep. His wife was attracted to Ilya and commanded that he come to her on pain of her complaining to Svyatogor of discourtesy. Ilya could but obey, but the next day he felt impelled to tell the hero of his wife's infidelity, whereupon Svyatogor slew her.

Presently Ilya and Svyatogor came upon a coffin, upon which was written: "This coffin shall fit him who is destined to lie in it." Ilya lay down in it, but it was too big for him, Svyatogor then tried it and it just fit him. But when he would raise the lid, he could not, nor could Ilya, though both tried with all their might. The breath soon left Svyatogor's body and he died in the coffin, though not before he gave Ilya his great sword.

One Easter morn, while Ilya was in church he vowed that he would say high mass that same day in the church in Kiev. He vowed also that he would go to Kiev by the straight way and would not stain his hand or his sword with blood on the way. Cloudfall, his steed, carried him swiftly through the air and it seemed that he would reach Kiev without incident. But as he approached Chernigov he saw three of the hated Tatar chiefs, each with forty thousand men, besieging the city. Despite his vow, Ilya had to stop and fight the Tatars. Snatching up a great oak tree as his weapon he attacked the besiegers and slaughtered them all and delivered the city.

Continuing his way to Kiev, Ilya then met Nightingale the Robber, a great bird from whose mouth and nostrils flames and sparks poured. Ilya broke a twig from a willow tree, set it in his bow, and shot the bird through the eye and bound him up and delivered him to good Prince Vladimir in Kiev. For his great deed Ilya was feasted and given great gifts and was received as a hero.

Ilya accomplished many other great deeds in the years to come, and his fame grew. His last effort was for the defense of Kiev against the attacking Tatars, who were led by Kalin. Ilya was at the head of the Russian warriors, and they were making good progress in the fight, killing great numbers of Tatars. But they began to boast and claim that if there were a ladder up to the heavens they would climb it and destroy all the heavenly hosts. They began again to slay the Tatars but for every one they killed two or three sprang up in his place. The Russian warriors were killed and the hero Ilya and his steed were turned to stone.

Oleg

OLEG, prince of Kiev, was the son of Vladimir, the first Christian ruler of Russia. Although Oleg was an actual, historical figure, the most famous episode connected with him is legendary, and is the subject of a well-known poem by the poet Pushkin.

While Oleg was on the way to do battle against the Hazars in Crimea, he met a sorcerer. Oleg asked him to foretell his future, and the sorcerer predicted that Oleg would conquer wide dominions and achieve his object of capturing Constantinople. He would go through great battles and wars, but he would not be harmed by arrow, sling, or assassin's spear. However, he would die through the instrumentality of his battle steed. Regretfully, then, Oleg parted from his courser, and set him out to pasture to live the rest of his days.

Oleg continued on his way and made the great conquests that the sorcerer had predicted. In later years Oleg inquired of his old steed, and, being told that it had died a long time ago, wished to see the bones of the animal. Oleg set his foot on the courser's white skull and asked whether it was from this that he was to find destruction. Just then a snake crept forth from under the skull, twisted itself around Oleg's legs, and stung him fatally, fulfilling the sorcerer's prediction.

Igor

A grandson of Oleg was IGOR, also a historical figure around whom legends grew up. Igor led the Russians against the pagan Polovtsi but was defeated by them at the River Kayala. He was taken captive, but with the aid of a guard, managed to escape and return to the Russians.

Sadko

SADKO was a musician of Novgorod who entertained at the feasts of merchants and nobles. But there came a time when no merchants or nobles called him to play at their feasts, so each day Sadko went down to the lake and sadly played his harp there. On the third day there emerged from the water Tsar Vodyanoi, the water king, who thanked him for the diversion he had provided the people of the lake. As a reward, he told Sadko how he might get rich. He was to go to a great feast where the guests would boast of their wealth and deeds. Sadko was to boast of three golden fishes in the lake. The guests would then wager their great wealth against this, whereupon Sadko was to come to the lake with a silken net and catch the fish with fins of gold. He would then become a rich merchant.

Events proceeded as the water king had predicted, and Sadko became very wealthy. One time he outfitted thirty ships and sent them to the Golden Horde in the east. There he bought all sorts of furs and gold and pearls and set sail for Novgorod. But on the sea his ships halted and would not move. Sadko realized the Tsar Morskoi, the sea king, was demanding tribute of him, so he ordered first gold, then silver, then pearls cast into the sea, but still the ships would not sail. Then Sadko offered to send one of the ship's company to the sea king, but the lot fell to Sadko himself.

So the rich merchant leapt into the sea, and he came to the ocean floor where the king had his court. The king wished him to stay and choose a wife, and Sadko saw that he could not refuse. But the Tsaritsa told him that if he would not kiss or embrace the wife he had chosen, he would return to Russia. It happened as the Tsaritsa predicted and Sadko found himself on the bank of a river, where his surprised men found him. Thenceforth Sadko sailed no more but dwelt and took his ease in his own town.

MYTHS OF BALTIC DEITIES

Perkúnas

PERKÚNAS was the god of thunder and lightning in Baltic mythology and the chief deity of the Baltic peoples. The thunder of which he was the god was his voice and it was the medium by which he made his wishes known to mortals. The outstanding myth regarding Perkúnas is that he freed the sun—which had been captured by a mighty monarch and locked up in a tower—and restored it to men so that they might enjoy its light and warmth.

Perkúnas hurled thunderbolts that struck down his enemies—devils and evil spirits and demons—and sent them to the lower regions, and he also sent the prayed-for fertilizing rains. Perkúnas had nine sons, two of whom were the Morning Star and the Evening Star.

Telyavelli

TELYAVELLI was the heavenly smith who had his forge in the sky, where he forged the Sun for Perkúnas and fixed it in its place in the heavens. He also made spurs, girdles, and crowns.

Perkune Tete

PERKUNE TETE was the mother of lightning and thunder. She took care of the Sun, who came to her every night, tired and dusty, at the end of a hard day's work, and she sent her out fresh and clean and rested, after a night's sleep, and ready to resume her labors. Perkune Tete, in some accounts, was regarded as the wife of Perkúnas.

Myths and Legends of the Finns

THE FINNS as a people with their own distinct culture are relative late-comers on the stage of history. They first appeared in the eighth century and, since they had embraced Christianity by about the twelfth century, they had little time to develop any extensive system of gods and goddesses. Those deities which did arise were chiefly simple personifications of the forces of nature such as the air, the forests, and the waters.

However, the Finns are the creators of the colorful legends which we know through their re-telling in the *Kalevala,* one of the great epic poems of the world. The stories of the *Kalevala* were long told and re-told by the people of Finland in the form of ballads celebrating the adventures of the national epic hero Wainamoinen and his brothers Ilmarin and Lemminkainen, but they were not arranged in literary form until 1835 when Dr. Elias Lönnrot went about the countryside and set down these old stories as he heard them from the lips of the peasants. The legends which comprise the *Kalevala* provide us with the greater part of this section.

ANCIENT FINNISH DEITIES

Jumala Ukko

JUMALA UKKO was the supreme god, the father of heaven. By his godly command, a wild duck or an eagle flew down to Ilmater, floating in space for seven centuries, and, using her lap as a nest, laid seven eggs in it, from which eggs the world came, with its islands and mountains and continents. Jumala Ukko separated air and water and created three beautiful maidens who scattered their milk over the universe.

Ilmater

ILMATER was the virgin daughter of the air. Tired of floating alone in space for longer than she cared to remember, Ilmater flew down to the bottom of the ocean, where she remained for seven hundred years, during which period she created heaven and earth from the seven eggs of a wild duck. At the end of this protracted period of labor, without benefit of aid from physician or midwife, Ilmater gave birth to a son, Wainamoinen.

HEROES OF THE "KALEVALA"

WAINAMOINEN, one of the three heroes of Kalevala or Finland, was the son of the Sea and Ilmater, virgin daughter of the atmosphere.

Wainamoinen was a great singer of songs and was once challenged to a singing contest by YOUKAHAINEN, a Laplander, brother of the beautiful AINO whom Wainamoinen wished to marry. Youkahainen claimed that he had been present at the creation of the world, had seen the earth shaped, the sun and moon placed in their proper positions, and the sky arched. Wainamoinen did not believe these extravagant claims and flatly called Youkahainen a liar. In his fury, the bard dared Wainamoinen to fight with him, but Wainamoinen instead began to sing a song of such power and beauty that Youkahainen's sled began to decompose into its original elements and he found himself up to his neck in quicksand. When the foolish challenger found that his life was in danger he saved it, but only at the last moment, by agreeing to let Wainamoinen marry his sister.

Aino had no interest in marriage in general and she had no desire to marry Wainamoinen, who was many years her senior. Seeking to escape, she swam to a nearby rock and was drowned when the rock crumbled as she sat on it and threw her into the raging sea. As she sank, several remarkable changes took place: her blood was transformed into water, her flesh into fish, her ribs into willows, and her hair into sea-grass. So sad was nature at Aino's death that it became a serious problem to decide who was to inform her parents of the unhappy event. The bear, the wolf, and the fox refused the unpleasant task of breaking the news, and after other citizens of the animal kingdom had rejected the responsibility, the hare agreed to carry the report, after the daughters of the sea threatened to roast him alive if he would not do as they commanded. When Aino's mother learned that her daughter was dead, three streams of tears issued from her eyes and formed cataracts between which arose three mountains of rock; on top of these mountains grew birch trees that gave refuge to cuckoos always and forever singing of love and sorrow.

After Aino turned him down, Wainamoinen travelled to POHJOLA, the cold country of the north, in order to forget Aino, if he could, and to try to find someone willing to become his bride. Youkahainen, the lying Lapp, tried to kill Wainamoinen with a poisoned dart on the way but killed his horse instead. Although Wainamoinen was not wounded he was left struggling in the water for eight years until he was rescued by a grateful eagle. Cuckoos, eagles, and other members of the bird kingdom had a friendly feeling for Wainamoinen because he did not fell the birch trees in the forest, declaring that the birds must have a place in which to build their nests.

Wainamoinen was carried to Pohjola on the back of an eagle. When he arrived there he was welcomed by LOUHI, ugly old hag, who was the mother of the MAID OF THE NORTH. She invited Wainamoinen into the house and fed him at her daughter's request. She agreed to give him a horse to take him home and her daughter's hand on condition that he make for her SAMPO, the magic mill, which would grind out riches and food aplenty. Wainamoinen stated that he could not make the Sampo, but he promised that on his return he would have his brother ILMARIN, the great smith, forge it for him.

Louhi then furnished Wainamoinen a sledge and a horse, and told him that he would have an uneventful trip back home—but only if he kept his eyes looking straight ahead. But Wainamoinen forgot this admonition and en route looked up into the sky to see Louhi's beautiful daughter spinning in heaven. He asked her to be his wife, but she set him to certain difficult tasks to prove his magic power; after this, she said, she might consider marrying him. Wainamoinen performed the tasks, but still the Maid of the North refused him.

Once back in Kalevala, Wainamoinen induced Ilmarin to forge the Sampo, promising him the hand of the Maid of the North if he would do so. Ilmarin assented and made the magic mill in four days. He then claimed Louhi's daughter. But the girl refused him, and he returned alone.

LEMMINKAINEN was the next hero to seek Pohjola's daughter in marriage. Louhi agreed, but only if Lemminkainen would shoot the sacred SWAN OF TUONELA, using one arrow only. Lemminkainen set off and found the swan in the treacherous waters of Tuoni, the river that flowed between the land of the living and the land of the dead. Just as he was about to draw his bow, a blind shepherd, whom Lemminkainen had earlier scorned, hurled a water snake at him. The snake wounded Lemminkainen sorely and he fell into the river, to be carried into Tuoni, where he was cut up into pieces and tossed into the river. Lemminkainen's mother learned of her son's fate and commissioned Ilmarin to make for her a rake five hundred fathoms long. With this she dragged the river for the pieces of Lemminkainen's body. She succeeded in finding them all and restored him to life by singing magic songs. Even then Lemminkainen wished to slay the Swan of Tuonela, but his mother dissuaded him, and he returned home.

Ilmarin eventually returned to Pohjola and this time succeeded in winning the Maid of the North. He took her back with him to Kalevala, but it turned out that she was cruel and deceitful. She sent one of Ilmarin's shepherds a loaf of bread with a stone hidden in it, and when he tried to cut it, he broke his knife. Angered, he turned the cattle into wild beasts which devoured her.

It occurred to Ilmarin and Wainamoinen that Pohjola, with the Sampo, was a happy land, and that it should be in their possession so that Kalevala might be happy. They, with Lemminkainen, set out for the land of the north to capture it. On the way Wainamoinen killed a giant pike, from the bones of which he made a *kantele,* a harp so wonderful that only he could play it, and when he did all nature listened, enraptured. When he played, men wept, even the player himself. Wainamoinen's tears dropped into the sea, where they became the first pearls.

The kantele was useful in the fight for the Sampo, for while he played, even Louhi and her followers were enchanted and the warriors of Kaleva snatched the Sampo. Louhi gave chase, transforming herself into an eagle to grab the magic mill. As she did so, it slipped from her grasp and fell into the sea, where it remains. But Wainamoinen noticed that pieces of its broken lid floated to shore, and so he knew that Kalevala would have some blessing from the Sampo.

The revengeful Louhi then stole from Wainamoinen the sun, the moon, and fire, and all homes in Kalevala were cold and dark. Jumala Ukko from his home on high hurled down flashes of lightning so that he might see what was going on. The lightning struck the earth, fell into the sea and was swallowed by a hungry pike in search of food. Its strange antics, with the ball of fire inside its stomach, attracted the interested attention of another pike, who swallowed the first one. When Wainamoinen found out where the lightning was located he began fishing patiently until the right pike pulled on his hook. He then cut the fish open, grabbed the lightning and, after burning himself severely, imprisoned it in an elm tree. In this manner was fire returned to man on earth. Later Wainamoinen, in the form of a pike, landed at Louhi's lair, defeated her sons in battle, found the sun and the moon guarded by a nest of snakes, which he killed.

Wainamoinen having grown feeble with the passing years, it was not long before he would have to give way to another great hero. It happened that the young maiden MARJATTA one day ate a cranberry, and soon after she bore a child. Her angry mother cast her out of her house, and Marjatta had to give birth to the baby in a stable. Wainamoinen foresaw that this child would be the warrior of the coming age. He built himself a copper vessel and sailed away into the west, singing his wonderful songs, and was never seen again.

Fairy Lore of Europe and the Orient

It was a prevalent opinion in the North of Europe that all the various beings of popular belief were once worsted in a conflict with superior powers, and condemned to remain till doomsday in certain assigned abodes. The dwarfs or trolls were sent to the mountains and caves; the elves to the groves and trees; the mermen and mermaids to the sea, the lakes, and the rivers. For all that, the creatures have refused to remain in their element: kobolds are spirits of the mine and quarry as well as of the household; trolls fly about in the air; and mermen and mermaids walk the streets at market-time; mountain spirits, wood spirits, and water spirits are constantly invading each other's realm.

The same confusion attends the attempt to classify the fairy folk by country of origin. There are too few differences among the ethereal creatures that can be accounted for on purely national grounds. The Irish *sidh,* or little folk, differ from the English fairy or elf and in turn from the German elf, but the similarities overwhelm the differences. And these "good folk" shade off into the French *fée,* who is more witch than fairy, apparently a thoroughly human woman with miraculous powers. And it is not true that these conceptions vary with the climate, sunny and warm in the South, sterner and wilder in the North. The spirit folk seem to be alternately benevolent and malevolent at whim, South or North, as capricious as nature herself.

Medieval superstition was not at one in explaining to origin of these lesser spirits. Some said they were descendants of an early race of gods, and that the fairy-like or semi-divine women—the *bonnes dames, dames blanches,* and *fées*—seen by streams or fountains or in forests were survivals of spirits and goddesses of river, lake, or earth. Others held that they were the souls of the dead, particularly of unbaptized children. The giants were looked upon as remnants of an earlier and more savage race of men, or as descendants of an older group of gods, titans dispossessed by newer deities and therefore hostile to them and to godlike man. The demonic spirits assumed their darker character through being associated with sinister aspects of nature, or with the dead.

Since the spirits, for all their crossing of boundaries, still maintain their identity for the most part with one of the four elements—earth, water, air, and fire—they have been classified as Earth Spirits, Water Spirits, etc. A special classification—Demonic Spirits—has been reserved for that malignant brood of beings which exist solely to prey on mortals. In this section we follow these general divisions in presenting information about the various groups of spirits.

EARTH SPIRITS

Fairies

The term "fairy" is usually associated with the beings popularly supposed to inhabit England, Scotland, and Ireland. They are called PIXIES in Cornwall, the AES SIDHE or SHEE in Ireland, and SITHS in Scotland. The Irish also referred to them as the Good People, a propitiatory term like the Greek Eumenides. Traditionally, they lived in fairyland which was another world adjoining our own; this might be under a lake or river or, as the Irish believed, under mounds or the roots of trees or in the side of a hollow hill. They are the native British equivalent of classical nymphs and fauns and hamadryads.

The size of fairies varied. Irish fairies were thought of as about the size of little children; English fairies seem to have been the size of full-grown mortals. Green was their favorite color, but their costumes might be any of the shades with which the earth decked itself, from yellow to green to brown. They were inordinately addicted to dancing, and the fairy rings—circles of rank or withered grass often seen in lawns and meadows—were said to be produced by the fairies dancing their "Lays" at a midnight revel. They were normally invisible to man, but through the use of a magic ointment some individuals might be permitted to see the little folk at their gambolling. They were, however, not to be spoken to.

Woe betide the farmer who put a scythe or plow to this hallowed ground. The sheep knew better than to take the smallest bite of the grass in these circles, and only the most careless of mortals would set foot upon the bare space inside, or fall asleep within the confines of the circle. If he took this risk, he was either stricken dead, or carried away to fairyland, or left with a body pinched black and blue. The punishment for an invasion of fairy rings overtook Fortunatus when he fell asleep on fairy ground.

Some held that the fairies were fallen angels; others, that they were the departed souls of men and women. They possessed the power to do good or to do harm, to foretell the future and to perform miracles. They could cause and cure most diseases and knew the virtues of herbs, plants, and minerals, birds, beasts, and the four elements, and they could apply and use them.

They had a passion for cleanliness and would, by pinching maids in their sleep, punish them for not sweeping their houses clean. However, fairies were also bountiful. They rewarded virtue and left unexpected gifts in the bottom of pails and bowls. Nevertheless, the dealings of fairies with mortals were always precarious. A gift of fairy gold would often change into withered leaves.

The practice of fairies of stealing children from their cradles and leaving a fairy substitute was a notorious one. In some accounts, these mortals were used by the fairies to pay their tribute to the devil. The changeling could be readily detected: it was mature and only seemed to be a child, and was usually ugly, deformed, and stupid. Sometimes human women were sought and abducted by the fairies to serve as midwives or nurses. Those who had actually gone to fairyland to perform these services brought eternal good luck upon themselves and upon their families. However, for a human visiting the land of the fairy folk there was the taboo that she must not eat of their food lest she be forced to dwell there forever.

The fairies were an organized people with a king and queen. Their rulers might have been OBERON and TITANIA of Shakespeare's play, or possibly QUEEN MAB. Fairies might have amours with mortals. The king or queen of the fairies, or one of their train, is frequently represented as having a fancy for a particular mortal; or a mortal as falling in love with a fairy knight or lady. The enjoyment of love between a fairy and a mortal usually involves some restriction or compact. The mortal is forbidden to utter her name or to see her on certain specified occasions or to do certain things; the breaking of the compact is the cause of calamity to the lover and all his race. The legend of MELUSINA is the best known instance of this.

Melusina was the daughter of the fairy Pressina and a mortal father, a king of Albania. By rushing in just after Pressina had given birth and seeing the fairy bathe her children, the father broke his agreement not to observe her at the time of her lying-in and was deserted by his fairy wife and offspring. Later, to punish her father, Melusina imprisoned him in a mountain. For this she was punished by her mother by being transformed every Saturday into a serpent from the hips down. She could be released only if she found a husband who would never see her on Saturday. Such a husband she found in Raymond of Poitiers, who by her means became rich and powerful. When at length her husband, yielding to curiosity, saw her taking the purificatory bath on a Saturday, she flew away in serpent form. Thereafter, her appearance and heart-rending cries heralded the death of one of Raymond's house, that of the Lusignans, or of a king of France.

Elves

ELF is a term most usually applied to a kind of Scandinavian fairy, identified in the Edda as a class of supernatural beings inferior to the gods. The elves lived in Elfheim (Elfhome), and their ruler was the Erlking (Erlkönig) or Elf-king, an evil spirit who inhabited forests and delighted in doing mischief to passersby. Division was usually made into White Elves, those which were benevolent, and Black Elves, those which inflicted sickness and injury.

The White Elves had fair golden hair, sweet musical voices, and golden harps. They were extremely fond of dancing in woods, hillsides, and meadows where the grass in the circle grew more luxuriantly than outside it. If at midnight anyone got within their circle, he might see them; children born on Sunday, in particular, had this power to see elves. The dancers had to disappear before cockcrow; otherwise they remained stationary but invisible and if anyone touched them unawares, sickness and pain would follow.

The Black Elves were an underground people, averse to the light. They appeared only at night because the beams of the sun could turn them into stone. They were ugly, long-nosed dwarfs of a dirty brown color. By listening to the underground people among the hills and rocks, the mountaineers learned a tune called the Elf-king's tune which they dared not play on their fiddles. As soon as it begins both old and young and even inanimate objects are impelled to dance. The player cannot stop unless he can play the air backwards, or until someone comes behind him and cuts the strings of his fiddle.

In Ireland and the West Highlands, cattle afflicted with some unknown disease were called elf-shot. They were supposed to have been wounded by an elfin arrow; the arrow-heads of the Neolithic period, sharpened flint chips, were adduced as evidence. In Scotland, cattle born with a mark were regarded as having been branded by the elves for mischief.

Danish legend connected their ELLE-FOLK with the rebel angels, who, when cast out of heaven, fell into the moors; or with Lilith's children by Adam. The males, who resembled old men, used to bask in the sunbeams. If anyone came too near one he opened his mouth wide and breathed upon the mortal; his breath produced sickness and pestilence. The females, who were beautiful, danced their rounds by moonlight. Their ravishing music, often irresistible to susceptible youth, produced fatal results. Their cattle fed on dew, and the cattle of men suffered by mingling with them.

Pixies

In Devonshire and Cornwall, popular superstition held to the belief in a form of elf called the PIXIE. According to the peasants, pixies were the souls of infants who died before they were baptized. They were small, generally handsome, and always dressed in green. Dancing was their chief amusement, which they performed to the music of the cricket, the grasshopper, and the frog—always at night. The pixie-house was usually a rock. By moonlight, on the moor, or in the dark shade of rocks, the king of the pixies held his court and, like Titania, gave his subjects their orders. Some were sent to the mines to lead the miner to the richest lode, while others were sent to draw him to some dead end by noises imitating the stroke of the hammer or by false fires.

The office of some was to lead travellers astray. If someone were separated from his friends by chance, the pixie would call him by his name and counterfeit the voices of his companions to seduce him. As Will o' the Wisp, the *ignis fatuus,* an imp would *pixy-lead* men on heaths and deserted places late at night. The elf was also adept at deceiving women: it would blow out the candle and kiss the maid with a smack; or make noises in the wall to frighten the household.

The Irish POOKA, the English POUKE are of the same family as the pixie. So too is PUCK, the original meaning of which would seem to be devil or demon. The word "pixy" is evidently PUCKSY, the endearing diminutive *sy* being added to Puck. Among other affectionate titles given the pixie were: *Hob, Lob-lie-by-the-fire,* and *ouphe.* PUCK, as an individual sprite, is identified with Robin Goodfellow (see next page under Brownies and Other Household Spirits).

Wights

The Eddic poems and the sagas tell of a class of spirits called VAETTIR or WIGHTS. These were tutelary spirits, guardians of the land.

These wights occupied the land unseen, except by those with the gift of second-sight. They dwelt in mounds at which offerings used to be laid, in trees too sacred to be touched, and in waterfalls. Consideration had to be shown them or else they would leave a district which would suffer in consequence. For this reason people would avoid a section known to be haunted by them, or settling in such a section. This fear of injuring their feelings led to the curious heathen law of the tenth century known as Ulfliot's law, which provides that a ship with a figurehead must keep its distance from the land. If the ship approached the land, the figurehead had to be removed, so that the Land-vaettir would not be frightened off by the sight of a ship fronted by gaping heads and yawning jaws. The Norse vessels had monstrous decorations for figureheads.

Though the wights were beneficent, with the coming of Christianity all such spirits were regarded as evil. Action was taken to expel them, by sprinkling the fields with holy water.

Brownies and Other Household Spirits

Of the class of domestic spirits, the BROWNIE of Scotland is identical with the German KOBOLD, the Danish NIS, the English HOBGOBLIN, or GOBLIN, and the French GOBELIN or LUTIN. Generally speaking the household spirit was kindly and useful, protecting the house from strange spirits. If well-treated he was the servants' friend and would at times take part in the household tasks. At night he was supposed to busy himself in doing little jobs for the family over which he presided. Farms were his favorite abodes.

If he became angry, all kinds of

misfortunes befell the house. Manual labor turned out badly and the cattle grew thin. Then he would annoy sleepers in the form of the nightmare, kissing them in their sleep so that painful blisters appeared on their lips, or tangling hair and beards in the night.

The brownies were brown or tawny spirits in contrast to the fairies, which were fair or elegant. They were covered with short curly brown hair, and wore a brown mantle and hood. They were small in stature, with wrinkled faces. They delighted in a bowl of cream and some bread, but were shocked at anything resembling a bribe or *douceur;* however, if the gift were given in a genteel and delicate way, they allowed their scruples to be overcome.

Two famous house spirits of legend were the English Robin Goodfellow and the German Hinzelmann.

ROBIN GOODFELLOW was a native British spirit whom early tradition identifies as a forest spirit and as a house spirit. From accounts about him Shakespeare seems to have derived his Puck from Robin. His chief function as a forest spirit or "merry wanderer of the night" consisted in misleading unwary travellers, and in frightening unprotected mortals. In his domestic capacity, he took up his sojourn with some particular family. Here, if he found everything to his taste, he aided in the domestic chores, doing in one night ten men's work. For these labors his standing fee was a bowl of cream and white bread. If displeased by his surroundings or the diligence of the maids, he punished the family by pinching, and went laughing away.

Puck was not a fairy, although Shakespeare so designated him in the *Midsummer Night's Dream.* He was both tall and broad, of the size of a full-grown man or bigger; lubberly in appearance and with a loud laugh. He had, however, the power of transformation and could change his shape to that of any animal or mortal at whim. He had an obsession about clothes and was mortally offended if any housewife took notice of his nakedness and laid out clothes for him beside his mess of bread and cream. "Hemton hamten, here will I never more tread nor stampen," he would declare.

HINZELMANN was a kobold who attached himself to the old castle of Hudemühlen and lived there for four years before he disappeared. He first made his presence known by acting like a *poltergeist* or knocking spirit, rapping within walls and speaking though invisible. He announced that his companions in the Bohemian forest would not tolerate him and that he would remain until his affairs were in order. After vainly trying to get rid of the kobold, the owner set a room apart for him, and regularly set a chair and plate for him. In return Hinzelmann scoured the pots and kettles, washed the dishes, cleaned the pails and tubs, and supervised the work of the servants. Everything thrived under his care.

Hinzelmann was fond of playing tricks, but he never hurt anyone by them. Servants were suddenly boxed on the ear or pinched, or set to fighting with each other when each in turn was assaulted from behind. Anyone whom the goblin could not endure he used to plague or punish for his vices. On the other hand he was very fond of society and particularly attached to two young ladies in the castle. Neither of these ladies ever married, for Hinzelmann frightened away their wooers.

Only once did he allow himself to become visible, at the prolonged entreaty of the cook, his intimate friend. Before sunrise one morning he appeared before her—in the shape of a naked child about three years old, with two knives sticking crosswise in his heart, and his whole body streaming with blood.

When the time came for him to depart he left a number of presents with the noble owner, and foretold that good fortune would attend the family so long as they were kept together and intact.

Leprechauns

The most famous of the tribe of fairies in Irish superstition is the LEPRECHAUN. He is described as a manikin less than two feet tall, in the form of an old man dressed in a cocked hat, laced coat, knee breeches, and shoes with silver buckles. The leprechaun was wont to infest the wine cellar, but his chosen occupation was that of making brogues. However, he carried out his profession in retired and secret places; his hiding place was often betrayed by the noise which he made hammering the brogues.

The leprechaun was reputedly fabulously rich. In order to get him to reveal the hiding place of his treasure, the human intruder on his secret refuge had to fix his gaze upon the imp and threaten to do him bodily harm. If, however, the leprechaun could divert the eye of his captor momentarily he was able to vanish and with him the prospect of wealth.

Sometimes the leprechaun took up his habitation in a farm house and as a domestic spirit made himself invaluable by rendering various household services.

Banshee

Another household spirit of Irish and Highland Scotch families was the BANSHEE. This spirit was noteworthy for becoming so attached to a particular family that it would wail grievously at the death of one of its members. The banshee sometimes is called the White Lady of Ireland.

Dwarfs or Trolls

In the countries of northern Europe the DWARFS were considered as spirits of the underground. The more usual appellation of the dwarf is TROLL, a word signifying evil spirit. Trolls, however, are not generally regarded as malignant beings.

The dwarfs were represented as dwelling inside of hills, mounds, and hillocks—whence they are also called *Hill-people*. They were stumpy little men, sometimes like Tom Thumb, no bigger than a finger, humpbacked, with long beards and feet occasionally like those of a goat or a goose. From dwelling underground, dwarfs were pale of countenance. The GNOMES, guardians of mines and quarries, were of the race of dwarfs.

In their subterranean dwellings the dwarfs had a beautiful kingdom, over which their king, Alberich, held sway. They came forth at night only, for sunlight was fatal to them, turning them to stone. They were clad in grey, but their king was more splendidly attired.

They worked in metals and wood and were skillful craftsmen. Among their most noted works were Thor's hammer and the ship *Skidbladnir* which they gave to Frey; this last was so large that it could hold all the gods together with their war and household equipment, but was so skillfully wrought that when folded together it could be put into a side pocket. Regin, a dwarf, made Sigurd's sword Gram, with which he slew Fafnir the dragon, and Regin himself.

The smith or other work of dwarfs was made available to mortals who laid the metal to be forged or the wool to be spun, together with a piece of money, at the mouth of their holes. Next morning the work was finished. Besides their skill in smith work, dwarfs were dowered with hidden knowledge and supernatural power. By means of their magic power they would sometimes give help to human beings, as in the well-known story of Rumpelstiltskin.

Yet, dwarfs were often hostile to men, and like other elfins, carried off women or girls to be their wives. They also, like fairies, substituted for mortal children stolen by them, their own deformed offspring. Troll-women were represented as exercising their seductive power over mortals.

When forced to exercise their skill dwarfs would cunningly curse the weapon made by them, so that it would bring disaster for generations afterward. Treasure forced from them as a ransom for their lives would also bring disaster to the new owners or their successors.

The trolls had a great dislike for noise, probably from a recollection of the time when Thor used to fling his hammer after them. Especially were they vexed by the ringing of church bells. When the people of Ebeltoft were plagued by thieving habits of the dwarfs, they hung bells on the steeple of the church and were soon rid of the trolls.

Danish legend connected its troll-folk with the rebel angels who, when cast out of heaven, fell into mounds and barrows.

Giants and Ogres

Giants figure largely in Celtic and Scandinavian myth and legend. They are beings, more or less manlike, but enormous in their size and strength and appetites. Boulders, rocks, even islands were said to have been dropped by them as they were carrying them from one place to another. Often they are pictured as wading the ocean.

Occasionally the giant is thought of as a kindly helper, benevolent if slightly stupid; sometimes he is the acme of stupidity; and very often he is an OGRE, a monster or hideous giant who lives on human flesh.

The giants of the Welsh are familiar to everyone through the achievements of Jack the Giant Killer over the fiendish but stupid man-mountains like Blunderbore and Cormoran and Galligantus. The giants Fingal and his son Ossian belong to the legends of the Irish. Fingal, legendarily, was the builder of the Giants' Causeway in Northern Ireland, bridging the channel from Ireland to Scotland. Fingal constructed it in order that the giants might the more easily pass from one country to the other.

A British legend of Celtic origin accounts for the race of giants in Britain, and their extirpation by the reputed founder of the country, Brute.

The emperor Diocletian had thirty-three infamous daughters, who murdered their husbands; and being set adrift in a ship, reached Albion where they fell in with a number of demons. The offspring of this unnatural alliance was a race of giants, afterwards wiped out by Brute and his companions when they reached Albion as refugees from Troy. GOG and MAGOG, the last two of the giant race were brought in chains to London, then called Troy-novant, and, being chained to the palace of Brute, did duty as porters.

Giants appear in the Eddic cosmogony. The first giant, YMIR, existed before earth and sea were formed. He and all his descendants, the Frost-giants, were evil. They lived in Jótunheim or in Utgard, outside the limits of earth and sea, a place assigned to them by the gods.

Some of the Scandinavian giants were monsters with many heads, varying from three to the nine hundred possessed by Tyr's grandmother. Giant women were sometimes beautiful and beloved by gods or heroes. Mostly they were hostile to gods and men, and as we have seen in our discussion of the Norse gods, Thor was their great opponent.

There were also giants who inhabited the hills and rocks and wild forest regions. Even in caves under the waters might giants be found, like Grendel in *Beowulf,* and Grendel's mother. These were called *eoten* and *thyrs.*

WATER SPIRITS

Mermaids and Mermen

MERMAIDS and MERMEN are usually pictured as having an upper body that is human and a lower that is fishlike. However, in many conceptions the water spirit was physically not distinguishable from mortals. Usually, the water spirits lived in deep waters such as the ocean and the big rivers, but they also liked to dwell in mill-ponds. They were called NIX (female, NIXIE) in Germany.

The Scandinavian mermaid was typical of the water spirits of most legends. She is represented as a pretty young girl who sits on the surface of the water, or on a stone near the shore combing her long yellow hair with a golden comb. When frightened she throws herself into the water so quickly that she often leaves her comb in the place where she was sitting. The male water spirit, like the female, is also a shy being who throws himself into the water on being observed by a human eye.

Mermaids and mermen also sought the company of people, especially at market-time or on fair-days. They appeared dressed as peasants, but they could be readily recognized: the left side of the merman's coat was always damp; likewise, a corner of the mermaid's apron.

When any person was shortly to be drowned, the water spirits could be previously seen dancing on the surface of the water. Among the Finnish-Ugric peoples it was believed that the drowned were transformed into water spirits and continued living in the water. They inhabited a magnificent region below the water. Mortals were sometimes conveyed to this watery underworld, enticed to their destruction by a mermaid. The legendary Lorelei was such a siren.

Lorelei

In the commonest form of the story the LORELEI was a maiden who threw herself into the Rhine in despair over a faithless lover. She became a siren who haunted a rock on the right bank of the Rhine, also called the Lorelei. There she combed her hair with a golden comb and sang a wild song, which enticed fishermen and sailors to destruction on the rocks and rapids. The men who saw her lost sight or reason; those who listened to her beautiful voice were condemned to wander with her forever. The tale is closely connected with the myth of Hulda, queen of the elves.

Undines

Sometimes water spirits were represented as marrying mortals. UNDINES were female water spirits who readily intermarried with human beings. An Undine who bore a child by such a union received with her babe a human soul. But the man who married her had to be careful not to go on the water with her, or at least not to anger her there, lest she return to her original element. Should this happen the Undine would seek to destroy her husband should he venture on a second marriage. In some stories, Undine is the name of an individual rather than merely one of the group.

Among the Finns there was the belief, allied to that of the Lorelei, that the water spirit was a musician whose wonderful music could be learned. The proper time for such instruction was Midsummer Night or before the eves of Lent and Easter. The person willing to learn had to take a violin with him and seat himself on a rock entirely surrounded by water. The merman would emerge and seat himself on the same rock. The lesson would begin just as soon as the mortal had promised himself to the water spirit and bound himself fast to the master. However, the ties would be made loose, so that they would become undone when the spirit suddenly precipitated himself into the water. The one who succeeded in passing through this ordeal became a great player who could make people dance even against their will. Sometimes the violin developed the wonderful quality of playing by itself and even its pieces would play when the violin was broken.

Neck, Nickur, and Kelpie

The Scandinavian water sprite, the NECK was a river spirit. Sometimes he was represented as sitting, on summer nights, on the surface of the water, like a pretty little boy with golden hair hanging in ringlets, and a red cap on his head; sometimes as a handsome young man above the water, but beneath like a horse; at other times, as an old man with a long beard, out of which he would wring the water as he sat on a cliff.

The icelandic water spirit was called NICKUR and appeared always on the form of a horse on the seashore; but he might be distinguished from ordinary horses by the circumstance of his hoofs being reversed. If anyone was so foolish as to mount him, he galloped off, and plunged into the sea with his burden. The epic *Beowulf* speaks of a water-monster, the NICOR.

Scotland also had its water spirit, called KELPIE, which in most respects corresponded with the Nickur. The mischievous water-horse would, like the Nickur, try to decoy unwary persons to mount him, and then plunge with his rider into the neighboring loch or river.

Drac

In the south of France there existed once a sort of fairy in human form called the DRAC, whose abode was the caverns under the rivers. Sometimes these dracs would float like golden cups along a stream to entice women and children bathing nearby; and when they attempted to catch the prize, the dracs would drag them under the water. This was said to happen to none more often than to suckling women who were taken by the dracs to rear their offspring. Sometimes, after the victim had spent seven years there, they were allowed to return to their homes.

SPIRITS OF THE AIR

The air was the medium through which many denizens of the fairy world moved, and likewise demonic figures such as witches with whom we shall deal shortly. We have considered earth spirits and water spirits, and next we take up fire spirits, but there are no familiar legendary figures whose exclusive habitat was the air. However, the Swiss alchemist and physician Paracelsus in the sixteenth century, developing a theory of the four elements, is said to have given the name SYLPHS to imaginary spirits of the air, and this use of the term sylph has been continued and followed by the various later writers.

(See also Gremlins in the section on "American Folklore".)

FIRE SPIRITS

We find fire spirits principally among the peoples of the Orient, and we shall discuss here the Djinn, Peris, and Deevs. However, continuing the reference to Paracelsus just given under spirits of the air, we may mention that Paracelsus is said to have given the name SALAMANDERS to spirits of fire, imaginary beings—not the small reptiles of the same name. (To complete the account of the four Paracelsus elements, we may add that his earth spirits were called gnomes, and his water spirits, nymphs or undines, corresponding to groups of spirits that we have already discussed.)

Djinn or Jinn

The DJINN or JINN (also GENE) of Arabian mythology was a sort of fairy, the offspring of fire. The djinn propagated their species like human beings and were governed by a race of kings called *Suleyman,* one of whom built the Pyramids. Their chief abode was the mountain Kaf, and they appeared to men in the forms of serpents, dogs, cats, monsters, and even human beings. When they chose to appear in human shape they were not to be distinguished from mortals.

They could however become invisible at will. They sometimes applied an ointment, *Kohl,* to human eyes, after which the person so favored could see an invisible djinn; or see treasure wherever it might be concealed. Frequently they gave onion peels which would turn into gold.

The good djinn were exquisitely beautiful, the evil djinn hideously ugly. Euphemistically they were addressed as *mubarakin*—"blessed ones." These were naturally hostile to men, though compelled sometimes to serve them as slaves. According to fable they were created from fire two thousand years before Adam was made. They dwelled in Jinnistan, under the domain of Eblis.

Peri and Deev

The Peri and Deev of Persia correspond to the good and evil djinn of the Arabs. Both alike were ruled over by Suleyman and dwelt in the mountains of Kaf, in Jinnistan. The bodies of both, too, were formed of fire.

The peries and the deevs waged constant war with each other. Like mankind, they were subject to death, but after a much longer period of existence. When the deevs in their wars made prisoners of the peries, they shut them up in iron cages, and hung them from the tops of the highest trees. Here their companions visited them and brought them the choicest odors to feed on, for the spirits lived on perfume. Perfume also had the property of repelling the cruel deevs, whose coarser nature was antipathetic to it.

When the peries were unable to withstand their foes they used to solicit the help of some mortal hero. He was given enchanted arms and talismans to enable him to cope with the gigantic deevs, and he was conveyed to Jinnistan on the back of some strange animal, such as the wonderful simurgh who spoke all languages, and who had knowledge of the future.

The deevs had the power of changing shape and becoming invisible. In their normal shape they were as ugly as the peries were beautiful. They had long horns and long tails, and great fangs.

DEMONIC SPIRITS

Witches

The witch was regarded usually as a human old woman who by some foul means, usually a compact with the Devil, acquired mystic powers of evil. Satan conferred the power and received the soul of the witch as compensation. However, the witch is often a spirit other than human, appearing in any form, even that of animals. Sometimes they had goose feet or several heads.

The witches were held responsible for the injury and illness of men and cattle. By using the paring of fingernails, a lock of hair, or some article touched or used by the victim, the witch could transfer an injury to him; the personal relic could be burned or pierced with thorns to the accompaniment of an incantation. In like manner, the witch had the power to raise storms, destroy crops, transform men into animals, and to work miracles. By an invisible arrow, the *haegtessan gescot,* the Scandinavian witch was supposed to bring disease or death to cattle. Like the fairies she was considered responsible, too, for riding the horses sweaty at night, and for making the cows give bloody milk.

Witches were supposed to have the power to transform themselves into animals to escape detection, and were believed to be accompanied by *familiars*—spirits who did their bidding. These familiar spirits were usually insects or cats. They were accused of bearing children by these spirits, thus breeding monsters. Sometimes witches were pictured as beautiful and attractive women who enticed lovers and then deserted them. Sometimes the nightmare was ascribed to witches or Hags (German *hexe* or "witch"). One afflicted with the nightmare was said to be hag-ridden.

In pagan Scandinavia the witches

as TUNRIDA or house-riders would sit on roofs or hedge-enclosures of a homestead to destroy it.

The witches were supposed to assemble regularly at a WITCHES' SABBATH, riding through the air to the place of meeting, and vying with one another in committing foul deeds and profaning Christian practices. The witch ride was performed on a *gandr* or "staff"—or more familiarly, a broomstick. Scandinavian witches or troll-women also rode on a wolf bridled with snakes.

This aerial flight of witches and sorceresses to a nocturnal gathering had widespread belief. The witch first anointed her feet and shoulders with the fat of a murdered babe, then mounting her staff made her exit by the chimney and rode to the place of rendezvous. The assembled witches feasted together, and concluded with a dance in which they all turned their backs to one another.

Bogie

The BOGIE is any imaginary thing that frightens a person. It is variantly called a BOGLE, a BUGBEAR, a BUGABOO and may refer to any malignant being which is invoked to cause fear, especially in children. Of such a bogie character is the HUCKAUF which superstition told would jump on one's back as he walked along the road at night.

Fée

Normandy was at one time infested by a kind of FÉE known as LES DAMES BLANCHES or White Ladies. They lurked near ravines, fords, bridges, and other narrow passes, and asked the passenger to dance, or to hand them over a plank. If he agreed, well; the fée would dismiss him after a round or two; but if he drew back, she would seize him and fling him into one of the ditches which were full of briars and thorns; or give him over to the LUTRINS, the cats and owls, and other beings which under her sway haunted the place and by which he would be cruelly tormented.

Another group of French fées, tradition tells, used to hold a fair at which all sorts of magic articles from their secret stores were offered for sale, and the most persuasive blandishments employed to induce those who frequented it to become purchasers. But the moment anyone did so and stretched forth his hand to take the article he had selected, the perfidious fées seized him and hurled him down the cliffs.

Nightmare Spirit

Primitive peoples and savages regarded nightmares as an oppression caused by the night-hag or riding of the witch. The nightmare, as the name suggests, was an *incubus* which was supposed to ride on or press the sleeper, even to the point of death. But the sleeper's feelings varied from great pain or oppression to mild or even voluptuous sensations. Consequently, it was assumed that the mare might be either a shaggy monstrous animal, or a male or female demon.

The MAHR was conceived of as the soul of a person which had left its body in order to torment a sleeper. A witch might cause her soul to act as a mahr; or it might be the soul of a woman secretly in love with the victim. In the guise of a man or woman the spirit might successfully pass itself off on an unsuspecting human as a being of its own kind. A male sleeper might find such a mahr desirable and offer the demon *succubus* love or marriage. When a Norse husband asked his nightmare wife how she had entered his room and she replied that she did not know, he showed her a knothole through which she might have come. Becoming small, she vanished through it. When a sleeper awoke after a visit from the nightmare and found himself grasping a straw or a piece of down, he was sure that the mahr had transformed herself into one of these.

Werewolf

In medieval Europe there was a widespread belief in lycanthropy—the power of certain individuals to assume the form of wolves, or in some regions, the form of the fiercest animal there existing—bear, tiger, hyena, leopard. The word WEREWOLF (French, *loup-garou*) means "man-wolf." The werewolf would attack men and infants, prey on cattle, suck the milk of cows, mares, and sheep, strangle horses, and cause cattle to die of plague. In England it was believed at one time that at changes of the moon, men could become wolves.

Among the Slavs it was held a child born feet foremost or with teeth would become a werewolf. A person turning into a wolf would run about the village casting plaintive glances at people, but without harming anyone. If enchanted he would retain his wolf-like shape until the charm had been removed.

In Eastern Europe the belief was advanced that every single family had its own werewolf, called VLKODLAK, which would try to harm the house; but that the house also possessed a good genius which would battle the werewolf and protect the household from him.

Estrie

The ESTRIE, of medieval Hebrew superstition, was the female counterpart of the werewolf. Included among the incorporeal spirits, she was none the less also a woman, a flesh-and-blood member of the community. She was an evil spirit who had adopted woman's form and spent her life among mortals the more readily to satisfy her gory appetites. She was a vampire whose particular prey was little children, though she did not disdain at times to suck the blood of grown-ups.

The estrie had the faculty of changing her shape as she willed and of returning to her original demonic state when she flew about at night. If an estrie were wounded by a human being, or seen by him in her demonic state, she would die unless she could procure and consume some of his bread and salt. When she was being buried, her mouth had to be stopped up with earth, lest she return to do more evil.

Vampire

Hungarian superstition was originally responsible for the legend of the VAMPIRE. The vampire was represented as the re-animated body of a dead person which had come from the grave and wandered about by night sucking the blood of persons asleep. Persons whose blood he had sucked became vampires in turn. During the day the vampire lay as a corpse, but by night, especially at full moon, it made its fiendish rounds.

Various Legendary Figures and Themes

Out of the experiences of the folk, their common joys and common tragedies, has grown a host of legends which almost defy classification. They have been grouped here under several headings which indicate that for all their diversity of origin, there is a common core of experience and aspiration which unites all people everywhere.

People have always had a dream of a better world, a more comfortable world, a Land of Heart's Desire, or the dream of finding a pot of gold at the end of the rainbow, as in El Dorado; or the dream of eternal youth discoverable in the Elixir or the Fountain of Youth. And the dreams have been translated into legends that for some became so real that they considered them true, and like Ponce de Leon set out in the vain hope of finding them.

People have shared everywhere too, the holiday spirit of joy implicit in the legend of Santa Claus and of Befana, a spirit of good will and humanity. And there has always been among all peoples an appreciation of mother wit, the barbed reply which common-sense (that sense which is common to all) makes to foolish questions and foolish acts. The Wise Men of Gotham and the legend of the Blarney Stone convey such a reply. And on the lighter side of life, a mixture of the sophisticated and the sentimental, is the gay or piquantly sad life depicted in the *Commedia dell' arte* or pantomime figures of Columbine, Harlequin, Pierrot, and Punchinello.

For people generally there is always tragedy to match the joy. There has always been the apprehension of evil in the world, of a devil in the form of a Mephistopheles or a Demogorgon, or of the sinister and occult, like the figure of the Pied Piper and the *Jettatura,* or the ironic, as seen in the domestic conflict of Punch and Judy.

And the people of all countries have crystallized in their legends the ideals of morality and conduct implicit in the actions of a Lady Godiva or a William Tell, or have used them to point a moral, as in the story of Fortunatus and of the captain of the Flying Dutchman.

The legends which we relate in this section came into special prominence in various periods of history and reflect their specific beliefs and interests. The Fountain of Youth and El Dorado had their vogue in the sixteenth century, the Age of Exploration and Discovery. The Elixir and Philosopher's Stone belong properly to the Middle Ages, the era of the alchemists and astrologers. Whatever their place or time or origin, however, the stories give evidence of universality, and have been taken up and spread most widely in ages receptive to their message.

DREAMS AND ASPIRATIONS

Atlantis

ATLANTIS was a mythical island of great extent which was anciently supposed to have existed in the Atlantic Ocean. It is first mentioned by Plato, and Solon was told of it by an Egyptian priest who said that it had been overwhelmed by an earthquake and sunk beneath the sea 9000 years before his time.

El Dorado

The name EL DORADO, meaning the Golden One, was first associated with a legendary ruler in north-central South America who one day a year was covered with oil and sprinkled with gold dust which glowed. Early Spanish explorers and later Sir Walter Raleigh sought such a chieftain and his country, but with no success.

The concept of El Dorado became the longed-for country of golden treasure, and the scene shifted to the west-central United States, where in the years 1540 and 1541 Coronado vainly searched for it. It remains the land of golden dreams.

Elixir of Life and Philosopher's Stone

The ELIXIR OF LIFE was the potion of the alchemists which supposedly would prolong life indefinitely. Some accounts made it a powder, others a fluid. *Elixir* also meant to alchemists the PHILOSOPHER'S STONE, a substance capable of transmuting baser metals into gold. According to one legend, Noah was commanded to hang a Philosopher's Stone in the Ark to give light to all creatures therein. Another relates that Prometheus' son Deucalion, saved after the deluge of Greek legend, put the stone in a bag yet lost it.

Fountain of Youth

The FOUNTAIN OF YOUTH was a mythical fountain supposed to possess the power of restoring youth. In origin the legend of such a fountain, derived from Indian Brahmanic legend, came to be confused in European thought with a legend of Semitic origin, that of the River or Spring of Immortal Life which was in Paradise and which confers endless health and life on those who have gone to heaven. Ponce de Leon, hearing of medicinal springs in northern Florida, sought these as the longed-for Fountain of Youth.

The Land of Cockaigne

The LAND OF COCKAIGNE (spelled also *Cokayne, Cocagne*) was in medieval legend a mythical land of pleasure, wealth, luxury, and idleness, a land in which the houses and streets and rivers were made of candy and cake and other temptingly good things, to which all could help themselves.

The Phoenix

A fabulous bird worshipped by the ancient Egyptians at Heliopolis, the PHOENIX was beleived to live from five hundred to a thousand years, then to make a pyre of spices in the Arabian desert, burn itself to ashes, and come forth with new life to repeat the cycle.

SPIRIT OF JOY

Santa Claus

The name SANTA CLAUS is a contraction of Saint Nicholas, the patron saint of children. The American legend of the jolly old man who comes from the North Pole over the snow in a sleigh driven by eight reindeer is crystallized in Clement Clark Moore's familiar poem *A Visit from Saint Nicholas* (1823), better known as "'Twas the night before Christmas." Santa is pictured as coming down the chimneys to leave gifts for the children, who have hung their stockings up for him.

In Holland, December 5, the eve of St. Nicholas' feast day, had long been associated with gifts from St. Nicholas for children. The English settlers in New York merged New Amsterdam's Dutch tradition of St. Nicholas with the English Father Christmas, moving the story to December 25 and joining it with the celebration of Christmas.

Befana and Babushka

BEFANA is the good fairy of Italian children, the female counterpart of Santa Claus, who is supposed to fill their stockings with toys when they go to bed on Epiphany or Twelfth Night. According to legend, Befana was too busy with house affairs to look after the Magi when they were on their journey to offer gifts to the Savior, saying that she could wait to see them on their return. They went back another way and Befana was punished by having to look for them forever. In spite of her Santa Claus character, her name is used as a bogie by Italian mothers to frighten little children.

In Russia, the joyful function of Befana is in the hands of the grandmotherly BABUSHKA who seeks out lonely children for special gifts.

WIT AND WISDOM

Blarney Castle and Blarney Stone

Two legends are connected with the castle of Blarney, in the village of Blarney near Cork. One has to do with the castle itself, the other with one of its stones.

Cormack Macarthy, according to the first, held the castle in 1602 and concluded an armistice with Carew, the Lord President, on condition of surrendering the fort to the English garrison. Day after day his lordship looked for the fulfillment of the terms, but received nothing but soft speeches from Cormack Macarthy, until he became the laughing stock of Queen Elizabeth's ministers and the dupe of the lord of Blarney. (Hence "blarney.")

In the wall of the castle at Blarney, about twenty feet from the top, accessible only with difficulty, is a stone with an inscription referring to Cormac Macarthy. Tradition says that whosoever can kiss this stone will be given the gift of easy speech.

Wise Men of Gotham

The legend is that King John of England, on his way to Lynn Regis, intended to pass through Gotham, in Nottinghamshire, with his army, and sent heralds to prepare the way. Alarmed at the expense of receiving the king and at the possible depredation, the men of Gotham decided to forestall the coming of the monarch and his army if possible. When the royal messengers appeared, wherever they went they saw the people occupied in some idiotic pursuit. Some were raking the moon out of the pond, some were making a ring of stakes to hedge in a bird. When the king was told of it, he abandoned his intention, and the "wise men" of the village cunningly remarked, "We ween there are more fools pass through Gotham than remain in it."

Till Eulenspiegel

TILL EULENSPIEGEL (the last name means "owl-mirror") was an actual peasant who is believed to have lived in Germany in the fourteenth century. A number of popular tales developed about him in which he is represented as the virtual embodiment of mischievousness. No one escaped his wit and roguery, which he exercised particularly on tradesmen, innkeepers, priests, and noblemen. His pranks were often scurrilous and obscene. Eventually he was sent to the gallows for his deviltry. He is the subject of a tone poem by Richard Strauss.

FIGURES FROM PANTOMIME

Pierrot

PIERROT is a favorite character of pantomime, a sort of clown lover. Pierrot is the lover of Pierrette or of

Columbine. His character has been evolved by time into a more romantic role, that of an artist lover of soaring imagination who grimly hides his real passion behind a comic mask.

Harlequin and Columbine

In some traditional pantomimes HARLEQUIN is a sprite supposed to be invisible to all eyes except those of his faithful Columbine. His office is to dance through the world and frustrate all the knavish tricks of the Clown, who is seeking to win the love of Columbine. He is a mixture of childlike ignorance, wit, and grace, always in love, always in trouble, easily despairing, easily consoled. He derives from *Arlecchino,* a stock character of Italian comedy, whose name was in origin probably that of a sprite or hobgoblin.

COLUMBINE has developed into a stock character of pantomime, as the daughter of PANTALOON and the sweetheart of Harlequin. Like him she is supposed to be invisible to mortal eyes.

SCARAMOUCHE as a stock character of pantomime has developed into the archetype of boastfulness and cowardice.

Punch and Judy

PUNCH and JUDY are the hero and heroine of the popular puppet show of that name, and their legendary conflict has spread throughout the world. The story is of Italian origin, Punch being a contraction of PUNCHINELLO.

In its essential outline, the story represents Punch as a humpbacked, long-nosed creature, dissipated, violent, and cunning. In a fit of jealousy he strangles his infant child, whereupon his wife, Judy, fetches a bludgeon with which she belabors him until he seizes another bludgeon, beats her to death, then flings the two bodies into the street. A passing police officer enters the house; Punch flees but is arrested by an officer of the Inquisition and shut up in prison. He beguiles the hangman into putting his own head in the noose and promptly hangs him. Finally he is visited by the devil whom he likewise vanquishes.

THE TRAGIC AND THE SINISTER

The Pied Piper

According to the legend, the town of Hamelin in Westphalia was infested with rats in 1284. A mysterious Piper, clad in a parti-colored suit—and hence called the PIED PIPER—appeared in the town and offered to rid it of the vermin for a certain sum. The townspeople accepted the offer, the Pied Piper fulfilled his contract, but then payment was withheld. On the following St. John's Day he reappeared, and again played his pipe. This time all the children of the town, in place of the rats, followed him. He led them to a mountain cave where all disappeared except two—one blind, the other dumb or lame. One version has it that the children did not perish in the mountain, but were led over it to Transylvania, where they formed a German colony which still exists there. Robert Browning popularized the story in his poem "The Pied Piper of Hamelin."

Bluebeard

The story of BLUEBEARD, the human monster who murders his wives and hides their bodies in a locked room, is an almost universal legend. The essentials of the tale—Bluebeard's prohibition to his new wife to open a certain door during his absence, her disobedience, her discovery of the gruesome secret, and her timely rescue from death—are to be found in the folklore of many countries. He is generally credited with the murder of seven wives.

Evil Eye and Mascotte

The superstition that certain persons have a blighting or malignant eye which deals death or ill-luck upon the one on whom it is turned is called the EVIL EYE. Under the name of JETTATURA it has flourished with extraordinary vigor in Italy, and is one of the most ancient of myths.

MASCOTTE or MASCOT is the term by which is identified some object, animate or inanimate, which, like the luck-penny, brought good fortune to its possessor. Through France and in other parts of Europe this myth of good fortune has become associated with the caul. The child born with it is not only lucky in himself, but also the source of luck to others.

Mephistopheles

MEPHISTOPHELES, of old German legend, is sometimes identified with Satan, sometimes as a subordinate demon. As the devil he is usually pictured as a spirit conscious of the good against which he is in revolt, a fallen angel who has not forgotten the splendor of his first estate. He is a melancholy fellow who tries not to be any worse than he must. In accordance with the old tradition he is dressed as a nobleman, all in red, with a little cape of stiff silk, a cock's feather in his hat, and a long pointed sword. His lamp indicates he is Lucifer fallen from heaven.

In his subordinate capacity, he is more the kobold of German myth than the devil of theology. Though summoned with terrible incantations, he proceeds to act the part of attendant and familiar servant. He not only waits upon and provides the legendary Faust with sumptuous fare, but he indulges in horse play and practical joking of a homely kind. He appears, too, alternately in animal and human shape.

Demogorgon

DEMOGORGON was a terrible deity whose very name was capable of producing the most horrible effects. He is first mentioned by the fourth century Christian writer Lactantius, who in so doing believed to have broken the spell of a mystery, for Demogorgon is supposed to be identical with the infernal power of the ancients, the very mention of whose name brought death and disaster.

Moloch

MOLOCH was a variant of BAAL, a sun-god who represented the sun in its destructive aspects. Moloch was worshipped by the early Canaanites and neighboring Semitic tribes. Moloch was described as having a bull's head with wide jaws, and long arms held out to receive the human victims who were sacrificed to him. He was worshipped by some of the peoples of North Africa, and sacrifices to him were made in Carthage as late as the first century A. D.

MORALITY AND CONDUCT

The Sword of Damocles

DAMOCLES, a courtier of the tyrant Dionysius the Elder, once remarked upon Dionysius' riches and power. Dionysius, to demonstrate the precariousness of one in his position, gave a banquet in Damocles' honor, which Damocles enjoyed to the fullest, until, upon looking up, he saw above his head a sword hanging by a single hair.

The Flying Dutchman

The FLYING DUTCHMAN was a legendary spectral ship, supposed to be seen off the Cape of Good Hope, and considered an omen of ill-luck. According to legend, an old Dutch captain, in the midst of a struggle with the elements, swore an impious oath to round the Cape even if it took an eternity to do it. The curse which was laid on him for centuries as a result would be lifted only if he found a wife willing to sacrifice everything for his sake.

Prester John

PRESTER JOHN, or John the Presbyter, was a fabulous Christian king and priest supposed in the twelfth century to have reigned over a wonderful country in the heart of Asia. According to the reputed travel writer Sir John Mandeville, he was a lineal descendant of Ogier the Dane, who penetrated into the north of India with fifteen of his barons, among whom he divided the land. John was made ruler of Teneduc, and was called Prester (that is, Presbyter) because he converted the natives. Another tradition says he had seventy kings for his vassals, and was seen by his subjects only three times in a year.

The Wandering Jew

The WANDERING JEW is a legendary figure doomed to wander over the earth until the Day of Judgment because he was said to have mocked at Christ on the way to Calvary. Under the name of Buttadeus he was said to have lived through the ages, and at the end of each century to fall into a trance from which he awoke a young man of thirty again. He was believed to have become gifted with supernatural wisdom, and his cruelty was turned to repentance. In his journeys through every land he exhorted men to be mindful of their sins and thus avoid the wrath of God.

The legend is the same in different countries but the identity of the figure varies. One tradition calls him Kartaphilos, doorkeeper of the Judgment Hall in the service of Pontius Pilate. In Germany he is called Ahasuerus, a cobbler; in Provence his name is changed to Boutedieu; in Belgium to Isaac Laquedem; in Spain to Juan Espera-en-Dios.

Lady Godiva and Peeping Tom

In the eleventh century, Leofric, earl of Mercia and lord of Coventry, imposed some very severe imposts on his tenants which his countess, GODIVA, urged him to remove. Thinking to silence her importunity, the earl said he would do so only after she had ridden naked through the town at midday. Lady Godiva took him at his word and actually rode through Coventry naked, on her horse. The earl then faithfully kept his promise. According to legend, all the inhabitants voluntarily confined themselves to their houses and resolved that anyone who stirred abroad should be put to death. However, a certain tailor peeped through his window to see the lady pass and was struck blind in consequence. Ever since he has been called PEEPING TOM of Coventry.

William Tell

WILLIAM TELL is the legendary national hero of Switzerland, whose deeds are based on a Teutonic myth of widespread occurrence in northern Europe.

Tell was the fabled champion of the Swiss in the War of Independence against Albert of Austria. He refused to salute the cap of Gessler, the imperial governor, and for this act of independence was sentenced to shoot with his bow and arrow an apple from the head of his own son. Tell succeeded in this dangerous assignment, but in his agitation dropped an arrow from his robe. The governor insolently demanded what the second arrow was for, and Tell fearlessly replied, "To shoot you with it had I failed in the task imposed on me." Gessler then ordered him to be carried in chains across the lake and cast into a dungeon filled with snakes. He was, however, rescued by the peasantry, and, having shot Gessler, freed his country from the Austrian yoke.

Fortunatus

FORTUNATUS was a hero of medieval legend—from Eastern sources—who possessed an inexhaustible purse and a wishing cap. He appears as a man on the brink of starvation, on whom Fortune offers to bestow either wisdom, strength, riches, health, beauty, or long life. He chooses riches, and she gives him the inexhaustible purse, but his gifts prove the ruin both of himself and his sons.

Myths and Legends of the Africans

THIS section takes up the myths and legends of the native peoples of Africa. Of the varied beliefs held by the many tribes and cultural groups in Africa, we deal with some of the deities and legends of the more numerous peoples, such as the Bantus and the Hottentots. Although these people are described as primitive, a reading of this chapter will indicate that they are not lacking in the imagination and humor that we have found in the more familiar myths and legends of the people who have contributed to our own Western civilization.

African High Gods

The HIGH GODS of the Africans are the major deities who are believed to live in the sky, but sometimes they live on earth, or at any rate, not as far away from people as heaven. For various reasons—usually their disgust at the way human beings act—they leave the earth and return to the sky.

One of the High Gods in African mythology, called BUMBA by the Bantu and some other tribes, was responsible for the creation. He instituted the laws and regulations to be followed by man, and he appointed agents or rulers to govern the tribes. When he felt that his work was completed he withdrew from the earth and went to live in heaven; when he wished to make his will known to his worshippers he did so by means of dreams and visions.

African High Gods are not necessarily, as Bumba seems to be, creators as we understand the term. Sometimes he is described as making man; sometimes man seems to have been created without any knowledge or action on the part of the god. In some legends, it is indicated that he made animals, but not men, who are represented as coming from trees, rocks, plants, and grass. In others, instead of being man's maker, he is surprised at his appearance and actually asks where he came from.

Many African myths also associate a High God with death; different tribes personify Death and call him different names, as KALUNGA, and WALUMBE, representing the latter as the son of heaven.

The African Bushmen worship the moon and other heavenly bodies, which are the center of their mythology. They also worship a large number of mythical creatures called different names by different tribes. As HUWU, TORA, GAUNA, they are symbols of the forces of nature connected with rain and they are prayed to by the Bushmen.

The Hottentots, like the Bushmen, worship the moon and pray to it for rain and food. They also call on many mythical heroes who are personifications of the natural elements that cause rain. Tsui-Goab, Heitsi-Eibib, and Gaunab, some of their outstanding heroes, differ only slightly from the creatures worshipped by the Bushmen. Cattle and water, both important in the economy of these tribes, play an important part in their religious customs and beliefs.

The Sacred Cat

Titishana was a young girl who had just been married and was about to move to her husband's tribe. Her parents urged her to take with her an elephant or an antelope, but she refused them, and insisted on taking their cat, an animal sacred to their clan. When she reached her new home, she built an enclosure for the cat and fed it well. But each night, the cat arose and took the husband's kilt and rattle and sang and danced. The husband saw this performance one night and killed the cat. At the same moment, Titishana fell down in a faint. On awakening she asked her husband to wrap the cat in a mat—she would die if she saw it uncovered—and they carried it to the clan of Titishana's parents. There the mat was unrolled and each member of the clan went up to look at the dead cat. As each one caught sight of the cat he fell down and died. So the entire village was wiped out. The husband told his friends that by killing the cat he had killed all these people, since their lives had depended on it. Furthermore, he complained, he had lost the dowry he had paid for his wife since there was no one left alive from whom he could claim it.

The Crafty Hare

A hare played a trick on a gazelle and induced her to get into a pot, whereupon the hare boiled her to death. He made her horns into a musical instrument which he played all over the countryside. A hippopotamus caught the hare, but the wily creature convinced the hippopotamus to free him, on the promise that he would teach him to blow the horns. The hippopotamus tried but could not learn to play them, so the hare convinced him that cutting off his thick lips might help. The hippopotamus then swallowed the horn, but the hare killed him and cut open his stomach, retrieving the horns. While he was washing the horns in the river, a cat stole the meat. In revenge the hare killed the cat and sold her meat, living for a time on the proceeds. When these gave out, he set to stealing from people's gardens, tricking the owners into fleeing by crying that the enemy was coming. In time this ruse was discovered, and the people attempted to catch the little thief by setting up an image of a woman covered with a sticky substance. But their plan miscarried, and instead they caught and killed their own chief, while the hare escaped.

Myths and Legends of the Polynesians

The Polynesians are the native peoples of many of the islands of the Pacific. Among the Polynesians are: the Maoris, early inhabitants of New Zealand; the Tahitians, Samoans, and dwellers on the Carolinas, Marshalls, and neighboring islands; and the Hawaiians. There is great similarity between the myths and legends of the Maoris and those of other Polynesian groups, though among the Hawaiians there were certain special deities. In our account we point out important local emphasis.

DEITIES OF THE POLYNESIANS

Versions of the Creation

Among the native Tahitians, Tiki was a god who existed from the very beginning. He floated on the water in a canoe, and he made or discovered the land by digging it up from the bottom of the ocean, where it was hidden.

In another version of the beginning of everything, Taaroa lived by himself in the heavens, or existed in total darkness in a huge egg from which he broke out. In heaven, Taaroa created a daughter and with her help he made the earth and the sea and the sky. Various legends have it that the egg was laid or dropped in the sea by a huge bird flying over the primeval bodies of water. Sooner or later the egg broke of itself and the result was the world.

Io, the supreme god among certain of the Polynesian groups, was a god who created himself. Io also created light and caused it to appear in the dark universe, and he separated the waters that surrounded the earth. A very special god, regarded by the priests as their own property, Io was prayed to at births, baptisms, and marriage rites connected with high-ranking people.

Rangi and Papa

Rangi (or Vatea), the Sky Father, married Papa, who was the Earth Mother. From their union came Tangaroa, Tane, Tu, and Rongo, the chief gods of Polynesian mythology.

Tane

Tane was the god of the light of the sun and of the birds and trees and forests. He is a chief figure in Maori and other Polynesian mythology. He married a number of wives, and they gave him as children trees, stones, snakes, mountain water, and grass. Not satisfied with such offspring, he complained each time to his mother, Papa, whom he had wanted to marry in the first place. She advised him to gather up the earth at the beach of Kurawaka. Doing as he was told, Tane hurried to the beach and scraped up the earth with his hands, shaping it into the form of a man, to whom he gave the name Tiki, or Tiki-au-a-ha.

Then from the soil of Hawaiki he shaped and gave life to woman, to be the wife of Tiki, and he called her HINE-AHU-ONE, meaning the "earth-formed maid."

In an entirely different version of this legend, Tane marries a tree who bears him trees, not men or women. Tane then goes to the beach of Hawaiki, mixes mud and sand and creates a woman. After he has shaped her properly and covered her he breathes life into her, and leaves her by herself for a short time. When he returns she is alive and intensely interested in everything about her. Seeing Tane, she laughs and marries him.

In some accounts, Tiki, not Tane, is a god, and creates man.

Tangaroa

TANGAROA was the god of the sea and of all the things and animals in it and the patron and protector of fishing and fishermen, both the group and the activity playing a very vital part in the economy of an island community. In a struggle with TAWHIRI, the tempest, one of his many brothers, Tangaroa escaped by diving into the sea when he saw that the battle was going against him.

Tu and Rongo

TU, the angry god, was the god of war and power, and, in time of war, the receiver of human sacrifices. He was a beneficent, as well as a belligerent, deity. In the battle against Tawhiri, in which Tangaroa jumped into the sea, Tu gained the victory.

RONGO, in contrast to Tu, was a peaceful god and a god of rain and fertility.

Kane

KANE was the chief god of Hawaiian mythology. A god of creation and procreation, he was worshipped by the chiefs and by those of humbler station as their common ancestor. He was believed to have shaped and formed heaven—two heavens, in fact—and earth: an Upper Heaven, for the deities, a Lower Heaven above the earth, and the Earth itself for the use of mortals; he also created plants, and animals, and, finally he made human beings, male and female, to live in the earth he made for them.

Ku, Lono, and Kanaloa

KU, LONO, and KANALOA were other leading gods in the mythology of Hawaii. They were generally mentioned together in connection with Kane and their names were associated in prayers and chants by the natives. Ku, god of fruitfulness, represented the male principle, and was worshipped as an ancestral god of heaven and earth. His counterpart was HINA, who represented the female force or principle. Ku was the god of health, long life, and success. His followers prayed to him that the earth might bring forth fruit and food and fish, and men and women.

POLYNESIAN HEROES

The Demi-god Maui

MAUI is the hero of many tales told by the Maoris of New Zealand, the early Hawaiians, and in various islands of Polynesia. These stories differ from island to island, but almost all versions agree that Maui was a resourceful, mischievous, wily figure who delighted in confounding the less well endowed. It was believed that shortly after his birth his mother wrapped him up in her apron and threw him into the sea. He was then taken up into the sky by supernatural beings, and from them learned his skills. When he reached maturity he determined to find his mother and brothers. His mother did not recognize him, but when he recalled the circumstances of his abandonment, she remembered and made him her favorite son. Maui's brothers were not conspicuous for their wisdom. It was said that they had no barbs on their spears and used eel-pots which had no trapdoors, wondering why they could catch no eels. Maui invented a barb for the spear and a trapdoor for the eel-pot.

Maui's brothers had the task of feeding an old relative, but they neglected her, eating the food themselves. Maui came upon her one day and found that one half of her body was already dead. He wrenched off her lower jaw and from it made a fishhook. The next day he and his brothers went fishing, but, since they thought he could not fish, they refused to give him a fishhook. Whereupon Maui pulled out his magic hook, baited it with his own blood, and cast it into the water. Soon, he felt a tremendous bite on the line and, hauling it in, found that he had hooked the land from the bottom of the sea. He ordered his brothers not to cut up the great catch, but they hacked at it with their knives, causing the land to struggle and flail about. For this reason the land is rough and rugged.

No task was too heavy for the great Maui. Once his mother complained that she could not dry her sheets of cloth properly because of the shortness of the day. Maui then determined to slow down the progress of the sun across the heavens. He obtained some strong rope and a magic club. As the sun rose in the east Maui noosed its legs and tied them securely to trees. Then he began to belabor the sun with his magic club. The sun begged for mercy and agreed to Maui's demand that henceforth he travel across the sky more slowly.

Maui noticed that every morning, before he and his brothers awoke, his mother disappeared. One morning he followed her and saw her pull up a bush from the ground and enter the earth through the hole thus made. Transforming himself into a bird, Maui followed her to the world below. Here he revealed himself to his mother and demanded food. But the fire was out, so Maui went to an old woman who was the guardian of the fire. He asked that she give him fire and she handed him one of her fingers, in which fire was concealed. But Maui took the finger and quenched the fire in the stream. She gave him other fingers and toes, except one, but each time Maui did the same. At last, angered by his mischief, the old woman set the world on fire with her last toe. Maui fled, calling on the rain and snow to aid him. They put out the fire and thus saved the world.

Mataora and the Journey to the Underworld

One day the youth MATAORA was visited by some people from the underworld, who were known as Turehu. One of their number, NUVARAHU, was very beautiful, and Mataora fell in love with her. They were married and lived happily for a while, but Mataora became jealous of his wife's attentions to his brother and he beat her. Nuvarahu was angry at this treatment and fled back to the underworld. Mataora, grief-stricken at her loss, resolved to follow her. He managed to find his way down and eventually came to the village of his father-in-law. Here the people laughed at him, for his face was painted with a substance which they could easily wipe off with their hands. His father-in-law showed him a permanent way of decorating the body, and Mataora agreed to have himself so decorated. This was the first use of tattooing. As his father-in-law applied the marks, Mataora cried out in pain, and Nuvarahu recognized his voice. She comforted him while his wounds were healing, and they lived happily in the underworld for a time.

But eventually Mataora longed to return to the world above and Nuvarahu agreed to accompany him. They took with them the young of the owl, the bat, the rail, and the fantail, who thus came to the earth. When they passed the door leading into the upper world the guardian of the door shut it, and thenceforth only the spirits of men were permitted to enter.

Myths and Legends of the Americas

AMERICANS of today know very few of the myths and legends of the earliest Americans, the Indians of North and Central and South America, yet here is a world of imaginative beauty and wisdom deeply set in the very soil on which we live.

Two points must be kept clearly in mind in considering the lore of the American Indians. First, is the fact that three great Indian civilizations rose to great heights of culture many centuries before the first white men set foot in this hemisphere. The Aztecs occupied the region which is now central Mexico, the Mayas, Central America and neighboring southern Mexico, and the Incas, Peru. Secondly, in the region which is now our United States there were many Indian tribes, with widely varying beliefs and legends, all living a tribal life far simpler than that of the Indian civilizations further south on the continent.

We take up in turn the deities of the Aztecs, the Mayas, and the Incas. Then we tell of the beliefs and legends of the North American Indian tribes. The section concludes with the deities of the tribal Indians of Central and South America who, like the North American Indians, lived entirely apart from the Aztecs, Mayas, and Incas, and developed their own beliefs and legends.

DEITIES OF THE AZTECS

Ometecutli and Omeciuatl

OMETECUTLI and OMECIUATL were the father and mother of the human race in the mythology of the Aztecs. They held the first and highest place in the mythological system of the Nahua race in ancient Mexico. Ometecutli, whose name means "two-lord," was identified with the god of the sky and the god of fire; and his wife, Omeciuatl, was identified with the goddess of earth. They were never born, as they existed from the very beginning of time. They were represented as dressed in the most elegant attire.

Tezcatlipoca

TEZCATLIPOCA, the supreme god of the Aztecs, began as a personification of wind or air and as a tribal god, but he became the chief god in time. He was represented with a mirror or a shield, in which he was able to see, by reflection, what mortals were doing. He had only one leg, having lost one when the gates of the lower world were shut on him in haste. He had both good and evil capacities. As the god who personified the breath of life, he was a giver of life, but he also took life. He was believed to be the originator of most of the Aztecs' arts.

Omacatl

OMACATL was the god of festivity and joy. His worship was limited to the extent that only those could honor him who were wealthy enough to do so in a manner that god himself thought proper. Easily offended if the feast and the decorations and the entertainment were not sufficiently expensive and elegant, the god would appear in anger before his worshippers to let them know without any doubt that he considered himself insulted and that they could count on being severely punished. Illness was the form of punishment that attacked all those who had participated in the celebration.

Opochtli

OPOCHTLI, the left handed, was the god of fishing and birdcatching and the inventor of important equipment, such as the harpoon used for spearing fish, the fishing-rod, and bird nets. Followers of these activities worshipped him by a special feast, the chief feature of which seems to have been the consumption of a tremendous amount of liquor. Opochtli was represented as nude and black in color, with wild bird plumes and a rose-shaped crown on his head. He holds a sceptre in his right hand, and a red shield with a white flower in his left.

Metztli

METZTLI, the Lady of the Night, was the goddess of the moon. She had good and bad aspects. As the kindly patron of harvests and of all growth, human and animal, she was loved and worshipped, but she was feared and hated as the goddess who brought the terrible things of night—cold, damp air, the poisons of the atmosphere, ghosts, and fright-causing shapes and shadows. The chief myth associated with her tells that it was necessary to make a human sacrifice in order to do away with the darkness that surrounded the entire universe. Metztli secured for the purpose NANAHUATL, a leper, threw him on the burning pile or furnace, and then walked into the flames. As she vanished with him, the night disappeared and the sun rose, the night being required to die so that the day or light might be born.

Mixcoatl

MIXCOATL, the cloud-serpent, was the Aztec god of the chase, and may have also been a god of air and thunder. As a god of hunting, he was represented as possessing the characteristic features of either a deer or a rabbit. He carried a quiver of arrows that represented the thunderbolts he used as weapons.

Yacatecutli

YACATECUTLI, the lord of travellers, was the god and patron of merchant travellers of old Mexico. They worshipped him when they returned from their journeys by giving splendid feasts in his honor, and they worshipped him when they arrived at a place where they planned to spend the night by packing their staves together in bundles and then sprinkling the pile of sticks with their own blood drawn from their noses, tongues, or ears. The traveller's staff was Yacatecutli's symbol and it was prayed to and bowed to and honored in every way with gifts of meat, flowers, incense, and tobacco. Human sacrifices —slaves—were offered up to Yacatecutli, and traffic was carried on in the buying and selling of slaves for sacrificial purposes and for eating at the ceremony after their being sacrificed on the altar. Yacatecutli had five brothers and a sister who were included in the sacrifices paid to him.

Ixtlilton

IXTLILTON, or the Little Black One, was the god of medicine and healing. As the god who helped mortals to recover from illness or who kept them always in good health he was regarded as the brother of MACUILXOCHITL, the god of good luck. His temple was filled with jars of black water which was given as medicine to sick children. If they survived the course of treatment or showed signs of improvement, the grateful parents gave a feast and ceremonial dances in honor of the god, whose statue was brought to the house of the parents for the celebration.

Quetzalcoatl

QUETZALCOATL was the god of the sun and the air. His name means "serpent dressed with green feathers," and the legend is that Quetzalcoatl, who was very ugly, wore the feather garment in order to hide his unattractive features. In addition to this godship of air and sun, Quetzalcoatl was also the god of wisdom and a teacher of the arts of peace, and his reign was a period of peace and plenty. He was represented with a long beard, and was dressed in a long white robe, holding a traveller's staff in his hand. He was credited with the invention of the calendar. As a sun-god he wore the well-known solar disk, so frequent in Egyptian art.

Tezcatlipoca, his rival, drove him out by means of his magic powers but he promised to return when he was needed. According to his myths, Quetzalcoatl threw himself on a burning funeral pile and was consumed by the flames, and his heart rose to heaven and was fixed there as the morning star.

The legend of Quetzalcoatl's return was put to good use by Cortes, Spanish conqueror of Mexico, who with his pomp and power could easily impress superstition-ridden people with the conviction that he was a god or the returning god.

Huitzilopochtli

HUITZILOPOCHTLI was the god of war. He was represented as wearing a headdress of bird feathers and carrying four spears and a shield. He was honored by human sacrifices on a wholesale scale and by an image of himself made of grain and various seeds mixed with children's blood; the image was then sacrificed, broken up into pieces and eaten by those participating in the ceremony. In addition to being a god of war, Huitzilopochtli was also the god of lightning, in the form of a serpent, and the god of crops and fruits.

Tlaloc and Mictlan

TLALOC was the god of thunder, rain, and moisture. His wife was CHALCHIHUITLICUE, the Emerald Lady, and his countless children were the clouds. He lived in Tlalocan, the Aztec paradise, reserved for victims of drowning, lightning, and dropsy, where they lived in eternal happiness. Those who did not die of such causes, and women who did not die in childbirth went to the dark and dreary Tlalxicco, ruled over by MICTLAN, the god of death and of the dead, where they endured an empty and meaningless existence.

Centeotl

CENTEOTL, the Aztec goddess and patroness of agriculture and nature in general, and of corn or maize in particular, was represented as a beneficent being, although she also had her evil side. In this latter phase, she was a beautiful woman who lured men to their death by her physical charms; her embraces gave pleasure, all too brief, to the unfortunate male, but they meant death. Merely to see Centeotl in her ravishing beauty was a fatal sign, foreboding ill for the future. Her worshippers believed that she lived in the west and that she caused sickness and pain.

DEITIES OF THE MAYAS

Itzamna

ITZAMNA was the king or lord of the Maya gods, the son of HUNABKUK, the first or creator god. Itzamna was the personification of the east and the rising sun. He was regarded as the Maya god of the sun and as the founder of their civilization. To him was attributed the invention of books and of writing. The names by which he was addressed, the "Master of the Dawn" and the "Man of the Sun," indicate the esteem in which he was held. Itzamna's wife was IXCHEL, the goddess of the rainbow and of childbirth and healing. Originally a tribal god, Itzamna rose to the headship of the Maya gods but was later displaced by Kukulkan. Tezcatlipoca was his Aztec equivalent.

Kukulkan

KUKULKAN, the feathered serpent, was the chief god of the later Mayas. Originally the god of life, and personifying wind, he was known as a builder of cities and a framer of laws. Various crafts were under his protection, and he was regarded as the inventor of the calendar, the use of which he taught to his people.

Chac

CHAC was the rain-and-thunder god of the Mayas. He was waited on by a large number of minor deities. His attendants, also known as Chac, the Red Ones, were his ministers. In religious rites they were represented symbolically by four old men who helped the high priest to carry out his tribal duties. Chac corresponded to Tlaloc, the Axtec rain-and-moisture god.

Ahpuch

AHPUCH was the Maya god of death and the one that was most feared and hated and cursed. He was the personification of all the forces of evil and of bad luck. He was constantly opposed to the good gods of life and fertility. He was represented as a skull devoid of flesh.

The Bacabs

The BACABS, four in number, were gods who stood at each corner of the world and held it up. At the Great Deluge all mortals and all the other gods were swallowed up by the raging waters, except the four Bacabs. Their names (variously given) were KAN, MULUC, IX, and CAUAC, and they symbolized respectively the east, the north, the west, and the south, and each point or quarter of the compass had its distinctive color, yellow for the east, white for the north, black for the west, and red for the south. The Bacabs were also gods of rain and of agriculture, and personifications of the four winds and the four cardinal points.

DEITIES OF THE INCAS

Manco Capac

MANCO CAPAC, the eldest of four brothers, all descended from the Sun-god, was the high-priest and the mythical founder of the Incas and of their ancient dynasty. According to one legend, he was born of a virgin, or, according to another, of the sun and the moon. Of his brothers, one was locked up in a sealed cave and left to die, and two of them were turned to stone. Having been commanded to travel through the country until he came to a place where his gold staff sank into the ground, Manco kept on searching for the promised land even after he had lost his three brothers. When he finally came to a spot where his wand was sucked into the earth he knew that he had reached the end of his journey, and he thereupon founded the ancient city of Cuzco and established the worship of the Sun-god.

Manco Capac was the brother-husband of MAMA OULLO HUACA, the patroness of the domestic arts and sciences, and with her as his companion he taught mortals the arts of peace. When they felt that they had carried out their task, the godly couple left the earth and returned to their home in heaven.

Viracocha

VIRACOCHA, the god of water, was one of the principal deities in the

Peruvian mythology. He was a culture god whose water caused things to grow, the creator and the possessor of all things, and the patron of growth in general. Gifts—land, cattle, offerings—were given to other gods by the Incas, but to Viracocha they gave nothing, because, as lord and master of the whole world, he needed nothing. Before the sun or the moon were made, he rose from the bottom of the waters of his home in Lake Titicaca and built wonderful cities and islands and then made both bodies of light and placed them in the sky properly. His next great task was to make stone images and then to give them life, thus creating the human race. In his travels he was set upon and attacked by the very beings he had created, but the lightning that he hurled, destroying the forests, soon showed them that he was their master. Granting them forgiveness, the god taught them the various arts of peace and agriculture, and religion, and gave them codes and institutions. Then, his work done, he disappeared, as he had come, into the deep waters of his lake-dwelling.

Pachacamac

PACHACAMAC was the god of earthquakes and the god of fertility of the Incas. He was not on good terms with Viracocha, his rival, and after defeating him he made the world over again, as he thought it should be made. When the Indians heard sounds in the earth, rumbling and murmuring sounds or deep noises believed to be Pachacamac's voice, they threw themselves on the ground in fear. The god's name was taken to mean creator or producer or sustainer of the world, in both space and time. Pachacamac was either the son, or the brother, of CON, whom he defeated in battle and drove away. In his shame and anger, Con took the rain with him, which accounts for the rainless seacoast of Peru. Both brothers, or father and son, lacked flesh and blood, but they were magically rapid in their movements and they could not be seen or touched.

Supay

SUPAY, the Shadow, was the god of death or of the dead. He was the king of the land of shades or spirits in the center of the earth. All those souls who were not fated to go to the home of the Sun went to Supay's underworld dwelling, which was a place of darkness but not hell, as we understand it.

DEITIES OF THE NORTH AMERICAN INDIANS

The Worlds of Sky and Earth

Though each of the Indian tribes had their local beliefs, certain large concepts are common to many regions. Widely held was the view that before the earth was formed and peopled there was a sky-world filled with the images of beings who were in time to become the peoples of earth.

The Great Spirit, known among the Algonquians as Manitou, pervades the universe, and among many tribes is worshipped as the visible Father Sky or as the Sun Father. With him is Mother Earth, and also their daughter the Corn Mother who presides over the fields and their fertility. Widely held was the belief that thunder was caused by the flapping of the wings of the Thunderbird, that lightning flashed from the arrows of celestial Archers, that rain was controlled by celestial Rainmakers. In related ways, the Indians accounted for other phenomena of Nature which so closely governed their lives.

Manitou

MANITO, or Manitou, was the Algonquian name for the spirit or force that pervades all nature, being either good or evil. Manito in one form or another, and under other names, was a concept believed in by virtually every Indian tribe. Manito was not thought of as a formal personality, and its nature is indicated by such equivalent names for it as Great Spirit, Great Mystery, and Master of Life.

Manabozho

MANABOZHO (or Manabush or Glooscap), the GREAT HARE, was, among the Algonquians, the creator of the earth and of life, the giver of food. He was the grandson of NOKOMIS, the earth. Various tribes had their own stories of the origin of Manabozho. Some relate that he was one of a pair of twins, the other being his brother CHIBIABOS, with whom he quarreled before he was born. Chibiabos killed his mother in his birth, and in revenge Manabozho slew him. Another version tells that his mother was the Flint, who made a bowl and dipped it into the earth; the bowlful of earth was dipped into blood and the blood was then transformed into a rabbit, which, in time, became a man, Manabozho.

Manabozho was a giant warrior and a master of wile. He destroyed the Great Fish, an oppressor of men and animals. Manabozho allowed himself to be swallowed by the monster and then he plunged his knife into the creature's heart, killing it.

Manabozho performed another great service for mankind. Complaining to his grandmother Nokomis of the cold on earth, he rode in his canoe to an island in the east, where an old man had fire. Manabozho, in the form of the Great Hare, came to the island wet and cold, and the old man and his daughters set him near the fire to warm him. When they were not looking he snatched a burning branch and dashed to his canoe, pursued by the old man and his daughters, but he escaped and brought the fire to Nokomis.

Many of the deeds of Manabozho were used by Longfellow in his famous poem *Hiawatha*. Hiawatha was one of the many names under which Manabozho was known. NOKOMIS appears in Longfellow's story, as does MINNEHAHA, of the Dakotahs, the lovely bride of Hiawatha.

Enigorio and Enigohatgea

ENIGORIO and ENIGOHATGEA, twin brothers in the mythology of the Iroquois, had nothing in common except the fact that they were brothers. Any good that one accomplished, the other undid or tried to undo. Enigorio represented or personified the Good Mind, and Enigohatgea, the Bad Mind. The former, with the best intentions in the world, travelled through the universe, creating streams and rivers, rolling plains and fruit-bearing trees, and doing other good works; the latter, motivated by malice, made naught of his brother's good deeds by causing whirling floods and thorns and deserts. Enigorio put up with his evil brother for a long time, but he finally lost patience and struck him such a blow that Enigohatgea was crushed into the depths of the earth. He sank out of sight forever, not to die but to become the king of the Indian underworld. There, he still lives, occupied in thinking and planning evil, and in receiving the souls of the dead into his kingdom. Enigorio and Enigohatgea, the Iroquoians believed, were the first two brothers of the human race, existing from the beginning of all things.

Atatarho

ATATARHO was the mythical king of the Iroquois tribes, noted for his greatness in war and for his skill in physic, as well as for his magic powers. The only clothing he wore was a robe or dress of black snakes, associated with healing, so that changing his suit was a comparatively simple matter: he discharged the snakes he was wearing and commanded another group of snakes to cover him.

Ioskeha and Tawiscara

The myth of the Iroquois brothers is duplicated among the Huron Indians in the story of another set of brothers, IOSKEHA and TAWISCARA, the White One and the Dark One. Their mother, a virgin, died in childbirth, and their grandmother, ATAENSIC, the moon, was the goddess of water, association between the moon and water being frequently met in the beliefs of American Indians. In a battle between the two, Ioskeha killed Tawiscara, whose drops of blood, as he ran for his life, became flint-stones. With the bad brother out of the way, the good one returned to his grandmother, created the human race, and went after and killed a giant frog that had drunk all the waters of the earth, thus making it dry and sterile. Ioskeha then guided the mountains of water into streams and lakes and rivers, and filled the forests with game. From the great tortoise that supported the world on its shell, he learned the secret of making fire.

Onniont

ONNIONT was a huge monster snake worshipped by the Huron Indians. According to the legends, he wore on his head a large, sharp horn with which he was easily able to cut his way through mountains, rocks, hills, and trees, or anything that ventured to get in his way. To have a piece of this horn, even the smallest piece, was, the Hurons believed, a great charm against evil and a sure bringer of good luck. Onniont was never found, the place where he lived never known, and his horn was never broken, although to find him was the highest wish of every Huron brave. The medicine-men of the tribe pretended that they had some fragments of the horn and they further pretended that they gave it, as war medicine, to the Huron warriors when they were summoned to take the war path.

Asgaya Gigagei

ASGAYA GIGAGEI was the god of thunder of the Cherokee Indians. He was prayed to or invoked when one was suffering from rheumatism; in the prayers made to him he was called both the Red Man and the Red Woman, which would seem to indicate that he was one of the hermaphrodite gods frequent in Indian mythology.

Esaugetuh Emissee

ESAUGETUH EMISSEE, whose name means the "master of breath," or "he who carries life or breath for others," was the god of the wind and the chief deity of the Creeks.

Ikto

IKTO, among the Sioux Indians, was one of the craftiest and cleverest of deities and was credited with having invented or discovered the art of human speech. In his slyness, which made it almost impossible for him to be deceived, he was the counterpart of the Algonquian Manabozho.

Haokah

HAOKAH, the giant god of thunder of the Sioux, was a strange creature, judged by ordinary standards. Hot and cold were, to him, cold and hot; he shook with laughter when he was miserably unhappy, and he groaned and cried bitterly when he felt merry and gay. The two sides of his face did not match in color. As god of thunder, he was pictured with horns on his head, or a forked headdress to represent the lightning. He used the wind as a drumstick to produce his thunder.

Tiwara Atius

TIWARA ATIUS, the chief god of the Pawnee Indians, was the author of creation and was credited with having created the sun, the moon, and the stars and with arranging them in their proper channels. His home was in the heavens and his messages were carried by the eagle and the buzzard. He was thought of not so much as a person as he was a spirit, being a Pawnee equivalent of the Algonquian Manito. Consequently, lesser powers had to mediate between Tirawa and man. Among the lesser spirits were the Sun Father, the Earth Mother, and the Morning Star, which was the herald of the Sun.

Wauhkeon and Unktahe

WAUHKEON, the Thunder Bird, a deity of the Dakota Indians, was engaged in an unending struggle with UNKTAHE, the god of waters. The changing luck of the contestants, victory going first to one and then to the other, is taken to represent allegorically, changes in atmosphere and nature. Unktahe, the Dakotas believed, was a master of magic and a master of dreams and witchcraft.

Ahsonnutli

AHSONNUTLI, or Estsahatlehi, was the chief god of the New Mexico Navaho Indians. He was worshipped as the creator of heaven and earth and was given the credit for having placed twelve men at each of the cardinal points in order to hold up the sky. He combined in himself the qualities of both sexes and was known as the Turquoise Hermaphrodite.

Italapas

ITALAPAS, the Coyote, was one of the chief gods of the Chinook Indians. His will was so powerful that he made the first prairie by "willing" the ocean to become land. He helped IKANAM to create man, and he taught men the arts of peace and agriculture. He also instituted many of the taboos associated with hunting. The Chinook Italapas, who was kindly disposed, was not like the Coyote of the California Indians, who was always looking for trouble and who made trouble when he could not find it.

DEITIES OF THE CENTRAL AND SOUTH AMERICAN INDIANS

Noncomala and Nubu

NONCOMALA is the creative god or deity of the Costa Rica Indians who is credited with having formed the earth and the creation of bodies of water. By his wife, RUTBE, a water-spirit, he had two children, the Sun and the Moon, who dispelled the gloom and darkness. After he had made man, Noncomala regretted his step when he saw how they lived and acted; in his righteous wrath he caused the whole earth to be flooded and all the creatures on it to be drowned. The serious consequences of his action were somewhat offset by NUBU, a kindly god, who managed to save man's life-seed and to sow it in the soil after the flood waters had receded. As a result, men were born again from the seeds that grew to ripeness, and monkeys were born from the undeveloped shoots.

Jurupari

JURUPARI is the chief god of various tribes of Brazilian Indians and is said to be their evil spirit. According to the myth of which he is the center, his mother was a virgin who gave birth to him after drinking a kind of Brazilian beer. As she did not have any sexual organs, she had to be bitten by a fish while she was bathing in order to give birth to her son. When Jurupari became a man he asked all his fellow tribesmen to engage in a drinking bout with him, but, according to the myth, the women of the tribe refused to prepare the necessary liquor. As a result, he hated women in general and became their enemy. He was finally killed and burned by the Indians because he ate all the children of the tribe in anger at their having made a feast of a tree that was sacred to him. From the ashes of the fire in which he was cremated grew another tree, believed to be the bones of the god; from this tree the men made many holy symbols, but, according to belief which was widely accepted, it is dangerous and may mean death for females to see or hear any part of the rites or ceremonies connected with Jurupari's worship.

Aricoute and Timondonar

ARICOUTE and TIMONDONAR, brothers, are worshipped by the Tupi Indians of Brazil. Aricoute, whose complexion is dark, is the god of night; Timondonar, the fair, is the god of light and day. The brothers are always fighting and always the result is the same, Timondonar, the day, overcoming and driving away Aricoute, the night.

Tamu

TAMU, also known as Grandfather and Old Man of the Sky, as a culture-deity of the Caribs of Brazil. He came from the east and he disappeared in the direction of the east, after having communicated the arts of peace and agriculture to his people. He promised them that he would give them help in the future and that when they died he would carry their souls to his palace in the sky. The Tamu of the Caribs is identical with the KAMU of the Arawack Indians, the KABOI of the Carayas, and the ZUME of the Guarani Indians of Paraguay.

Bochica

BOCHICA is the god of dawn of the Muyscas Indians of Bogota. A long time ago he taught them how to cultivate the soil, how to build houses, to make clothing, and to tell time, and how to live under a code of laws that he drew up for them. When he finally decided to disappear from the earth, he divided it into four parts and gave the responsibility of governing to four chiefs who from that time on saw to it that Bochica's laws and principles were carried out to the letter.

Chia

CHIA, the moon, is also the goddess of water of the Muyscas Indians. A bad-tempered deity, she flooded the earth out of spite. If a warrior saw her in a dream, he dressed himself in female clothing, engaged in feminine tasks and pretended to be a woman, in the hope that he would deceive the goddess as to his sex and so escape her anger and its evil effects.

Pilian

PILIAN, the chief deity of the Araucanians, an Indian people living in Chile, is worshipped by them as the god of thunder. He is noted for his remarkable speed, for his redness, red being the color of flash of lightning, and for his hasty temper. He lives on a mountain and can be appeased by dropping liquor into mountain streams.

Aka-Kanet

AKA-KANET, who is called the father of evil, is the god of fruit and grain of the Araucanians. He is the patron of the harvest and his throne is in the Pleiades. Although sometimes associated with evil, Aka-Kanet is prayed to by the priests as a well-disposed deity and is looked upon as the grandfather and protector of the race.

Amalivaca

AMALIVACA is one of the gods worshipped by the Orinoco River Indians. He taught them the arts of agriculture and how to understand the secrets of the soil. His return in time of need is expected by his worshippers.

American Folklore

THE IDEA that America has a body of popular tales which can be referred to as "folklore" is of quite recent origin, but the fact that the American people have been creating these tales virtually since their arrival on this continent has long been recognized. In this section we discuss some of the best known heroes of American folklore. Most of them were real persons whose achievements have been exaggerated through the countless relations of their exploits. Apart from these folk characters, there are the new, tiny, imaginary creatures, the Gremlins. Of the legendary figures, the most famous is Paul Bunyan, whose size and prowess are of truly epic proportions.

Paul Bunyan

PAUL BUNYAN, the "mightiest and greatest of all the boss loggers," is the lumberjack hero of the Great Lakes and the Pacific Northwest. In the stories of Paul Bunyan exaggeration is the keynote. Paul's place of birth is not certain, Maine, Michigan, Minnesota, or the Canadian woods being some of the regions that contend for the honor. But although it is not known exactly where he was born there is no doubt about his powerful strength, which he began to exhibit from the very beginning, or about his startling growth, which was so rapid that he outgrew his cradles quicker than his father—who was a good carpenter—could build them. When he was a month old, being then twenty feet tall, and still growing, he got out of his cradle while his parents were arguing, slung it on his shoulder, left home, and began his travels. He invented a huge hotcake griddle so large that it had to be greased by men skating on it with strips of bacon tied to their feet.

His sway extended from the winter of the Blue Snow (when the snow fell and later melted into ink) to the spring when the rain came up from China. That winter was a cold one, so cold in fact that Bunyan had to use blow-torches in order to thaw out the shadows of his crew when they froze on the walls of their cabins, and so cold, too, that the curses the men used froze in the air, not thawing out until the following spring or the Fourth of July, when they exploded with a bang.

Paul Bunyan was surrounded with companions, both animal and human, who were worthy of his greatness. One of these was BABE THE BLUE OX, who measured forty-two axe handles between the eyes and a plug of chewing tobacco, with an appetite that matched his size. Others associated with the Samson of the lumber camps were HOT BISCUIT SLIM, as fine a cook as any giant could want; FEBOLD FEBOLDSON, a Swede, who kept the tools sharp and the pots and pans in proper shape; LITTLE MEERY, who killed and brought in the food that Slim cooked; JOHNNY INKSLINGER, good at figures, and the bookkeeper of the logging camp; SHANTY BOY, who could sing any song known and make up any others; and GALLOPING KID, who gave up being a cowboy after the humiliating experience of being thrown by a bull.

Davy Crockett

DAVY CROCKETT is known to history as one of the heroes of the Battle of the Alamo, where he lost his life. But as a figure in American folklore, the heroic aspect of the man is less emphasized than is his ability as a teller of tall tales—a homely Tennessee backwoodsman around whom a host of legends have sprung up. Many of these stories he told as he went about the countryside trying to drum up the votes which elected him magistrate, state legislator, and sent him three times to Congress. The character of his stories can be judged from his own telling of how he treed a wolf:

"The snow war as deep as my middle, the wind blowed so hard that I went into a hollow tree to warm myself. I hung kill-devil up and began to thrash my hands, when a wolf cum along, and looked in. He stared right up in my face, as much as to ax leave to pick a breakfast off of any part of me he wanted. I war so astonished at his imperdence that I stood right still a minit. Then the wolf turned about, and war going off, when the end of his tail stuck through a big knot hole in the tree. I ketched hold and pulled his tail through. He jumped and twitched and tried to get away, and screeched like a dying hawk. I tied his tail into a big knot and fastened it with a strap, so that he couldn't haul it out, and left him thar to amuse himself."

Johnny Appleseed

JOHNNY APPLESEED, who flourished in the first half of the nineteenth century, was an eccentric New England pioneer. He built up an apple nursery in Pennsylvania, gave saplings and apple seeds to families who were moving west, and went up and down the country planting apple trees in Ohio, Indiana, Illinois, and Pennsylvania. He thought nothing of travelling hundreds of miles in order to take care of his orchards. Long before he died, legends began to develop about him and his peculiar ways, his torn and ragged clothing, his wild appearance, his knowledge of the secrets of the woods, his religious ecstasy, his aid to pioneers and settlers in growing their own orchards and in protecting them when danger threatened, his knowledge of the ways of the animals of the forest, and his kindness to them. Familiar with various seeds that had or were supposed to have healing powers, he was looked up to by the Indians as a combination of a saint and a great medicine man.

In real life, Johnny Appleseed was John Chapman; who his parents were, where he was born, and when, are not known with certainty; it is believed that he was born about 1774 or 1775, and in Massachusetts, either Boston or Springfield. The care he gave his apple trees led to his death, on March 11, 1847, after he had caught pneumonia following a long and hard journey to one of his orchards.

He travelled a good deal, spreading the gospel as well as apple seeds, but is generally believed to have made his home in Ohio, about 1810. Since his death, legends and "tall tales" of which he is the center have continued to grow. Outside the realm of legend and in the field of authentic fact was his warning to white settlers in 1812 of approaching attacks by the Indians. Chapman roamed freely through forests filled with unfriendly redskins but they never harmed him in any way.

Jim Bludso

JIM BLUDSO, of the *Prairie Belle,* was a heroic steamboat engineer on the Mississippi. When the *Prairie Belle* caught fire, Jim held the nose of the burning boat to the shore until all the passengers were safely landed, he himself going down to his death with the vessel he loved. His sacrifice was immortalized by John Hay in his *Pike County Ballads.* Jim Bludso and Casey Jones (see below) belong to the same tradition: both were heroes, both saw their duty and did it, with a full realization of what it meant. In both cases, the stories and legends have a basis in actual events and characters.

Tony Beaver

TONY BEAVER, the West Virginia lumberjack, is a Southern version of Paul Bunyan, whom he resembles in size, powerful strength, and impossible feats. He had his camps "up Eel River" in the Cumberland Mountains, "way up in the Smokies," and in other regions. Of an inventive turn of mind, he is credited with having invented peanut brittle when, in order to halt a raging flood, he threw a huge surplus crop of molasses and peanuts into the stream. Tony Beaver was a mighty logger, a miracle worker, a demigod, a product of fantastic imagination, of exaggeration, of bragging, of "shooting one's head off," and of the ability to tell lies on such a grand scale without a trace of shame that they seem to be or to take on the appearance of truth.

John Henry

JOHN HENRY is the Negro hero of a cycle of American songs, ballads, and tall tales. Sometimes he is a railroad steel-driver, sometimes a Mississippi River roustabout, but he is always a man of superhuman strength. The legends tell of the supernatural events that characterized the day he was born, when he weighed forty-four pounds, of his singing a river song, of his talking to his astonished parents, of his "getting mad" at not being fed, when the dogs and hogs had already had their supper, of his smashing his cradle, of the huge meal he ordered, of his climbing out of bed and leaving home—all on the day of his birth.

It was his strength that made him the hero that he was and it was his strength that killed him. Proud of his power, John Henry made up his mind to show that he was stronger than a steam-drill in driving steel; he beat the machine in a contest, but the strain was too much even for his mighty frame and he died, with his hammer in his hand, a victim of man and muscle against the machine. This most famous feat of John Henry appears to have some historical basis in a real steel-driver, perhaps John Henry by name, who took part in such a contest in 1870 or 1871, the scene of the struggle being the Big Bend Tunnel on the Chesapeake and Ohio Railroad, in West Virginia. As with all mythical and legendary heroes, details vary widely in different songs and stories, although agreeing on fundamental points, such as strength, courage, magic skill in handling a hammer, and pride in that skill.

Casey Jones

CASEY JONES, whose real name was John Luther Jones, is one of the great names in American folklore. A famous locomotive engineer and a hero, he died in a train smashup, sacrificing his own life so that others could jump to safety. The wreck occurred on April 30, 1900, and when they found his body in the wreckage of "old 638" one hand was on the whistle cord and the other on the airbrake lever. Casey worked for years on the run between Jackson and Water Valley before being transferred to the Cannonball Express of the Illinois Central. The song or ballad that first made him famous—there have been many songs and stories since—was made up by WALLACE SAUNDERS, his Negro engine wiper, who idolized him, as did another Negro, his fireman, SIM WEBB. It was to Webb that Casey Jones shouted his last words and his last order, "Jump, Sim, and save yourself." Apart from the heroism that has made his name a magic one, Casey Jones was noted for other qualities, not heroic, perhaps, but human: he always laughed or smiled, he never drank, he was loved by all those who worked with him, and he could do things with a locomotive whistle that no other railroad man could. His widow described it as "a kind of long-drawn-out note that he created, beginning softly, then rising, then dying away almost to a whisper." Her husband Mrs. Jones recalled as a lovable lad, six feet, four and a half inches tall, dark-haired, gray-eyed, always in good humor, with his Irish heart as big as his body. His nickname came from the town of Cayce (Kentucky), pronounced in two syllables, exactly like "Casey."

Gremlins

Not so long ago, air pilots, air navigators, and others invented a group of imaginary gnome-like creatures whom they called GREMLINS. When there is trouble with an airplane engine or anything unusual in any part of a plane, a gremlin is said to be at work. And, apart from airplanes, gremlins can be referred to as explaining any unexpected interference nowadays. Gremlins are a contribution of the Air Age to the world of myths and legends.

Topical Index

General Index

Key to Pronunciation: ā, as in *fate;* ă, as in *fat;* â, as in *fare; a* as in *comma;* ah, as in *father;* ē, as in *see;* ĕ, as in *bet; e,* as in *dozen;* ī, as in *bite;* ĭ, as in *hit; i,* as in *habit;* ō, as in *dole;* ŏ, as in *not;* ô, as in *orb, call; o,* as in *random;* o͞o, as in *soon;* o͝o, as in *good;* oi, as in *boil;* ow, as in *how;* ū, as in *cue;* ŭ, as in *but;* û, as in *cur, fern; u,* as in *circus;* ü, as in the French pronunciation of the word *début* and in the German word *über;* K, as in the German word *machen* and the Scottish pronunciation of *loch; th,* as in *thing;* TH, as in *this;* zh, as in *azure, vision.* The primary accent in a word is indicated by a single stroke (′); the secondary accent is shown by a double stroke (″).